RICHARD DIMBLEBY

RICHARD DIMBLEBY

a biography

by

JONATHAN DIMBLEBY

HODDER AND STOUGHTON
LONDON SYDNEY AUCKLAND TORONTO

For Daniel in memory of his grandfather.

Acknowledgments

I have received much help from many people in the preparation of this book. To all those who were kind enough to write to me about my father I am grateful. I thank the following for allowing me to trespass upon their time to draw on their memories and judgments: Kenneth Adam, Roy Annette, Michael Balkwill, the late Donald Boyd, Richard Cawston, Evan Charlton, F. W. Chignell, Anthony Craxton, Henry Cunnington, Robin Day, Robin Duff, Mary Elliot, George Eynon, Richard Francis, Malcolm Frost, Charles Gardner, Frank Gillard, Cecilia Gillie, Arthur Godfrey, Sir Hugh Greene, Norman Hackforth, Stuart Hood, David Howarth, Jeremy Isaacs, Robert Kee, S. J. de Lotbinière, Joan Marsden, Sir Ralph Murray, John Morgan, the late Duke of Norfolk, John Norman, Lord Oakshott, Dudley Perkins, Arthur Phillips, Laurence Pollinger, Harvey Sarney, Jane Seymore, John Shuter, Tony Smith, Godfrey Talbot, Professor Hugh Trevor-Roper, Wynford Vaughan-Thomas, Reg Ward, Woodrow Wyatt and Grace Wyndham-Goldie.

I am indebted as well to the staff of the London Library, the British Newspaper Library, the Thames Television Library, Dr. Nicholas Cox of the Public Record Office, Bernard Chiesman of the Foreign Office Library, and in particular to Dorothy Phillips of the BBC Written Archives Centre whose painstaking research went far beyond professional obligation.

ACKNOWLEDGMENTS

I have a special debt to Charles Hailstone from whose research into the early history of *The Richmond and Twickenham Times* I have drawn heavily, to Michael Peacock for his long outspoken hours about Panorama, to Anthony Wigan who wrote extended and helpful notes for me about the BBC of the Thirties and early Forties, to Leonard Miall who has given me valuable advice and to Ian Churchill-Davidson, my father's friend and doctor, who gave me great assistance.

It was at the urging of Malcolm Muggeridge that I finally started work on the book. My secretary, Brenda Perrin-Jaquet not only organised me, but translated my labours into a legible manuscript.

I am grateful to my family for its support; and especially to my mother, without whose loving sympathy and help this book could not have been written, and to my wife, Bel, to whose wisdom this book owes much.

Contents

Chronology

1913   Born in Richmond, Surrey.

1927   To Mill Hill School for boys.

1931   Leaves school to work on *The Richmond and Twickenham Times*.

1934   Joins staff of *Bournemouth Echo*, living in Lymington, Hants.

1935   Joins staff of *Advertisers Weekly*.

1936   Joins BBC as Topical Talks Assistant, becoming first BBC reporter.

1937   Marries Dilys Thomas.

1939   Reports from Spanish Civil War, as first BBC war correspondent.
Becomes first BBC reporter to cover a Royal Tour (in Canada).
To France to join British Expeditionary Force.

1940   To Middle East GHQ, Cairo.
To Sudan.
Lybian Desert Campaign.
Greece.

1941   Cairo and Desert.
Eritrean Campaign. Battle of Keran.
Iraq, Syrian Campaign, Turkey, Persia.

1942   Cairo and Desert.
Recalled London.

1943   First bombing raid on Berlin.
Becomes BBC air correspondent.
Helps prepare BBC reporting teams for D-Day.

1944   Reports D–Day assault.
        Becomes Head of BBC War Reporting Unit.
        Reports Air war.

1945   Reports crossing of Rhine.
        First correspondent to enter Belsen Concentration Camp.
        First Allied correspondent to enter Berlin.
        Resigns from BBC.

1946   Awarded OBE.
        Twenty Questions starts.
        Commentator at Victory Parade on Opening Day of post-
        war television.
        Becomes Editor-in-Chief of *The Richmond and Twicken-
        ham Times*.

1947   Begins Down Your Way.

1948   Starts London Town.

1950   First cross-channel television programme.

1952   Lying–in–State and Funeral of George VI.

1953   Coronation of Queen Elizabeth II.

1954   Becomes Managing-Director of F. W. Dimbleby and
        Sons Ltd.

1955   First General Election Special.
        Start of Panorama.

1958   First televised State Opening of Parliament.

1959   Awarded CBE.

1960   Princess Margaret's Wedding.

1961   First BBC transmission from Moscow.

1962   Inaugural Telstar programme.
        First live transatlantic television transmission.
        Reports from earthquake disaster in Skopje, Yugoslavia.
        Appeal for victims raises £400,000.

1963   President Kennedy's Funeral.

1965   Funeral of Sir Winston Churchill.
        First visit by Pope to United Nations.
        Enters St. Thomas's Hospital in October.
        December 22nd dies.

Foreword

A LITTLE AFTER NINE O'CLOCK IN THE EVENING OF December 22nd, 1965, St. Thomas's Hospital announced that Richard Dimbleby had died. Almost at once, ITV and then BBC programmes were interrupted to report the news. At ten o'clock, Frank Gillard, the Director of Radio Broadcasting, gave the BBC's first reaction with the words: 'This is news which will bring sorrow to almost every home in England, and the sense of deep personal loss to millions of people, in Britain and the world, who never had the chance of meeting him but who nevertheless have long regarded Richard Dimbleby as a close family friend.' A little later on BBC television, in a forty-minute tribute, carried immediately afterwards by ITV stations, Huw Wheldon, the Controller of Television Programmes, said:

> He was the voice of the BBC on thousands of occasions, and on hundreds of occasions I think he was even the voice of the nation. To an extent, I think, incomparable in the history of radio or television so far as this country is concerned, he was the voice of our generation, and probably the most telling voice on BBC radio or television of any kind in this country so far. It is in this sense I feel he is irreplaceable, and what can we do except mourn him?

At Buckingham Palace, where she was dining with the Prime Minister and the Archbishop of Canterbury, the Queen was informed of the event, and at once sent a telegram expressing her deep sympathy to the family.

The next morning, the first of many thousands of tributes from all over the world arrived at the BBC and at our home in Sussex: from the European Broadcasting Union, from German Radio, from Moscow ('A great voice has gone off the air'), from the Commonwealth, and from the United States, where Fred Friendly, President of CBS, cabled: 'Richard Dimbleby—BBC—was a dateline all in his own right like Coventry, Parliament, Trafalgar, and Dunkirk. His voice, the voice of Britain...' By the end of the next week, the Post Office was delivering letters of condolence by the sack. Some were neatly typed and came from elegant addresses; others were painfully and carefully printed on pieces of rough paper by those who did not have the habit of writing.

'I shall be grateful all my life for the tremendous amount of pleasure, not to say education and uplift given to us by your father, through the medium of television especially. Any child, even, listening to a commentary of his on a Royal Occasion, could feel they were being drawn into history itself,' wrote one woman from Dartmouth in Devon. 'As a nation,' wrote another from Liverpool, 'we have lost the greatest-ever broadcaster, and television for me is now dimmed and quite desolate.'

'I am writing to you on behalf of the Postmen at the above office,' wrote one of the workers at the West Brompton sorting office, 'who would like to send their deepest sympathy at the loss of a great broadcaster.' 'The wife and I mourn his loss, as if he were one of the family, as he had been so near and dear to us in the world of radio and television for so many years,' wrote a couple from Glamorgan, 'on occasions and all events of importance, he was the means of bringing them all so real to so many countless thousands of homes poor, and rich alike.'

Among others, Princess Alexandra and the Queen Mother wrote personally, the latter recording that she: 'shared the sorrow of millions of other people'. From State House, Lusaka, President Kaunda wrote: 'The name of Richard Dimbleby will long be remembered by those who knew him or came into contact with him'. From Banstead in Surrey, a woman wrote: 'To so many in ordinary little homes like mine, he showed the good example of perfect English, beautiful manners and integrity.' 'I do not know how to start first as I have no words to express myself clearly,' wrote a worker from Coleshill in Warwickshire, 'it is a great shock to learn through the T.V. News the sad news of the death of your Gentleman Father, Mr. Richard Dimbleby.'

'It is with tears in my eyes I learn tonight of Richard Dimbleby's death,' wrote another, 'it is as though a part of

England itself had gone'. 'I'm just a young housewife with three small children but I feel that although I have never met your husband that I've lost a friend,' wrote a woman from Hampshire. From Edinburgh another wrote, 'You felt he was speaking just to you. Oh! it is so sad and I, like MANY others feel lost. I cannot realise I shall never hear that much-loved voice again.'

The thoughts were repeated thousands of times: 'Richard Dimbleby was BBC television and personally that ended last night'; 'There was only one Richard Dimbleby. Today even our local fire station flies its flag at half-mast in tribute'; and 'in the same time this hour of sorrow for everybody's feeling,' wrote an Italian worker living in Germany, 'will you be so kind to have my personal feeling of regret for all family's BBC for such big loss. I am very sorry if I am ask you for a favour and to send my feelings as unknown friend, to Mr. Dimbley's wife and my warm cuddle for his sons, David and Jonathan in this hour of big sorrow for them.'

On the last day of 1965, as the tributes continued to arrive, my mother opened a fund for cancer research for those who had wished to send flowers. It was called the 'Richard Dimbleby Cancer Fund'. Within two days, it had received 6,000 letters, containing £14,000. Within a month the total had reached £50,000, and the money continued to arrive. (A year later, when more than £100,000 had been raised the trustees of the Fund, the family, established a fellowship in cancer research at St. Thomas's Hospital. The hospital built a special research laboratory which was opened in 1966, by the Queen. Now, ten years later, with the Fund standing at about £400,000, and £25,000 arriving each year, the fellowship has been elevated to a professorship of London University, the Chair still being held at the hospital.)

On January 4th a Memorial Service for Richard Dimbleby was held at Westminster Abbey. The Dean and Chapter of Westminster had offered the service as their tribute to his broadcasts from there. In the event it became an occasion of national mourning, watched on television by 5,000,000 people in the middle of a Monday afternoon, and by a further 6,500,000 in a recording late that night.

It was a damp, bleak day, with a wind blowing from the Thames, whipping through the Dean's Yard. Yet from the middle of the morning men and women had started to queue in the cold to attend the service. By early afternoon, the Abbey was full, every seat taken, the side aisles filled with standing people. In the cloisters hundreds more stood waiting to watch the service on monitors. Many more stood outside. By four o'clock a large crowd had gathered at the front of the Abbey, standing still and quiet. There were pensioners in best felt hats and long overcoats, businessmen with bowlers who had left early from the City, housewives, hair freshly permed, schoolgirls on holiday, students muffled in college scarves, secretaries, clerks, and workers in their Sunday best. None of them had met Richard Dimbleby; for them he existed only through the medium of television. Half as a joke, half in affection, he had often called them 'my public'. Now his public were there; they did not smile and they did not talk. They had come, in the cold, to do him honour. It was the largest congregation—apart from on a State Occasion—which the Abbey had ever witnessed.

Inside with the family and with friends, a phalanx of distinguished broadcasters and journalists, representatives of the Queen and the Prime Minister, politicians, ambassadors, church-leaders and mayors, took their place beside the ordinary men and women who did not normally share such occasions—except vicariously, through the voice of the man they now mourned.

The Abbey was bright with arc-lights; technicians in morning-suits noiselessly efficient, moved back and forth with cameras trailing fat coils. Microphones hung low over the choir, as it and the congregation sang, 'Praise My Soul the King of Heaven', 'Jerusalem', 'The Old Hundredth', and 'All People that on Earth do Dwell'.

The Dean of Westminster conducted the service, George Reindorp, the Bishop of Guildford, gave an address, and Lord Fisher, who had just retired as Archbishop of Canterbury, spoke of the gifts of 'mind and heart' which had allowed Richard Dimbleby to establish 'a new art and a new profession of communicating to the people by a commentary, the outward and the inward meaning of great occasions both in church and state'. The BBC Symphony Orchestra, conducted by Sir Adrian Boult, played Elgar's 'Nimrod'. There was a two-minute silence; and as a camera zoomed slowly in to the empty platform on the Triforium from where Dimbleby had made his commentaries, his colleague Wynford Vaughan-Thomas reminded the millions who sat at home: 'Today that place is vacant and that voice is still.' Afterwards, with the sound of Bach's Toccata and Fugue resounding through the Abbey, the family led the way slowly out, past row after row of unknown weeping faces towards the crowd outside who stood with heads bowed while the muffled bells of Westminster rang out against the rush-hour traffic.

Even the professional communicators seemed stunned by what one of their number had created. 'It was the televising of the service, the commentary on the passing of the commentator, that made it unique,' wrote Peter Black in *The Daily Mail*, 'it was a once-for-all event ... It was, in fact, a State Occasion of its own. The first and probably the last to be created by television.' Angered that no member of the Royal Family had seen fit to attend the service ('It was, perhaps, fitting that with his death they seemed to vanish from the scene') Nancy Banks-Smith found the service 'both simpler and more moving than a Great Occasion'. And when on television she watched the 'nobodies standing in the black January night', paying their last respects, 'she suddenly felt very affectionate towards the British. The eternal audience. It was their service.'

In the midst of this public grief only one quizzical voice was raised. In the House of Commons, after paying his own tribute, the Rt. Hon. Iain Macleod wondered of the Abbey service: 'Are we not losing our sense of proportion when we thus pay homage to a television personality?' In the prevailing mood, it was a courageous question, but he was unanimously condemned. 'The remarkable wave of regret and grief for Dimbleby,' wrote the distinguished columnist, Robert Pitman, 'is, I think, due precisely to the fact that he was much more than a TV personality ...'

The Times had already written that he was: 'A truly international figure'; and *The Daily Mail* editorialised that: 'The name of Dimbleby is secure in the history of our times, for it is unique.' The same feelings were expressed in many thousands of words in hundreds of newspapers in every continent of the world—from *The Bath and Wiltshire Chronicle* to *The New York Times*; from the *Statesman of Delhi* to the *Glasgow Herald*.

No Englishman in recent times, except Sir Winston Churchill who died in the same year, has been accorded the outpouring of sorrow which greeted Richard Dimbleby's death. It was not only that, at fifty-two, he had died too young; it was not only that, as one colleague said, having suffered from cancer for five years, 'he died with dignity, as he lived and worked with dignity'; it was not only that he had come to occupy a place in British life that he had created for himself, and which made millions of people believe that he was their friend; but, implicit in all that was said and written, and sometimes explicit, was the sense that his death signalled the end of an era, not only in the history of the BBC or of broadcasting, but in the life of the nation.

Richard Dimbleby's broadcasting career began in 1936 and lasted nearly thirty years. It was a period of accelerating social change; by 1965, the Britain of the Thirties had been transformed absolutely and irrevocably. In the process the BBC became one of the dominant cultural influences in Britain, speaking to, and later from, the people, reflecting, judging, and even forming their values and aspirations.

The BBC itself was profoundly transformed. From small and frail beginnings, it had become by 1965 the biggest and most powerful purveyor of information in the world. Cautiously independent in the Thirties—by the Sixties the BBC was an apparently indestructible institution of the state. Radio, reaching its zenith, had yielded to a new medium, television, which was to have greater effect on the lives of the people than any social invention since the printing press. In each of these major developments, Richard Dimbleby played an intimate and dominant part. If Reith created the BBC, it was commonly said, then Dimbleby was its voice.

Against that background this book is an account of my father's life from his birth in Richmond, where the family owned and ran local newspapers, to the day of his death from cancer fifty-two years later. I have tried to explain some of the passions and convictions that guided his public and private life; to analyse his contribution not only to the art of broadcasting but to the history of the BBC; and, as well, to unravel some of the strands in the relationship between Richard Dimbleby and his public, placing it in the context of an era in which he was 'the voice of the BBC'.

I am even more aware now than I was when I began of the dangers and difficulties that beset a son who is foolhardy enough to write about his father: I have not escaped them. I am aware too, that some who knew him intimately and others who knew him not so well, would have seen my father (and the BBC) through different eyes: I hope that they will forgive me my errors. Although, where it has been relevant, I have sought to be objective and critical, I am not dispassionate. I offer this book in the belief that my father made a contribution to his important public profession which has not, and will not, be emulated.

I

First Years

Think of what our nation stands for
Books from Boots and country lanes.
Free speech, free passes, class distinction,
Democracy and proper drains.

JOHN BETJEMAN

ON THE LAST SUNDAY OF MAY 1913 THE PEOPLE OF
London fled the city in their thousands. They went according to
their means by motor-car, charabanc, train or bicycle. Some
carried hampers of food, most wore their Sunday best, all were
escaping the oppression of a heatwave in the first mass exodus of
the year. After a week on a sweaty factory floor or behind a sticky
office desk the weekend offered a brief reprieve; in a field or by a
river-bank the temperature, hovering in the low eighties, could
be enjoyed for the first time in seven days.

The Royal Borough of Richmond on Thames was uncertain
about the weekend invasion by the day-tripping masses, who
(now that the excursion business was doing so well) seemed to
arrive in greater number every week. Of course it was good for
business; the High Street was thronged by window-shoppers
admiring the smart little jewellers and the high-class tailors. The
cafés and restaurants did a roaring trade and the Castle Hotel,
serving tea and scones to a multitude on the lawn, was about to
have its best year ever.

From their riverside houses, taken for the season, the gentry
down from London viewed the invasion of the masses as an affront
to their birthright. What, they wondered aloud to each other, was
their Richmond retreat coming to? Cars and omnibuses filled the
streets, forcing horses and carriages and people to shelter in back

alleys; petrol fumes seeped through tightly closed windows into elegant drawing rooms; the raucous cries and laughs of the day-trippers made relaxation impossible; and for those whose windows opened onto the river, the blaring of the gramophone on the steamers weaving a dangerous zig-zag through the punts and skiffs, drowned the sound of a band which was the one bearable expression of popular taste.

A little way from the river, up Richmond Hill, above the sound of the populace enjoying itself, Gwen Dimbleby waited calmly with a nurse at her side and a small dog on her bed for the birth of her first child. Downstairs in the drawing room her husband Fred for once had forgotten the affairs of the family business which normally preoccupied him at weekends. The Dimbleby family owned the local newspaper, *The Richmond and Twickenham Times*, which was much involved in the traffic-congestion controversy that had split the town. Some wanted to widen the road, others would ban the buses. The Dimbleby news-paper came down firmly on the side of conservation, arguing in its leader column that weekend: 'There is a soul in the stones of Richmond Bridge, in its time-stained arches, its shadows and its outlines. Once they are disturbed and the spell is broken, what was before a bridge of character becomes a mere structure of stone.' Fred Dimbleby, who combined a full-time job in Fleet Street with the post of Editor in Chief of the family paper was, like most of those in his position, proud of Richmond. Though he was pre-pared to accept inevitability of progress he would not countenance 'change for change's sake'; the replacement of the bridge by a mere 'mechanical combination of strains and stresses obedient to the laws of nature' was unthinkable.

This weekend, however, he hardly glanced at the paper, as he waited for the word to go upstairs and admire his firstborn. He was one of twelve children, seven of whom had died at birth, so naturally he was anxious. He need not have been. At midday Gwen was delivered of a screaming baby which the nurse thrust under her nose (not altogether to her delight) with the time-honoured observation 'Mark my words, ma'am, he's a fine baby, he'll be a great man one day.' They decided to call him Richard. Fred was delighted that he had a son who could one day take over the family business and become the fourth generation of the family to make journalism his life.

Richard's great-grandfather Jabez Bunting Dimbleby, the son

of the Superintendent of Hull Gasworks, was born in 1827. His family was strict Methodist and he had been named after the most prominent Methodist of the first half of the eighteenth century. The original Jabez Bunting was a stern disciple of his master and the most forbidding advocate of Wesley's notorious advice to Methodist parents: 'Whatever pain it costs, break the will if you would not damn the child. Let a child from a year old be taught to fear the rod and to cry softly; from that age make him do as he is bid, if you whip him ten times to effect it.' In the struggle between radicalism and orthodoxy in the Methodist Church, Jabez Bunting stood ruthlessly on the side of reaction, believing that his Church should promote 'the loyalty of the middle ranks as well as subordination and industry in the lower orders'. It is certain that the young Dimbleby who bore his name had a disciplined upbringing in Hull. The family were highly respectable members of the lower middle class. Their Methodism imposed on them devout sabbaths followed by diligent weekdays. It was obedient to authority (both of the Church and the State), politically conservative and spiritually cheerless. Jabez Bunting Dimbleby must have had a stout constitution for although he became a devout Wesleyan, he escaped the worst effects of what one contemporary writer called an 'appalling system of religious terrorism... fitted to unhinge a tottering intellect and to darken and embitter a sensitive nature'. He sang gloomy hymns, preached gloomy sermons, but made his way in the world.

He was sent to a private school in Hull, moved from there as copy boy on to a local paper, soon became a reporter, and some years later moved south from Yorkshire to Chelmsford in Essex. There he set up home with his wife and two sons and went to work for the *Essex News*. He was a man of some worldly ambition and social aspiration. To satisfy the first, he devised a shorthand dictionary and prepared it for publication, only to discover that a certain Isaac Pitman had got there before him—an untimely intervention which Jabez Bunting Dimbleby was convinced had robbed him of an assured place in history. To satisfy his feeling that the Dimblebys were a little better than their financial status might suggest, he set about exploring the origins of his family, spending much time and money searching painstakingly through old manuscripts in public libraries for a hint of the truth. After many years' work, slender evidence led him to the conclusion that the family had first arrived as members of the noble retinue of William the Conqueror; they had put down roots in Lincoln-shire and had given their name to the village of Dembleby, being known in the area as the Dimblebys de Dembleby. His findings, flattering as they were, entered the family mythology for ever, so that more than half a century later his great-grandson Richard not only made a sentimental pilgrimage to Dembleby but blithely informed a succession of innocently inquiring reporters that yes, it was true, the Dimbleby family had settled here in Norman times, and yes, he Richard Dimbleby was descended from the Dimblebys of Dembleby.

In Chelmsford (where the truth was that he was a journalist of moderate means and talent) Jabez Bunting Dimbleby brought his sons up in the Methodist tradition. One of them, Frederick, soon became a zealous follower of Wesley, and had preached his first sermon before he was fifteen. When the family moved to London (where Jabez Bunting was to work at Waterlows as a foreign reader, the wretched dictionary having failed absolutely) father and son were soon spending evenings and weekends preaching salvation to the poor in the slums of the East End. The young Frederick was fervent and devout, and he threw all his spirit into his mission. It was nearly his undoing. The East End may have seemed promising soul-saving ground but it was pro-foundly unhealthy. Frederick fell ill. The doctors ordered rest and feared consumption. Thus alarmed, Jabez Bunting, refusing to hear any contrary argument, arranged for his son to move out of London away from the danger to the more congenial climate of Richmond on Thames.

Frederick arrived in the town in 1874, at the age of twenty. Almost at once he was offered a job. *The Richmond and Twickenham Times* had been founded one year earlier by Edward King—a bizarre character filled with a liberal crusading passion which sought to transform Richmond, bringing enlightenment to the benighted, and hope to the oppressed. Already in less than a year *The Richmond and Twickenham Times* had aroused the ire of many local dignitaries by its editorial commitment to giving 'promi-nence to the exposure of local evils'. In a town which much preferred the high Toryism of *The Richmond Comet*, rumours were put about that King was a little unstable, even mad.

Sensing in Frederick Dimbleby a kindred passion, King offered him a job as a reporter. Within two years Dimbleby was the editor's assistant; and they became close friends. Soon they were a famous pair in Richmond, always together and always arguing. Their leading articles, constructed with great care out of King's wild (and frequently libellous) flow of invective and Dimbleby's dogged reason, were required reading in the town. Councillors shuddered under the onslaught. Local dignitaries were castigated as 'arrogant and domineering', 'infirm of temper' and 'blind to the signs of the time'; the mental 'fossilism' of one councillor, thundered *The Richmond and Twickenham Times*, 'would fill the minds of his constituents with painful and grievous amazement if they could see him about his elected business'.

Dimbleby was not so romantic as King. It was he, not the editor, who started to worry when advertising fell away, as offended worthies one by one transferred their allegiance to *The Comet*. He was beginning to learn the first rule of a local paper— that although it could proclaim 'we take an *independent* position as we cannot believe in an infallible party on either side of the house', economic necessity is a dictator who demands caution. Where injustice and suffering were plain to all, then *The Richmond and Twickenham Times* could speak out. Otherwise, in matters of controversy it would have to learn when to hold its tongue. It was a matter of survival that it should seek to give offence to as few as possible without quite being all things to all men. *The Richmond and Twickenham Times* had to learn that moderation in all things did not make eunuchs of men, but was rather a virtue, born of necessity, to be held in the highest esteem.

The strains of editorial crusades and subsequent writs for libel gradually exhausted King. In 1896 he was certified as a lunatic and incarcerated in a local asylum. Long before that Frederick Dimbleby had started to guide the paper's fortunes. Now he was in sole charge, and the company became known as F. W. Dimbleby and Sons.

If Dimbleby adopted a more cautious tone in his paper than King, in some matters he was as unyielding. His fierce Methodist principles made him a redoubtable foe. He belonged to the Order of Good Templars, who believed that the path towards Virtue was to be found in the valley of self-denial. They did not drink, or smoke, or gamble, or swear. Dimbleby obeyed the rules rigidly, and when he married, he imposed them on his wife and then his children. Like most of his class in late Victorian England he believed that poverty and disease amongst the lower orders were evils caused by the chronic moral frailty of the sufferers, not the faults of the system. Frederick was a considerable orator, much in demand at public meetings all over the country, and later in Europe and the United States. What he lacked in insight he made up for in eloquence. 'I suppose we have met tonight,' he would proclaim, 'to encourage one another in fighting against the greatest preventable evil that ever affected a nation.' The enemy was the demon drink, the root of all wickedness and suffering, and only when it was banished from the land could his vision of the ideal world be realised—a world of 'humble homes, sanely ordered, temperate, serene, sweet with human affections, yielding the fullness of the brightness of life'.

In time Frederick became a local councillor, a Justice of the Peace and a Poor Law Guardian. He reached the exalted rank of Grand Counsellor and Grand Chaplain of the Good Templars and travelled the land for his cause. Each Sunday he walked seven miles out of Richmond to a little village where he preached in the Parish Church, took Sunday School and visited the poor. His reputation as a stern judge of lesser mortals was tempered by the recognition that 'he was imbued with the spirit of earnest piety'.

Like his soul, his business thrived. The paper may have lost its crusading edge (though he refused all advertisements for liquor, at great cost both to the advertising revenue and his reputation among the town's licensed victuallers, hoteliers and publicans) but it was much respected. He was a founder member and vice-president of the Institute of Journalists, whose committees found him 'clear of sight as of speech, frank, courageous, courteous...'

On his death in 1908 Frederick bequeathed to his family a secure position in Richmond society. No-one who was anyone in the town was absent from his funeral, and the tributes, printed at great length in his newspaper, were fulsome to a fault. *The Richmond and Twickenham Times* was a solid thirty-five years old and spoke with the authority of approaching middle age. It reflected the values by which its proprietor had lived and which he had instilled into his children. It was established, respectable and not overburdened with imagination. It revered family life, hard work, compassion tempered by realism, and a modest righteous prosperity. It was now in the hands of his two sons Percy (who became Managing Director) and Fred. Five years later Richard was born into a family which already seemed to have roots deep in Richmond.

Fred had left school at fourteen to learn the family business from the bottom. In 1898 when he was twenty-two, frustrated by the apparent limitations of his father's suburban life, he determined to break away, and make his mark beyond Richmond. He found work in Fleet Street as a sub-editor, in rapid succession on *The Sun*, *The Star*, *The Daily News* and *The Evening Standard*. He worked hard, combining Fleet Street with his editorial control of *The Richmond and Twickenham Times*. By 1913, he had a comfortable income of around £500 a year—enough to pay for a nanny for Richard, a daily help, a gardener, and a 'living in' maid. He also ran a car. It was a comfortable house and he and Gwen lived a comfortable life—punctuated each year by conferences of the Good Templars, whose stern cause had dominated both their childhoods.

Gwen was the daughter of a Bath surveyor, whose family, like the Dimblebys had 'signed the pledge' and supported the Liberal Party. The humdrum life prescribed for a young Victorian girl in Bath soon irked her. She was what family friends would describe as a 'spirited girl': against her father's better judgment, for he thought it immodest, she insisted on learning to ride a bicycle; and when she was older, to his dismay, she sometimes lingered a little long in the Park at dusk before her nice young escort delivered her home. By the age of eighteen she was a young woman of considerable and renowned beauty, with a passion to go on the stage. Her father was distraught, but after long heart-searching permitted her to go to London and stay with her aunt, who, having scandalised Bath by divorcing her husband some years before, had moved to London to become a theatrical agent where, to make matters worse, she lived in sin with a theatrical impresario called Bannister Howard. Though the two had soon legalised their relationship, it was with trepidation that Mr. Bolwell saw his daughter on the train to London, and the West End. She emerged from the experience unscathed, though not before her father had threatened to disown her if she accepted her aunt's invitation to go on tour in pantomime. Her youthful infatuation with Fred Dimbleby (for whom the Bolwells had that respect which the middle classes reserve for one of their number who is a little more prosperous than they) promised to steady her. He was ten years older, and showed at first little sign of reciprocating her affection. When he at last made plain that he had fallen in love (for the first time in his thirty-five years) the union between

the two temperance-obeying, low-church, middle-class families
was welcomed by both sides.

By the year of Richard's birth the middle classes must have
come to believe (even if they had not yet come to express it in such
terms) that they had never had it so good. The Liberal Government was doing enough but not too much: the poor had their
relief, the workers their insurance, and the Trades' Unions their
Party (which mercifully most of their members did not support).
The rich were being taxed a little more heavily but not enough to
spoil the high jinks which made such vicariously exciting reading
in the papers next morning. The middle classes, no longer
squeezed between rich and poor, were becoming more prosperous
and more powerful. They knew their place, but then so did those
above and below them. Peace and prosperity seemed assured.

As befitted the main organ of local information *The Richmond
and Twickenham Times* did not permit itself to share entirely the
complacency of most of its readers. Among the reports of whist
drives, exhibitions, parades, garden parties and first nights, the
details of which it dutifully recorded down to the last name, it
found space for another world. It was not a world about which
many in Richmond knew very much, and it rarely impinged on
their lives. Fred Dimbleby believed that the duty of a local paper
was sometimes to remind its readers that not all mankind shared
their blessings. The paper devoted much space to a meeting of the
British Federation for the Emancipation of Sweated Women
which made a virtue of rescuing girls from far away in the East
End of London where 'thousands of people [were] grinding their
faces in the dust of poverty' and training them 'for some kind of
useful domestic work' in more salubrious surroundings. (It was an
incidental factor, which the paper forbore to point out, that such
'rescue' had a remarkably beneficial effect on the chronic shortage
of good servant girls.)

Fred Dimbleby's paper regarded the Federation with much
approval, combining as it did the Victorian faith in charity on
the one hand and self-help on the other as the solution to most
social evils.

Fred did not reflect much on greater, more threatening events.
In the month of Richard's birth he read about the labour troubles
on the Clyde, the strike in the Liverpool Docks and the Welsh coal
pits, and he knew of the threat of the 'Triple Alliance' which
some thought would rock the fabric of British society. He read

too about Northern Ireland where Sir Edward Carson had demanded rhetorically of his Unionist audience: 'What is Ulster going to do?' (about the Liberals' Home Rule Bill) and they had roared back at him: 'Fight!' At the Curragh the British Army was contemplating mutiny, and senior Tory politicians were promising their secret support. In the East End of London on the very day of his son's birth mounted police charged a crowd of twenty thousand who had gathered to hear Sylvia Pankhurst speak her emancipated and revolutionary mind.

In Richmond such problems seemed far away—not serious enough to disturb the even tenor of Richmond life, or the Dimbleby household. How long such complacency would have endured is unknown; but the opportune intervention of the First World War ensured that for a time at any rate the middle classes could continue to ignore the portents of upheaval—the workers' strikes, the female demonstrations and the Ulster jingoism. The advent of war filled the people with a sense of urgent patriotism that buried social unrest. And the middle class values, to which the burghers of Richmond so tenaciously held, were allowed to flourish long after their time was past.

The war made no difference to little Richard. Untouched by the turmoils of peace, Richmond was equally free from the pressures of war, though some of her children were killed at the front, playing what Tawney described as a 'profitless part in a game played by monkeys and organised by lunatics'. Like other Richmond women Gwen Dimbleby knitted balaclava helmets and socks for the boys at the front. *The Richmond Home Journal* in the lounge urged its readers 'to continue as far as possible our everyday habits and arrangements as they were before the war' and noted contentedly a few issues later that 'Richmond in wartime is exceedingly like Richmond in peace'. Gwen had ordered her nanny that Richard should be taken out in the pram each day for an hour 'in all weathers except fog' and once a week while he was taken onto the Green or along the towpath Gwen went to help prepare and serve food at the soup kitchen for the wives and children of men at the front.

Richard's progress was lovingly recorded: the first smiles and gurgles and words that were much admired in the High Street, first steps taken on a summer holiday in Cliftonville where the family regularly took rooms. There, one afternoon, a military band came marching down the road outside. He heard it,

clambered up to his feet and staggered to the window to gurgle his
delight at the colours and sounds of the pageant below. It was
the start of a long, long affair with ceremony.

Richard Frederick Dimbleby was incurably friendly, the first
indication of an expansive personality being given when he still
had a dummy. He had been alternately sucking it and throwing it
into irretrievable corners much to the irritation of Gwen, who
seeing a dustman outside told him that some children never had
dummies at all and that he ought to consider himself lucky and not
behave in such a spoilt way. Mortified, he stumbled down the
stairs out into the road and presented his possession to the bemused
dustman with the words: 'For your baby 'cos he hasn't got one.'

By the time he had reached the age of five the Dimbleby family
had moved from Richmond Hill to a mansion flat on the edge of
the river, beside Richmond Bridge. It had a fine view over the
river, and Richard spent much of the time gazing out at the
activity of the river. He soon asked for, and was given, a boat—a
diminutive dinghy with oars he could hardly lift from the water.
He spent all his afternoons rowing fiercely along in competition
with the skiffs and the steamers, and then resting by the bank or at a
mooring. He soon knew all the boatmen, who would hail him like
an old salt and indulge him with sweets as the youngest boatman
on the Thames. He was happier with them than with children. His
parents soon resigned themselves to the fact that, unlike most
children, he had few friends of his own age. He went to infant
school, a local day school and then, when he was ten, to a
preparatory school near Battle in Sussex, called Glengorse. Out of
school and during the holidays he spent all his time by the river
or alone in the flat, playing clumsily with Meccano, or more skil-
fully on the piano. His gifts were those of personality rather than
intellect. He was amiable, cheerful, and well liked by his elders
who admired the way in which his father had instilled into him
at an early age the virtues of good manners and courtesy. His first
report from Glengorse (where, since he was eighteen months
younger than the other boys, he ended one from bottom of the
class) made the kind of non-commital judgments about him that
were to pursue him throughout his school career. At Games he was
'rather clumsy'; at History he was 'doing well'; at Mathematics
he had 'tried hard' and was 'a keen worker'; at Latin he showed
'great improvement'. Only in Music (where he was top of the
form) and in English (where his teacher judged firmly 'he will be

good at this subject') did he show real promise. His academic progress, from indifferent to poor, was much more a matter of laziness than stupidity. Throughout his school life a series of frustrated teachers would complain, more and more vociferously, that if only he would 'try harder' or 'apply himself more whole-heartedly' he could do very well. Richard preferred to bask in the goodwill which he spread around him and which was readily reciprocated. He was excessively idle. His sister Pat who was born when he was nine, and who doted on him, remembered him always 'mooching around doing nothing. He always seemed to be bored.' Only the river, or the piano, and later the car, sparked him into life. To his family and their friends he seemed a very pleasant, very ordinary little boy.

Sometimes in the summer the family would load up their tourer and set off down the Great West Road to Bath to stay with Gwen's parents. Those were very special occasions. They left at five o'clock in the morning, driving steadily, stopping frequently, and they did not arrive until teatime. Richard had to travel in the open in the dicky seat, which he loved—so much so that they once reached his grandmother's with Richard soaked to the skin from a long violent rainstorm on Salisbury Plain, which his parents had forgotten and he had not noticed. He loved Bath. His grand-mother's house on Newbridge Hill was late Georgian, broodingly Victorian inside. The garden behind was a mystery of wisteria, honeysuckle and roses. There were secret drooping ivy corners, moss-covered tracks and woody bowers. Here he could lie in the shade, away from the family, and doze and dream. Already in his teens he began to nurture a romance with the country: one day he would live in rural England—'in the real England'—the England of green fields, lazy cows, old oaks and cosy white-washed farmsteads. The schoolboy romance, founded on little but a love of peace and quiet, was to become an adult passion which (enflamed by experiences he had not yet had) would convince him that 'country life' embodied all the values that made Britain great.

His father, Fred, was a simple patriot. On the outbreak of war he had at once heeded the call for King and Country. However, at the age of thirty-eight he was deemed too old to be sent to the front line, and was seconded instead to Whitehall, where he moved from department to department ('on secret work' as he told Gwen) for two years. In 1915, he came out into the open and began a brief but highly successful Whitehall career. He was sent to the War Office, and later to the Ministry of National Service under Sir Aukland Geddes. There he helped plan the propaganda campaign to woo civilians into the Army to replace their fallen comrades. At the end of the war he was enlisted to prepare yet another propaganda campaign to convince those he had sent out that there would be homes and jobs for the survivors and they would not be forgotten by a grateful nation when they returned home. Soon he was given the title of 'Director of Publicity' to the Government, becoming the first of what would later become an army of Government public-relations officers. He spent much time with Lloyd George, who had become a family hero, sometimes accompanying him on speaking tours and frequently being summoned to Downing Street. Once Gwen went with him to tea at Downing Street and was thrilled when Megan Lloyd George confided to her that Fred was 'such a reassuring presence—when he's around we know everything is going to be all right'.

Richmond was much impressed by Fred Dimbleby's standing— a friend of Cabinet Ministers, a confidant of Lloyd George, he travelled the country on the Government's behalf speaking to all the leading editors of the land, dealing with demobilisation, resettlement, strikes in the pits and on the railways (which the Government had ruthlessly crushed). His achievements in the world beyond Richmond had a definite, if subtle effect on the family's social standing. For many years the Dimblebys had felt themselves uneasily poised between the 'trading' and the 'professional' middle classes. They were, in a sense, in 'trade' as proprietors of the local paper, but their trade—journalism—was regarded as a professional activity. Such doubts were not readily voiced, though Fred's mother would frequently demand of her son, 'Fred, we're not in *trade*—are we?' and later Gwen was uneasy when the firm's Twickenham Office blossomed into a stationer's. Fred's success in Whitehall banished all fears: the Dimblebys now most definitely belonged to the professional classes. It was inevitable as a result that Richard should be sent to a public school, becoming the first in the family to make that momentous step into that form of social respectability.

In 1927 Richard Dimbleby was enrolled as a pupil at Mill Hill School for boys. His parents had chosen the school on the northern outskirts of London for three reasons: it was not too far from home, so they could see him frequently; a friend of the family had sent a son there who emerged 'with such good manners and a

nice speaking voice'; and, most important, the school subscribed
to the values and traditions by which the Dimbleby family had
thrived and prospered. Mill Hill was one of those institutions
established in the middle of the nineteenth century to cater for the
social aspirations of the new middle class thrown up by the
industrial revolution. It was filled in the main by the sons of
merchants and industrialists from the North of England, who by
reason of their birth and Low-Church Christianity were not
acceptable at the old established public schools. By 1927 Mill Hill
had not greatly changed, though it had a greater sprinkling of the
professional classes—the sons of the methodist clergy (of whom
Kingsley Martin, who had left a decade earlier, was the most
illustrious), lawyers, doctors and academics.

The school rules belonged to public-school orthodoxy. All boys
were 'expected' to have a hobby and 'required' to take part in
school games—'the express object' of these regulations being to
prevent 'the habit of "loafing" and its attendant evils' (which
were either too dire or too obvious to mention). Parents were
earnestly requested to encourage their sons to take 'active exercise'
every day; the school prayer urged them 'to labour diligently and
faithfully' in the pursuit of virtue, excellence and God; and those
who had been judged to 'exercise a beneficial influence in the
school by their character, position and attainments' were rewarded
by high office, being chosen to become school monitors.

The school ethic had been admirably summed up by the
previous headmaster: 'England', he avowed, 'has always put a
higher value on character than excellence, and Millhillians, who
are the direct descendants of the Puritans, are imbued with their
spirit . . . the moral standards of the country today are a monument
to the glory of the Puritans.'

Like so many of the sentiments of Low-Church morality, the
Puritan ethic which Mill Hill espoused allowed its adherents to
believe in that kind of virtue and morality which seemed positively designed to ensure their material as well as their spiritual
well-being. The non-spiritual aspirations of Millhillians were
neatly expressed for Dimbleby in his first term by the School
Magazine: 'to us here at school the coming life seems to hold all
that can be possibly desired—motor-cars, cigarettes, wealth, perhaps even something higher.'

Richard Dimbleby was not the stuff of which public-school
heroes are made, but fell in readily with the school routine. He

returned to school on time; he rose every morning at seven-thirty, washed in cold water, had a cold swim, sat in the refectory eating ill-cooked bacon and eggs and hard toast with margarine; he stayed quiet (but inattentive) in class, and played rugger in winter and cricket in summer. But despite such valiant attempts at self-effacement, he did not easily merge into the background. Even as a teenager he was uncommonly large, not flabbily fat, but tall and broad and heavy. His face was round and ruddy, and he matured early. In school photographs, even at the age of fifteen he looked like a man among boys. With a cheerful face and large ambling figure, he was well known to everyone, but he was reserved, not easily entering into the games and intrigues and affections of public-school life. With the cruelty of schoolchildren he was punished for his size with the nickname 'Dropsy'—a hated name which humiliated him, though he soon learned to hide it (so much so that less sensitive souls came to think that he did not mind). He was acutely sensitive about his size. Years later, as a famous broadcaster, he would suffer the indignity of reading a rabble of critics (who had never lost the cruel instincts of childhood) discuss his weight and build as if it were a personality defect, in terms which never managed to disguise a fastidious distaste for the outsized. It never ceased to be painful.

It must be said that he did little to help his image. He spent part of most afternoons in the tuck-shop, which was for him a delightful retreat from the rigours of school. The array of artificial cream-cakes on the counter, the Mars bars on the shelves, the rashers of bacon and the boxes of eggs by the stove, the gurgle of hot sweet tea in the urn, the mixture of smells and promised tastes behind the steamed-up windows which hid the grey reality of winter afternoon outside, became a drug. He did not gorge but sat at a little table, usually alone but sometimes with his friend Henry Cunnington, nibbling, nodding, listening and observing. It was almost impossible to dislike him. Schoolfriends and teachers remember that he was never bullied, that though teased, he never became the persecuted 'fatty of the fourth'. There was something about his manner and personality which warned would-be tormentors not to take liberties.

His record of academic achievement was dismal. He moved slowly up through the school, in the lower half of every form, scraped through his school certificate, and found himself (fortunately with his best friend) relegated to the academic back-

woods. Instead of joining the sixth form he was dumped unceremoniously in Shell which was reserved exclusively for those who in a more enlightened era would be described as having 'a learning problem'. Dimbleby was a dud, incapable it seemed of mastering the intricacies of mathematics or science. Only in French and English did he reveal the slightest sign of promise. His standard in English bordered on the excellent: he was a fluent writer and eloquent speaker—'If he would think more and talk less' admonished one end of term report: 'he would do very well'.

Dimbleby failed to compensate for his failure in the classroom by excellence on the playing field. At rugger he was slow and clumsy though (much against his will) he was frequently included in minor teams because his bulk made him invaluable in the front row. He intensely disliked those afternoons in the mud, followed by the steaming showers and wet floors of changing-rooms where his clothes got damp and smelt musty. The summer was a little better. He loathed cricket, for which he had no talent: but when dragooned into a weekly compulsory game he could stand at long-stop for the entire afternoon making daisy chains.

Only in music did he excel. He was in the choir and was accompanist (and sometimes singer) for a select group who called themselves the Savoyards. They took their singing with great seriousness, rehearsing for forty-five minutes almost every night of the summer term—at the end of which they would perform not only to the school but to distinguished outsiders as well. His housemaster who conducted the group thought him uncommonly proficient. He was one of the few boys at the school who had the right to play the school organ whenever he wished. As he gained the privileges of age he was even permitted to forego rugger for the lofty independent calm of the chapel. Sometimes friends would steal in to listen to him work his way through a repertoire which ran from Mahler and Schubert to Gilbert and Sullivan. It was the custom at the end of morning chapel for the organist (if he were boy not master) to herald the departure of the last teacher from the chapel by switching from solemn fugue to latest pop song. Dimbleby was so famed for his transitions that even teachers would linger outside to marvel how smoothly Bach could become 'Tiptoe through the Tulips'. He was jealous of his rights in the chapel, sometimes going to great length to prevent others who shared those rights to the organ from exercising them. He had one particular rival, a boy called Lunt who went on to

B

become a distinguished organ scholar at Cambridge. One after-
noon with the assistance of Henry Cunnington, when he had
exhausted his allotted hour, and Lunt was due to follow him,
Dimbleby went through the elaborate process of clambering
inside the organ, and dismantling some important intestines.
When Lunt arrived he found Dimbleby surrounded by pieces of
pipe and wood engaged on an apparently complicated repair job:
'Sorry Lunt,' he was told, 'not a hope of playing any more today,
Middle C is not ciphering.' Lunt, being a trusting fellow, retired;
Dimbleby and his friend hastily put the organ together again, and
had the whole of the winter afternoon blissfully to themselves.

Behind his modest exterior he also began to reveal himself as
something of a showman. At end of term films, which were invariably old and silent, he took it on himself to emulate the best of
the theatre organists, whom he revered. Henry Cunnington
remembers him playing right through a showing of *Metropolis*
(which ran for eleven reels) without once flagging. Long before
the end of the film it was suggested he might like to rest, but
Dimbleby relished such marathons. At the end he banged lyrically
into the final crescendo, finished, rubbed his hands together, and
said: 'I enjoyed that.'

At home Gwen's thespian aspirations (and talent) were no
longer thought unbecoming. She was a leading member of the
Richmond Operatic and Dramatic Societies. As a small boy
Richard, dressed for silence in plimsolls, had delighted in the job
of call-boy, bustling back and forth behind the stage, knocking on
dressing room doors with the warning 'five minutes to go'. The
Dimbleby family took amateur dramatics with great seriousness.
And to Mill Hill drama Richard brought some of the professional
attitudes that he had acquired in the Richmond theatre. His performance as Ralph Rackstraw in *H.M.S. Pinafore* was judged to
be 'admirable' by the School Magazine's critic, who was generally
thought sparing in praise. Certainly he took less kindly to
Richard's performance in an end of term revue. His sketch was:
'the longest of all and the least successful: not that it wasn't acted
well—it was, . . . but it was not original, and the wit (of which
there was plenty) smacked rather of the set performance and the
professional stage than that of a family party'. Like his size, his
great 'professionalism' would in later years be one of the most
formidable critical barbs hurled at him. In this case, however, he
was unscathed, choosing to interpret a jibe as a pat on the back.

At Mill Hill he was as isolated from the real world as he had been in the bosom of his family in Richmond. The school stood on the top of a ridge looking south towards London and north into rural Middlesex. It was surrounded by fields and wood, a criss-cross of minor roads, and the village houses of affluent commuters. The boys were forbidden to go into the shops or cafés of Mill Hill village; or communicate with anyone who did not 'belong' to the school. They were forbidden to 'break bounds', to travel by motor-car, to go for a walk or ride a bicycle without permission. Preserved from much contact with anyone from a different class at home, the school rules ensured that they would not remedy the deficiency at Mill Hill. Thus by stealth the school imposed upon its pupils the blinkered view of society by which its preservation was assured. An indication of the social myopia which prevailed at the school can be seen in the reports of the School Debating Society to which all those 'with any taste for speaking, any gift for self-expression' were urged to belong. The technical standard of debate was high, verbal felicity was much in evidence, but the ignorance was extreme. Debating the issue of prohibition one speaker (sounding as Richard Dimbleby's grandfather must have done) avowed that if 'a working man' could get drunk, he would, and that as a consequence he should be compelled to abstain—while the Opposer argued that if he could not buy beer the 'working man' would either buy more tobacco, or take home more money to his wife, in which case she would 'take it away and spend it on something equally bad'. Such attitudes in 1931, when Britain teetered on the edge of mass unemployment, spoke a frightening ignorance and complacency.

If Richard Dimbleby did not drink in the spirit of Mill Hill with enthusiasm, he was not disposed to reject it outright; for the moment he was content to let his school days slip by as painlessly as possible. Seniority brought its own rewards for those who had not offended. Richard acquired a study and a fag. The fag prepared his food and cleaned his shoes. His study became famous, not for its enlightened discourse on the affairs of the world, or for the intellectual diligence of its occupant but for its comfort and good food. In a cold and draughty building Dimbleby's study was always warm; it was filled with thick cushions to lounge on; his table was piled with magazines of a not too demanding nature; and his tuck box was always crowded with cakes and bread and

jam. It was cosy, friendly, and welcoming. By his last term, when
he was eighteen, he had only one worry in the world.

His academic record had borne out earlier anxieties. He had
twice failed his matriculation examination, because of his poor
mathematics. If he was worried he contrived not to show it, and
his father (who had left school at fourteen and did not expect his
son to go to university) was not unduly perturbed. His son, he
thought, would be far more profitably employed learning the
craft of journalism, and preparing himself to run the family
business. But Richard was not so certain about a career in journalism. Although he had no strong inclination for any other career,
he had tentatively added 'doctor' to 'journalist' on the 'intended
career' list which the headmaster liked each pupil to fill in. Years
later when it was thought important to have attended university,
Richard fostered a myth that he had been prevented from 'taking
up a course at university' by a sudden (and largely illusory)
collapse in the family fortunes. The same insecurity prompted
him to confide that an ambition to be a surgeon had been dashed
by the same family misfortune. Though surgery fascinated him
he had no inclination or talent for academic life.

There had in fact been something of a family misfortune,
though it was much less critical than he led people to imagine.
In May 1931, after a furious row with the editor, Fred Dimbleby
stormed out of his job at *The Daily Mail*. The issue was politics.
After the fall of the Liberal Government Fred Dimbleby had
chosen to leave Whitehall, refusing to serve MacDonald's Socialist
Government. He had become devoted to Lloyd George and for
a long time the family had voted Liberal. Lloyd George's mixture
of radical rhetoric and conservative action was calculated to appeal
to men like Fred Dimbleby with his roots in the non-conformist
tradition which sought a better world with no poverty but no
loss of what the fortunate had been given and the diligent had won.
The Liberal Party was the Dimblebys' natural political refuge.
Fred had gone to Whitehall out of patriotism, had stayed because
of Lloyd George. In 1928 he became the old man's publicity
manager. He was to mastermind Lloyd George's campaign to
publicise the growing threat of mass unemployment, by which
they hoped to revive the flagging fortunes of the Liberal Party.
Unfortunately the campaign was a flop, the Liberal Party's decline
continued, and there was little Fred could usefully do for the Party.
He joined *The Daily Mail* as a Parliamentary Correspondent.

Lord Rothermere, the *Mail's* proprietor, was a man of little talent who had deluded himself that he could play Kingmaker (and a lot more besides) to the Tory Party. For a brief and ludicrous period the *Mail* promoted at first ridiculous and then sinister causes. Of the stormtroopers in Germany, it had few criticisms, and it did not find the antics of their leader Adolf Hitler in any way offensive. In addition *The Daily Mail* took an adulatory fancy to the young Oswald Mosley and his New Party, observing that he 'combines the fervour of the Evangelist with the grace of the matinée idol'; the New Party ought 'to shake the complacency of the parliamentarians'; and the Mosleyites were 'taking on the present Parliamentary system.'

Fred Dimbleby bore Rothermere's flirtation with fascism in silence for a little. Then he complained. Then he spoke out. He was a man of strong and simple opinion, and the reaction of his friends in Westminster to what his paper published confirmed his own instinctive feelings. In May he stormed out of *The Daily Mail* office and left Fleet Street for ever. Although he had thus lost his Fleet Street income, catastrophe was by no means imminent. He decided to return fulltime as editor of the family papers. Much more important than the financial suffering, was that his departure from the *Mail* meant the disappearance of the job which he had arranged for Richard in the paper's Paris office.

At Mill Hill Dimbleby's delight at the news that he had passed matriculation on the third attempt was tempered by the news about Paris. For the first time Henry Cunnington saw his friend really depressed—'My father's left the *Mail*. I can't go to France. I shall have to work at Richmond. Oh God!'

As he left Mill Hill for the last time at the end of that summer term for the shop floor of F. W. Dimbleby and Sons he carried in his pocket his last school report. It spoke highly of his character and ability, his conduct, his industry and his progress. It went on: 'He has taken a very keen and active part in the school life and can always be relied upon to do his best. He has got on here very well with masters and boys alike. I feel confident that he will make a success of life.' His father was unimpressed: 'Huh!' he grunted to Gwen, 'Is that what we sent him to public school for? I could have that said about a poodle.'

2

The Young Reporter

Happy is England! I could be content
To see no other verdure than its own;
To feel no other breezes than are blown
Through its tall woods with high romances blent.

JOHN KEATS

A WEEK LATER, WHILE SOME OF HIS FRIENDS FROM MILL
Hill set off on extended holiday before going up to Oxford,
Richard Dimbleby found himself in the composing room of
The Richmond and Twickenham Times. It was typical of his father
to suggest with some brusqueness that there was 'no point in
wasting time'. He wanted his son to make a mark in the world
just as he had, and the sooner he set about it the better.

Richard did not regret *The Daily Mail* or Paris or university
for long. Later an occasional belligerence towards undergraduates,
an irritation with what he thought was their sharper-than-thou
tittle-tattle, was the only indication that he gave of the intellectual
insecurity that some non-graduates affect not to feel. Otherwise
when the subject of university arose he pointed to his own achievements as evidence of the unnecessary indulgence of a university
career. What if he *had* spent three years at Oxford or Cambridge?
He was eighteen; he had led a secure and unadventurous life in
a household which had a traditional suspicion of 'ideas' and respect
for 'facts'—the things which Fred said 'you could see and hear'
(and, he would almost add, 'put your trust in'). It was a view of
life which if simple was at least conducive to a good digestion. If,
in 1931, Richard had gone to university he would have been
plunged into a world of intellectual ferment. England seemed
poised on the verge of nobody quite knew what: there was a

National Government; the economic crisis was at its peak; unemployment was reaching towards three million; the Hunger Marches were about to start; Mosley was preaching a new and frightening faith to the East End of London; fascism, infant of the depression, was struggling to its feet in Europe; serious intellectuals hailed Stalin's Soviet Union as the new hope of mankind. In the universities the sons of the middle class wrestled with new concepts, conflicting passions and opposing politics. Only dullards could remain unmoved—and whatever the fragility of his intellectual training Richard Dimbleby was no dullard: he had a quick mind, a fluent tongue. Inevitably he would have been involved, taken sides. As it was he took no part, remaining imprisoned by the limitations of a happy home and the family business. The traumas of the early Thirties passed him by.

At Richmond he worked in the composing room, learning how to operate a linotype machine, on the 'stone' discovering how to 'make up' a page (and developing in the process an undying obsession for trying new layouts); and on the press which he loved: 'the creaking sound of paper tautening (five miles of it on every reel), the beginnings of vibration, and within a few seconds the building is echoing and trembling'. Like all apprentices he was teased and made a fool of; but he learnt the intricacies of the art of newspaper production, and to relish the damp smell of fresh newsprint.

There was much bonhomie on the shop floor of *The Richmond and Twickenham Times* and by some Richard was regarded with real affection. But no-one could forget that he was the boss's son doing his stint before moving on to better things. F. W. Dimbleby and Sons had a poor reputation. The print unions were weak so managers and overmen felt free to behave as they would. It was not uncommon for young apprentices to be (literally) kicked around by bullying overmen who, with the gift of overtime at their disposal, wielded great intimidating power: 'You have to go faster than that, you know!' a Works Manager could bellow at a hardworking compositor, and fear no Union reaction. The Management men were tough and they were hired for it. The family remained above the battle, its hands unsoiled. Occasionally when 'they' came down (be it Managing Director Percy, Editor in Chief Fred or 'Mrs. Fred') the staff would mind their manners, and some, to the amusement of their fellows, would adopt the alien mannerisms of the middle class to ingratiate themselves with the bosses.

Once—in extremis—the family had very firmly stepped into battle. In the week of the General Strike of May 1926 many readers of *The Thames Valley Times* (which came out on Wednesdays) were surprised to find their copy of the paper dropped through the letter box as usual. Nearly every other newspaper in the country was shut down. Three days later on Saturday *The Richmond and Twickenham Times* (whose delivery was also a surprise) carried a leading article, which bore the authentic imprint of Fred Dimbleby. It began:

A WONDERFUL WEEK—a week that has illustrated all the strength of the British character, a week that in a Latin country might have culminated in revolution and bloodshed . . . nobody doubts that the British spirit will win through, grave though the position of the country may be, and that Britain will emerge from one more sea of troubles with head unbowed.

'Steady' is the watchword. It is annoying to see our trade dwindling, to have few newspapers, to be idle through no fault of our own . . . It is irritating, in the leisure-loving south, to reflect that we are suffering in many ways because of some trouble that has occurred in the remote industrial areas. Yet we can all carry on . . . The appearance on Wednesday of *The Thames Valley Times*, when most of the newspapers in the country were shut down, has created a good deal of comment. Publication of that issue, and of today's paper, is entirely due to the loyalty and good spirit of the staff.

Which was not quite the whole truth. On the eve of the strike, Percy Dimbleby had offered the workers two choices. They could join the strike, in which case they would be sacked, or they could carry on working, ignore the strike call, and be assured of the company's future benevolence. Eight men obeyed the General Strike call and duly lost their jobs. The rest, facing the prospect of no work, with families to support, behaved with due 'loyalty and good spirit'. The Dimbleby family was Victorian not only in morals but in business: six years later when Richard was in the Works the memories of 1926 had not been entirely erased from the collective mind of the shop floor.

It was not a happy paper. Percy and Fred Dimbleby were quite opposite characters. Percy was small, frugal and enjoyed a reputation for great meanness far beyond the office: the principle that money was for saving and not for spending had been elevated by him into a passion. He married but produced no children, lived in the same house for almost his entire adult life, and rarely left Richmond. He was jealous of, and never really forgave, Fred for leaving the confines of Richmond and making a name for himself in the world beyond. He resented the assurance with which Fred had left the *Mail* and then at his own convenience returned to the family business full-time, while he, Percy, had been left alone for so many years to manage its affairs. The Managing Director determined to assert and maintain his authority over his wayward brother.

Within months the two men were quarrelling. Fred, whom Percy regarded with great suspicion, wished to improve the paper, buy new plant, and hire more reporters. Percy would not countenance such extravagance and he had a maddening way of reminding the Editor in Chief that the Managing Director's word was final. On numerous occasions the Editor in Chief would storm into the Managing Director to demand that Percy accede to his plans for the paper. The Managing Director would listen for a little, then lean back in his chair, adjust his spectacles and say primly: 'No, I think not Fred.' His brother who had a short temper would explode with frustration, his voice echoing out far beyond the confines of the Managing Director's office. Then Percy would deliver the coup de grâce: 'Well, when you've finished, Fred, I think we'd better leave it there, I've got a lot of work to do.' And Fred would storm out of the office slamming the door in rage behind him.

Percy was cordially loathed by nearly all the workers in the company. To them he seemed cold, remote, mean, a bully. 'Mr. Fred,' though he had a bad temper was at least a human, if sometimes a frightening boss. He wore a monocle, and workers who were summoned to his office went in some trepidation of his disapproval. On one occasion he sacked a worker for refusing to do overtime on the orders of a much disliked Works Manager. One by one the other men who had also refused to obey orders, were called to his office for sentence: 'I am not giving you fourteen days' he told each of them, fixing them with a frown that was truly fearsome, 'this is a warning. When you're told to do overtime, you do it. Understand?' And the offenders, reprieved, went away grateful for his leniency.

Fred imposed his own standards on reporters, and particularly on Richard when his son moved up into the reporters' room. He would never lay himself open to the accusation of 'being soft' on 'Mr. Richard'. No reporter was allowed to leave the office without a hat on; young reporters were forbidden to grow beards. The hapless employees of other firms who were ignorant of Fred's Victorian hauteur suffered greatly. On one occasion the Tax Office sent a clerk along to see him. He walked into the Editor in Chief's office forgetting to remove his hat. Fred was furious: 'Now just you go back to your office and tell your Inspector that if he wants to speak to me, he may do in person by appointment, and tell him that if he sends a clerk along on his behalf again, who does not have the good manners to remove his hat in my presence, I'll knock it off for him.'

From long years of training Fred was an excellent editor. Reporters who went on from Richmond to Fleet Street remember that he always wrote what he wanted to say first time, deliberately, on small sheets of paper, at an even pace. No word was crossed out, no comma out of place. As he wrote one sheet, a messenger took it down to the compositor's room while he wrote the next. Fred expected his reporters to aspire to the same standards. Under his father's guidance Richard acquired a journalistic speed, fluency and neatness which was to serve him well. Fred was severe with those who failed to live up to his standards, but his gruff praise when work was well done was generous.

Richard did not find the work of a local reporter congenial. To him it was a survival test rather than a training ground. It is true that under his father's critical gaze he learned to be accurate, to spell the names of vicars and bridesmaids correctly; to count the number of guests at garden parties and funerals; to repeat the jargon of the Court Room and make it intelligible; to remember that in the mind of a speaker the words which he chose to open *this* fête were just as important as those chosen by someone else at *that*, and that therefore they should be noted exactly and fully. He learned to be polite to boors and courteous to bores, to listen to old jokes and old complaints with a sympathetic ear, and to write it all up quickly, finishing two stories in the hour, all neat and tidy with beginnings, middles and ends. It came very easily to him. He went to law courts, police stations, inquests, christenings, marriages, funerals, hospitals, mortuaries, town halls, council meetings, political rallies, and garden fêtes. And he was bored.

His father would have condemned any display of disaffection, so Richard hid it from most of his colleagues. They enjoyed his good humour, the assurance which seemed so in advance of his years, and his ability to make others think they mattered. They noted too the blossoming of a great energy. At home and at school he had been slothful. Now it was as if he had suddenly woken up, and realised that he wished to move in the world. The frustration of his daily round on the local paper, soon made way for a desire to move on and out of local journalism. He had the ability (denied to most talents) of disguising his frustration and he wore his ambition lightly. He began to work furiously to drive out boredom and frustration.

In 1931, for the first time in his life Richard Dimbleby fell passionately in love. During his last term at Mill Hill his pocket money had been sent to him on his father's behalf by Fred's personal assistant, a girl of eighteen called Dilys Thomas. They met for the first time, just before he had left school, in his father's office. He had never had a girl friend, and was awkward and embarrassed in front of women. He stammered out a 'Hello, Miss Thomas' and fled. Dilys had come to the paper almost straight from school after a quick secretarial course. Her father, Arthur Thomas, knew Fred through their membership of the National Liberal Club. They were very different men. Thomas was a thoughtful reflective, intellectual Welshman, possessing in abundance those qualities of his native land which are so despised and envied at the same time. He loved poetry, books and music, and was a brilliant raconteur. A man of strong emotions, he was subject to bouts of great depression: tormenting himself with the sufferings of the world, sitting in his armchair with tears in his eyes, saying to his wife: 'Kathleen, Kathleen do you realise what is happening . . . ?' He was a graduate of Dublin University, a barrister of some distinction, an author, a Chairman of the London County Council's Education Committee, a Liberal candidate, and an ardent social reformer. His eldest daughter, Olwen, was a ballet dancer, and a member of the company at Sadlers Wells; his second daughter, Myfanwy, who had just become the first woman to win an external law degree at London University, was practising as a solicitor; and his youngest, Dilys, wished to become a journalist. Fred Dimbleby, who came to regard Arthur with a respect which bordered on awe, was delighted to give Dilys a chance in the office.

Her start had not been auspicious. On her arrival at Dimbleby's

she was summoned to the Editor in Chief's office. She rushed up
the stairs, red in the face, out of breath, hair flying, coat undone,
and umbrella half open. She stood panting in the room waiting
for her new boss to welcome her. When he looked up, removing
his monocle, he greeted her: 'So you want to be a journalist?'
'Well, I er...' she was overcome with confusion, words failed
her, she dropped her umbrella and spent the next few moments,
mumbling apologies, kneeling on the floor trying to extricate
the umbrella from the coat, and her notebook from the umbrella.
But Fred took to her and soon allowed her to go into the reporters'
room and 'be a journalist'. Each evening the reporters' room,
filled with smoke and beer bottles, echoed to the sound of argument, which was often long and frequently acrimonious. In these
heated evening discussions about unemployment, the economy
and the fascists, only Richard Dimbleby took no part. Dilys stood
firmly and powerfully in the Liberal middle, defending the
traditions of both their families. Richard who had no taste for
controversy, and who suspected that argument was wasteful of
time and talent, watched on as Dilys held forth. With that air of
vulnerability and defiance so irresistible to men with a powerful
protective instinct, she never lacked eligible escorts, and enjoyed
going out with whom she liked, and whom she could accommodate in her busy reporter's schedule. She liked Richard. Once
he had overcome his initial bashfulness, he was a delightful companion: irrepressible, and filled with exciting ideas for trips and
outings. They started to go on reporting assignments together,
and then out to lunch, and then to each other's homes. Their
friends noticed long before he thought that it was evident that
he was in love. It was the first time that Richard had ever felt
really serious about anything; Dilys came to dominate his life.
His friends saw a touching quality about his love. He was so
obviously and openly proud of his conquest, and always a little
bewildered that, from an array of suitors, she chose to be with
him. There were always, he felt, other, more glamorous men
who would steal her away. He was devoted and, a little to his
own surprise, filled with an immense passion. When he was
away he started to write letters to her. They were tender, romantic
and, as he grew more confident, less and less inhibited. Until
their marriage seven years later, they were also invariably humble.
He never forgot to remind her that he was aware that she had
not given her promise, that it was 'if' not 'when' she would marry

him. The passion for Dilys was the first time any strong emotion had affected him; the first time that he, or others, realised that he was a man of unusually strong feelings which once roused did not easily go away. The letters to Dilys which he wrote whenever he was away in the next fifteen years never lost their first intensity.

To begin with, Richard's father was not enthusiastic about their infatuation, believing it would interfere with his son's work, and affect his career. He was fond of Dilys, but they were too serious too young. Richard (in his view) had a long way to go, and matters of the heart should not be allowed to get in the way. He made it clear that he did not expect either of their performances at *The Richmond and Twickenham Times* to be affected by their emotions. Thus they had to adopt elaborate ruses to be alone together. The News Editor, a soft-hearted man who smiled on their romance, was enlisted on their side, suddenly discovering that many local matters which until then had been adequately covered by one reporter now required the attendance of two—especially dinners and dances. The Editor in Chief had to know nothing about it. Later, when the families became close friends, Fred, relenting, gave his blessing, but frowned if Richard arrived home late. They spent nearly every evening together, either on a story, or at the office, or out in Richard's car which he had bought for thirty shillings and which was notoriously and conveniently unreliable. It frequently, and sometimes genuinely, broke down far from home late at night. On one such occasion they had to leave it at Brentford where it had caught fire and walk to Dilys's home at Ealing, arriving at three o'clock in the morning. They had never been so late before and were terrified when they saw that the light was still on in Arthur Thomas's study. Dilys pushed him into the house: 'I'm sorry, sir, you see the car . . .' Her father stopped him: 'No explanations, no explanations now. You must both be exhausted—come and have some coffee'. Accepted by the family, Richard became possessive, unable to bear Dilys spending time with anyone else. On the occasion of the Local Press Ball which his grandmother's death made it unseemly for him to attend, he stood outside the hotel where it was being held, until long after midnight waiting to make sure that she did not leave with any other man.

Although he was bored with Richmond, it was a painful day when in the spring of 1934 he left *The Richmond and Twickenham*

Times to move to Lymington in Hampshire where Fred had arranged for him to work as a reporter on the local paper. Of his time in Lymington, he subsequently wrote,

> I was on the editorial staffs of the *Southern Echo* and the *Bournemouth Echo*, and was local correspondent in the New Forest area for the leading London Dailies and News Agencies. I represented both these papers at the same time over an area of a hundred square miles, sending each separate stories of all news events, principally from the New Forest area . . . I became used to all forms of rapid news work, at any hour of the day or night.

Although (in a job application) he made his work sound dramatic and not a little important he found Lymington rather like Richmond, but without Dilys, and he hated it. Whenever he could, he drove out into the country, to the New Forest or up into the hills, on the edge of the cliffs, where he would make himself a pot of tea on an old primus stove, sit and dream and write letters to his love.

From one of his favourite spots overlooking Studland Bay he wrote a few weeks after arriving in Lymington:

> I haven't been extravagant—coming out here, as I had plenty of petrol in the car, and I've made my own tea here. I know that the country for miles round here is beautiful—moorland and hills—but I feel so lonely, and my old heart aches so much. If only you were sitting by my side. I felt I couldn't stay in Lymington today—you know what it looks like on Sundays! But somehow now I feel that I was silly to come here. It's so lonely. Only the cries of the seabirds, and an occasional cuckoo. You can hear the noise of the surf in the distance, and about a quarter of a mile away there are some children playing, and I can hear their voices. That's all—these Purbeck Hills can be terribly lonely sometimes. I feel that if I have to stay here alone much longer I shall *scream*—I know it's childish but you, I believe, will understand. I have a confession to make to you— which I would only tell you—I hate Lymington and its district. It's gradually getting me down. It's so much the village—so horribly quiet after London. People say: 'Oh! you'll get used to it—but I don't *want* to. I would be all right if I were in a

pretty little cottage in the country but it's living in a horrible smug country town that I loathe.

His impatience with Lymington became more acute every month. As his frustration grew so did his ambition. He wrote to Dilys:

I have never tried to write short stories or special articles of any kind and for that matter you haven't either. I wonder if we have any leanings that way. It has occurred to me that if you and I were more 'writers' than 'journalists', our time would be so much more our own and we *could* travel and tour and see places . . .

In another letter he wrote:

You know, if only I can discover the right sort of market for writing, or get an 'assured income' in some way or other, we can have our caravan and be as free as the winds . . . You must think I'm always writing to people and never effecting anything. But you *do* see, don't you, that it's only by writing all the time and repeatedly trying to place stuff that one can *ever* have any success?

He started to write in earnest, drawing on his experience as a reporter: 'I realise' he wrote in a foreword to a collection of his articles, 'that I have seen many things that were beautiful, many that were sad, but all of them things which at the time seemed to be just the happenings of routine.' The articles were an attempt to record 'the innermost secrets of the country, glimpses of the heart of England that come with breathtaking unexpectedness to the country reporter on his rounds'. Each of them was a resolution of the frustration of the local reporter's lot, an attempt to fill the gap between reality and the tedious list of names and irrelevant facts that had to fill his daily 'copy'. One of them reflected his hostility to the 'smugness' of country life. It was entitled Feudal Fete:

It is opened by a florid woman hired for the occasion for the price of a huge bouquet whose speech is greeted by the music of subdued clapping led anxiously by the vicar. The coconut shy is under the direction of old Admiral Z who twenty years ago rendered his country conspicuous service 'somewhere in Whitehall' and has never been able to forget it. After a little the florid lady is wondering when she will be able to slip away to a sherry party—very fashionable in the country—without being seen by the populace; and as the local people drink lemonade and ginger beer, in a little while the Generals and Admirals will slip round the house to the study where a thoughtful host has left a decanter or so, and a few syphons and bottles. The treasurer counts the takings and by the look of beatific joy on his face, it is not hard to imagine that the annual deficit on the church heating fund has once again been considerably reduced; and the florid lady who tells the vicar 'that she is delighted by all she has seen', is helped into her limousine . . . and they say that feudalism is dead in England!

Richard Dimbleby was never reactionary but his instincts were deeply and romantically conservative. He preferred to observe than to judge. So he wrote of a gypsy encampment deep in the New Forest where the caravans

twelve of them, stood in a wide ring round the smooth green lawn of the enclosure, tall, gaunt, and throwing long, gloomy shadows from the setting sun. And in front of each one glowed twelve pinewood fires . . . the air was filled with the smoky smell of burning wood, mingled faintly with the odour of grass, of trees, and of the mysterious undergrowth.

He had gone there nervously to meet the mother of a boy who had been drowned in a forest pool, and whose inquest he had to cover. As he left 'somehow affected by the silent grief of that dark gypsy woman' he realised that he was not alone: 'Looking round I saw not without alarm that a dozen men and women had come silently from their fires and caravans to escort me to the gate.' Later, after the inquest, he drove home, pausing on the edge of the forest and saw that 'far away, lost in the midst of a sea of burnt gorse and sunbaked turf five tiny figures were making their way towards the tall pine trees to the west.'

Richard Dimbleby's view of Hampshire life was highly selective. He allowed a rose-tinted filter carefully to screen out from his perceptions those things which were unpleasant, or wicked or degrading, those things which would unduly disturb his sensibilities. Occasionally he went to Southampton, to the cinema or to hear the Bournemouth Symphony Orchestra (especially when it played Mahler). Had he chosen to look a little more closely at the city he would have been shocked. In October 1934, a colleague of his called, Douglas Ashley, who had been his predecessor in Lymington and was now based in the Head Office at Southampton, was so outraged by the conditions in which hundreds of Southampton families were living that he decided to start his own weekly paper, to expose their degradation and the failure of the Council to do anything about it. The first issue sold out. He wrote:

> I have been shocked and revolted. In some of the houses in the Town Ward, and in Swaythling, families with three or four young children apiece are sleeping on sacks on the floor . . . It struck me that if it were true that one half of the world does not know how the other half lives, the position here is that one eighth of Southampton doesn't care how the other seven-eighths are living.

The article detailed cases of men and women selling their possessions to buy food, of families evicted and sleeping rough in the street, of men wearing out the soles of their only shoes in the search for work. It was a brilliant piece of journalism. For a young reporter with campaigning instincts *The Southern Weekly Sketch*, as Ashley called his paper, might have seemed to offer some relief from the frustrations and limitations of the *Southern Daily Echo*. But Dimbleby did not seek to join the new paper; nor did it occur to Ashley to ask him. It was not that he would not have cared; his concerns (for the moment) were elsewhere.

There were signs in some of his articles that there was more to his romanticism than a dreamy perception of rural life. His observations contained and began to express an attitude, a nostalgia, a yearning almost, for a pattern of life which was ordered and unchanging, and which he only dimly (and a little sentimentally) perceived. He had gone to interview an old man and his wife on their diamond wedding anniversary, and afterwards he wrote:

> He spoke to me of the forest, the fields and of the weather . . .

When I asked about his life, he had nothing to tell. He could remember every detail from his boyhood, but it was of no interest 'to the newspaper' he thought . . . I like to believe that I saw deep into the soul of England that morning, by gazing into a pair of old blue eyes . . .

When the old man died he went to the funeral:

Thirty mourners stood in the exposed churchyard facing a warm May breeze, as the tall, white-clad vicar murmured the last words of the familiar service. The next morning there was no obituary, no carefully written 'memoir' in England's papers. Even locally, ten brief lines recorded the death and funeral 'of a ninety-year-old man'. But beneath the mass of flowers, all of them labelled 'Tom', which lay like a summer carpet in the churchyard, lay buried the spirit of England . . .

His romance with the English countryside became inextricably entwined with his passion for Dilys. His letters became increasingly insistent (though he was still respectful about the possibility of marriage) about the future:

I love to think, when I'm feeling a bit miserable that my staying and working here *may* mean that I shall have you and your loveliness, your beauty, your kindness, with me forever . . . Just now I was building a shelter for the 'meth' stove with some bricks I found, and it occurred to me that if you and I were out caravanning I would have been building one for you. I suppose it sounds rather ambitious but if I can't afford 'Sleepy Dell' (the name they had given to an imaginary cottage in the country) just as soon as we are married—again, of course, *if* we are—we could buy a comfy trailer caravan and have a wonderful time.

We could go all over the country at weekends, 'days off', and holiday times and apart from being together, and having a sort of country cottage with us all the time, we could sit by our caravan in the evening and have a camp fire and listen to the wind, and look at each other . . .

And in another, later:

We'll be so happy together. We must hunt out some place in the country, just a tiny place, which will be home, and then when we've got more money we'll find a *tiny* flat 'somewhere in London' and we'll have our third home, the travelling one, so that we can go just where we want to.

We'll do all those things, you and I. I'm determined we shall, and somehow I feel deep down in my old bones that it's going to happen.

He stayed in Lymington for eighteen months and longed to be away. There were some compensations: he played the organ at the church in the evening alone; he stirred the Christmas pudding at the Eynon's house—George Eynon, a 'rival' from another paper had befriended him; and occasionally Dilys came down for the weekend. Then he drove to Brockenhurst station to collect her off the London train, and took her back to stay (in separate lodgings) in the town. They would walk, go to a cinema, eat dinner out and wonder if Myffy (Dilys's lawyer sister) had forgiven Richard for some proposed extravagance with which Dilys had unwisely acquainted her. They both lived in need of her good opinion, and she was not frightened to make her judgments clear; when Myffy was cross with them for lack of caution they were filled with gloom. His desire to live as he wished (for which he would need more, much more money) intensified his ambition to escape the confines of local journalism. And though he had not managed to find a publisher for his articles, he became increasingly confident of his abilities. It began to show in his reports for the paper as he sometimes omitted the guest list from a wedding or the opening words from a speech and began instead to substitute his own phrases. As a result his reports lost their factual edge and gained a descriptive touch. Sub-editors at Head Office began to complain 'there's never anything in Dimbleby's copy'—and in their terms they were right.

George Eynon remembers that 'Richard was always original— he didn't do the obvious thing like the rest of us'. On Armistice Day, other reporters went to the biggest local church service. He went alone to Buckler's Hard from where Nelson's Fleet had once set sail. And there he wrote of the past, of Britain at war, of soldiers and sailors who had died for their country; of a wet autumn day, the smell of mud at low tide, a few wandering gulls, silent boats at anchor—of images to remind his readers of 'the soul of Britain'.

In one of his last letters to Dilys from Lymington he wrote

complaining of the 'boring work' of the local reporter ('I've got
to hear the New Milton Operatic Society in *San Toy* tonight.
Oh! Gawd!') and promised himself a move from Lymington and
then 'something much better than journalism.' In December 1935,
after a little over a year, he decided, not least because he wished
to be nearer her, that he must return to London. He resigned
from the staff of Southern Newspapers and applied for a job on
a trade magazine called *Advertisers Weekly*, which he could just
claim had brought him to Fleet Street. His father strongly disapproved of his working for an 'advertising rag' and urged
patience upon him. But since he was vaguely considering that
the 'something better than journalism' which he sought might
lie in advertising or public relations, he had no sense that he was
squandering his journalistic integrity.

Jobs in Fleet Street were hard to get. It was a time when
graduates were unemployed in large numbers. In journalism
everybody was, more than usual, after everyone else's job. Half-
employed journalists roamed Fleet Street in search of work. The
owners (particularly on magazines like *Advertisers Weekly*) exploited the situation unmercifully. One error, one lunch-time
too long, one late arrival at work, one missed story, invited not
a reprimand but the sack. The *Advertisers Weekly* was suffering
chronically from the effects of the recession. Nearly all the news
was trade news filled out by 'special features' which were no more
than advertising supplements. Competition for advertising was
intense, and it was the reporter's job to help find firms willing
to take space in the paper in return for advertising space. The
work was dull but demanding. Richard Dimbleby was hired as
a reporter for £4 a week. Three months after he joined the
paper—so rapid was the turnover, so eager and large the queue
of aspirant journalists prepared to accept pitiful wages—Richard
Dimbleby was appointed News Editor; a post which made him
at the age of twenty-three, as he wrote with some pride, 'the
youngest News Editor in Fleet Street'. The work was hard and
the hours were long: 'I am having hard experience here' he wrote
'as this paper has a reputation for weekly exclusive stories, and
is regarded as one of the boldest and most go-ahead trade or news
papers in the country'. It was soon apparent however that the
work was unlikely to satisfy the aspirations of a young man who
seemed to those who worked with him to be in a considerable
hurry. He determined to move as soon as he could.

By now he was living in a bed-sitter in Bloomsbury, looking after himself for the first time in his life. In Lymington he had lived in lodgings, with his meals provided. He thrived now in London on doughnuts which he bought from a delicatessen across the road, and milk which he drank in great quantities. Occasionally he cooked a 'celebration' dinner for Dilys, when they ate spaghetti and drank wine. Otherwise when he was not out he sat alone with his doughnuts.

He used to listen to the evening news bulletin on the radio and like most people of his age thought that it was stuffy and dull. One evening it occurred to him that there was no irreversible law of nature which made this so. What was more, it was obvious how it could be improved. The next day he went into the office and told his staff: 'I'm going to write to the BBC and get a job there'. He said it, as he now said everything, with such an air of assurance, and in such an ebullient manner, that no-one thought to ask him whether he was serious. The BBC was an august institution; each year scores of graduates of Oxford and Cambridge with good degrees trooped eagerly to Broadcasting House in the hope of joining the Elect, and serving the Nation under the lofty rule of Sir John Reith. To belong to the BBC was to join an exclusive club whose members (men of discerning intellect and civilised spirit) were enjoined to share with the Nation, through the medium of wireless, their appreciation of all that was best in the realms of information, education and entertainment. It was not immediately obvious how Richard Dimbleby could contribute to such worthy, if unworldly undertakings. He had a quick mind, he was a competent reporter, he was hard working, and more ambitious than he seemed—but such qualities were by no means unique. What he had not so far revealed was that he was a man of unusual energy, filled with original ideas, which he could express with a formidable confidence and flair. But he did as he said he would. In his Bloomsbury bed-sitter one evening in the summer of 1936 he sat down and composed a letter to the BBC asking for a job in the News Department.

3

To Broadcasting House

Oh my England
that free speech without free radio is as zero

EZRA POUND

IT WAS A FORTUNATE ACCIDENT THAT RICHARD DIMBLEBY
had a singularly robust ego. At his first interview with the BBC
it was made plain to him that the Corporation was not in
immediate need of his services. He was unperturbed. A few weeks
later he wrote again to the BBC, to the Chief News Editor, John
Coatman.

45, Torrington Square, W.C.I.

Dear Mr. Coatman,

You may remember that a few weeks ago you were good
enough to give me an interview at Broadcasting House when I
enquired about possible vacancies on your staff.

Since then I have been hoping to hear from you, but I quite
understand that the possible opening you mentioned may not
occur for some time.

Meanwhile I am daring to make a suggestion concerning the
news bulletins which you may care to consider. Naturally, I
should very much like to assist with it myself, but that is not the
only reason for which I make it.

It is my impression, and I find that it is shared by many

others, that it would be possible to enliven the News to some extent without spoiling the authoritative tone for which it is famed. As a journalist, I think I know something of the demand which the public makes for a 'News angle', and how it can be provided. I suggest that a member or members of your staff—they could be called 'BBC reporters, or BBC correspondents'—should be held in readiness, just as are the evening paper men, to cover unexpected News for that day. In the event of a big fire, strike, civil commotion, railway accidents, pit accidents, or any other major catastrophes in which the public, I fear, is deeply interested, a reporter could be sent from Broadcasting House to cover the event for the bulletin.

At the scene, it would be his job, in addition to writing his own account of the event, to secure an eye-witness (the man or woman who saw it start, one of the survivors, a girl 'rescued from the building') and to give a short eye-witness account of the part he or she played that day. In this way, I really believe that News could be presented in a gripping manner, and, at the same time, remain authentic.

Everyone, I think, finds the agency reports a trifle flat after a time, as, indeed, they are bound to be. It is for that reason, I take it, that you keep an observer at Geneva, and incorporate a short talk in the bulletins on some topic of the day. But these talks are always academic—they come from some authority on the subject. There can be no vital authority on a sudden news event, unless it be the man in the street who was on the spot.

Technically, the scheme should present no difficulties. Through the Saturday Magazine and In Town Tonight, you already know that the rather uncouth voices of Londoners and countrymen can be recorded or transmitted satisfactorily, and you are used to last minute arrangements. The description of the event, in addition to the story written by the reporter and agency matter which you may care to use, could be transmitted from the studio, to which your representative could bring the eye-witness.

Alternatively, if that person should be unable to come, it should be possible to record his or her brief description in the mobile van you keep for actuality programmes. Such a news bulletin itself would be a type of actuality programme. I do submit, however, that a journalist should be given the job of assisting with its presentation, rather than a BBC producer.

I do not propose that the whole of the news should be treated in this way, although a staff man at the regional centres could cover you in the same way, and big events of the type could be relayed for the news from these places. The usual foreign, political and personal news would still be supplied by the agencies or by your own representatives direct.

The principle of enlivening news by the infusion of the human element is being followed in other spheres, as you know. The newspapers, of course, have demanded interviews for their big stories for many years, and I myself have had to obtain eye-witness accounts and personal interviews for hundreds of stories of all types.

The newsreels are following suit, The March of Time being an example. In this, as you may have seen, the method followed is not only that of showing the news, but telling why, and how, it happened. That is what I suggest the BBC could do with great success, not only with sudden events or catastrophes, but with all types which at present come to the listener from the pen of a Press Association or Exchange Telegraph man who gives the same story to hundreds of provincial evening papers and London dailies.

If the news service is to be extended, both for home programmes and those to the Empire, would this not be a valuable part of the programme? It does seem to me that in the future and particularly in the event of national emergency, the BBC will play a vital part. Recorded news bulletins of the type I suggest would also prove valuable libraries of this century, for the next.

If you put this scheme into operation, or even included part of it in your future scheme, I should be happy if I were able to play a part.

I have had the type of experience needed, both among country people in the provinces and in the suburbs. Now I am in Fleet Street, and it may possibly interest you to know that I have been appointed News Editor of the *Advertisers Weekly*—I now have, I believe, the doubtful honour of being Fleet Street's youngest editor, a position which my father enjoyed thirty-five years ago at the same age.

But I have detained you far too long already. I hope that you have found time to read this long letter, and that it may be of some use. I do hope that there may be some opportunity for me in your department in the not too distant future, for I really am interested and confident that I should be of use to you.

Yours very truly,

RICHARD DIMBLEBY

It is improbable that Richard Dimbleby was aware of the heresies enunciated by this carefully self-deprecating letter. In 1936 his proposals were not only revolutionary; they threatened to open a Pandora's box of inconvenient and even menacing issues.

The BBC had no reporters. For news it relied exclusively on the news agencies like Reuters and the Press Association—and small teams of men in Broadcasting House spent long hours ensuring that the nightly news bulletin, read in sombre tones by a dinner-jacketed announcer, should be studiously bland and soporific. It was not an accident. Not surprisingly John Coatman did not feel the urge to request Dimbleby's immediate attendance at Broadcasting House to put his plans for the BBC into practice. Instead, impressed by his enthusiasm, he suggested that the ambitious young man apply for job as a sub-editor in the News Department. Dimbleby did as he was bid, sending another long letter of application—and the job went to someone else. It was not until September 1936, nearly six months after he had first sought to join the BBC, that he walked through the swing doors of Broadcasting House as a member of the BBC staff.

'Here I was,' he wrote later, 'at a small empty desk in a small and otherwise empty room about to tackle a job which did not yet exist and about which I knew nothing at all.' Yet his arrival at Broadcasting House signalled the beginning of a profound change in broadcasting. The approach, style and techniques which were to create a new form of journalism, which were to distinguish programmes from War Report to the World at One, and which were to be borrowed and adapted with even more effect by television, had their origins in Room 525, where Richard Dimbleby sat late one Friday afternoon in September 1936 and wondered what to do next. He was a Topical Talks Assistant, on a salary of £350 a year.

The British Broadcasting Corporation was about to celebrate its tenth birthday (though the original British Broadcasting Company had been formed fourteen years earlier in 1922). Among other duties, the BBC had been obliged by its 1927

Charter 'to collect news of and information relating to current events in any part of the world and in any matter that may be thought fit and to establish and subscribe to news agencies'. It was a deceptively bland injunction.

The BBC was the creation of Sir John Reith whose ideals and morality became its own. Reith was a Scot, a son of the Manse, into whom the spirit of Calvinism had bitten deep. His outlook was narrow, his principles were rigid, but, as he said of himself (with typical modesty and some truth): 'we were vouchsafed a measure of vision'. 'Our responsibility,' he had declared, 'is to carry into the greatest possible number of homes everything that is best in every department of human knowledge, endeavour and achievement, and to avoid the things which are, or may be hurtful.' Within the BBC his fierce look, his gaunt face, his great height and austere manner made him a formidable, and awesome personality. Few dared cross him; none did so with impunity.

If Reith's vision was exalted, he had walked enough in the mud of the real world to discover that 'the conscious social purpose' with which his BBC was to be charged could only flourish if he had the freedom to fly where his moral dreams would take him. Between 1922 and 1926 he fought a protracted battle on three fronts against a phalanx of businessmen (who were the share-holders of the company and greedy for profit), press lords (who feared the rivalry of broadcasting) and politicians (who were filled with blind panic at the prospect of the airwaves filled with voices speaking freely). By 1927 he had rid himself of the businessmen and established the BBC as a non-profit-making broadcasting monopoly, which drew its income from the licence fee collected by the Post Office.

However, the press lords and the politicians were still oppressed by him. Their traditionally conflicting interests found common ground on the issue of 'News'. When the press lords argued that all news broadcast by the BBC should be bought from (and compiled by) the agencies, the Government nodded approvingly that this would give 'some sort of assurance that the news was of the general type of uncoloured news'. The message was plain: the question of 'News' was inextricably tied up with that of 'Controversy'. Important news was always controversial—the more the BBC was tied to the 'uncoloured' offerings of the agencies, the less risk there was that this dangerous new instrument of communication could be used to incite the masses to civil commotion. As it happened, Reith had no taste for either news or controversy. Yet to establish his freedom Reith was bound to assert his right to deal in both: 'The service,' he had written of the BBC, 'would either be conducted within clearly defined and narrow limits or else there would be no limits at all.'

By the Thirties Reith was under the impression that he had won the battle. It was an illusion. The press, it is true, had compromised and retreated. The Director-General had asserted the BBC's rights to gather and broadcast *more* news, *more* frequently and the press lords were quiescent. But news bulletins of the early Thirties, unadventurous and obediently colourless, were no threat to Fleet Street.

The Government too had relented: controversy was no longer banned from the airwaves. Like the press lords, it discerned no threat in Reith's high-minded urge to take the best of drama, music, education and religion into the homes of the people.

Constitutionally Reith had won the independence he so much cherished. But he lacked the urge to put the principle to the test: free to let radio news flourish he allowed it to wither; free to be controversial he eschewed debate. From the fact that he was able to press his moral crusade with impunity, he allowed himself to draw the dangerously false conclusion that the BBC was free.

The real limits of freedom permitted to the BBC had been brutally laid down in one week of May 1926. On May 4th, with the Fleet Street presses silent and the news agency tapes blank, the BBC broadcast the first bulletin of the General Strike. Lacking any sort of news organisation it could not have expected to make an impressive debut: 'The sudden change from the bulky newspaper to the short bulletin cannot be perfected in an instant,' explained the announcer (by turns bland and apologetic): 'Moreover, the world has been asleep and not active for the last eight or ten hours and therefore there is bound to be comparatively little news...' It was a disastrous beginning, made worse by the admission that the BBC would try to fulfil its grave responsibilities to the public, 'in the most impartial spirit that circumstances permit'. Reith was soon in deep trouble. With Churchill fretting to press-gang the Corporation into Government service as a weapon against the strikers, the BBC was soon forced into humiliating compromise.

When the Archbishop of Canterbury sought to broadcast a

message of conciliation, the Government forbade it. Reith wrote to the Primate:

> We are in a position of considerable delicacy at the moment. We have not been commandeered, but there have been strong representations to the effect that this should have been done ... It would therefore be inadvisable for us to do anything that was particularly embarrassing to the Government, by reason of the fact that it might lead to the other decision that we are hoping to obviate.

Meanwhile as the middle classes rejoiced in the BBC the workers muttered in angry dismay. With the survival of his Corporation at stake Reith confronted a terrible dilemma: if he stood firm against the Government he might lose the BBC; if he did not, he would risk its reputation. When the High Court declared its dubious verdict that the 'so-called General Strike by the TUC is illegal,' he clutched at the legal straw; at once Reith's brave BBC was declared to be 'in this dispute on the side of the Government'.

Reith was conformist by nature, instinctively on the side of authority, and of the State. The moral values which he sought to propagate were those which were deeply rooted in the system. The shock of 1926 was the more severe because Reith was quite unprepared for confrontation of that kind. When his vague commitments to impartiality, whispered timorously before a Government with its blood up, were so cruelly brushed aside, he was being spurned by those whose political principles and traditions he treasured and which his BBC would impart to the masses. It was perplexing as well as humiliating.

Reith never recovered from the General Strike. As he directed the BBC into the Thirties, he seemed above all concerned that the Corporation should never again face the indignity of Governmental contempt. The moral crusade would continue, the 'consoling voices of the air soothing the sightless, cheering the bedridden' would still bring comfort; but in those areas of broadcasting where the BBC was in danger of burning its fingers, Reith would guide the Corporation well clear of the fire. Throughout the Thirties the tyranny of 'safety first' stifled adventurous talents and gave the orthodox their tongue.

More seriously the BBC managed to turn a blind eye to the reality of that decade. In an age of economic crisis, of political uncertainty, and of unemployment—where the poor 'have no possessions but pawn tickets and debts' and their children 'lack food, lack fortune, lack opportunity, lack joy'—the BBC was content to purvey the general goodwill of a country vicar at a vestry tea party. Inside the Talks Department there were furious protests (and even resignations) at Reith's iron rule.

All Talks were carefully screened before reaching the airwaves. 'There are many pitfalls to be avoided,' C. A. Lewis (the BBC's first Director of Programmes) had written in 1924: 'anything which is likely to cause offence to any of our vast audience' had to be excised and the fault rectified, before the script (*all* Talks were pre-scripted) was approved, stamped, signed and (thus neutered) delivered. By the Thirties little had changed. It did not stimulate originality: spontaneity was impossible. Those who could not (or would not) write standard scripts and speak in standard accents simply had no voice. Radio was a medium through which the few who ran things spoke to the many who did not, in terms which seemed designed to fly over their heads or send them to sleep.

The News Department (which was part of the Talks Department) was ruled even more fiercely by the dead hand of orthodoxy. A few weeks before Dimbleby's arrival in 1936, the bland tones of the Ullswater Report (after which the Charter was renewed for another ten years) were an unnecessary reminder to Reith of the need for caution:

> The influence of broadcasting on the political life of the country is brought to bear not only by speeches, talks and reports, but also by the provision of news. It is, therefore, of the utmost importance that the news distributed by the BBC should be a fair selection of items impartially presented.
>
> The present arrangements for the collection of news appear on the whole satisfactory... In the presentation of news, simplicity is desirable and the BBC should be as impersonal as possible.

Richard Dimbleby's letter with its breezily innocent suggestions for 'enlivening' the news challenged every broadcasting orthodoxy of the day. His proposals, which sounded technical, were in fact political. At the heart of his letter were ideas about the content, style and presentation of programmes which raised

questions that the BBC had carefully avoided for a decade. If the
BBC were to heed his ideas, it would find itself embroiled in the
turmoil of the real world. In his scheme the news would be
'gripping' not colourless; it would be 'human' not impersonal;
BBC reporters would describe events (like strikes) in their own
words, not those regurgitated from the agency tapes; ordinary
men and women would speak as they saw, without scripts,
unvetted, in their own 'uncouth' tongue; their words would sometimes even be recorded (a practice which was still regarded as a
form of deception); more of them would be heard in many more
places; and, more than that, BBC news would not merely report—
it would explain 'why and how it happened'. They were fundamental changes. But the most disturbing implication of all lay in
Dimbleby's suggestion that 'in the future and particularly in the
event of national emergency' the BBC, through its news service,
would play 'a vital part'. To a BBC still haunted by the spectre
of the General Strike, that prospect was far from enticing.

The effect of all Dimbleby's proposals would have been to
summon news from the back row of the BBC's chorus into the full
glare of the footlights, a transformation which, had Sir John Reith
wished, could have been brought about long before. The adventure into radio journalism advocated by Dimbleby was regarded
with a distaste which bordered on fear: it would take much energy
and persuasion to cajole the BBC into taking the first tentative
steps into the unknown.

The self-effacing restraint of his letter to Coatman was out of
character. It soon became plain to his new colleagues that Richard
Dimbleby was obsessed by the broadcasting vistas which his
romantic nature now contemplated. Broadcasting House was to
be the centre of a huge network of information, with facilities
unrivalled in the press (which would become quite subordinate
to radio) or in any other broadcasting organisation in the world.
A fleet of cars—preferably Lagondas, which were both large and
impressive—with BBC NEWS painted dramatically in large
letters on the doors, and a flashing light on top, would stand ready
in every part of Britain to rush to disaster. Sometimes reporters
would telephone their news directly to Broadcasting House and
onto the air, more often they would make 'on the spot' recordings
and hurry with them to the nearest studios. The BBC would hire
an army of 'stringers'—local press correspondents—to keep the
BBC newsroom in touch with regional issues. The BBC reporter

would be a man of distinction and authority, who would have access to the mightiest in the land and would be welcomed by the humblest, whose voice and name would be recognised wherever he went. He would make the BBC respected throughout the world for the brilliance and authority of its news service.

Dimbleby was not so naive as to describe his dreams in quite these terms except to his closest colleagues. But once he began to expound his theme, he expressed himself with such massive confidence, that he could not help but take the floor. The writer, David Howarth, who worked with him then and became his most trusted confidant, said later: 'Richard set about reforming the presentation of news by starting a kind of underground movement, infecting people here and there among the staff with his own excitement at his own ideas of radio news reporting. I was drawn into it early because he discovered I was prone, like himself, to wild enthusiasm.' To Kenneth Adam (later to become the BBC's Director of Television): 'it seemed as if he had a sense of mission, he never gave up—his energy was remarkable.' According to Charles Gardner, who soon became the BBC's second Topical Talks Assistant: 'Richard was the pioneer. There is no doubt about it, that it was he who had the ideas and the driving force to carry them through—the rest of us followed his lead.'

To others he was a disconcerting presence. Years later when he had already been acknowledged as 'the voice of the BBC', and when he kept his intense frustrations with the Corporation private, he wrote with affection of the Thirties: 'The BBC in those days still had the atmosphere of a big family firm. It had led a sheltered life and was modest and retiring. It could be very stuffy and very old-fashioned; sometimes it could be as dithery as a maiden aunt.' Time had made Dimbleby gentle. In the late Thirties he spent many hours with David Howarth devising elaborate and extremely painful deaths for his superiors who seemed happy only when obstructing his plans.

In the two years before Dimbleby joined the BBC there had been tentative advances. No longer was it possible for the BBC to boast (as it had done in 1930) that when there was no news worth broadcasting, the bulletin would be cancelled—on one occasion the announcer had said (as if it were the most usual occurrence): 'Good evening. Today is Good Friday. There is no news.' By 1936 there were more bulletins, and under Reith's watchful eye the News Department had been expanded.

In 1934 Reith had appointed John Coatman to the post of Chief News Editor. Coatman had been an officer in the Indian police and then Professor of Imperial Economic Relations at the London School of Economics. Reith had chosen him, not for his journalistic potential—Coatman knew nothing about news—but to act in Reith's quaint phrase as a 'right-wing offset', to balance the leftish threat which the Director-General had detected elsewhere in the Talks Department. Mercifully Coatman proved to be as independent of mind as Reith: on his first day in office he was irritated by a persistent buzzing from the wainscotting beside his desk: 'That's Mr. Siepmann's buzzer,' explained his secretary anxiously, 'that means he wants to see you.' Siepmann as Head of Talks, was Coatman's immediate superior. The ex-Indian police officer was not amused; he reached down, yanked the offending buzzer from the wall and stalked into Reith's office to inform the Director-General that no one buzzed for him, and that if he were to stay he would require absolute independence from any other department. Reith, doubtless astonished at such a bravura performance, arranged at once for the separation of News from Talks. It was an important change.

Under Coatman the News Department, no longer to be regarded as a mundane offshoot of Talks, hired more staff and produced more bulletins. Coatman gathered a group of talented individuals: Kenneth Adam (who was to have a distinguished BBC career) came from *The Manchester Guardian* to be Home Editor; R. T. Clarke, also from *The Manchester Guardian*, a military historian of repute and a classical scholar (who had published a translation of the Characters of Theophrastus), became Foreign Editor; Michael Balkwill, a winner of the Newdigate Poetry prize at Oxford, a man of rare ability who chose to spend his entire BBC career in the News Room, and who was to be responsible for more BBC radio (and then television) bulletins than anyone else, became a sub-editor. Another sub-editor's post went to Tony Wigan who had arrived from the *Belfast Telegraph*, and was destined to become the BBC's longest-serving New York correspondent; and in charge of News Talks (the tender young offshoot of the News Department) was Ralph Murray, whose intellect and temperament later summoned him to the Foreign Office, an Ambassadorship in Rome, and later a Governorship of the BBC.

As Murray put it, 'we were mostly a graduate lot with some

serious thoughts and criteria between us, most of us had more
or less newspaper or news agency experience, a fair aggregate of
intelligence and large areas of ignorance. Richard was not only
five years younger than the bulk of us—he was not a graduate'.
Murray was plainly disconcerted by the exuberance of Dimbleby's
manner; 'Mentally, he was the antithesis of us all, whether of the
slightly conceited, sceptical young graduates or of the disciplined,
self-critical, professional sub-editors. He was enthusiastic, uncritical, unintellectual. He not only knew none of the answers, he
never even bothered about the questions.' Those who felt irritated and even rebuked by his enthusiasm and energy nicknamed
him Bumble—because, as Murray put it, 'he was fat and buzzed'.
Sometimes, perhaps unconsciously, they indulged in a little mild
deprecation: 'Very quickly,' wrote Murray, 'he was popping up
with ideas, suggestions, contributions. Very soon he had worked
his fat, quick, bouncing personality into a partnership in our team.
But he was never arrogant, never impertinent, always loyal . . .' If
Dimbleby ever sensed that he was being patronised, he never
showed it.

The News Room of 1936 was quite unlike its sophisticated
television successor of forty years later, where what is absurd and
what is tragic becomes a 'story' to be cut, dried, packaged,
labelled and then sold in the nation's sitting rooms as the truth.
In 1936 the News Room had a casual leisurely air. Their bulletins
were gentle and discursive; and, by the standards of later years,
amateurish. R. T. Clarke ruled with a gentle touch, was excessively lazy, devoted to 'his boys' as he called his staff, and incapable
of an angry word: 'Are you sure that is wise, dear boy?' was the
nearest to a rebuke that he could bring himself.

Officially Murray was Richard Dimbleby's boss. The two men
were opposite personalities with very different tastes. Dimbleby
admired Murray's cool intellect. Murray was affectionately
amused by Dimbleby's zeal and disarmed by his charm. A
journalist, observed Murray (with instinctive distrust), is required:

to describe, judge, criticise, or examine matters on which he
necessarily cannot possibly possess much if any expertise, and in
relation to which not only his judgment but even his description must rest on incomplete information. He must have the
confidence, perhaps one should say the blind confidence,
constantly to pronounce his judgment or publish his findings

on this inadequate foundation ... Plenty have it, and become in various degrees perspicacious, opinionated, analytical, waspish or portentous as their natures and professional opportunities allow. Perhaps fewer have it combined with charm; not merely charm of manner but charm of nature such as Richard had.'

In October 1936, Richard Dimbleby undertook his first reporting assignment for the BBC. It was not a strike, or a hunger march, or a political rally in the East End, but the annual conference of the Council for the Preservation of Rural England. Though his report from Torquay (where the conference was held) revealed heroic attempts to inject some life into the bucolic ruminations of the assembled delegates, England must have rattled to the sound of turning-off switches in living rooms throughout the land. However much he rolled his tongue around the names of the assembled delegates ('His Majesty's Lieutenant for Devon, the Rt. Hon. The Earl of Fortescue, the Rt. Hon. The Earl of Crawford and Balcares, the Rt. Hon. Sir Halford Mackinder ...'), it was impossible to disguise the fact that it was an event of some-what less than major significance. Even Sir Halford's sensitive social observation that when the trippers arrived the 'sandy shores (of Devon) during the summer months resemble the penguin rookeries of the Antarctic Islands', which apparently, 'raised a laugh', failed to rescue Dimbleby's report from broadcasting oblivion.

However, he had cause never to forget it. The next day he walked into the office for the editorial conference. R. T. Clarke looked at him. 'You know that Sir Cecil Graves was on the 'phone to us directly after you broadcast last night,' he said. Dimbleby looked pleased that the Deputy Director-General should have taken notice of a contribution by so humble a member of the staff. 'He said that you started your piece with an inverted sentence and that you are not to broadcast again.' Sir Cecil Graves was almost as august a figure as Sir John Reith, his judgments treated with awe. Fortunately R. T. Clarke was of an indepen-dent nature, and he was less offended by Dimbleby's error than Sir Cecil. After a short absence from the microphone, Richard Dimbleby was quietly permitted to continue his career.

His next big assignment took him to a farm in Hampshire where a cow called Cherry had astounded the agricultural world by her milk production record, and stood poised on the verge of becoming world champion. The script still survives:

COW NOISE
[Richard Dimbleby] That is not Cherry—although we spent the best part of an hour today trying to persuade her to say a few words to the BBC listeners—but it is one of the great herd of cows we found at Red House Farm, Alton, and it can serve to introduce the heroine of the day...

It was not the stuff of great broadcasting, though the discerning eye would have noticed some promising passages: 'the old wooden roof with its grey rafters, the corrugated iron walls, and the single smoky lamp hanging from a centre beam'. It was, however, the first occasion on which he put into practice some of the techniques suggested in his letter to Coatman. Instead of returning from the farm, with his report (as if he were for a newspaper) and then broadcasting it 'live', he went with the mobile recording unit (which was a converted laundry van) and recorded, not only the moo of a cow and splashing of milk, but an interview with the farmer and his cowman. In London he edited the discs—by marking with chalk those parts of the recording which he intended to use in the broadcast: a snippet of interview here, a 'cow noise' there. Then he wrote a script designed to dovetail with the recorded extracts, and marked his instructions on it—'fade in, hold and fade down milking noise, then hold under'—and then broadcast his report 'live' raising his hand at the appropriate moment to 'cue' the relevant recording. It was a cumbersome process (though he and the engineers soon worked out ways of working at astonishing speed) but it transformed the craft of the radio reporter.

After a few months, when Dimbleby had been joined by Charles Gardner, they were left much to their own devices. No-one ordered that they report this or that: they decided between them what they should cover, and who should do it. There was, however, a tacit understanding that their subjects should be non-controversial. It was not a restriction that bothered either of them. The two BBC reporters covered shipwrecks and fires; they visited lighthouses in distress and crumbling sea-walls (it seemed from their reports that Britain was in constant danger of being washed away); they travelled on veteran car rallies and Air Raid Precaution tours; they opened cathedrals and they went down mines. And they explored new methods and new techniques. To Gardner, 'Richard was *the* driving force of the Department— he was always trying out new ideas.'

It was Dimbleby who discovered that the telephone box made a perfect BBC studio. Often he and Gardner found themselves with their precious discs stranded far from Broadcasting House, too far to get them back in time for the News. 'Could we not,' he suggested to Howarth, 'fix an amplifier and a microphone to a telephone, and broadcast straight into the studio?' They decided to find out, and spent days (quite unsupervised and quite illegally) dismantling GPO 'phone boxes all over the south of England, recording into the receiver, and rushing back to London to hear the results. It worked.

It was Dimbleby who suggested and organised a network of 'stringers' to keep the News Room in touch with the provinces. With no formal authority he 'hired' dozens of local reporters to 'phone in whenever a 'story' seemed about to break. He discussed ways in which their contacts should 'in some way announce their identity to PBX so that the telephone operators know automatically that they are our news contacts coming through with a story or suggestion'; and he arranged their payment, at first, out of the petty cash fund. Dimbleby also thought up a means of communication between the News Room and the 'observer' out on his assignment. The early evening bulletin habitually ended with the announcement: 'The Sports News will now Follow.' Dimbleby suggested that if the sub-editors wished him to make contact with them—a story had changed or another one seemed more important—they should turn the phrase round to: 'Now follows the Sports News.' Although it was illegal to communicate in this way, it was very effective and soon became the News Room's standard practice. He also ascertained from Scotland Yard that the police would have no objection to the 'flashing blue light' of his dreams, though the BBC, thinking it a vulgar idea, demurred.

Nothing mattered as much, however, as the recording car. The laundry van, which *was* the mobile recording unit (apart from two huge pantechnicons) imposed intolerable restrictions. It was slow, heavy and large, and the equipment it carried was portable only in the sense that it could be transported by lorry. They could record only where the lorry could take them. Dimbleby lobbed unmercifully for a mobile recording car, complaining, 'We can never compete with Fleet Street without it,' to a BBC hierarchy which in any case shrank from that prospect. When finally in 1938 the recording car arrived, Dimbleby, to the amusement of his colleagues (some of whom could not quite understand what all the fuss was about) behaved like a schoolboy with a new toy. At once his horizons became limitless; he made a point of discovering events which took place a long way from London, just to prove how invaluable the new car would be. Howarth, who was his frequent companion, and who suffered constant night-time calls from him, stood in awe of his 'mental and physical constitution—he never seemed to get tired; the more difficult and distant the assignment the happier he seemed to be'. Later, with justifiable pride, Dimbleby wrote weightily: 'It is no exaggeration to say that the whole vast network of BBC News recording has developed from the introduction of that solitary vehicle.'

More important than technique, Richard Dimbleby brought a new style to broadcasting. The news bulletins had been lucid and sometimes elegant; they were always impersonal and neutral; they were read in anonymous tones by unknown voices. Reith had thought of broadcasters as

> aloof and mysterious... They neither receive nor do they desire, the attention of the street and the market place... They are personages of much importance in the land... In many ways I think it is desirable that they should continue in their comparative obscurity... The desire for notoriety and recognition sterilises the seeds from which greatness might spring. A place in the stars is of more importance than a place in the sun.

Reith's mystical musings were not attractive to Richard Dimbleby. He, quite unashamedly, wanted a place in the sun. And in any case he could never be anonymous: his style was immediately distinctive—and not to everyone's taste. Murray in particular winced: 'he seldom wrote what he was reporting, but rather recorded or transmitted it straight off his tongue: he had a rolling fluency in delivering it, but at a terrible stylistic price. I cursed him and slashed his copy and blue-pencilled his adjectives and called upon him to think what language meant... It was to no avail.' Others in the Department marvelled at his self-confidence before the microphone and the way that he never stumbled for a phrase. No-one else could do it. Being of a school which believed in clarity, brevity and objectivity above all else, which was concerned with the word more than the message, R. T. Clarke looked on sympathetically but disconcerted.

Michael Balkwill, more perceptive about the future of radio, was more sensitive to Dimbleby's approach: '...he found words that blew a wind of change through BBC bulletin style. Perhaps there was still the odd newspaper cliché, but he was beginning to find how to convey grandeur without being emptily pompous; how to be vivid and colloquial without cheapness and gimmicks.' It was a personal style. His voice was light and slightly breathless—as if he had just that moment run into the studio to deliver his report—and he told his story *to* his audience, he did not broadcast *at* them. It was not surprising that the BBC began to get letters asking 'What is the name of your news observer...?' Not surprising either that he became the first reporter (though a little later) to be named in the bulletin, not just as 'our observer' but 'our observer, Richard Dimbleby'.

At the end of 1936, an event occurred which, for the first time forced the BBC to recognise the power of the on-the-spot radio broadcast: the Crystal Palace caught fire. It started after the final editions of the evening papers, which meant that the News Department of the BBC had the story to itself (a predicament which it did not greatly relish). The flames from the burning glass could be seen for miles; when the BBC put out a special news flash, it seemed that the whole of London came out to see the spectacle. The roads of south London were jammed with vehicles. In vain police tried to clear a path for bell-ringing fire engines. Most of the BBC staff joined in the scramble. (There is hardly a BBC man who does not remember having played the leading part that night in transmitting the drama to the listening multitudes.) Richard Dimbleby and David Howarth were stuck in the traffic jams in the laundry van. By the time they reached Sydenham they found to their consternation that the outside broadcast unit was already there. Dimbleby disappeared into the smoke, calling out with delight as he went that he had found the head of the fire brigade: 'It's perfect, David, his name's Firebrace!' A few minutes later he emerged, eyebrows singed, face blackened, and made for the 'phone. According to Howarth he was ecstatic. It was a sombre occasion, but he could broadcast live, with the sound of the flames, the crowds, and the fire-engines behind him; and he had 'scooped' Fleet Street—it was a milestone in the history of broadcasting.

The official policy of the BBC was that there was no competition between its News Service (which was still almost entirely compiled by Fleet Street news agencies) and the newspapers. Dimbleby and Gardner—enthused by the Crystal Palace episode— decided to create their own scoops. It was not always easy. When Tommy Sopworth's yacht *Endeavour* was lost on its way back from America in the Atlantic, Dimbleby suggested that they should be the first to discover her. It would be a great BBC adventure: one of them would go to Plymouth, the other to Southampton. They needed tickets for the train and the News Department had not yet realised that 'observers' required expenses (a discovery that Dimbleby later forced upon the BBC to its lasting displeasure). There was, however, a cash box in the office which was supposed to contain £10 for emergencies—but as usual it was empty except for a sheaf of IOUs signed by the News Editor. So the two reporters were short of £3 and no-one in the News Room could make up the difference. Eventually they went

across the road to the Queen's Hall where a performance of the
BBC Promenade concerts was in progress. They informed the
lady at the kiosk that they were BBC 'observers' (a title which was
still almost unknown) and demanded £3 in return for their IOU.
After a lengthy display of persuasive charm they got it, and the
next day had their scoop. Gardner was the first to discover the
Endeavour, which had been found drifting off Land's End;
Dimbleby was the first to go aboard the yacht when it reached
Southampton where he was granted an exclusive interview with
Sopworth and was invited to celebrate with him the safe return
of the famous yacht. He also drank some of the yacht's drinking
water. Next day he became ill and doctors diagnosed paratyphoid
and (as if in disapproval of his 'scoop') the BBC took much persuasion before they would help with his medical expenses.

At this period, since it offered them no threat, the press did not
usually feel compelled to notice the output of the BBC's News
Department: but in March 1937 Richard Dimbleby hurried to
East Anglia to report the invasion of the Fen Floods: 'It is about
time someone put in a word for the BBC and their work in
making known the flood danger in the Fens this past fortnight,'
wrote *The Star*. 'The special observer's comments from the dykes
have on more than one occasion been thrilling to listen to . . .' And
The Star's reporter observed with the air of one resolving a
baffling puzzle: 'I understand that the BBC had a mobile recording
van on the spot; Mr. Dimbleby of the News Department (it was
the first time that his name had been mentioned in the national
press) spoke a summary of the situation in the late afternoon each
day into the microphone there.'

The floods provided Dimbleby with precisely the opportunity
that he needed to demonstrate the potential of radio. He stayed in
the fens for nearly a fortnight reporting on the daily advance and
retreat of the floodwaters; interviewing farmers and housewives,
bargees and river authorities, councillors and policemen; recording gurgling pumping stations, rowing boats, motor barges,
sloshing water and pouring rain. But he had not been content
merely to report the story: 'Contact between the Great Ouse
Catchment Board Headquarters in Ely and workers at various
points has been maintained by means of messages broadcast by the
BBC,' observed *The Times*. The 'contact' was inspired and
organised by Dimbleby, who arranged for the installation of an
'open' line between Ely and Broadcasting House and then com-

mandeered every portable radio he could find in shops and private houses. He had them distributed to launches and tugs and key points on the banks of the Ouse, and arranged to interrupt programmes whenever he wished to broadcast instructions to the working parties in the fens: 'The service of broadcasting the latest information about the behaviour of the waters,' applauded *The Star*, 'was of tremendous value to the Fenlanders.'

Michael Balkwill, who had to edit his copy, noticed another facet of Dimbleby's reports from the Fens—the obsession with accurate detail:

He did not deal in vague descriptions of 'hundreds of acres inundated in the grim fight against the encroaching waters'; he found out and explained in his reports what the complete situation really was—and explained it in terms of exact locations, comparative water levels, pumping stations and sluice gates, with proper use of technical terms...

Another distinctive feature of the reports was his tone of voice and choice of language. There was nothing anonymous or detached in his report of March 16th, 1937:

It was deathly quiet in the Fens last night. Nothing could be more peaceful than the view from the banks of the Lark, with the glimmering lights of Ely away in the distance, and the yellow light of the Prickwillow Pumping Station, and away down the stream the moving pinpricks of light that were the lanterns of the men working to close the cracks in the bank.

Today the scene has changed: a cold wind is sweeping across the flat marshland—rain is falling... Perhaps at this moment you can hear the wind as it roars round us.

The Fen people are calm. So far there has been little alarm: but they are deadly serious too. Every available man is at work... heedless of the rising wind and rain, watching only the level of the inky river.

Not everyone was impressed by Dimbleby's dedication to this novel form of broadcasting: with a revealing dryness Murray remembered that 'he sploshed around for days over-reporting some fen floods'.

The most important event for Richard Dimbleby of 1937, of his whole life to that moment, was his marriage to the girl he had first met six years before in the office, Dilys Thomas. In the tradition of both families it was not a modest occasion. The Thomases had moved from London to a little village in Sussex called Copthorne, and on July 3rd before a large congregation, 'a journalistic romance culminated at the altar of Copthorne Church'—as the *Southern Daily Echo* reported (in the language each of them had employed on numerous similar occasions before). They sang the traditional hymns, 'Love Divine, All Loves Excelling', and the organ played the traditional 'Wedding March' and the 'Bridal March' from Lohengrïn. Afterwards on the lawn, they drank champagne in the sun, and the two families and entire staff of the Dimbleby papers basked in mutual delight. After the cake was cut, and the speeches done—which were not too short or too long (the bride's father being a barrister, and the groom a broadcaster—and in any case both families taking pride in doing these things well), Richard and Dilys drove off in a car lent to them by their friend and Richard's colleague, Tony Wigan, for a week in Cornwall—after which Richard was to return to the BBC for a week before they took a month together 'on the Continent'.

The honeymoon in Cornwall was quiet and uneventful, though the journey was enlivened by a traditional but embarrassing drama. On the first night, they stayed in Salisbury, at a small hotel with rooms over a book shop. In the evening after dinner, Richard crossed from their bedroom to the bathroom on the other side of the corridor to run a bath for his bride. Having turned on the taps he returned to the bedroom. Fifteen minutes later, they were reminded of the existence of the bath by the sight of a trickle of water, which promised to become a flood, seeping under their bedroom door. They leapt up, rushed out to find the bathroom and the corridor awash. Summoning a porter and some mops they did what was possible; but being a wise old man, the porter reminded them of the old oak floorboards and the gap between each plank—and the bookshop below. He advised them to leave their money and depart the hotel at daybreak. And so after an anxious night, waiting for the knock at the door, just after dawn they tiptoed along the creaking corridor and slipped guiltily out into their first full day of married life.

Their wedding present from *The Richmond and Twickenham Times* was £100, and despite the disapproval of their Uncle

Percy, they decided to spend it all on the European holiday. Again they borrowed a car—on this occasion an open 1½-litre MG with the registration lettering AMO, which Richard, who had a skill at such manoeuvres, had persuaded out of the MG car company. In 1937 it was still a considerable adventure to drive through the Continent, and they kept a detailed log of their journey, which afterwards they wrote up, neatly typed, with photographs and little cartoons drawn by Richard.

'We left 20 Cedar Court [their new flat in Sheen] in AMO at twenty-five minutes past seven and reached Dover at 10 o'clock'—they began, with the formal and exact detail with which they disguised their excitement at the trip. They recorded in detail the problems of Customs posts, of driving for the first time on the wrong side of the road, and of the 'crazy' motoring in Paris. They went to the Paris Exhibition, keeping their ticket, and took photographs. They were 'shocked beyond measure' by the British pavilion:

> the first thing we saw on entering was an awful tableau of Britain's sporting few in the pink. Not only did this, and, in fact the whole of the pavilion, suggest that huntin', shootin' and fishin' were all of which Great Britain is capable, but the models themselves might have come from the cheapest tailor's window. There was also a photo montage of the Prime Minister looking like a mouthful of teeth. Of course, he was castin' a fly! We were honestly ashamed to think that Britain could take such little interest as to allow so poor an impression to be stamped into the minds of the millions who visited Paris this year.

They drove south from Paris towards Switzerland, worried at their fuel bills with petrol at over two shillings and three pence per gallon, eating picnics on the way of raw carrots, bread and wine. In Switzerland, which they found 'the most beautiful country we have ever been in', they drove through high mountain passes (the height of each they recorded with precision); they took a steamer on Lake Lausanne, crossing to the French border and back (for two shillings 'if we stayed on board'); they went to Andermatt, 'quite obviously one of the "genuine" towns, not just built for tourists'; and two weeks later, after seeing altogether five European countries, as innocently and completely happy as they had been when they left, they arrived back at Dover, where, since they had spent precisely £100 they had to borrow money from a friendly AA patrolman to buy petrol for the journey back to Richmond and the BBC.

By the end of 1938 the News Department had a staff of thirty-one, an increase of twenty-five in four years. The bulletins were better written and better presented. The amount of air time allotted to news had more than doubled to ninety-five minutes each evening. Seeking even greater expansion, R. T. Clarke reminded his superiors in a long memorandum that news had 'become an essential service to the public'; News Talks (Dimbleby's Department) had 'undergone a radical transformation'.

Clarke was not afraid to distribute credit where it was due. Without exception the successes and the ideas upon which his report dwelled had been Dimbleby's.

> As far as the organisation of a recorded news section is concerned, that is easy. It is most emphatically Dimbleby's province, and I think I ought to say here how greatly I value his services in this connection, and also pay tribute to him for the devotion with which he has succeeded in making himself a first-class broadcaster in this type of programme.

As if that was not accolade enough, he continued his report by giving his support to Dimbleby's dream. 'The News Department,' he wrote, 'could usefully expand if the BBC could have ready a whole fleet of cars available to cover a story in almost any part of the country.' It seemed that the BBC News Department was poised on the edge of a new era in which Richard Dimbleby's views about broadcasting were no longer the exception but the rule. But the key phrase in Clarke's memorandum was: 'the difficulty here is more one of policy than anything else'.

The advances made in the News Room had been technical; in the sensitive areas—on that dangerous ground where the 'facts' are in dispute, and where the 'truth' is bogged down in controversy— 'policy' intervened: 'We were finding our way,' Murray has said, 'we were cautious, not certain where we were going. We had no support or direction from on high and we were left very much to ourselves: we were not prepared to risk very much.' Reith's personal aversion to news and his reluctance to offend the political establishment had become ingrained in the minds of the BBC's hierarchy. Despite Clarke's pleas to extend his Department, no more mobile recording cars were produced and no more reporters were hired. Between 1936 and 1939 neither Dimbleby nor Gardner nor Murray covered any important industrial, economic, social or political issue in Britain. For the coverage of every sensitive issue the BBC relied exclusively on the Fleet Street news agency reports—which could be re-written for broadcasting in a manner calculated to be as inoffensive as possible to all sides. It became plain to some in the News Room that there was a huge discrepancy between the techniques which were used to cover the insignificant, and those which were used for what mattered: in the one the craft of the radio reporter was allowed to grow, in the other it was forbidden.

Perhaps the most shameful example of this timidity was the BBC's attitude towards the Spanish Civil War. From 1936 until 1939 the BBC relied exclusively on the agencies for its coverage of the war (although every newspaper maintained a reporter on the ground). No member of the BBC News Department was permitted to go to the war. Richard Dimbleby (who had argued passionately but to no avail that he should cover the Abyssinia war—where Mussolini's invading army was systematically destroying the native resistance) now argued along with the rest of the News Room that one of them should cover the Spanish Civil War from the front line. The BBC would not countenance it: the Spanish war was an acutely sensitive issue.

From the beginning the Foreign Office had taken a close interest in the BBC's coverage and as Franco's forces gained the upper hand the pressure increased. By 1938 when British public opinion was still overwhelmingly on the side of the Republicans, the British Government was confidently but secretly hoping, in the words of the Foreign Secretary, Lord Halifax, that Franco soon: 'would settle the Spanish question'. The BBC under the temporary leadership of Sir Cecil Graves (who had succeeded Reith in 1938) was even less resilient than before: the News Department was enjoined to exercise extreme caution. The word 'rebels' (to describe Franco's forces) was replaced by the more respectable-sounding 'insurgents'; R. T. Clarke took to guiding the news bulletins into a position mid-way between *The Daily Herald* (which supported the Republicans) and *The Daily Mail* (which was on Franco's side). But even the most anodyne bulletins

were subject to scrutiny and criticism. At one point the pressure
on the Department reached such proportions that the normally
equable R. T. Clarke was moved to protest. Marching into the
Director-General's office he stated, in no uncertain terms, that the
pressure on 'his boys' would have to stop, and came out
slamming the door angrily behind him. It is said that Graves—
showing the courage of the weak—immediately ordered his
dismissal. It was only after a hastily organised 'round robin' of
protest landed on the Director-General's desk twenty-four hours
later that Clarke was reprieved.

It was in this atmosphere at the beginning of 1939, with
Franco's forces poised for victory, that the BBC summoned up
the courage to send an 'observer' to the war. Richard Dimbleby
arrived in the village of Le Perthus on the Franco-Spanish border
high in the Pyrenees at the end of January. The war had been
fought with ferocity and without restraint. Already half a million
people had died from bullets, starvation or disease. Now as
Franco's forces moved northwards into Catalonia, Republican
soldiers and civilian refugees fled in panic towards the French
border. It was cold and wet; they were hungry and exhausted. At
the border there was no water, no food and little shelter; yet in
one week nearly half a million refugees (of whom one hundred
and seventy thousand were women and children) crossed over
from Spain into France. It was a pitiful scene.

For the first time in his life Richard Dimbleby had witnessed
intense suffering; to see it on such a scale had an immediate and
profound effect. It produced reporting from him of a kind that
had never been heard before on radio. Writing many years later
The Daily Mail's television critic, Peter Black, remembered the
indelible mark that 'most memorable broadcast' from Le Perthus
left on him:

> In my memory this broadcast is inextricably linked with the
> growth of radio news, with the fear, relief and shame of the
> Munich settlement, with the curious change of mood in the
> ensuing twelve months, and with one of Hitler's speeches
> relayed from a Nazi gathering in the Berlin Sportpalast...
> young Dimbleby's broadcast from Spain, carefully neutral
> because the BBC news had to be neutral, nevertheless aroused
> something to which its hearers had to respond: the stirrings of
> dread, disgust, anger and determination.

Thirty years afterwards, Dimbleby wrote:

> It was my first experience of war, and a pretty shattering one. The sky was lit up with gunfire and bursting bombs... But I don't think that I was so much moved by the proximity of war as by the awful appearance of these desperate people... It was the first time that I had seen the innocent victims who suffer so terribly in war...

At Le Perthus he had helped carry across the border those who had died of exposure, while the French troops held the starving women and children at bayonet point. He had been angered by 'the rough, arrogant methods—there had been something very Nazi about them—of the *Garde Mobile*'. The conditions of the concentration camp at Argeles into which the defeated Republican troops were herded by the French authorities were atrocious—'not much difference really between Argeles and Buchenwald'.

At the time those judgments had to be kept to himself. In his first report he spoke, without a script, of the human suffering:

> There was an old woman at the international station at Cerbere last night, the colour of deep sun-burn with dirt, and with dried blood on her face from a deep gash in the cheek. She told me how she and her children, and eight other old people, lay down in the open to sleep. It was she said—and for this I can vouch—bitterly cold. In the morning three of the group, one of them her daughter, were dead...

He spoke in a quiet voice, deceptively matter-of-fact, but taut as if controlling great emotion with difficulty.

> Some of them are in the last stages of exhaustion. They're hungry—starving, many of them—and numbed with cold.

He saw a woman with tears streaming down her face:

> begging a guard to tell her where her baby was: the guard trying to soothe her in broken Spanish, and a Frenchman, who'd come in from the Barcelona area with these refugees, telling me that she'd gone mad. The baby she was looking for was killed in a raid more than a week ago.

Two days later he was speaking 'live' on the border: 'with one foot in France and one foot in Spain', into the ten o'clock news. For the first time in the history of broadcasting—depressing achievement—listeners heard the sounds of gunfire and bombing in the background as he spoke:

It is, I think, the first time that a microphone has been here... Since early today—early this morning when we got here— there have been crowds, masses, lines of wretched torn and tattered soldiers going by, throwing down their guns, their rifles and their pistols at the guards on the frontier... There are machine guns by the dozen stacked up just behind me—I'm sorry I'm pushing my way past the *Garde Mobile* in order that I can get well onto the frontier line: he didn't like it very much... Now here comes another procession of lorries. I'm going to stop for a moment and let you hear it go by. The first one is a Russian lorry piled high with soldiers... The second carries a heavy gun... and behind it is another lorry with two soldiers in it, four or five sheep and a cow piled up in the back of the lorry. This would be almost comic if it weren't such an appalling tragedy to watch down here...

The BBC had never broadcast anything of the kind before: and it was delighted by the achievement. Dimbleby returned home to London, chastened by what he had witnessed, to the accolades of his colleagues, and—unprecedented tribute—a commendation for his coverage from the Board of Governors, who were doubtless as pleased that the BBC had emerged from the exercise un- scathed as they were about the brilliance of Dimbleby's broad- casting.

It was obvious that Richard Dimbleby could no longer remain anonymous. So while the announcers who read the bulletins, soon to be famous themselves, remained mysterious unknown voices, 'our observer' became 'our observer, Richard Dimbleby'. He was now the BBC's senior reporter. Each major assignment fell to him as of right: the return of Chamberlain from Munich and the first-ever broadcast coverage of a Royal Tour. By 1939 he had demonstrated to the satisfaction of the most sceptical that his ideas about broadcasting could work. Yet as Britain stumbled towards September 1939 the BBC took no steps to transform the

News Service into the kind of organisation which he had urged upon the Corporation for three years.

In 1936 Richard Dimbleby had told a sceptical Broadcasting House: '...that in the future and particularly in the event of national emergency, the BBC will play a vital part'. When that 'national emergency' finally occurred, when Britain declared war on Germany, the BBC still had two reporters and one mobile recording car. It was not an auspicious beginning to the most dramatic and desperate five years in the nation's history.

4

War Correspondent

... war began, that is, an event took place
opposed to human reason and to human nature ...

LEO TOLSTOY

ON THE DAY THAT WAR WAS DECLARED THE BBC'S
radio schedules were cleared, solemn music was played, lengthy
news bulletins were read, Corporation staff left for secret centres
all over Britain, and Richard Dimbleby became the BBC's first
war correspondent.

He was not unprepared. He had been at Heston Airport when
Chamberlain arrived back from Munich promising 'Peace in Our
Time' and had grunted to a colleague: 'Huh! I wish that were
true.' Like others in the BBC he had felt outrage at the
Government's 'appeasement' of Hitler. When Hitler marched
into the Sudetenland, he had gone to Germany in the hope of
accompanying the international force which was to supervise the
absorption of the little state into the Fatherland. Neither the force
nor Dimbleby made it. It had astonished Dimbleby that the BBC
had permitted him to go to Germany at all at such a delicate
moment—and he intended to make the most of it. He and David
Howarth were met at the German frontier in their recording car
by a delegation from the Ministry of Propaganda in a row of
elongated Mercedes. Swastikas, boots and uniforms abounded.
The German authorities, it was plain, intended to show the
representatives from the BBC who would win the war of
propaganda. Dimbleby was unabashed. As the entourage swept
into Aachen with the BBC recording car squashed in the middle,
he ignored the frosty stares of his hosts and dispensed Nazi

Salutes and 'Heil Hitlers' in the manner of the Fuehrer himself. The Germans were at a loss—'Was the man serious? Was the man mad? Or was he (could he dare?) ridiculing them?' When they arrived in the city Dimbleby went a step further. With earnest air of one seeking to learn a new craft he asked his hosts to demonstrate for him the intricacies of the Goose Step. The Germans did as they were bid, whilst Dimbleby looked on, and then with studied innocence, did his best to emulate his hosts. A few days later in Hamburg Dimbleby (who had an observer's taste for low life) asked to be shown the night clubs of St. Pauli. They took him to the Zillertal where it was the custom to invite the guests to conduct the Bavarian band. Howarth watched as the baton was handed to Dimbleby: 'They agreed to try "A Bicycle Made for Two" and the band found that Richard knew how to conduct. Then... Richard made the Bavarian band play "Tipperary". A Norwegian from the next table came over, bowed, shook Richard's hand, and congratulated him on his courage in calling for that tune at such a time.'

Back in London, on the eve of war Dimbleby was frightened and excited. A week earlier, and in secret (even the BBC did not know what he was doing) he had driven the BBC's recording car onto a cross-channel ferry for France. He loved intrigue and it delighted him that 'our only official document was a letter from the War Office stating that we were engaged on an important mission and should be allowed to pass without hindrance'. At Dover, 'I produced my letter of authority, explaining that I regretted very much that I could not tell them what was in the car or where it was going'. Before they left he had telephoned Howarth who was on holiday in Ireland and asked him conspiratorily whether he would like to 'break off your holiday and go for a "trip"'. Howarth did not hesitate but returned at once to England. Now the two of them with recording engineer, Harvey Sarney, drove to Paris and hid the car in an underground car park, where they covered it with camouflage paint and dollops of mud. They returned to London and went to Austin Reed with a BBC chit (signed by the Chief Cashier) authorising the purchase of military uniforms, which the War Office had instructed they should wear. Then he put his affairs in order, checked his insurance policies and his will, and went down to Cuddington, a little village outside Aylesbury to say goodbye to Dilys.

Richard Dimbleby's childhood romance with the country had not ended with marriage nor had his yearning for 'Sleepy Dell'. Reality had forced upon him a flat in Sheen, which because it was his first marital home, he would always regard with nostalgic affection. But it was not merely the threat of war and air-raids which in June 1939 had made him, whilst he was in Canada as the BBC's first correspondent to cover a Royal Tour, spend much time cabling England not merely with reports of the Monarch's activities, but with offers of money which he did not possess for a country cottage in Surrey which the owner did not want to sell. When he heard from Dilys that the man's decision was final, he wrote one of his long letters to her speaking of their 'miserable disappointment'; and refusing to give up his cottage, he promised 'to do everything I can do to make [him] change his mind. There is just a chance that a direct plea from the royal train may do the trick'. It did not. However, so determined was he to live in the country that he instructed Dilys apologetically ('I am sorry to deliver long lectures from this seat in a Canadian train') to let their flat, advising her 'we can quite easily rent somewhere cheap,' in the country, 'even if we do not like it terribly much, and then start looking round all over again'.

A few weeks later they became (with a friend) the tenants of a big old-beamed, open-fireplaced cottage in Cuddington, which in Tudor England had housed three families.

The parting was difficult. Richard had never liked to be away from home for more than a few days, and when he was abroad he wrote repeatedly of his 'terrible loneliness' away from Dilys. Though neither of them mentioned it, both feared that this war would be like the last—and that they would not see each other again. Worse, they now had an eleven-month-old baby, David. Richard doted on his son, expressing his delight in letter after letter, and threatening all manner of punishment for him, if the infant did not recognise his father after he had been away.

It was a middle-class custom of the day to keep a 'baby record' charting the early weeks and months of the child's growth—to be filled in by the mother. Yet 'The Little One's Log' for David was recorded for his first six months by Richard. The first entry observed, with a loving attempt at clinical detachment,

the birth was normal...there was great difficulty at first over feeding, and on the third day, mother had a temperature of

103° ... the temperature remained high for two days. It was far above the rise of temperature often expected on the third day. Meanwhile the baby was fed on mixture given on page 11, being first put to the breast at each feed. He was lazy, however, and went to sleep instead of sucking ...

There were compensations however. In an obviously important footnote, he added, 'both nurses considered the baby unusually strong, with unusual control of the head'.

Richard had no urge to say goodbye to his family. He resolved the problem by taking Dilys to Aylesbury, where he could catch a London train. There he bought her a bicycle, and they walked a little out of town, then he turned the bike towards home, placed Dilys upon it, and with the instruction not to turn round, pushed it away down the hill.

He returned to London, collected his uniform from Austin Reed, changed into it and marched with some aplomb into Broadcasting House to say farewell. It seemed that the entire BBC staff had arrived to see him leave. There were smiles at his uniformed rotundity, but when R. T. Clarke said farewell to one 'of his boys' he had tears in his eyes. The BBC Administration, symbolising a relationship which had started badly and would get worse, was unmoved: 'Whilst they are on service, these members of staff will have to pay for their messing, and will have to buy petrol,' wrote one member of the Accounts Department, 'I therefore propose to arrange to make them an advance of £60 for these purposes, paying £20 into the account of each of them. This division is in case of any of them meeting an accident'.

Collecting the car from Paris, Dimbleby, Howarth and Sarney drove to the headquarters of the British Expeditionary Force at Arras. The largest hotel in town, the Universe, was already filled with officers, and so they found rooms in a shabby, third-class hotel down the street. It had no heating, little hot water, poor food and lumpy beds. Arras, dismal at the best of times, seemed bleak. But, filled with the drama of war, they transformed an attic room into a makeshift recording studio and waited for hostilities to commence.

At the Universe Dimbleby soon made himself known to the assembled officers, and by dint of considerable charm and a manner which belied his twenty-six years, he soon talked himself

into private drink and dinner parties. He had no doubt about
the role he should play. In his own estimation he was no mere
reporter, he was the representative of the largest broadcasting
organisation in the world: in France at least, he *was* the BBC.
Traditionally the Army was suspicious of journalists; it viewed
broadcasting with consternation—the reporter, with his microphone ready to record stray words, was a menace. The restrictions
of all war correspondents were severe. No reporter could leave
Arras without a 'conducting officer'; nor could he use a telephone;
nor could he report without being censored by a blue-pencil
mind which instinctively regarded all information as secret, and
journalists as irresponsible muck-rakers. For the BBC it was
worse: less understood, it was more distrusted. It took very
great skill to break down the barriers. Later in a confidential
BBC memo, Dimbleby revealed how he set about the task:

> I regard it as an honour to be an accredited war correspondent
> and I think my view is shared by the few of us who had the
> privilege of being the first correspondents to go to France
> with the Army in 1939. We were the people who had to
> break some very thick ice and establish ourselves as trusted
> observers. We managed this successfully... But it was not
> enough to be on friendly terms... You must show a sense of
> military discipline and bearing... We simply must fit our-
> selves into the landscape and conduct ourselves in accordance
> with the rank whose privileges we enjoy. We must remember
> that in the eyes of the Army we are all officers...

The first despatch that Dimbleby sent back to the BBC
revealed the problems of the war correspondent without a war.
There was little to say and the censors ensured that he said less.
He had set out to report the drama and heroics of battle and
now he had to report the 'mood' of the troops at rest. He set a
cheery tone:

> I and my colleagues have come back to out billets tonight
> impressed to the point of amazement by the cheerful optimism
> of the British Army. Men of every rank have spoken to us in
> terms that make it impossible for us to be mistaken. From the
> Colonel on the staff to the P.B.I. (if those of you who know
> it will excuse the expression) squatting over a smoking wood

fire, cooking a great pile of sausage meat buns, with faces as solemn as owls, there is the same feeling. These people don't think they will win—they *know* it.

Occasionally he managed to convey the atmosphere of the depressing and bitterly cold winter months of 1939 and 1940. He arranged, after long negotiation, to have himself attached temporarily to the French Army, and drove the three hundred miles from Arras down to the Saar frontier, on roads so icy that the recording car, fully loaded with the three BBC men and their equipment, skidded into the ditch no less than seven times on the way. On the border German and French outposts stood facing each other in resolute inaction. It was both eerie and absurd. The front line was on the edge of a wood. He reported:

I could hear the birds singing in the wood, the rustle of a hare that leapt away from us ... this wood had been shelled ... nearly every night it was visited by German patrols... We found a machine gun mounted in a small trench, manned by three men. Fifty yards along the edge of the wood was the second gun. We were only three hundred yards from the German position... I suppose we were in full view of the Germans ...

Later he walked back towards the shelter of the Maginot line and stopped in a deserted village:

There were curtains in the windows and outside the houses pigs and hens were roaming together. There was manure piled high on the pavement... Outside one house lay a young pig that had clearly been dead for some time. I stepped over it, pushed open the door and went into the living room ... In the room at the back there was an unmade bed. There was the remains of a fire in the kitchen. The living room had been left in a state of turmoil; drawers had been pulled out and the contents spilled on the floor. It was covered with letters, newspapers, old photographs and bills. There were some dead flowers from an upturned vase, and alongside them a large brown envelope with a German inscription on it addressed to the owner of the house. It contained a brightly coloured catalogue, and offered for sale some beautiful spring bulbs from Cologne.

Dimbleby was always offended by such scenes: to a man brought up in ordered security such desolation was a violation of human dignity. And he valued the right to dignity—to live in self-respect without fear—above almost all else. He was to witness many similar scenes in the next five years. They never failed to move him, and he never failed to notice and report the tiny details —the unmade bed, the dead flowers, and the catalogue from Cologne.

On the same trip he persuaded the local French commander to take him through the deserted streets of Strasbourg down to the Kehl bridge which separated the French from the Germans. 'Why don't you do anything, why don't you fight?' asked Dimbleby. The Commander shrugged: 'Why should we start anything, it is better like this.' The reporter decided to record a commentary standing on the bridge looking at the German lines (he could not bear 'fakes'; and was outraged when less punctilious colleagues later in the war pretended they were where he knew they were not). He moved out from behind the sandbags. At once a German officer from the other end of the bridge did the same: 'Come back, come back,' implored the French Commander. Dimbleby ignored him, finished his recording and then returned slowly to the bunker, the German following suit. But French censorship was rigorous: 'You cannot say where we are,' he was informed. 'I want to say only that we are in France.' 'I am sorry, Monsieur, it is forbidden.' 'But everyone knows we are in France and everyone knows that the French Army is in France.' 'I'm sorry, it is forbidden.' 'For God's sake,' exploded Dimbleby, 'what shall I say then, that we're on the front line in the middle of Switzerland!'—but he did not get his way.

Dimbleby longed to record the sound of war on disc, and spent much time trying to persuade the French to open fire. They always refused, saying: 'If we open fire, they open fire— and then what?' 'Then you fight and you win.' 'No,' replied the French, with ominous resignation, 'it will not be like that.' Eventually he did manage to record the sounds of battle, and gleefully he informed Broadcasting House of his 'scoop'. The *Radio Times* which habitually devoted much space to Dimbleby's doings in France, fanfared the forthcoming attraction:

Listeners will hear in due course these broadcasts from the advanced forts of the Maginot defence zone. They will hear records of quick-firing guns of all calibres including the great howitzers and the famous '75's, while scenes will be described in English of the progress of the battle as it presented itself to the eyes of the British wireless observers.

The tone of the *Radio Times* did not endear itself to all listeners; a certain Captain Byron was outraged and wrote to the *Yorkshire Post* to complain: 'I am wondering if the BBC have any feelings for those mothers and fathers, brothers and sisters, wives and sweethearts who have their menfolk out in France.' And the *Post*, with every show of sincerity, rallied to his support:

What are the BBC aiming at in these broadcasts? If their object is to give listeners a thoroughly realistic impression of modern warfare, they are surely attempting something which is not only misguided but unattainable. The idea of radio reporting is itself good; it has proved its value on many peacetime occasions and may now be welcomed as a valuable adjunct to the despatches of war correspondents. But what will listeners sitting at home want to hear from the army areas across the Channel? Not, surely, sounds suggesting, however imperfectly, the grim ordeal of battle... What listeners are most likely to welcome is an evocation of the quieter and more human aspects of the daily life of the troops...any attempts to reproduce the sounds and atmosphere of a battle, or even of a trench raid, should surely be ruled out.

The apparent outrage of the *Yorkshire Post* reflected a general concern among the press magnates about the possible re-emergence of broadcasting in wartime as a threat to the supremacy of Fleet Street. The Newspaper and Periodicals Emergency Council demanded that Dimbleby's war correspondence: 'should not be transmitted until after newspaper reports of the same event had already been published.' The Corporation repeated the traditional weary reminder: 'that the BBC did not seek to damage newspaper or other interests' but added with newfound courage that 'a return to the pre-war arrangement in respect of news would seriously damage not only the reputation of the BBC but, what was of far greater importance, the prestige of the nation as a whole'. For the first time the newspapers' bluff had been called. There were more skirmishes (indeed the press and the BBC spent much of the war complaining about each other's special privileges). But the *Yorkshire Post's* attempt to relegate the BBC to a subsidiary role was a dying gasp from the press.

If the public was uncertain what it required from the BBC in war, so was the Corporation itself. The Controller of Programmes shared the *Yorkshire Post's* view about the undesirability of broadcasting the sound of the Maginot line guns, although the programme (when he relented) aroused almost no critical reaction. The guns, it must be presumed, were at least more inspiring than the interminable voices of Government ministers exhorting a reluctant nation to do battle in what was still, palpably, a non-war.

The confusion about the role of the BBC in wartime was absolute. As a consequence of the BBC's timidity in peacetime the Government had not found it necessary to consider what should be done with it when war broke out. So while Goebbels prepared to mastermind Germany's massive propaganda campaign the British Government and the BBC began a long and bitter wrangle over the future of broadcasting—for the first time confronting issues which should have been raised a decade before. For ten years the BBC had sidestepped every important question about broadcasting; now in war it not only had no answers, it scarcely knew what the questions were. What was it to be, objective? neutral? impartial? How was it possible? Under what conditions? According to whose values? Now in war the questions no longer seemed relevant. But because they had never been answered, the BBC had no independent political base from which to respond to the demands of Government.

For its part the Government was as befuddled as the BBC. While the Corporation's Director-General, W. G. Ogilvie, had thought that the BBC should broadcast the famous Bagley Wood recording of the 'song of the nightingale' on the eve of war, as an earnest of 'Britain's peace-loving intentions', the British Government (or at least Neville Chamberlain) was rumoured to be of the opinion that, 'broadcasting had no part to play in modern war and should cease as soon as war broke out'. Even if the BBC's survival were not at stake (except in the unhappy mind of the Prime Minister) its independence was. In 1935 the Committee of Imperial Defence had decided that in the event of war the Government would take 'effective control of broadcasting and the BBC', the Ministry of Information becoming responsible for 'censorship control over the programmes of the BBC'. However, in July 1939 the Government appeared to change its mind, announcing that it would not 'take over the BBC in wartime'; nonetheless the new Ministry of Information (destined to be despised and ridiculed for most of its mercifully brief life) produced a memorandum stating that one of its officials would become 'Director of Radio' on the outbreak of hostilities.

The Ministry of Information suffered the misfortune of being a new Department in Whitehall. Its powers were never clearly defined; it lacked experience and expertise and it ruined the political reputations of its first three ministers—one of whom was Sir John Reith. Moreover its officials had to spend much of the time reminding other Departments and the Armed Services, of its existence, demanding—with a marked lack of success—that it, not they, should handle relations between the Government and the BBC. The Ministry and the BBC were destined for a stormy relationship.

On one thing only did they agree. In 1939 the BBC discovered that the public had an appetite for news: 'News feeds on crisis and at all critical times the BBC's news bulletins stand out as the most important part of its service in listeners' estimation,' proclaimed the BBC Handbook for that year. The Ministry gave fulsome support to the view that 'the dissemination of British news should be speedy and widespread'. They *seemed* to agree on one other matter too. In the Thirties the BBC had built up a reputation for the truth, and it was on this reputation that British propaganda was to be built. 'All British publicity' proclaimed the Ministry 'should be truthful and objective'; 'The BBC, no less than the three fighting services, has been under orders since the war began' asserted a brave-faced Corporation. 'The most important of these orders has been to tell the truth—in war as in peace.' The confident tone hid a painful reality. All were agreed that the BBC should tell the truth. But whose truth? And how much of it? And when? And to whom?

The most intelligent account of the role of the 'democratic propagandist' in war was given by Harold Nicolson, who served briefly as a Parliamentary Secretary at the Ministry. The BBC, he wrote, should concentrate on 'the rapid provision of plentiful and accurate news. In doing so [it] should remember that accuracy is more important than speed...' Then, unwittingly

begging the question about truth, he added 'There will be many
occasions upon which, for reasons which it is not possible to
explain, information has to be delayed or even withheld.'

The conflict between the Government and the BBC was
precisely about whether and under what conditions news should
be 'delayed or even held up'; it resolved itself into the issue of
the BBC's independence. Was the BBC directly under the orders
of the Ministry of Information? Was it an extension of the
Ministry? Or was it free but bound to take guidance from its
officials? Like the slide from 'whole truth' to 'half truth' to 'lie',
the transition from 'independence' to 'subservience' is gentle and
seductive. For an enfeebled Corporation, bullied by a Department
of Government piqued by the disdain shown for it by the rest of
Whitehall, and bent on self-assertion, a Government 'takeover'
was a real risk.

In France Dimbleby was unaware of the hostilities between
Government and BBC; of the confusions and conflict about the
role of the BBC he knew and learned nothing. Two years later
he was to pay dearly for their hostilities and his ignorance. For
the moment, wrapped against the cold in an Arras attic, he
thought things simple enough: Britain was at war; the BBC was
at war; he should try to help win the war. By Christmas 1939,
in the phony war, it had become a depressing task. Like
everyone else, he was cold, bored and frustrated. His trips along
the Maginot line filled him with foreboding. His reports, breezily
optimistic, bound by the tightest censorship of the war (he once
had 'tommy-gun' scratched out of a disc moments before it was
due for broadcasting) belied his feelings. He had noticed the guns
of the line pointing in the wrong direction; he had been
dismayed by the low morale of the French; it seemed plain that
if the Germans wished to advance, nothing would stop them.
'Am I mad?' he turned to David Howarth on one occasion and
asked, 'or are we going to witness the biggest shambles in
history?'

In Arras they waited and brooded. He soon ran out of 'war
correspondence' and, more out of boredom than duty he turned
himself into an impresario, organising and chairing broadcast
quizzes in which soldiers in Arras competed against their sweethearts in London; introducing a 'family favourites' from the
front; and sometimes producing a weekly variety concert. He
brought Gracie Fields to the microphone, watched George

Formby play his ukelele in the slush outside his hotel, and in a bedroom of the Universe strove to keep the peace between Noel Coward and Maurice Chevalier as the two quarrelled (in the politest terms) about who should have top billing that evening. On Christmas Day, in his roles as correspondent and entertainer he organised and took part in no less than five broadcasts, 'trying to act' as he put it 'as some kind of link between the men stranded in this frozen unlovely part of France and their people back in Britain'.

In France, even more than in London he became a law unto himself, jealous of his territory: he was BBC representative, features producer, quiz-master, public relations officer, policymaker and impresario—and he wanted to do all this alone. To the growing irritation of the News Department in London he refused simply to be what they thought he should have been—their 'observer'.

In his self-imposed role as 'Mr. BBC' he began to dispense largesse—not very great by normal standards, but by the BBC standards of the time calculated to cause the Administration apoplexy. One of his Christmas programmes was recorded in a casualty clearing station and in a gesture of goodwill towards the staff (who had no way of paying for extra food) he offered to buy them turkeys, mincepies and plum puddings—not realising that more than one hundred and twenty people were invited to the feast. The cost came to £30. He felt bound to write a humble letter of explanation to the BBC:

> I feel that the money will be well spent, as the BBC is making fairly heavy demands on the Army... Also many newspapers are putting on special shows and 'comforts' for the troops, and I feel we shall get back in goodwill and co-operation much more than I have spent. I do beg your pardon for not having consulted you—but this question was one I had to decide on the spot and I felt confident that the Corporation would support me...

He also bought a 'British warm' which cost him ten guineas 'which I considered excessive, but was assured was very reasonable in view of general prices here. However, as I know I could have got the same thing at Austin Reed's for eight guineas, I am putting that amount only on the enclosed expense sheet. I will happily bear the balance in the good cause of feeling really warm'.

Dimbleby's unusual humility had its origins in an unhappy relationship which developed in the Thirties between him and the Corporation's Administration. To the admiring consternation of Charles Gardner, he spent much of his early career doing for BBC expenses what he had done for the News Service. It did not endear him to a BBC which regarded any expenditure of Corporation money as a mortal sin. The parsimony was not without humbug. In the Twenties the BBC well understood the need for 'hospitality'; spending large sums to maintain a house in London primarily for the purpose of entertaining visiting dignitaries. But humble employees of the Corporation were not expected to show generosity in the same way. Among their other duties Gardner and Dimbleby were charged with welcoming visiting speakers in the News Talks programme. The BBC maintained a room and a drinks cupboard to help them— though it was a firm (if unwritten) rule that a guest should only be offered one drink before a programme, and nothing afterwards. The BBC men were to exercise the same self-restraint. To enforce compliance with the regulation, each bottle was covered with a label on which Dimbleby or Gardner had to mark the new level of the liquor with their name and the date every time they dispensed the Corporation's hospitality. Though Dimbleby drank little himself, his liberality to others caused much irritation.

Dimbleby had tastes and aspirations which sent a shudder through the Administration and a frisson of delight through less courageous colleagues. Charles Gardner remembers that Dimbleby led him in numerous assaults upon the all-powerful and much-hated Administration: ' "they" challenged the need to buy a pint of beer for someone who had helped us. Fighting "them" became the joy of our lives.' When he stayed away from London he became the first BBC employee to live in the style to which he would like to become accustomed: 'I remember him ringing all the bells in sight in one splendid hotel and ordering a manicure, drinks in the room, and expensive sandwiches,' wrote Gardner, 'mainly I think to enjoy seeing the look of shock on my face.' In 1939 when he returned from six weeks' covering the Royal Tour in Canada (which brought him high praise from the Board of Governors) the Accounts Department queried his 'incidental' expenses of £94 for the trip. He composed a memo of mock (but convincing) grandeur: 'Do you expect me to account for every half penny when I am with my King?' He won the day, but his arrogance was not easily forgotten by Administration officials who suspected—correctly—that the young man who had dared to challenge them held them in some contempt. It was unwise—but he did not change his ways. Later, harbouring the grudge against him, 'they' would get their own back.

Now in France Dimbleby continued to spend Corporation money, and spent much time accounting for it. 'I am afraid I have been rather irregular in money matters during the last day or so, in view of quite unexpected events,' he wrote early in January 1940. The 'unexpected event' in question (Dimbleby never lost the power of dramatisation) was 'a rush visit to Paris with a conducting officer'. The conducting officer was a Captain (brought out of retirement) by the name of The Honourable Harry Tufton. Dimbleby was intrigued by his first contact with the British aristocracy. Tufton had a country house with seven gardeners, maintained a suite permanently at the Ritz and complained to a wide-eyed Dimbleby that after the war he would have 'merely £5,000 a year, dear boy' on which to survive. Dimbleby who had aspired for 'something much better than journalism' and who earned less than a tenth of his conducting officer's income, found the style alluring.

The justification for the Paris jaunt was to resolve a dispute between the BBC and the French authorities which threatened to make daily broadcasting to London impossible: 'By dint of a frontal attack on the Quai D'Orsay,' Dimbleby explained to a dubious Corporation, 'and a little expensive entertaining (which included, though he did not mention it, giving a bouquet of flowers and lunch to the wife of the relevant civil servant) I cleared things up ...'

The Administration, which disliked his panache at the best of times, must have been even less amused by the rest of his letter: 'My conducting officer happens to be an "Hon." in private life, and insisted on staying at the Ritz to meet many of his friends. He has similar ideas on feeding and entertainment, so the visit was expensive. Anyway I had to cash a cheque in Paris for twenty pounds. I have not spent all of this, of course ...' The BBC accepted his explanation but without a smile.

By March, nearly seven months after leaving London, Dimbleby had run out of anything to say about the war. He had visited nearly every front-line unit, had interviewed generals and privates, and was a well-known figure. He wanted to move on.

A month later he took an Imperial Airways Flying Boat for the Middle East. As befitted the BBC's 'Senior News Observer' (with Charles Gardner with the RAF in France, Edward Ward in Finland, and Bernard Stubbs replacing Dimbleby with the BEF, the BBC had four observers) the BBC advertised his departure: 'He will make his headquarters in Cairo ... he will be away between two or three months ... he goes essentially as a News Observer ... On this tour Dimbleby goes alone.' More than two years later after covering the war in fourteen Middle East countries and travelling more than fifty thousand miles he was to return home, a famous name, but an unhappy man.*

The tour of duty started well. Even the press gave him a send-off, admitting publicly for the first time the existence of his craft: 'The radio war correspondent—a new skilled and dangerous profession—has come into being' announced *The Star*:

> His despatch comes to us by word of mouth, a medium which must at times be more vivid and more thrilling than the printed word. The voice of a man who may have risked his life a few hours earlier, and who has, in any event, undergone severe physical and emotional strain, conveys more than he may intend. But the very catch in the voice makes the heart beat faster in sympathy ... It is a man's job these young adventurers have taken on. Its importance from the point of view of public confidence cannot be exaggerated.

Making allowances for Fleet Street hyperbole, it must be admitted that the press was far more alive to the potential of radio in wartime than was the BBC itself. Dimbleby found Cairo exciting:

> a babel, a yellow and white, dusty, smelly city of shouting, screaming men and women, of screeching trams and crazy buses, of lunatic motor drivers and dreaming pedestrians, of starved and beaten cabhorses, mangy dogs, of rabies, venereal disease and dysentery. Anything can be bought in Cairo, if you are willing to pay the price; any price can be lowered if you are willing to argue ... Cairo [is] unbelievably corrupt and, sometimes, incredibly beautiful.

* See map on page 408.

After he had been only a month in Cairo the war in Europe began in earnest, and the British started their scramble back towards Calais. Dimbleby was intensely frustrated. He wrote to a close friend at the BBC:

> The outbreak of things on the Western Front—and tragic as they have been, I shall never forgive myself for having missed them—has put a different complexion on my work here (where the war has not yet begun), and I have dropped many things which would otherwise have been of more than usual interest . . . I get very upset inside when I hear of places I knew so well in France being blown to bits, and I am anxious to know how my team fared. I try not to think of my wife and child—I can only hope to God that they're all right where they are.

In the same letter he raised issues which were to assume great importance later:

> The censorship has been much tightened in the last few days, and I have just heard that my last two cables to News were stopped altogether. The trouble is that the censors here don't tell us if they're stopped. Everything has to be censored twice, by the Army and then by the telecommunications people for the Egyptian Government. I have a third one for broadcasting . . .

The second issue was propaganda:

> Now that the BBC has paid for me to come all this way, and I have made all my contacts with the Government and army people in the Middle East, I cannot help thinking that it would by a waste of money to fetch me back again . . . when the news from elsewhere is sad, I am convinced of the practical value of solid, not too cheerful, but confidence-giving stuff from other places where things aren't so bad . . . [also] the propaganda people at the Embassy here seem very anxious for me to stay in this part of the world. I don't believe in BBC people being parties to too much propaganda, but there are times when everyone must help the good cause, and it appears that I am considered to have been helping from here.

D.

Dimbleby had been given no instructions from London about the role of the BBC correspondent in war—largely because the BBC was still uncertain itself. His attitude, naive as it may have been, sprang from his ignorance of the BBC's views and his own absolute commitment to helping the war effort. The BBC did not reply to his letter.

On June 10th 1940, to no-one's surprise, Italy entered the war—and the extraordinary, sometimes ludicrous, often bloody, occasionally chivalrous, usually miserable, struggle for the control of an empty desert began. It was an old-fashioned battle, a relentless back-and-forth across a dead earth dotted with names like Sollum, Capuzzo, Mersah Matruh, Tobruk and Benghazi— names which might have been conjured up for a historical romance. There was no front-line, or if there was, it was momentary, always shifting like the sand storms which blew up from the Sahara, obliterating all vision for days at a time. It was a General's playground where the maps revealed no inconvenient towns filled with women and children. It was a tactician's dream: water-holes here, ports there, ravines and passes, and square mile upon square mile of open ground. The Desert War belonged to another age and it was fought with different rules. In Europe they dropped indiscriminate bombs to terrorise the people; here both sides refused to poison the wells upon which their survival depended. The enemy was admired. And once in the no-man's land of the desert the enemies played football. Both sides sang 'Lillie Marlene'. Weeks of boredom and discomfort in the sand, when it was no longer amusing to fry eggs on jeep bonnets, were followed by sudden confusing action in the swirling dust. Once, carried away by the valour and romance of his 'Army of the Nile' Churchill spoke of its 'glorious cavalry charge' across the sand. Others who find absurdity in human folly need only look at the Desert War for their symbol—where midget men in midget tanks chased each other endlessly and fruitlessly across a wide expanse to conquer a desert. It was an almost impossible war to report.

Dimbleby left for his first trip into the desert in June. Characteristically he made sure that he and his driver would lack nothing. His truck was filled with tents, sleeping bags, camp-beds, pressure cooker, stove, folding table, chairs, oil-lamps, crates of food, fruit and beer. A crescendo of bottles rattling, clattering, breaking announced the imminent arrival of the one-man caravan almost before his truck bumped into sight over the sand dunes. He was at once entranced by the desert:

> There was no movement, and until I grew accustomed to its dimension, no landmark on which to rest the eyes. In those moments when I saw the desert for the first time, I experienced a queer humble feeling. I think I realised more keenly than ever before how tiny a man is in such surroundings; how tiny even a hundred or a hundred thousand men can be, and how insignificant. Here in the desert where you live with the strict relentless rhythm of the sun and the moon and the stars, you come to a closer understanding of your own unimportance . . . the feeling of humility never left me when I was living in the desert. Sometimes at night I used to walk away from the camp and stand alone in the moonlight . . . I thought the desert remained cruelly aloof and though men fought and died on its bosom, and were buried in it to a depth of six feet, their graves no more than scratched its surface and all the noise and confusion were only tiny sounds in its emptiness.

Two days later they ran into a sandstorm—'the desert roused to fury, flaying us with a thousand whips of sand that stung our faces and knees unbearably, choking us and covering our bodies and luggage with a yellow screen'. That evening he saw his first battle at Capuzzo, the first tank engagement of the Middle East war:

> I can see field guns ready in position to shell the Italian artillery [he reported to London]. To my left some of our tanks are moving slowly . . . others, larger tanks, are moving relentlessly about the open plain, like terriers sniffing the ground . . . I look at my watch; it's zero hour. And as I look up again there's a flash from our field guns—the whoosh of shells in the air—and then the boom of the guns . . . The light is fading; the sun is down . . . but we can still see the little black shapes of the tanks moving in and out of the smoke.

That night, still excited by the battle, he tried to sleep. A truck came bumping across the desert to where they had pitched their tents and a Captain got out and came over to them to ask directions. He was delivering the post:

> That is life in the desert [wrote Dimbleby]. All day man fights

his battle; he is cut and bleeding, perhaps he dies in the burning sun, or he lies there with the flies gathering on his blood until a stretcher bearer or an ambulance reaches him. But at night tank-fighting must stop. So does noise and movement, heat and dust. Men breathe and are refreshed; they wash and eat and sleep, and across the wilderness to the battle zone of tomorrow comes a solitary man, bringing the post from home.

In Cairo General Sir Archibald Wavell surveyed his Command. He was outnumbered six to one by the Italian Army; he was short of equipment, of artillery and tanks, of supplies and transport. He was defending a vast area of the Middle East, Asia Minor and Africa. He was in no condition to go on the offensive though he was confident that he could hold the Middle East against the Italians, and so protect the important supply routes to the Far East and even more the oil wells of Persia and Saudi Arabia without which Britain could not wage war.

In London Churchill was anxious for action. In the summer of 1940 he summoned Wavell to London to give him marching orders. It was a disastrous meeting. The two men were incompatible. Wavell was cool, detached, a brilliant strategist, who regarded war as a 'wasteful, boring, muddled affair', flinching from the passionate romantic urges of the Prime Minister. 'The discussions,' noted Churchill, 'were severe. As usual I put my case in black and white.' Wavell was obdurate and noted drily: 'I found that Winston's tactical ideas had to some extent crystallised at the South African war.' By the end of their meeting Wavell was convinced that Churchill did not trust him and would not leave him alone. He was right. Churchill was afraid that the Italians would overrun the Middle East and doubted that Wavell would be able to stop them. The acrimonious meeting between the obdurate General and the stubborn Prime Minister signalled the beginning of a battle between the War Cabinet and the General Headquarters of the Middle East Command which was to last nearly two years and which would lead to the dismissal of two of Britain's greatest Generals. As the BBC's observer in the Middle East, caught unwittingly in the struggle between London and Cairo, Richard Dimbleby would become its innocent victim.

In the autumn, as expected, General Graziano led his Italian troops across the Libyan border, into Egypt. As he had planned, Wavell allowed his forces to drop back before the advancing might of the Italian Army. Richard Dimbleby, who had been carefully briefed by the British commanders, sent back his first despatch:

> It may not yet be called an attack for the enemy in their advance have found nothing in front of them to attack. They have plunged into wide open and nearly empty spaces . . . but somewhere between Cairo from where I am speaking now . . . somewhere in the three hundred and fifty miles of desert the British forces are ready and waiting.

Three days later (on September 17th) he broadcast:

> it must be admitted that the Italian advance has been very rapid . . . But this does not alter the situation in general—which is causing no anxiety; and which, it cannot be too strongly emphasised shows no danger to the British forces or to Egypt . . . There is no direct evidence that the Italians intend this advance to be the forerunner of the grand attack on Egypt. In fact there is evidence to the contrary. It seems more likely that Mussolini is staging a demonstration designed to appear as a territorial conquest and to keep up his end of the Axis . . .

He must have been astonished the next day to receive a curt telegram from the BBC: 'Beg frankness stop infinite damage done minimising enemy advantages. Signed A. P. Ryan.' Ryan was new to the BBC and had never met Dimbleby. He had been seconded from Whitehall to act as the Government's man in the Corporation and had charge of the most crucial area of the BBC's affairs—its news coverage of the war and its relationship with the Ministry of Information. He demanded, and was accorded, the title of 'Controller (Home)' and was one of the most important men in the BBC. He had daily access to War Cabinet Minutes; he knew the thinking of the Government and he was not disposed to ignore it. Dimbleby's despatches filled him with dismay: they were in complete conflict with the War Cabinet's view of the situation. Dimbleby had reported that there was no cause for 'anxiety'; the War Cabinet thought that Egypt was facing 'mortal danger'. It was an intolerable position for the Corporation which Ryan regarded as 'the fourth arm' (along with the Army, Navy and Air Force) of war.

Dimbleby was furious but contained himself, cabling back:

You mention minimising enemy advantages can only assure
you every word my material and my interpretation event
completely accurate according to official information and guidance supplied Army Headquarters here stop from own knowledge assure you my suggestions future event here also right
stop can only think that official guidance London must differ
from that given here stop events near future will supply you
necessary proof stop . . . reference your request frankness am
already being so frank as to annoy some authorities and would
remind you every one my despatches subject four sometimes
five time separate censors . . . in spite your horrible insinuations
me I remain full admiration your general presentation news . . .
Regards Dimbleby

In the event Dimbleby's confidence proved correct. The Italians
halted their advance at Sidi Barrani, fifty miles short of the British
lines at Mersah Matruh: Egypt was *not* about to fall. His inspired
guess about the conflict of 'guidance' was also correct. He received
no word of apology from Ryan—which did not augur well for
their future relationship. Instead Ryan wrote to the Ministry of
Information to give vent to his anxieties about Dimbleby's
despatches 'which come through the official mill in Cairo . . .',
which refer constantly 'to the useless nature of places to which
the Italians advance . . . and which, if there was a danger of an
Italian victory, would be most damaging to home morale.' The
Ministry replied endorsing Ryan's fears and stressing the need

to avoid over-confident versions of the Egyptian situation being
published . . . [Colonel Neville of Army Public Relations] has
been discussing the matter at the War Office and has been in
communication with Cairo on the subject, but is not yet satisfied that things are as bad as they should be. *He proposes to take
the matter up at the War Office and to use your letter as an
illustration of the difficulties produced by divergent handling of the
situation . . . it would be wise to make quite certain that Dimbleby's
material and other material on the African campaign is discussed with
Neville or his people here before it is broadcast* . . . [my italics].

So the BBC, committed to broadcasting the 'truth' had two
alternatives: it could transmit the truth according to Wavell or

the truth according to Churchill. The BBC in London had no doubt which was the more convenient of the two. The fact that Dimbleby (broadcasting the Wavell version) was correct was irrelevant. Henceforth Ryan judged his Middle East observer as unreliable and over-confident; and he did not forget it.

There had been murmurs too about Dimbleby from another quarter—the Accounts Department. In the lull between the Capuzzo battle and the Italians' timorous invasion of Egypt he had travelled down the Nile to the Sudan. It had been a miserable journey in a humid and overcrowded steamer. And Dimbleby was unwell. By the time he reached Khartoum (after thirty-six hours on a slow train) he had a fever, but with other correspondents he staggered into a meeting with General Platt, who was guarding the Sudan from invasion by the 250,000 strong Italian Army in Eritrea. As he came out of the meeting, Dimbleby, who had not told anyone of his fever, collapsed. He was rushed to hospital where a doctor confirmed that he had diptheria. A frightened and subdued Richard Dimbleby lay on his back for a month, isolated from the world, save for his nurse, and, once, a huge spider which crept into his bed at night and which he was convinced (at least for the benefit of his children in later years) was a tarantula.

He recovered only to receive a telegram from the BBC complaining that he was spending too much money. The Accounts Department had been sniping at frequent intervals since his arrival in the Middle East. While the Fleet Street correspondents lived on lavish expense accounts (and some of them had their wives installed in Cairo as well) Dimbleby felt bound to explain:

I must live as normal a life as possible, and therefore I must buy glasses of orangeade in this infernal climate, cigarettes, and occasional books. Those are normal items of expenditure which in the ordinary way would come from my own pocket. I fully expect that they shall but I would ask the indulgence of the BBC in one point only that the extremely high prices here shall be remembered.

I have obtained the maximum reduction in my room here, which is a very ordinary one, placed on the hot side of the hotel [the Continental]. I *must* stay in this hotel as all the other correspondents are here, and it is the great centre of news and gossip in the city. I am doing my best to keep expenses down and such entertainment I give is either in reply to invitations I have had to accept, or is necessary and profitable from the business point of view . . .

From Khartoum he replied to a further complaint from London:

Much regret always this feeling unpleasantness accounts and appreciate have spent lot money but one cannot represent BBC half way round world in tropic summer [he had already travelled over 10,000 miles] without doing that stop might also point out accounts I have now been separate wife child nearly a year on solid BBC work have suffered diptheria on job and am covering only British land fighting will not mention such trivialities as several Italian bombings one machine bombing from air . . . would not ask money if not needed but am twelve hundred miles from base with hospital and return journey totalling forty pounds to pay.

Richard Dimbleby was the first BBC man ever to spend such time away from home, and he suffered (as all pioneers) the effects of the limited sensibilities of bureaucrats in London. In London one or two BBC officials allowed the rumour to circulate that Dimbleby was a spendthrift at the BBC's expense, and that he was unresponsive to criticism into the bargain. In a bureaucracy of modest talents, where to commit yourself to paper is to lay your professional life on the line, it began as a whispering campaign, which almost certainly reached Ryan. By the end of 1940 (such is the way of all rumour) it was thought by many in Broadcasting House that Dimbleby was lazy, lived too well, hob-nobbed too much with afternoon alcoholics in the bar of Shepheards Hotel, and had ideas above his proper station. In the Middle East, for the first time disconcerted by the peremptory telegrams from London, Dimbleby began to wonder if he had done something to offend the BBC. But he had little time, and little inclination to let this worry him for long.

In October, when it was plain that the Italians were not going to launch an attack on Cairo, he went to Turkey, which, being a neutral buffer state between the Axis and Allied Forces, was beginning to assume increasing significance, and where, as a consequence, the BBC wished to set up radio communications between Ankara and London. The journey gave him the first of several opportunities to fulfil a boyish dream. He was given the exciting responsibility of taking some diplomatic bags from Cairo to the British Embassy in Ankara: 'Two of the bags contained general correspondence; the third held documents of a more important nature . . . I had a courier's passport.' He set off with glee and a forgivable air of restrained self-importance. He went through Jerusalem into Syria ('where Axis agents, representatives of the Gestapo and a number of German officers in mufti had already arrived . . . only my diplomatic status allowed me to pass through and then without the smallest degree of security. I became acutely conscious of my position . . . at all costs no-one must be allowed to tamper with my diplomatic bags'). Without mishap he reached the St. George Hotel in Beirut which was filled with French colonials who 'had been playing and swimming all through the agonising months of 1940, and they were playing still. They didn't care what happened as long as life remained quiet and amusing'. He decided that he would make an imperious entry. Summoning a porter to carry his precious diplomatic bags he marched into the dining room.

> Our entrance was quite a success. Perhaps I looked very English; certainly I was dressed the English way. The mailbags with their big seals were unmistakably diplomatic . . . There was a hush in the conversation as I walked down the long room followed by the porter. The maître d'hôtel fluttered up and although I can speak French, I asked in English for a table . . .

He sat at a table near some German officers. At the end of the meal he marched out as he had entered: 'This time there were faint acknowledgments and one elderly man deliberately lifted his glass as I passed . . . although I knew it was foolish, I felt vastly better for having shown the flag to the enemy.'

From Beirut via Tripoli, and Aleppo, he took the Taurus Express to Ankara. On the day he arrived the news came through that Greece and Italy were at war. He made at once for Athens, fighting his way into the city through the chaos of a mobilising Army. There, with another correspondent and a photographer, he hired an elderly Packard saloon, piled it high with rugs, overcoats, vacuum flasks and typewriters and headed for the Albanian border. It was intensely cold.

The experience of those days in the Greek mountains stayed with him. Afterwards he wrote:

People with my sort of job are habitually careless and casual; they are always moving from country to country, making and breaking friendships as they go. They have no roots. Now I saw clearly what love of home and family was worth. The men of Greece fought and died at the front, their women worked as nurses or stayed in the village ploughing and digging. They and their children bowed their backs to the winter sun to keep the farms going . . . The old people who could not work on the farms went out on the roads and toiled through the blizzards to keep the surfaces in good repair. They were not made to go; they were not paid. They went for the love of Greece.

The three correspondents were the first British to drive through Greece north to Albania after the outbreak of war. They flew a Union Jack at the radiator, and, believing that they were an advance party from the British Army, the old people dropped their tools, and stood waving and cheering as the Packard swept by. As they climbed up higher into the mountains it got colder. They passed Greek convoys—old lorries belching fumes, moving slowly. And they passed mule trains. The roads were covered in ice and there was a high wind. At one point they saw a mule caught by a gust of wind lose its footing and slip onto its knees by the side of the road:

The driver tugged at it, but the poor beast was terrified by its fall. It heaved and jerked up, but each time the weight of its load forced it down again onto the icebound road. It began kicking and struggling in panic. The man was on its outside and he was bending down to release the load when the wind hurled itself out of the valley again. Slowly man and mule together slid struggling to the edge of the precipice and as we watched, they dropped out of sight into the snow swirling about the abyss.

From then on, the journey ceased to be a glamorous adventure. Further on they were held up at a mountain village by another convoy of mules which filled the road. While they waited a cluster of Italian bombers flew overhead, circled and dived. The first bomb fell on the outskirts of the village, the second fell nearer and the third dropped beside them. The car rocked violently, the windows shattered and the three correspondents crouched on the glass-strewn floor. As the bombers wheeled off, they got out of the car and looked dazedly around. One man had been hit by shrapnel. He was sitting in a doorway crying for help. The entire front had been ripped off the house nearest them and in the snow: 'it looked like a cake from which the icing had fallen away. Two old women were standing, gaping at it . . .' Fragments from one of the bombs had mown down nearly a dozen mules:

> Two were lying on their sides, kicking convulsively as the blood poured from them. As we were approaching a driver took out his rifle and shot both of them through the head. The rest lay in a hideous tangle, heads blown from bodies, legs bent and snapped with bloddy bones sticking through the skin. The entrails of one had been blown round its neck in a slippery red garland. Another had been laid open from muzzle to tail, as though by the slaughterer's axe . . .

It was not a sight that was easily forgotten. 'Since that day,' he wrote, 'I have seen many corners of battlefields where human beings have been torn apart by weapons of modern war, but never have I seen such a surfeit of carnage. These were only the remnants of animals but we felt sick.'

When Dimbleby left for France the war had seemed a chance for excitement, even glory. It had been between nations. Now he saw that it was between men. Good was still fighting evil but there was nothing glamorous about the struggle. The massacre of the mules, the women staring at their ruined house, the man with the shrapnel wound became a few of hundreds of images to be stored up, permanent reminders of the reality of war. At the front-line he saw the Greek resistance in action—the tortuous advance by a guerrilla army against the massive force of the Italians. He watched the soldiers on the mountains through a periscope:

> I felt like someone looking into a seaside camera obscura, where the shapes of innocent people are thrown on a white table for

your amusement. These little crawling shapes, moving in absolute silence on the face of the mountain, were living fighting soldiers . . . There was a horrid fascination in watching them.

He saw dead and wounded men, Greek soldiers labouring to drag old guns through the snow and ice into the firing line— patriots fighting for their country:

Our soldiers smirked at the Greek Army and our Air Marshall had 'never heard of' the Greek air force. But when Greece went to war our eyes were opened. I saw the Greek army fighting and dying in the snow, with its thin blankets and old guns. I saw the Greek air force fly away in its handful of old machines to meet the enemy, knowing it was flying to its death . . . These men, in the Greece of 1940, were superb.

His despatches made no pretence of objectivity: 'Let me add my voice to the chorus of praise to Greece. We have a new ally,' he cabled, emphasising the Greeks' need for 'aeroplanes, aeroplanes, aeroplanes' if they were to deal 'a mortal blow to the enemy,' it was natural for the Greeks to turn to Britain for even more support...' He had not chosen a very good moment to rouse the British to the Greek cause. Although King George VI had cabled the Greek Government: 'Your cause is our cause; we shall be fighting against a common foe' the War Cabinet, pressed on all sides for help, had already agreed that 'any assistance we may be able to give Greece cannot be given until the German-Italian threat to Egypt is finally liquidated, the security of Egypt being vital to our strategy, and incidentally to the future of Greece'. For the BBC, therefore, Dimbleby's despatches were yet again inconvenient, although he sent fervent cables urging the Corporation to use *his* despatches instead of news agency reports, claiming that he and his companions were the 'only British observers to reach foremost Greek positions', but there is no record of his reports from Greece being broadcast by the BBC.

•

5

On Six Fronts

Always they must see these things and hear them,
Batter of guns and shatter of flying muscles,
Carnage incomparable, and human squander.

WILFRED OWEN

AT BROADCASTING HOUSE A. P. RYAN DEBATED HOW
to tell Richard Dimbleby that the BBC no longer required his
services in the Middle East. The Corporation's senior observer had
already been an embarrassment to him through his cheerful (if
innocent) support of Wavell against Churchill and his inopportune
championing of the Greek cause. Ryan wanted his BBC
reporters to be very much less obtrusive than Dimbleby and to
set their sights very much lower. In September 1940, he had
drafted a cable for his Middle East Observer commending him
for some 'very good stuff' but urging him 'to tell us only what
you are told or hear or see on the spot... Don't include
generalisations about the war at large... Avoid general apprecia-
tions of strategy, unless they come straight from the horse's
mouth... Your greatest value to the BBC is as an eye-
witness describing simply and vividly what he has seen...' And
he added a telling note in the margin to the News Editor, R. T.
Clarke: 'Would you let me know how you would alter it, and
then let us have it delivered to Master Richard.'

The implication was obvious: Dimbleby had ideas above his
station—though no-one yet had the courage to tell him so. In a
sense, though, Ryan was right. The BBC's Middle East Observer
was not content merely to record what he regarded as the colourful
minutiae of battle. His conception of the role of BBC reporter

was (given the inevitable and proper restriction imposed by the censors) that he should report on the grand scale, interpreting mood, analysing plans, describing the broad sweep of battle—acting in effect as a full-blooded foreign correspondent. He should not spend all his time sending back despatches which could have been compiled by a moderately competent journalist writing articles for a women's magazine. Moreover, he had scant respect for the agency reporters in the Middle East (upon whom Ryan wished to rely for the broader picture) and his access to 'the horse's mouth' was already far greater than any other correspondent in Cairo. In the eyes of the Middle East Command he *was* the BBC, and he was treated with very special consideration as a result.

Ryan sensed this in 'Master Richard' and did not like it. It was the more disturbing by the end of 1940 because for weeks Churchill had been pressing Wavell to throw the Italians back out of Egypt into Libya in a major assault, and was irritated with Wavell's reluctance to move. When the Middle East Commander did move (in his own time) he signalled the War Office warning against 'undue hopes being placed on this operation'. Churchill thundered to the Chief of the Imperial General Staff: 'If, with the situation as it is, General Wavell is only playing small and is not hurling his whole available force with furious energy he will have failed to rise to the height of circumstances...' Unmoved by the Prime Minister's intemperance Wavell summoned the Middle East war correspondents to his office and told them: 'Gentlemen... we have advanced in the Western Desert. This is not an offensive and I do not think you ought to call it an offensive yet. You might call it an important raid.'

It was at this point that Ryan decided to recall Richard Dimbleby. At all costs he wished to avoid a repetition of the previous September: Dimbleby's replacement would much less likely cause a similar problem. Edward Ward had made a name for himself by some vivid reporting of the war in Finland a year before. His manner and style were quite different from Dimbleby's. He was colloquial, he was lighter, and he would know his place. He would make no attempt to broadcast on matters of what he himself sardonically would call 'high strategy'; nor would he try to step beyond the formal bounds of the relationship between Army and correspondent; neither seeking nor expecting special consideration, he would be content to record the details of battle and the 'colour' of war. He would certainly not regard himself as the voice of the BBC in the Middle East. He would suit Ryan well.

Ryan's urge to replace Dimbleby was intensified by the rancour which now marked the relationship between the BBC and Whitehall. By the end of 1940 relations between the Corporation and the Ministry of Information were strained almost to breaking point. Ryan who had been sent to the BBC as Whitehall's man, had become the Corporation's fiercest (and ablest) champion. But he confronted a Government, Parliament and Civil Service, which (in his own view) had lost confidence in the BBC; which regarded the Corporation as disobedient and irresponsible. The charges were absurd but dangerous. Ryan was forced to devote nearly all his time to rebutting the allegations against the BBC. He complained that Ministries gave conflicting instructions, and paid only 'lip service' to the value of propaganda, which had for a long time been officially defined as a fourth arm of war (alongside the Army, Navy and Air Force) and which included 'the dissemination of prompt, accurate and full news, as well as of British views'.

In his struggle with Whitehall, Ryan was fighting to preserve, not to extend, the role of the BBC. The news bulletins (he was to write with approval late in 1941) were 'taken largely from agency reports, official hand-outs received from the Ministry of Information and the BBC's own monitoring of what enemy and other broadcasters have been saying'. The question of the Corporation's own men providing the bulk of the BBC News had not yet arisen and Ryan had neither the time nor the inclination to contemplate the prospect. So in 1941, when the war was being fought in the Mediterranean and the Middle East, when it was about to be fought in Russia and the Far East, it did not occur to him (or to anyone else in the Corporation) that to have just one reporter beyond the shores of Britain was absurdly inadequate.

But how to tell Dimbleby he was no longer wanted? Ryan made copious notes of possible ways of doing it: Ward (he mused) was a better reporter, of that there was no doubt. So either Dimbleby could be told to remain in Athens or in Cairo, or he could return home. At this point he revealed a sudden and convenient solicitude for Richard Dimbleby's health. Somewhere in the BBC files was a note which had originated in Khartoum advising that Dimbleby's heart had been affected by his attack

of diphtheria. it would be unwise, Ryan now avowed, for the
BBC to 'take the responsibility of sending a man not in perfect
health to face the inevitable hardships of the desert campaign.' The
same applied to Athens. 'Dimbleby,' observed Ryan, generously,
'is not a man to spare himself' and he would be bound to indulge
in strenuous trips into the Albanian mountains where 'we are
already getting an adequate Reuter service'. So that left one
alternative.

What Ryan appeared to overlook was that in August Dimbleby
himself had cabled from Khartoum: 'Apparently watch heart
after diphtheria', and subsequently, while the BBC showed no
anxiety whatsoever for his health, he had reported the first Italian
advance, and the start of the Greek campaign in the Albanian
mountains. Someone must have realised that Dimbleby would be
unconvinced by the Corporation's sudden concern for his health,
for the matter was never raised again.

Ryan's desire to present the case for Dimbleby's withdrawal
in the most diplomatic terms was motivated less by concern for
his 'observer's' sensibilities than fear that it would provoke the
Middle East Command to rush angrily to Dimbleby's assistance.
In the end he decided to summon him home, instructing the
News Department:

> . . . get in touch with him as quickly as possible to prevent
> him arriving in Egypt (from Athens where he had been in-
> formed of the renewal of desert hostilities) and hearing a garbled
> version of the re-arrangements from GHQ Cairo. We must
> make it plain to him that he is being recalled for a rest after
> competent service . . .

Ryan's fears were well grounded. Dimbleby received his cable
on the way back to Egypt. He was unimpressed:

> For Ryan stop received your very surprising cable . . . sincerely
> hope there's some worthwhile job waiting at home as can't
> help being reluctant leave Mideast now things starting grand
> scale stop . . . shall unchange original plan go front tonight as
> it must be covered . . . Dimbleby.

GHQ Cairo was upset, as Ryan had feared. An urgent SOS
was sent to the War Office from the Middle East Command
urging that Dimbleby should stay. A fortnight later (such was the

Richard Dimbleby

Richard, aged 3 weeks, with Gwen

With Gwen and Fred, aged 5

Aged 10 with Gwen and his baby sister, Pat

Richard at Mill Hill School where 'his record
of academic achievement was dismal'

With Dilys on their wedding day, June 26 1937,
at Copthorne Parish Church

In the Libyan Desert in 1942 as the BBC's first War Correspondent:
'victim of a conflict between the War Cabinet and the Middle East
Command of which he knew nothing'

In Saudi Arabia—neutral territory. On the back of the photo he wrote,
'I look tough but look at the man who's waiting to kill me!'

Kassala, March 1941. Recording his first despatch of the final Eritrean Campaign

At the battle of Keren—'It was bitter, vicious fighting'

The houseboat on the Nile which gave him a reputation at the BBC for reckless extravagance

At the Brandenburg Gate in Berlin 1945—the first British correspondent into the fallen city

(Bl

Dimbleby (behind and to the left of Churchill) reports the Prime Minister's tour through the ruins of Berlin

Recording the entry of
the Australians into
Beirut at the fall of Syria

In Berlin, giving a live
commentary on the
triumphal entry of the
Allied Troops into the
defeated city

In the studio recording an interview for London Town, the first television programme to use 'back-projection'

The commentator

For London Town he went down sewers and up fire engines

fragility of the BBC's position, and so impossible was it to give the real explanation for withdrawing Dimbleby) that Ryan, perhaps the most powerful man in the BBC, was forced to reverse his decision. He cabled Dimbleby to inform him that he would stay in the Middle East after all as 'co-ordinator' of the BBC and Dominion broadcasts in the Near East. The concept of 'co-ordinator' was a face-saving fiction: already Dimbleby was up in the desert pursuing the British advance against the Italians. General O'Connor's troops were hustling the Italians west back towards Tripoli. Dimbleby followed, passing

> gutted tanks and armoured cars blistering in the sun, petrol and diesel lorries with burst tyres and broken backs, exploded ammunition trucks standing like black skeletons in the pools of their debris. The Italians themselves lay tangled in the mess with the desert fleas crawling over them and the savage flies tormenting their swollen faces. The desert is an ugly place in which to die . . .

Capturing Sidi Barrani (rendering 'glorious service' purred Churchill 'to the Empire and to our cause') they reached the little port of Bardia. The town was heavily fortified with barbed wire, minefields and bunkers. The Allied forces surrounded it, cutting the water supply and the Italians' only escape route, and then began shelling. Mussolini had cabled General 'Electric' Bergonzoli instructing him to: 'defend Bardia to the last'. 'In Bardia we are, and in Bardia we stay,' was the gallant reply.

Next day, with three other war correspondents, Dimbleby drove up to the town through continuous shelling—'shells went throbbing incessantly overhead, and pillars of black smoke shot suddenly into the air . . . Through this tanks, bren carriers, and we ourselves, moved up . . .' Within a few hours the Italian resistance had crumbled. In the evening the war correspondents were with the first Allied troops to enter the town. It was an astonishing sight:

> On either side of us in the gloom [reported Dimbleby] were gathering crowds of enemy officers and men—*with* their arms. They had not been captured and they should have been fight-ing . . . they did nothing; they just stood and watched us drive through . . . they were gathering voluntarily to surrender to

the first British troops they saw . . . several actually ran up to me with their hands up, crying 'Surrender'.

The town was aflame; its neat white houses blackened by smoke, its streets filled with rubble. Prisoners stood in desolate groups—altogether more than 300,000 of them—waiting to be disarmed. Above all else, Dimbleby remembered the sight of a young boy lying on the ground with a gaping stomach wound. All the British ambulances were filled with Allied casualties; but he stopped one of them and helped a gunner lift the boy inside. There was some cursing at having to make room for 'a bloody wop' but two of the wounded, seeing that he was a boy, made a pillow for his head and another covered his body with a coat. The boy's friend stood watching the ambulance disappear into the gloom. Dimbleby went over to him: 'I gave him a hand to the edge of the road, where he lowered himself onto the hard ground. Then he burst into tears and cried more bitterly than I have ever seen a man cry before.'

The correspondents decided to drive back that night across the desert to Mersah Matruh, 170 miles away. The fall of Bardia, 'was a major event in the Wavell offensive and its propaganda value was great,' wrote Dimbleby. 'Official and unofficial accounts of its capture had to be transmitted as quickly as possible, preferably before the enemy had time to invent and broadcast doctored reports and explanations.' They set off already exhausted. Dimbleby, who would never admit to tiredness, was excited at the prospect of a dash across the desert to his deadline and offered to drive. Alan Moorehead was one of the correspondents in the back: 'We drove on slowly, endlessly, chilled to the bone . . . Just before dawn we were approaching Mersah Matruh, Richard Dimbleby driving . . . [we were] too frozen to move but beyond sleeping. Only Dimbleby slept.' The truck hit two concrete drums placed across a new bridge and

plunged into space over the ditch beside the road. They were unhurt, but out of the gloom emerged an engineer who stared glumly at the wreckage for a moment. Then in a tired voice he said: 'I've been working for a solid month in this bloody hole. I built that bridge. I finished it today. I was just putting up a nice little sign to say "Bridge begun by the Twenty-first Company of Engineers, December 1940. Completed 1941." I don't suppose it matters now. Or would you like me to say "Destroyed by war correspondents January 1941?"'

In Cairo Dimbleby sent back his account of entry into Bardia to Broadcasting House (where, much later it was judged by the Controller of Overseas Broadcasting to be 'one of the outstanding radio reports of the war'), and briefly met Edward Ward, who headed for the desert, while he began his job as 'co-ordinator'. Within a few days he heard once more from Ryan. The cable was phrased in his characteristically blunt style:

Please strictly observe stop Ward sole official commentator stop send all Ward verbatim except censor's cuts stop tell Ward we want personal factual descriptive stories every day stop where are our stories query Times good stuff daily stop don't want official communiqués or general observations stop acknowledge stop Ryan.

Perhaps the Controller was still smarting at his humiliation by the Middle East Command, but since Dimbleby knew nothing of this, and had no idea that he was out of favour with Broadcasting House, he was dismayed at Ryan's acrimonious tone.

In the nine months that he had been in the Middle East, he had heard hardly a word of approval from London, and no praise for his report of the fall of Bardia. Now this man Ryan, whom he had never met, was not only being offensive, but, by implication, was yet again, impugning his integrity, as he had last September.

Dimbleby cabled back in some irritation and pain: 'Your orders received stop confess puzzled their peremptory nature as unaware them yet contravened any way stop . . .' He went on to say that he would never cut Ward's despatches unless forced to do so by censorship; that he only sent an official communiqué because it was the quickest way of transmitting the news of the capture of Tobruk 'at least three hours ahead of other services'; that communications between the front and Cairo were so bad that daily despatches from the desert were impossible; that *The Times* had daily reports because Fleet Street 'pooled' the despatches of their frontline correspondents; and that in the absence of any reports from Ward, he thought that the best way to compete with the press was for him to send whatever he could from Cairo. After this exposure of the BBC's ignorance of the problems of war reporting, he ended his cable: 'Presume by naming Ward quote sole official commentator unquote you unwant me broadcast any more stop if you have reason believe my work here unsatisfactory can only apologise as have done my best alone generally in difficult conditions et against powerful competition. Dimbleby.'

His point by point rebuttal of the Controller's cable could not have endeared 'Master Richard' to Ryan though the BBC Controller was sufficiently chastened to send a mollifying (if disingenuous) reply: 'This to clear misunderstandings stop Single Libya correspondent necessary comply military press regulations stop no reflection you stop unwished us. Ryan.' For the moment at least all was forgiven.

In February there was a lull in the desert war. Under instructions from London Wavell halted his offensive in order to send some of his troops to the assistance of Greece. Rommel was on his way to North Africa to support the failing Italians. Dimbleby's substitute, Edward Ward, was in Cairo to await the renewal of desert hostilities. So Richard Dimbleby took the boat again to Khartoum, heading for Eritrea where the British were preparing their final assault on Italy's last stronghold in her East African Empire. In Khartoum he was shocked by the high life: 'our East African Army was engaged in its bloody and exhausting battle against the Italians in Eritrea (while officers and civilians in the Sudan) were living at pre-war standard. Cocktail and tennis parties, river sailing, dinner jackets . . . these were the order of the day.' One evening while he waited in his hotel for some minor repairs to his truck (he had been joined by a BBC recording engineer, Donovan, complete with his equipment) an Army jeep drew up. A man staggered out:

> a shocking apparition. His clothes stained and torn . . . his hair was long and matted about his neck with grease and sweat . . . his face was lined and old . . . his hollow cheeks were pale under the covering of bristle and beard . . . He did not smile or speak but tottered across to a basket chair and fell into it.

It was Kenneth Anderson, a fellow war correspondent and friend. Travelling by truck, camel and on foot, he had journeyed deep into Abyssinia to watch the Ethiopian guerrilla army in action against the Italians. On the return journey, finding himself lost, he had headed in the general direction of Khartoum—walking for more than one hundred miles through the bush and desert, travelling for six days in terrible heat before he ran out of food and water. He had been saved from death when he stumbled across a roving British platoon.

It was with some trepidation a few days later that Dimbleby and Donovan set off along the same track for Eritrea, in an elderly unreliable Italian truck. It was a dreadful journey over a dead land of intense heat, sandstorms, rutted tracks, deep soft sand, no animals, no people, no shelter. Only one day from Khartoum, Dimbleby stripped the gear box trying to free the truck from a sand drift; for the next two days they drove using only first and top gear. By the time they reached Kassala they were exhausted. There, while Donovan waited to repair the truck, Dimbleby hitched a lift in a British Army staff car and made for the front-line.

The battle of Keren was one of the bloodiest of the Second World War, yielding numerous tales of individual gallantry, hand-to-hand fighting and heroic death. The town of Keren, perched high in the mountains of Eritrea, was the northern outpost of the Italian colony, protecting the route southward into Abyssinia. Only one road crossed the mountains, twisting up from the plains through Keren, where the might of the Italian Army was firmly entrenched. The only way to get through was to storm the town. Protected by the black jagged peaks of the mountains it seemed impregnable.

The battle for Keren lasted nearly six weeks. Names like Brigs Peak, Sanchal, Cameron Ridge and Dologorodoc were to enter the history books of the regiments that fought there, celebrating victories won at terrible cost. Young commanders were breezily bold ('now a lot of you chaps will probably get killed tomorrow but you don't want to worry about that'); and older officers uttered First World War slogans ('there is only one degree of resistance—to the end'). Entire battalions were destroyed as they tried to scale the black peaks against machine-gun fire, mortar, and the hand grenades lobbed down from above. In one skirmish three hundred men died on the way to the top of Brig's Peak. Those who got there destroyed the Italian post, killing its last defendants in hand-to-hand fighting.

Dimbleby witnessed the last fortnight of the struggle. It was an ordeal. On his second day he narrowly missed death when a British 'stringbag' bombed the Allies' base camp by mistake killing six soldiers a little way from his tent. He climbed up the rock-face to Cameron Ridge, where the temperature was over 120 degrees, and looked through binoculars at the Italian mortar position apparently a stone's throw away above them. As he moved up for a better view there was the whine and smack of a bullet on the rock above his head. He half leapt, half fell back behind the ridge, falling on top of a none-too-happy sergeant in the process: 'Funny, they don't usually fire at this time of day. It must be your size,' joked a private—'thought you were a general I expect.'

Down below there was some light relief. Oliver Baldwin (the son of the ex-Prime Minister) arrived in a truck rigged up with a gramophone and loudspeakers. He positioned it facing the Italians and then 'to demoralise them' as he explained to Dimbleby, played some extracts from Puccini and Verdi, to make them homesick. Dimbleby noted in his diary: 'some at the front claimed that the enemy could be heard singing arias, echoing down the rocks from the Italian front line.' Others were not so moved. Baldwin spent much time sheltering from shells clearly directed at eliminating the propaganda.

A little way away from the main camp Dimbleby had installed himself in some comfort. He and Donovan set their bivouac against the truck under the shade of a huge tree. They dug a latrine ('and fitted a seat brought all the way from Khartoum'), and rigged up a canvas bath behind a nearby shrub: 'I put my patent table and tools inside the lorry bivouac and we were snugly established . . . When it was getting dark I opened my valise, blew up my air bed, trained a mosquito net over it and lay down to sleep under the stars. It was cool and pleasant...' At daybreak he returned to the reality of war:

> It was bitter, vicious fighting...There was little mercy in this battle. Some of the wounded Italians lay out in the sun in full view of our positions. The Indian bearers crawled out to bring them in. The enemy machine gunners watched them and waited until they were bending over their stretchers. Then they opened fire and mowed the bearers down.

Every day there were the wounded to be brought down from the mountains to the field hospital below in Happy Valley:

> It was an unending procession of stretchers, lowered slowly

and painfully down. I watched the twisted faces of the men from Britain and India, the men with torn backs lying on their stomachs groaning, the men with heads buried in bloody bandages, and the lucky ones, the lightly wounded, limping and wincing over the loose stones: those who died were left to the end, their bodies bloated in the sun.

On the day that Keren fell he drove into the fortress town past the abandoned Italian positions and their dead. He passed an Eritrean soldier sitting on the ground behind his gun:

He had been shot through the face by the first infantry tank to break through but the grip of his dead hands held him in position . . . day after day [he] sat there behind his gun. Each morning he was a little blacker, a little more swollen . . . One morning he rolled over on his back, but his hands stayed in the same position before him. He seemed to be praying for mercy.

For a month afterwards the dead lay in the mountains. Those who had to pass through held handkerchiefs to their noses, and vultures were black in the sky.

Dimbleby pressed on with the Allies forcing the Italian Army back towards the Red Sea. At one point the Advance guard went too far. Dimbleby stood talking in the middle of the road with a brigadier when an Italian mortar position opened fire on them. The first shell landed short; the second over their heads; as they ran the third landed just where they had been standing; and one of the group was wounded. They fell on the ground and waited: 'I was pressing myself tightly to the earth . . . the shelling continued . . . one round came sobbing down, louder and louder and louder and right overhead. "This is it" I thought. It landed six feet away, silently. It was a dud.'

Asmara the capital of Eritrea fell without resistance. Dimbleby entered with the first tanks. It was like Bardia again: rows of defeated Italians lining the route; guns, ammunition, field-glasses, compasses and water bottles lying abandoned on the side of the road. They walked into the main square of the city—the first British troops—and met no resistance. At the hotel they found elegant, cool Italians sipping imported Camparis. Feeling most inadequate, the conquering heroes, dirty, unshaven and sweaty, humbly asked if there was a room for the night. 'After the mighty

battle of Keren and the collapse of the Italian army,' wrote
Dimbleby, 'it was an anti-climax.'

They moved on towards Massawa, the Red Sea port, and the
end of the road. Admiral Bonetti who commanded the Italian
Fleet at first refused to surrender: 'The Italians,' he declared, 'will
stand in Massawa to the end.' Two days later the Admiral relented
—after a brief bout of shelling—and raised the white flag. A small
group of war correspondents, with Dimbleby at their head were
the first officers into the town. Mistaking them for the British
General's advance party, Admiral Bonetti formally offered them
his surrender. They graciously accepted and with much dignity
the good Admiral led them to the Harbour's edge to contemplate
the half submerged and smoking hulks in the water, the last
remnants of the Italian East African Empire. Dimbleby watched
him sit down by the water and place his ceremonial sword across
his knee to break it: 'But it only bent, and in disgust he threw it
into the harbour . . .'

That evening, dangling his feet in the water, Dimbleby recorded his despatch on the fall of Massawa. 'It's strange, but
comforting,' he recorded, 'to realise that now that Eritrea is under
British control, there is an unbroken chain of British or Allied
territories spreading thousands of miles west from this point, right
across Africa to the Atlantic Ocean.' Back in Khartoum forty
days after they had left for Keren, they walked up into the hotel,
tired and dishevelled. A dinner-jacketed young man looked up at
them superciliously: 'Good heavens, has there been a battle somewhere?'—'Yes, there has been a battle. A bloody battle. A bloody
awful battle.' Long afterwards Dimbleby wrote: 'I still dream of·
Sanchal and Cameron Ridge and if I stand on an English hilltop
and breathe the words Brigs Peak and Dologorodoc, I can almost
smell the horrible sickly stench of Happy Valley.'

Dimbleby returned to the Western Desert. In GHQ Cairo there
was depression. Rommel's troops had driven the British back
towards Egypt; the Germans had pushed the Allies out of Greece;
and rumour was rife that the Nazis were fomenting uprising in
the Near East, that German Airborne Divisions were about to
land in Vichy-controlled Syria, and that Hitler would pressurise
Turkey (the neutral buffer between the Axis and Allied powers)
to join the Nazi cause. In quick succession Dimbleby went to Iraq,
Syria, Turkey and Persia.

In Iraq he drove through the desert with the Transjordan

Frontier Force to make contact with the legendary Glubb Pasha whose Araba guerrilla army was skirmishing with Raschid's Ali's Iraqui forces. Raschid Ali had staged a pro-German coup d'état, threatening the oil pipe-line running across the desert between Kurkur and Haifa. It was the kind of warfare that Dimbleby thought he would enjoy:

'We stormed across the rutted desert, keeping our formation. Far out to the right and left of me, I saw the truck bouncing and banging along with the Arab troopers leaning forward with their headclothes streaming behind. It was an exciting picture.' But when they made contact that night with Glubb Pasha and the Arab Legion, he was more circumspect. He listened to their plans for the assault on an Iraq position, and wished himself elsewhere. Only journalistic self-respect forced the question from him: 'Can I come with you?' Glubb Pasha looked at the round young man in front of him: 'Are you used to crawling on your belly, may I ask?' 'No, I'm afraid not.' 'Well, we shall probably travel the last part of the journey on our stomachs, two miles or so. Perhaps . . .' With relief Dimbleby took his cue, and watched the Arab Legion disappear into the night.

From Jerusalem, he marched into Syria with the Allied troops. His first despatch contained much detailed observation but also one of those ringing declarations of faith, to which the BBC took such exception:

> . . . we can and must afford to ignore the feelings of the Vichy authorities and the French Army in Syria, dangling like a red and blue puppet on the end of a string jerked by Hitler. We can with clear consciences adopt the attitude suggested by one Australian commanding officer to his men before they crossed the frontier. He said: 'Spare no effort to prevent action with the French but if they start firing on you treat them as an enemy.'

They did open fire and it was a bitter five-week war. There were poignant moments of absurdity. On one occasion Dimbleby was with some Free French forces from the Foreign Legion when they found themselves ranged against a sister battalion from the Legion who had gone over to the Vichy side. The troops prepared to open fire and then realising what they were about to do pointed their guns at the sky. With a fine sense of the inevitable the

commanders of both sides, met and agreed to a mutual withdrawal: 'It's not easy,' Dimbleby reported to London, 'to invade
someone's land and persuade him you're doing it for his own
good; nor is it easy to persuade him that there are, in fact, such
things as Nazis in Syria when all the power of the German
propaganda has convinced them that there aren't.' The Syrian
French did not easily succumb to British truth.

When Damascus finally fell he drove into the city with the
Free French General Le Gentilhomme. That night he sat on his
hotel balcony and recorded another distinctive report:

> There has not been a victory at Damascus. For many of the
> Free French it has been a homecoming and there have been
> some tearful and joyful reunions between families and old
> comrades . . . in the distance there is singing. Damascus is quiet
> at this summer midnight, but to lean on this balcony, to watch
> the twinkling lights and hear the crickets chirping, is to realise
> that today another blow has been struck for freedom.

By August 1941 he was back in Turkey and, by the end of
the month, preparing to leave for Teheran, the capital of Persia.
With the Iraqui revolt crushed and Syria subdued, the War
Cabinet wished to secure Persia against the risk of Nazi control.
The Persian campaign was the first joint exercise of the war by
the British and the Russians. 'We welcomed the opportunity,'
wrote Churchill, 'of joining hands with the Russians and proposed
to them a joint campaign.' The defence of the Persian oilfields,
the need to pass 'munitions and supplies of all kinds' to the Soviet
Union, and the 'future strategic possibilities' of the area, made
the arguments for the invasion of Persia compulsive. With James
Holburn of *The Times* Dimbleby made for Baghdad where they
hired an old Chevrolet and a driver to take them across desert
and mountains on the eight-hundred-mile journey to Teheran. As
usual Dimbleby had contrived to get himself a diplomatic passport. It was a notoriously dangerous journey. The driver had been
reluctant to go, and agreed only when *The Times* and BBC
said they would pay him £50. Towards the end of the first day
when they were driving along a mountain road towards the town
of Karmanshah they rounded a bend to confront a group of ragged
men in tattered uniforms who waved sticks and rifles and left
no doubt about their intentions. The driver, frightened, yelled

'bandits, bandits' and went to slow down. 'Drive on, damn you!' shouted Dimbleby, who was in the back seat, pushing the terrified man hard in the back of his neck. Holburn urged him on from the front seat, and with little to choose between the bandits and the wrath inside the car, the poor man put his foot down and drove at the men barring the path. At the last moment the crowd scattered, but one grabbed a door pillar and another jumped onto the boot lid. Somewhere a rifle went off. Dimbleby grabbed hold of a Thermos flask and brought it crashing down on the hand of the man clinging onto the side of the car, and he let go. The Chevrolet roared forward, bouncing and banging, the man on the back fell off and all the luggage fell on top of Dimbleby—but they arrived at Karmanshah alive.

There Dimbleby went to see the Major in charge of the local British brigade: 'I would like a military escort please to Teheran.' 'I'm sure you would' replied the Major, unimpressed, 'but you don't expect me to spare my men for everyone who has trouble in this godforsaken place, do you?' 'No, but I am carrying secret diplomatic mail and this'—he flourished his courier's passport— 'gives me the right to demand in the name of the King that you give me protection.' The Major was suitably abashed and at once provided him with a convoy of two army trucks to accompany him on his way. By the time they left, the town was deserted. They had been to the police station to report the attack and as soon as the word got round every house and shop was barred and shuttered against the marauders. Holburn and Dimbleby, feeling they had had a near escape, vowed to return by another route. (The next day German radio announced that two British correspondents had been captured in Persia—before the two reporters had had time to report it—and ever afterwards Dimbleby was convinced that the ambush had been arranged by the Germans to silence him.)

The two Allied powers moved on Teheran in a pincer movement from the west and the east and Persia offered no resistance. At the outskirts of the city (once they had passed through the British lines) a police post tried to stop them—'but', his diary records, 'I thundered so convincingly in French and English, and waved my passport so fiercely, that they were intimidated and let us pass'. (Many years later, when he had come to be venerated as a BBC totem, younger journalists were astonished by his formidable displays of outrage at incompetent or officious bureaucracy.) The terms of the armistice agreement between the Allies and the Persian authorities required the eviction of the German population from the country: the women and children to Turkey and thence home to Germany; the men (many of whom had escaped from Syria and Iraq) to internment camps in Russia and India. It was a bizarre process. Every German in Persia had been rounded up and held in the grounds of the German legation. But most of the Persian authorities were pro-German, and the Nazis themselves were using all kinds of delaying tactics. The Russians were anxious for the deportations to begin; the British, better versed in the sophistication of diplomacy, tried to soothe the Russians, while discreetly threatening the Persians. Dimbleby wished to become the first foreigner to broadcast from Teheran. There was a cabinet meeting to discuss the matter, and the Persians finally agreed. The broadcasting station was on the outskirts of the city, and manned by German engineers.

It was a glorious opportunity to play the Nazis at their own game. I went into the control room where there were two surly Nazis [all his Germans were surly, sullen or cruel] . . . 'Listen,' I said as brusquely as I could, 'the Allies are in control here now. You are going to an internment camp as soon as the Persians have replacements for you. I'm here to relay to London and you'd better see that it goes through'.

The next morning he went down to the railway station to watch the departure of the first Germans. With the Counsellor at the British Legation, Dimbleby strode up and down the platform inspecting the 'prisoners'. As the train pulled away, a few of the Germans shouted out a departing 'Seig Heil', at which the Embassy staff and Dimbleby burst out laughing and cheered. A few days later his close relations with the British Legation paid dividends. He was told confidentially that the Shah had abdicated, and that the Soviet and British troops were advancing up the city to maintain order. He was thrilled, noting in his diary:

Got all details and wrote 1000 words, which broadcast direct ex-Teheran to London on 19·87 at 1.30 pm. Complete world beat—justifying journey here!!!' BBC led 2.30 and all evening bulletins, quoting in extenso, and new Shah having heard me denounce obstruction of Teheran police in getting Germans away, at once sacked chief of police!

That afternoon he drove to the edge of the city to witness the first meeting in the Second World War of Britain and Soviet troops. He managed to charm his way into the British military attaché's car, which went ahead of the other British representative to the Russian forward position. After close scrutiny by the Soviet guards they were allowed up to the Russian field headquarters. There General Novikoff and the British Colonel saluted, shook hands and sat down for the first Allied vodka of the war. Dimbleby was introduced as one of the Legation and sat down with them. Another Russian, like him in plain clothes, joined them. Dimbleby assumed that he was a secret serviceman and decided to play a similar role, nodding inscrutably at his Soviet counterpart as one professional to another and occasionally darting what he imagined to be conspiratorial glances around the table. Afterwards, when the limits of the Soviet advance into Persia had been agreed, they consumed liberal quantities of vodka, and departed—the Colonel repeating exuberantly again and again, 'Splendid fellows those Russians, yes splendid fellows.'

A few days later Dimbleby travelled a long, slow route by road and train, back to Turkey. Apart from the battles (indelible images of suffering) and the victories (brief exultations) his life had been the war correspondent's round of frustration and exhaustion. He had travelled nearly twenty thousand miles, most of it along rough roads; he had suffered breakdowns and punctures; he had slept rough and in flea-infested road houses; he had been ambushed, sniped at, bombed, shelled, and machine-gunned; he had kept his patience while Army censors haggled over his every word and scored his carefully spoken discs with excising penknives; he had rushed to catch planes which did not arrive, to reach cabling facilities which did not work and telephones where there was no reply, to make contact with a BBC which did not seem to care. Back in Turkey he hoped for some rest: he found himself instead at war again with Broadcasting House.

6

The Battle with the BBC

Suppose he'd listened to the erudite committee,
He would have only found where not to look.

W. H. AUDEN

TURKEY ENTHRALLED DIMBLEBY. ANKARA WAS A MELT-
ing pot of intrigue; of diplomatic missions from Britain, the
United States and Germany; of Allied and Axis agents masquerading as commercial travellers and shop assistants. Gossip,
rumour, half-truths and lies filled the correspondent's day.
Dimbleby was in Turkey, on and off, for four months. In that
time he met nearly every Allied official and most Allied agents;
he was on nodding terms with German diplomats and saw
German spies behind every foreign smile. He had friends in the
Turkish secret police who followed everyone, even each other,
all the time. He went on an endless round of Embassy parties
and unofficial private dinners with First Secretaries and Military
Attachés. As if to symbolise the absurd confusion on one
occasion at a Government banquet he saw the wives of the British
and German Ambassadors arrive at the same moment in identical
evening gowns bought from the same elegant couturier. As they
saw each other and turned away in mutual horror, their sequined
dresses became entangled, and with due ceremony he walked
across to them and freed them from embarrassment.

The reporter who wanted to drive fast Lagondas through
France at the dead of night and who thrilled to the courier's
passport was entranced by the mystery, excitement and danger
of the spy's life. In neutral Turkey where German and British

propaganda competed openly and in secret for the hearts and minds of the Turkish authorities, he was able to indulge his taste for the fantastic to the full. For part of the time he broadcast for Britain and Europe on what his colleague, Edward Ward, called disparagingly 'high strategy'—on the state of Turkish morale, on the demoralised state of the Germans on the Russian front, of atrocities that the Nazis had perpetrated against nationalists in conquered Europe, and on the importance of a tough British stand in Persia. With that work done, he could sit and romanticise.

In all Dimbleby wrote four books about the war; two autobiographical accounts of his experiences, a novel, *Storm at the Hook* and a thriller which he called *A Voice in Asia*—which was never published. *A Voice in Asia* is a story of espionage, romance, dramatic flights, earthquakes, and murders. It is set in Turkey, in the early summer of 1943 and the hero of the adventure is called Richard Tresmayne, who, the foreword explains, is 'a war correspondent [who] has acted on many occasions as a diplomatic courier and has carried out duties which have taken him behind the scenes in the allied conduct of the war. He may perhaps be described as an informed observer well known to the public at home and abroad for his many despatches . . .' Tresmayne has an intimate knowledge of the Middle East, and is free to wander without suspicion almost everywhere in the area. In the story he is sent to Turkey by the British Secret Service (after a long briefing at a secret headquarters in Pimlico) to help discover the route of an overland radio communication system linking Berlin to Tokyo which had been nicknamed by the Germans the '*Sprach Rohr*'— the 'voice pipe'. British Intelligence wishes to intercept the radio signals between the two capitals; and it can only do so if it can find one of the links in the chain. Tresmayne has a series of improbable adventures—he is given a bodyguard by the British Embassy in Ankara (a man who had been his driver in the first Libyan campaign), and together they go to Istanbul where he meets a beautiful cabaret dancer who pulls a gun on him, then breaks down and gives him an important clue, which leads the SIS to send him into the Pamir mountains in northern Afghanistan. There he flies to a secret landing strip at night, discovers two enemy agents, knocks out one of them, and shoots the other dead. He returns to Turkey with more clues, raids a house on the island of Principo in the Sea of Marmara where he finds the headquarters of the German 'voice-pipe' organisation; has a chase, a fight, sees his bodyguard killed, and finally himself shoots down the head of the German network on the Island of Dogs.

It reads like a script for a 'B' movie (though it is exciting enough) but Dimbleby added a preface: 'Much of it will seem fantastic in the setting of the Second World War but though we can honour the convention by which all its characters are "fictional" the story is based so closely on the truth that it could not be written until now.' (And in the synopsis he repeats: 'vital security considerations have prevented the telling of its extraordinary adventures for a full five years after the happening'.) The implication is plain; most of the adventures happened, and Richard Tresmayne, no-one was to be left in any doubt, was Richard Dimbleby.

Even more bizarre is the fact that in May 1948 in one of a long series of talks which he did for the North American services of the BBC, called 'Off the Record', Dimbleby retold much of the story from *A Voice in Asia*. It was subsequently reprinted in the BBC magazine for overseas listeners—'London Calling'—where it was introduced, with no suggestion that it was fiction, in these words: 'While on a secret wartime mission in Asia Minor, Richard Dimbleby . . .' In the broadcast, which he called 'The Girl with the Red Rose', he outlined the entire adventure of Richard Tresmayne, though he rather coyly chose to 'draw a veil over the creature comforts of the Pamir mountains'; and of the dénouement on the island of Principo he said cryptically,

> A number of fantastic events happened on that island, so fantastic that looking back on them after five years, I can hardly believe them. Only one or two souvenirs on my study shelf remind me that they were true, and that I had the good luck— I suppose it was that—to be mixed up in one of the strangest adventures of the war . . . The ringleader of the German organisation is dead—how and when he died I cannot tell you even now. But he is buried in Turkey and there is no monument over his head. And, as for me—well you know what I am doing.

By a resolute suspension of disbelief it is just possible to imagine that Dimbleby did carry out some of the exploits he describes in *A Voice in Asia*. In the Second World War (and afterwards) journalists were invited to undertake some bizarre adventures on behalf of the British Intelligence Service: it is quite likely that an 'amateur' like Dimbleby initiated into some of the ways of the service, might have carried messages and reported back on the conditions of those countries through which he travelled. He certainly had close links with the Secret Service in Turkey and frequently referred to his BBC travels through Asia Minor as 'secret'—and when he had to leave Turkey to replace Edward Ward, who had been captured in the Western Desert, he noted curiously in his diary: 'Don't really want to go to desert as if I'm captured, as five war correspondents have been—really believe I shall be shot after my work in Ankara.'

Against that there is apparently no evidence in either BBC or Foreign Office files that Dimbleby was in Turkey in late spring of 1943; it is most unlikely that a 'voice pipe' between Berlin and Tokyo did exist (although, according to Professor Hugh Trevor-Roper, senior members of SIS might well have believed in it—'their little heads were capable of believing in anything'); and even if the Secret Service had used him, it is only remotely possible that they would have allowed him to carry out such a James Bondish operation.

It is more likely that *A Voice in Asia* is a fantasy created out of a heady mixture of his own adventures in the Middle East and the secrets he gleaned from indiscreet friends in SIS over late-night brandy. This leaves unanswered the question of his broadcast on the North American Service of the BBC. It is just possible that he prefaced the broadcast with a warning that it was fiction (though no *caveat* appears on the transcript). Otherwise it seems that Richard Dimbleby, who by 1948, was a broadcaster of repute, allowed himself to perpetrate upon his unsuspecting listeners an elaborate fantasy which some critics would feel bound to call a lie. Dimbleby was an incurable romantic with a boyish delight in adventure and espionage but he was not much given to fantasies, he was not a congenital liar, and it seems unlikely that he would have risked a successful career for the fun of a hoax. Yet unless the *Adventures of the Rose* took place that is just what he did.

Whether it was true, half true, or wholly false, Dimbleby was never left alone with his fantasies for long: reality in the shape of the war and the BBC soon intervened. By the middle of 1941 Dimbleby was once more out of favour with Broadcasting House. In May A. P. Ryan sent a note to R. T. Clarke, the News Editor, complaining that neither Dimbleby nor Ward 'is delivering the goods or paying for his keep' and, much more revealingly, he complained that Dimbleby 'is also disobedient'. R. T. Clarke, who until then had made no criticism of the work of either of them, saw a chance to strike a decisive blow in an internal BBC wrangle (which had started from the moment when Dimbleby first set foot in France). Richard Dimbleby would be his foil.

Clarke prepared an elaborate reply for Ryan. It was true that the work of Dimbleby and Ward had been disappointing—but there was an explanation, at least in the case of Dimbleby, (though it required some re-writing of history). Dimbleby was sent to France as an 'observer', wrote Clarke, but gradually he turned himself into a 'representative . . . and neglected the original and in my opinion paramount news duties'. His replacement when he moved to the Middle East, Bernard Stubbs, had taken 'a more orthodox view of his duties as a news man'. (Clarke omitted to mention that Dimbleby had been in France throughout the 'phoney' war while Stubbs witnessed—very briefly—the start of the real war.)

In Egypt, the 'evil system' continued, wrote Clarke, 'Dimbleby's reputation fell considerably and it was decided to replace him by Ward whose reputation was very high', but 'in the new un-controlled circumstances [Ward] proved no better than Dimbleby'. Clarke then launched into an extraordinary attack on both of them: 'Their output has been meagre; their work much below their own former standard; they have acted on their own; they have been impertinent without justifying impertinence with success. I could add more . . .' Mercifully he did not. The usually mild Clarke then revealed the purpose of his onslaught:

> When a correspondent receives no instructions, gets answers to urgent cables very late or not at all and has no idea to what person he is responsible, he is apt to interpret loyalty to the Corporation as doing what he on the spot finds most attractive...
> I want my own control of them and others to be as absolute as that of the Foreign Editor of a newspaper over his correspondents.

Clarke's schoolmasterly anger reflected the frustration of a man caught in a bureaucratic trap: Dimbleby had become a law unto himself not merely because it was in his nature, but because he was answerable to no one department in the BBC. Two years after the outbreak of the war, the concept of a 'BBC reporter' was still so novel that his duties had not yet been adequately defined on paper; in a bureaucracy this meant that no-one had either the power or the responsibility to dictate his movements.

Unaware that his reputation was being used in a struggle for power in Broadcsating House, Dimbleby chose this moment to send a trenchant cable to London which could only have reinforced the Corporation's anxieties about him:

> Please pass this message highest proper quarter in Corporation stop As it appears that Russian development may have greatest bearing Middle East situation and obviously affects whole course of war [The German Army had just invaded the Soviet Union] do you feel Corporation should be represented stop Understand Russia not accessible from Britain but can quite easily go from here in fairly short time with full approval Middle East Command . . . This may be ideal opportunity for Corporation to make proper contact with Russian Broadcasting Authorities never before possible . . . beg you consider this carefully as I feel we should not leave biggest development of war totally uncovered . . .

In a Corporation which still wished its correspondents to behave like junior local reporters, Dimbleby's muscular self-confidence was an irritation. Until Dimbleby's telegram arrived in Broadcasting House, the BBC had not even considered the possibility of sending a correspondent to the Russian front. Now they sent back a temporising cable 'indicating' Dimbleby noted in his diary: 'that they intend me to go Russia if ban on foreign broadcasters can be lifted.' But a day later in conjunction with the Ministry of Information, the Corporation decided there was 'no urgent reason' why the BBC should send a correspondent to Russia.

Unaware of this, Dimbleby sent another cable to London again urging enthusiastically that he be sent as a 'representative', if it was not possible to broadcast from the front, adding: '[I am] sure personal contact necessary'. In high excitement he then prepared for the overland journey to the Soviet Union, arranging for a new passport, and searching for a suitable two-wheeled trailer 'for petrol and luggage'. Three weeks later he had still heard nothing from the BBC. In August he cabled again even more energetically and expansively:

> For powers concerned stop Have received from our Am-

bassador Cairo promise full diplomatic facilities in any journey Russia stop . . . meanwhile would draw your attention general situation further East Unknown extent your information but advise you that likelihood violent extension war to Far East is great and close at hand stop every point that can be affected by such extension conflict whether India Singapore Australia China or Pacific is easily and quickest reached from here . . . As your senior observer outside Britain I have full confidence military and diplomatic authorities in any journey necessary and I urge you regard me not just as observer Middle East but as floating representative outside Britain . . . sorry present such sweeping canvas but in view highest standing Corporation throughout these areas and publicly accepted fact of news observers feel we must envisage next developments broadcast scale stop am anxious go wherever can do most useful work . . . for your own ear my wife is quite happy me being away as long as she feels me serving Corporation and doing useful job . . . Dimbleby.

By this time Clarke had won his struggle for control of the Corporation's observers and in reply to Dimbleby's inoffensive if energetic cable he chose to make it clear who was in charge:

Arrangements revised re. home news observers abroad . . . now onwards directly under self who addressing all instructions . . . suggestions ex you always considered but considerations here take first place argumentative re-statements ex you deplored situation herewards necessarily unknown you Example your Russian scheme embarrassing view negotiations here . . .

If he imagined this would tame Dimbleby he was mistaken. In November, with signs that the 'violent extension war to Far East' (as he had written in August) was imminent, Dimbleby cabled London again suggesting 'a Far East trip'. He received no reply. He cabled again, asking to go to Singapore. In London Ryan was asked for a decision. He instructed Clarke: 'Your cable should include a firm choke-off of this suggestion, saying that the question of correspondents outside the Middle East is no concern of Dimbleby's.' Ten days later a perplexed Dimbleby noted 'At last cable from Clarke—rather bad tempered.'

When Japan at last declared war at the beginning of December he sent another telegram to London noting in his diary: 'could catch Wednesday flying boat if they replied quickly. Waited all day, but by midnight—no reply! How typical of BBC and how sickening it is. However went ahead with preparations.'

So certain was he that the BBC would send him to Singapore— with war in Russia, the Middle East (where there was a lull) and now in the Far East, he was the BBC's only correspondent outside Britain—that he sold his much loved Chrysler ('for £140, ten pounds more than I paid for it over a year ago') and had his bank account transferred to Singapore. But the next day he wrote in his diary: 'Really am getting mad with BBC. Have sent three urgent cables since Sunday and they haven't even acknowledged them . . . Meanwhile flying boat 24 hours late, thank God, so may be able to catch it after all.' It did not cross his innocent mind that the BBC (in consultation presumably with the Government) did not have any intention of sending a reporter to Singapore to record the fate that had already been decided for the island—its downfall.

The next day the BBC at last replied: 'Singapore Rightout stop Cover Libya . . .' For once Dimbleby felt really depressed: 'Crushing disappointment . . . Oh God! I've sold the Chrysler and transferred moneys to Singapore. Now I've got to undo it all and go back to that *filthy* desert . . . feeling like suicide.'

In the nine months he had been away from the desert the monotonous to-and-fro across the sand had continued. Rommel had arrived early in 1941. Outwitting the British commanders, his troops had turned 'Wavell's Way' across the desert into 'Rommel's Way'. Churchill had taken the opportunity of British setbacks to rid himself of Wavell. General Sir Claude Auchinleck had arrived in his place and was proving just as able and obdurate as his predecessor, frequently reminding the impatient Prime Minister that 'to launch an offensive with the inadequate means at our disposal is not, in my opinion, a justifiable operation of war.' Meanwhile Churchill fumed, 'It is impossible to explain to Parliament and the Nation how it is that our Middle East armies have had to stand for four and a half months without engaging the enemy.' In the autumn the Auk finally launched his attack with the words of Churchill ringing in his ears: 'The Desert Army may add a page to history which will rank with Blenheim and Waterloo. The eyes of all nations are upon you. All our hearts are with you. May God uphold the right!'

Unfortunately God was not disposed at this time to indicate which of the struggling armies he was supporting: the battle raged indecisively for more than a month in the worst desert conditions. Then on December 18th Rommel retreated. In Cairo there was what Dimbleby later called 'a dangerous surge of optimism'. As he left for the front he sent back 'a powerful piece' based on communiqués released at GHQ which announced 'Germans in full retreat in disorder with front broken everywhere'. In reality, GHQ in Cairo must have known that Rommel 'retreated with deliberation and was never in serious difficulties'.*

From this moment on for the next six disastrous months, the task of the war correspondent became all but impossible. The battle moved so fast and on so many fronts that no-one could form a coherent picture of what was happening before yesterday's victory had become today's defeat. Just before Christmas 1941 Dimbleby set off for the front-line with his new recording engineer, F. W. Chignell, who had just arrived from London. The weather was atrocious; nights of frost following days of dust-storms. In the rush to catch up with the advancing army Dimbleby had forgotten his compass and they were frequently lost; but when there was a lull in the storm they were able to watch the British convoys 'surging over the desert like ships of the line . . . wonderful sight'.

They spent Christmas night in the middle of the desert in their bivouacs with a sandstorm outside; Dimbleby tied a guy-rope to the rear wheel of this truck for extra security. It was cold, so dawn broke before Dimbleby got to sleep—just as they should have been ready to move on. Only their driver was awake. He decided to test the truck after the sandstorm; got in, revved up and accelerated sharply out of the soft sand. He had gone ten yards before he noticed in his mirror that a large piece of canvas was flapping from the back of the truck and behind it, sitting in the sand with a look of blank incomprehension on his face, was the figure of the BBC's senior war correspondent, staring at his departing tent.

The next day, they lost the way again. They drove for an hour before they suddenly realised that they must have arrived in the notorious Sidi Omar minefield. They sat for a moment with featureless desert all around them, terrified to move. And then slowly, inch by inch, they backed out along the exact track

* Corelli Barnet: *The Desert Generals*.

by which they had come in, and escaped. By the end of December they had arrived in Benghazi. It was New Year's Eve and a party was in progress: Chianti, tins of captured German sauerkraut and sausages were there in abundance. Much recovered, Richard Dimbleby (whose prowess was well known) was asked to play the piano. At midnight, he started on 'Auld Lang Syne'. As if on cue, the air-raid warning sirens started up and a few moments later bombs were falling all about them:

> I banged the old piano unmercifully, trying to drown the din outside. A stick of bombs fell with resounding crashes that shook the whole building. The louder the raid, the louder we sang. Our guns were sending their shells moaning over the roof, and a bomb whistled down and swayed the building as it burst... in the darkness we bellowed our song in defiance of the Germans above.

The air-raid was an omen. Within a few days the Allied troops were on the retreat again, back across the desert through the towns which they had taken, lost and retaken again, losing them once more. Needing urgent repairs to his truck and his recording equipment Dimbleby and Chignell went back before them. It was a bad journey, across 1,200 miles of desert to Cairo; at times they only managed 90 miles a day. At Mersah Matruh where they spent their last night, the Germans launched a bombing raid:

> I sheltered behind a wall with two German prisoners from the Halfaya contingent (captured at Halfaya Pass) which was lined up just by us. The two, very young said: 'bombs! bombs!' I said in my best German: 'Shut up! What are you worrying about, they're your planes aren't they?'

They arrived back in Cairo that night.

Four days later, while Chignell was still trying to have the truck repaired, Dimbleby received another of the now traditionally curt telegrams from London, recording in his diary: 'Feel somewhat depressed because of R. T.'s (R. T. Clarke) cable saying why wasn't I in Libya.' The following day he was told that General Auchinleck had asked if Dimbleby could fly up to Eighth Army Headquarters: 'as soon as possible'. His diary for the next ten days gives some indication of the frustrations and difficulties of the job.

28th January 1942

Got to Heliopoly at 6.15 a.m. I had to fly in the body of the machine sitting on a pile of luggage in the dark and looking at the rear gunner's feet. Felt rather ill, and nearly died when he let off his guns to test them . . . Saw the C-in-C who said 'very glad to meet you' . . . Lunched in C-in-C's mess and found they'd decided to move Army at 3.00 p.m.

29th January 1942

Shearer [the Deputy Director of Military Intelligence] apologised yesterday for having brought me up on a day when Army moving, saying: 'I hope you forgive me, Richard.' Don't know if I do! Today I drove in a broken-down utility back to Sidi Azeis on the frontier where Army supposed to be going. Hard tiring journey . . . at the end of couldn't find Azeis so bedded down in a wadi. Feeling rather ill, shivering and a temperature. Also sore throat and glands. Probably a dose of sandfly fever.

30th January 1942

Set out this morning, still feeling wretchedly ill, and located Army, being horrified to hear the C-in-C had pitched a battle HQ near Gazala and wasn't coming to Azeis . . . Saw doctor and got some captured Nazi pills and gargle which had good effect.

31st January 1942

Feel a bit better today and when called at Army found a signal telling me that Chignell (who had followed him forward in their recording truck) at Gazala. Decided to return there. At 8.00 p.m. came our first air-raid. Again at 3.45 a.m. when a stick fell pretty near and shrapnel was around. And again at 5.00 a.m. Seven sticks around us altogether. Helped Chig and driver dig a slit trench!

1st February 1942

This morning heard from Fielding (Public Relations) that 7th Brigade, cut off in Benghazi, had fought their way out . . . set out at once to find them and located them near El Aden aerodrome . . .

2nd February 1942

First thing today helped Chig cook sausages and onions then wrote long cable . . . then set off . . . Ran into one of the worst sandstorms I've ever suffered. Groped our way to a petrol dump. Drew twenty gallons. Sandstorm so bad we had to stop

at 2.30 p.m., huddled in back of truck, turn on radio, and
stick it out . . .

3rd February 1942

Set out on our journey . . . I heard that the Germans had
pushed through Timmini and that 4th Div. had had to bail out
of the Dema position and retire. That means the 8th Army
has moved since Sunday and everything must be retreating . . .
Heard from 30th Corps at Bugbug that Army had gone to
Safafi . . . arrived after dark.

4th February 1942

Found Safafi was only the report centre. Army HQ going to
Kilo 110 near Sidi Barrani. What chaos! No-one knows what's
happening and some people say we can't hold the Germans.
Having torn my tent, slept coldly in the back of the truck, left
early in the morning. Chignell having lost an essential piece of
7-point cable decided to make for Cairo where I *must* get
proper transport and a general view of the situation . . . Truck
passed out on track south of main road—we couldn't get it
going though we took carburettor and petrol pump to pieces,
so we had to bed down again! Boiling engine due to following
wind had used up most of our water—so we were in a fix.

5th February 1942

No-one having come by at 9.00 a.m. this morning Chig and I
spun a coin. I lost and set out to walk for help taking part
of the water in my bottle. Felt like Captain Oates, not knowing
how far I'd have to go. [Fortunately after a walk of a little more
than two hours he reached the main road and got help.]

6th February 1942

Two punctures. Waited for four hours on main road while
driver went back to Bogush to get new wheels and tyres from
workshop.

The next day they arrived back in Cairo, exhausted to face
yet more trouble from the BBC.

Life in Cairo offered a sharp contrast to the rigours of the desert:
officers and civil servants played golf or tennis or polo at the
Gazira Club; there were tea-parties and picnics at the Turf Club;
Shepheards Hotel served good dinners, fine wines and cool drinks;
clubs and bars stayed open until dawn, and the city light shone.

The BBC office which opened early in 1942 was a rented room
in Sharia Gameh Charkass, in the crowded market area of the

city. It was excessively noisy. The smell of rotting food, garlic and goats wafted up into the studio from the market stalls below. A café blared constant music. Dogs, cats, pigs and goats wandered freely about the building. The two floors above the BBC office were rented by ladies of extremely dubious virtue. Occasionally eager young soldiers would walk into the office with a look of hungry expectation only to retreat in embarrassed haste when they were confronted not by the nubile girls of their imagination but the sternly masculine form of a less than welcoming Richard Dimbleby. Once or twice recordings had to be halted until the groans from above the dangerously swaying ceiling had reached their crescendo and died away: 'What a place,' Dimbleby noted in his diary, 'in which to record Generals.' The office faced the sun and there was no air conditioning. Dimbleby was not only uncomfortable, but ashamed of the office, regarding with some irritation the parsimony of the BBC which forced him to maintain the Corporation's Middle East office in a slum. When the Minister of State came to broadcast, Dimbleby noted acerbically: 'I see no reason why when he is used to certain standards he should have to remember the BBC office as the most squalid he's visited.' Dimbleby went there as seldom as possible.

When he was in Cairo he spent much of the day either at his hotel, at GHQ, or at the Shepheards Hotel, which was the city's main meeting place and centre of gossip. In the evening his main form of relaxation, usually alone, but sometimes with Chignell, was to go to the cinema, where he watched an interminable succession of romantic Thirties musicals, recording fondly in his diary afterwards judgments like 'I love Joan Fontaine'. He drank very little, noting with disapproval one evening that a friend bought two bottles of champagne: 'which I won't drink in wartime'. When he had little work to do, he was bored and felt guilty. He soon became oppressed (as he had in Beirut and Khartoum) by the soft life in which so many of his fellow country-men seemed to indulge to excess: wherever he went, colleagues and friends would gather round him—at dinner, at the bar, in a private house; he was jovial, he was warm, and he was invariably optimistic, but he did not enjoy excess. When the British ordered all bars in the city to close at 10.30 p.m. he was delighted. He had become increasingly worried about what he called the 'war effort'. 'Not happy about it,' he noted in his diary on February 14th, 'Cairo is a bad place—for work and energy. There is too much drinking and no-one's working enough.' A few days later, he broadcast on the Egyptian radio service to that effect. It caused consternation. He was attacked from all sides with great vehemence—hardly any section of the community failing to identify itself as the specific object of his attack. A few days later the Deputy Director of Military Intelligence chastised him for the broadcast: 'I found him most upset in the name of GHQ about my talk . . . I tried to explain that I wasn't attacking anyone in particular but rather a dangerous frame of mind. Tonight I wrote him [the DDMI] a long letter suggesting that widespread action should be taken to get to the realities of Middle East.' The sensitivity of GHQ to criticism was acute, and for days afterwards Dimbleby was subjected to a barrage of hostility. He was unrepentant: 'a nasty issue would be raised if they wanted to stifle criticism of themselves.'

It might seem curious that by now Dimbleby's reputation for profligacy had reached fantastic proportions at Broadcasting House. Men like Donald Boyd, the influential new Head of News Talks (who, like Ryan, had never met Dimbleby) was convinced that his Middle East correspondent was a self-indulgent ne'er-do-well, and his ascetic nature was appalled. The myth of Dimbleby's extravagance—that he lived like some latter day Middle Eastern potentate, eating, drinking, living and loving with a reckless disregard for his health and the BBC finances—was sedulously fostered by envious rivals. Feeding off rumours from Cairo, his colleagues chose to confuse style with extravagance—and the BBC's Accounts Department was not disposed to put them right.

Dimbleby was an ebullient personality with a taste for the dramatic. For much of the time in Cairo he rented a houseboat on the Nile, where he had a servant, and gave occasional (but famous) parties. He bought a vast old Auto-Union which had been captured from the Italians in the winter of 1940, and when he was off duty he dressed up his Egyptian driver in an extraordinary mixture of robes and cumerbunds, and gave him a turban in the Dimbleby 'colours'. Inevitably, and by no means to his dismay, he became a well-known figure in Cairo. But the entire cost of the little vanity was much less than the price of a good room and much liquor at the Continental Hotel. In his first eighteen months in the Middle East he had to account to the BBC for precisely £2,202—about £28 a week. He had bought a car and truck (with the BBC's approval); he had repaired both constantly; he had travelled more than 35,000 miles by road, air, boat and train; he had paid hotel bills; he had bought tents and clothing for the mountains and for the desert—and he had spent little more than half what a colleague from Fleet Street would have expected to spend in half the time.

Unaware of the reputation he had been given in London, Dimbleby was both astonished and angry when he returned in February from his exhausting desert trip to find a letter from one of the BBC's most august figures, Sir Richard Maconachie, reprimanding him for his extravagance.

Dimbleby used the opportunity of his reply to Maconachie to range far beyond the matter of expenses, revealing for the first time the schism between the BBC and its senior news observer:

You describe me as a young correspondent [wrote Dimbleby] which if my rapidly approaching thirty years and my wife and family at home allows me in these days to be considered still 'young' is an accurate enough description. But please remember that in such a country as Turkey (where the disputed expenses had been incurred) no-one had ever set eyes on a BBC man before although they listened regularly to our programmes and regarded the BBC as an institution. When one represents the BBC one is not in the same category as a correspondent of a newspaper of which the country visited knows little or nothing. You are representing something that the foreign people as well as one's own diplomatic representatives regard as part of their lives. Therefore as the representative of the BBC, you are the BBC, and your arrival is quite an event . . .

I don't think anyone working at Broadcasting House in London who has not represented the BBC (and how few have) realises fully the important part played by the Corporation in the lives of other nations. Is it realised that many people know the BBC and its transmissions better than they know their own national stations? I have been amazed to find throughout the dozen or more countries in which I've worked out here, that I am known by name, and well known, to thousands of people of all nationalities . . .

I cannot help the fact that the BBC enjoys much fame abroad; nor can I avoid appearing as the living embodiment of the BBC wherever I go. It has its advantages. The doors are open to you and you can extract better facilities of work and tap higher

sources of information than any other correspondent or observer. You can meet all the prime and foreign ministers, all
the chiefs of staffs and all the ambassadors you want, and if
they are likely to be of use you do . . .

You are willy nilly, just what in your letter you say one is
not—'a diplomatic correspondent'. It is something even more
than that, because you are received not only as a working
observer, not only as a personality, but as the official envoy of
a very great and powerful national organisation.

If Dimbleby, through bruised dignity, allowed a little vainglory
to creep into his letter, he nonetheless spoke the truth (and in
his case an inevitable truth—years later the Corporation was to
promote him as the living embodiment of the BBC). But in 1942,
when the BBC was still insecure and weak, it did not wish its
young men, particularly those engaged in the delicate task of
'observing', to assume so prominent a role.

Little knowing how his words flew in the face of the myth
Dimbleby went on to remind the BBC that he was not a
spendthrift:

> Your 'young' correspondent although en garçon . . . is regarded
> as a suitable object of entertainment by everyone . . . He cannot
> accept invitations from scores of people (nor can he refuse
> them without offence) over a period of several weeks with-
> out reciprocating . . . Therefore he does just as much enter-
> taining as he *must* and no more. He eschews liquor (whisky
> is eight shillings a tot) and when he isn't being entertained,
> retires to bed with a book if he isn't broadcasting, and sits up
> until the relay time of 2.00 a.m. drinking cups of coffee if he
> is. I hope it is realised that I do not throw Corporation money
> about carelessly.

Neither the facts nor his moral indignation affected the widespread
belief at Broadcasting House that Dimbleby was a profligate; and
although for the moment the issue was dropped, it was not
forgotten.

Dimbleby guarded the reputation of the BBC jealously. At the
beginning of the Desert Campaign war correspondents were
treated by the Middle East Command at best as irrelevant and
at worst as fifth columnists. Dimbleby had painstakingly sought

to convince the authorities of the importance of broadcasting as a weapon of war; by 1942 by a mixture of diligence and charm he had impressed his view upon GHQ with such effect that he enjoyed the prestige and respect in Cairo that would normally only be granted to a senior diplomat. He dined with Auchinleck's senior officers and closest friends; he went to the cinema with Government officials; and he was a confidant of the Acting Minister of State, Sir Walter Monkton. He was not disposed to see this unique relationship with the Authorities undermined. So when the BBC sent out a small team from London to man the Cairo office he was anxious and suspicious that they would let him down. He lost no time in summoning the 'new recruits—very raw' to a meeting, 'giving a short lecture on the general position and trying to make clear what position the BBC and its representatives here enjoy'. He was soon reassured that 'they meant well' though furious when one of them (his friend Arthur Phillips) innocently accepted a flight in a Blenheim which had not been cleared by Army Public Relations. 'Such things are bad,' he scribbled in his diary, 'I try so hard to make people here regard us as official—as part of the Government. If we are involved in anything like an "escapade" this can't be done.' His irritation with his new colleagues was not always burdened by the sense of his heavy BBC responsibilities but by simpler feelings. When one of them complained that a 'message' programme linking wounded prisoners in Cairo with Britain was a 'stunt', he noted furiously 'Impertinence! Does he really think that giving forty cripples the chance of speaking to families after being in enemy hands is a *STUNT*.' With D. F. Aitken who was to administer the office ('and who has been given very explicit instructions not to interfere with me') he soon had a good relationship—so much so that the new arrival was soon writing to Broadcasting House on Dimbleby's behalf.

The issue, which had arisen before, was Dimbleby's freedom of movement. Throughout February 1942 he had written a stream of cables and letters seeking permission to leave Cairo and go to Syria, Iraq, and even India (which Auchinleck had persistently suggested he should visit).

> It seems to me that it is unreasonable [wrote Aitken to the BBC] that he should be strapped down by rigid control from London, when London cannot possibly have knowledge of the prob-

abilities on which a decision must be based. Dimbleby . . . has inside information on what is happening and what is likely to happen . . . Dimbleby has been in the Middle East for something like two years. He knows the geography, the forces set-up and journalistic ropes. He has access to sources of information which are far higher than any that are available to even the best newspaper correspondents . . .

Dimbleby's frustration was intense. Rommel's New Year Advance towards Egypt had halted. By February it seemed plain to British Intelligence that it would be at least three months before he would have enough supplies to move further. As the Eighth Army was not well enough equipped to start a counter-offensive, Auchinleck had made clear he had no intention of launching an offensive against Rommel until June at the earliest. In Cairo the BBC's only war correspondent outside Britain had nothing to do. While Broadcasting House mythology had him enjoying the fleshpots of Cairo he fumed at the inactivity—'I shall go mad if I have to hang around here much longer'; 'I find I get moods of depression . . . not having enough work to do and being kept here by London.' Like Aitken he could not understand why the BBC would not let him leave Cairo. 'I must move East,' he noted in early March, 'there is nothing in Libya and they are granting leave from the Eighth Army—so nothing can be imminent.' He even persuaded Sir Walter Monkton to send a cable to the War Office urging that he be allowed to visit other fronts. It was to no avail: nearly a month after his first request to move he got a reply from London, in Aitken's words, 'ordering him peremptorily to stay in Egypt and Libya'.

By this time Dimbleby was referring in his diary to the 'sickening' behaviour of the BBC and the 'pigheadedness' of its officials. Matters got worse in April when Dimbleby saw a cable addressed to Aitken informing him that Ryan 'was considering the position of overseas correspondents and that the whole question of Middle East was being discussed'. Well versed in the ways of BBC bureaucracy, Dimbleby jumped at once to the correct conclusion: 'That can only mean that after two years London has woken up to the fact that the Middle East is important, and they're going to send out some "senior official" they want to get rid of to take charge.'

Three weeks later Aitken received another telegram telling him that a new 'Middle East representative to co-ordinate all activities had been appointed.' Despite his premonition Dimbleby felt 'rather staggered' at the news: not only was the BBC apparently giving part of his job to someone else, it had not even had the courtesy to tell him. The next day he sent a cable to the BBC which he judged to be 'polite but pretty firm . . . I'm learning that you get nowhere with the BBC unless you push yourself'. The cable was a summation of his frustration, disappointment and hurt at his treatment by the BBC.

> Please place before highest appropriate authority stop Must ask definite and serious consideration me repeated requests go a new front ex Middle East stop Have now been here over two years longer than any other correspondent et feel entitled ask for change stop recent developments BBC arrangements make me no longer indispensible . . . decision appoint representative co-ordinate all BBC work Middle East . . . makes my position finally impossible stop outwardly it must appear that self superseded . . . sincerely feel cannot continue here under new arrangement . . . Please regard this request as urgent stop Dimbleby.

He received no reply.

Six weeks later when a telegram did arrive for him, containing details about the new representative, and no more. Dimbleby could contain himself no longer and cabled back to Broadcasting House: 'Beg London spares me life history Liveing and Secretary until we've disposed of Egyptian invasion. Regards Dimbleby.' An unsigned hand has pencilled on the BBC copy: 'It looks as though Dimbleby's waist and head measurements are becoming more nearly equal'. Relations between the BBC and their senior observer were deteriorating fast.

Inexplicably the BBC at no stage saw fit to explain to Dimbleby why they had so resolutely refused him permission to move from the Western Desert. And his increasingly impatient demands to move ('I do feel very strongly that if I have to spend BBC money I should at least be allowed to go where it is most productive,' he had written in one letter 'As long as I am kept here, I cannot extract news from, nor manufacture it in, Libya.') were used to confirm the London prejudice that he was arrogant and obstinate. In fact the reason why the BBC required him to stay in Cairo was simple: Broadcasting House was certain in March that the war in the desert would soon be resumed.

By early 1942 the conflict which had poisoned the relationship between the War Cabinet and the Middle East Command for the first two years of the war was raging once more. Churchill pressed again and again for Auchinleck to renew the offensive, judging it 'lamentable' that the British 'should stand idle for so long a period at enormous expense while the Russians were fighting desperately and valiantly along their whole vast front'. Auchinleck, quiet and dignified, resisted the political pressure. 'The permanent and overriding object is to secure Egypt from attack,' he insisted. 'We could not afford to take the offensive in Libya. We should rather concentrate on strengthening our defences in the Middle East.'

Broadcasting House, knowing that Churchill might force the issue at any time, did not dare let Dimbleby leave—and worse, by broadcasting from Iraq or India as 'our Middle East observer', give the impression to the rest of the world that the lull in the desert was likely to last. Dimbleby, in ignorance of the row between the soldier and the politician, innocently assumed that the BBC was merely being 'pigheaded'. The misunderstandings and bitterness between the BBC and Dimbleby soon got more serious.

In the middle of May Dimbleby was given a special briefing by his friend Tony Philpott, the Deputy Director of Public Relations and an intimate colleague of Auchinleck. 'He says all signs suggest Germans in desert on defensive and not preparing attack.' Dimbleby wrote in his diary, 'He suggests that I should emphasise our general defensive measures, showing them to be preliminary attack.' A few days later he duly broadcast in his regular War Review that: 'Fundamentally our task in the Middle East has been, and still is, defence'—having no idea that an impatient Churchill had just ordered a deeply reluctant Auchinleck to launch an offensive before the middle of June. By allowing Dimbleby to be briefed in these cautious terms, Auchinleck was making sure that no-one should be in any doubt about the military priorities in the Middle East: the defence of Egypt mattered more than the rout of the Germans.

Richard Dimbleby's position was now unenviable. He drew his information from the Army High Command and he broadcast the results in the name of a BBC which was under the direction of a Government locked in conflict with that same Command. Since he knew nothing of the conflict, he became—inevitably—its victim.

On May 27th, unexpectedly, Rommel attacked. It was the start of a month of military disaster for the British. The German Army moved forward with a speed and cunning that left the British commanders numbed and bemused. At the 8th Army Head-quarters there was dismay. Out of touch with the front line, unable to keep pace with the unexpected speed of Rommel attacks and counter-attacks, British Intelligence was at a loss. While his Army fought towards defeat General Auchinleck cabled Churchill, 'Fierce fighting is still proceeding and the battle is by no means over . . . but whatever may be the result there is no shadow of doubt that Rommel's plans for his initial offensive have gone completely awry.' In his tent at Army Headquarters, Dimbleby had an uncomfortable night: 'German planes began coming over and kept up continuous procession until nearly daybreak, bomb-ing nearby, machine-gunning and cannoning the road, letting down parachute flares and generally making life dangerous.' The BBC's reporter, attempting to report the war single-handed, had decided to stay at Army Headquarters. The battle was moving so fast that the confusion was absolute; the armies advanced, retreated and wheeled on so many fronts at once, over so vast an area that it was impossible to form any coherent picture of what was happening except from Headquarters. And even there, as he soon discovered, it was all but impossible.

On 6th June, he began to suspect the confident noises being made by British Intelligence and Army Information were mis-placed: 'Things don't seem to be going too well,' he noted, 'I think there's been a failure of liaison or plan somewhere.' A week later his fears were justified: 'Disastrous news today . . . our people ran onto enemy anti-tank guns and suffered such heavy losses that today "I" [Information] announced that enemy had three tanks to our one'. Yet on the same day, General Auchinleck, who had flown up to Battle Headquarters to see General Ritchie the Commander of the 8th Army, returned from the meeting with the feeling: 'the atmosphere here good. No undue optimism and realities of situation are being faced calmly and resolutely.' Two days later, on a visit to 13 Corps Headquarters Dimbleby spoke to a senior intelligence officer who judged 'situation much steadier and not as bad as might be. We still hold a coast road open to

Tobruk by strong mobile columns. Meanwhile enemy is short of infantry . . . and certainly suffered heavy losses against us during the weekend.' Accordingly he sent a despatch to London (and was encouraged that during this period he was being quoted 'in extenso . . . BBC positively plugging me): The successful reformation of our infantry . . . [has] been a difficult and dangerous operation but in achieving it, a much better complexion has been put on the whole Libya position.' The next day, the 18th June, Army Headquarters was on the retreat again and Dimbleby recorded in his diary: 'Intelligence once again out of touch with situation. It's very hard to get news or to locate formation head-quarters at the moment. Don't think much of situation.'

Three days later Rommel's forces burst through the defences of Tobruk, and within twenty four hours had captured the port, the symbol of British might in the Middle East. It was the darkest day of the war.

For the Prime Minister the news of the fall of Tobruk could not have come at a worse moment. He was in Washington seeking to persuade the United States to join the war. The disaster of Tobruk cut the ground from under his feet, turning a negotiator into a supplicant. As if that was not enough he returned to London a few days later to face the loss of the Malden by-election and a motion of 'No confidence' in the House of Commons. A mood of intense gloom descended over the War Cabinet, the Chief of the Imperial General Staff, Sir Alan Brooke, and Churchill himself.

It reflected a public mood. The British had been encouraged to believe that Tobruk would never fall, that it contained within its whitewashed walls the spirit of the Free World, the hopes and aspirations of the British Empire. Its collapse was a shock and a mystery. Churchill at once asked Sir Stafford Cripps to report to the Cabinet on the loss of public confidence. The Lord Privy Seal had little trouble in isolating one major cause of the gloom as 'over-optimistic news reports from Cairo'.

'It is true,' wrote Cripps, 'that these reports are in no sense official, but they must necessarily be influenced by the information given to the press by military authorities, and their general line of this reporting has undoubtedly done much to emphasise the shock of the loss of Tobruk and the retreat to Mersah Matruh.'

Just over a month earlier, at the beginning of June, a few days after Rommel had launched his whirlwind assault towards

Tobruk, GHQ Cairo had sent a cipher cable to the War Office:

> Dimbleby now has access to battlefield information highest
> source and is sending quick-transit daily despatch. It is urgently
> requested that Dimbleby's facts be considered authoritative and
> that the tone for Libya news in all bulletins be taken from him
> in preference to all newspaper or agency reports.

It was an extraordinary cable and when Ryan received this
message, he at once passed it on to the Director-Generals of the
BBC (Sir Cecil Graves and Robert Foot) with the observation:

> It would not be true to say that the very sketchy messages we
> have had from Dimbleby support this telegram. We do of
> course use his material in preference to anything else since he
> is our man. If we relied on it solely we should not get anything
> like a full account of the action now being fought.

But it was not only the problem of full coverage of the battle
which worried Ryan. The cable to the War Office had confirmed
doubts that had been planted nearly two years before when he
had seen fit to cable Dimbleby during the Italian advance of 1940,
'beg frankness'. The doubts had become fears when Auchinleck
replaced Wavell; were reinforced by Dimbleby's urgent demand
(at the General's instigation) to leave the desert during the spring
lull; and this cable made him certain: Dimbleby was a mouthpiece
for the Middle East Command—which was bad enough. When
the Command was in dispute with the War Office it was—for
the BBC—disastrous. The BBC reports from the Middle East
during the terrible month of June did nothing to dispel Ryan's
worries.

A few days after the Cripps memorandum to Churchill about
'the over-optimistic reports from the Middle East', the Ministry
of Information, in the person of the Director-General, Cyril
Radcliffe, asked to see all Dimbleby's despatches for June. Ryan
at once did as he was bid, including with the reports a letter:

> There is no doubt [he informed the Ministry] that Dimbleby
> says what Auchinleck wants said. There is equally no doubt
> that this reveals a grave misunderstanding by Auchinleck about
> public opinion in this country and all over the world outside

the Middle East. I have warned all three services from the beginning to cut Dimbleby according to our lights, but knowing a little of the heated (in all senses of the word) atmosphere of news work in Cairo, I am sure that if Dimbleby were told by the BBC he was going astray on policy he would get angry and sympathetic support from the highest soldiers.

Once again the 'divergence of view' (as Auchinleck had called it) between Cairo and London was the cause of what had now become a crisis for the BBC in London (and though he did not yet know it) for its correspondent in the desert. Auchinleck had never attached the same symbolic importance to the defence of Tobruk as Churchill. For the Middle East Command the loss of the little port was a shock but not a catastrophe. As he had stated so often, Auchinleck was much more concerned to preserve the 8th Army as a fighting force to defend Egypt than with heroics in the desert of only marginal strategic significance. Unlike his superiors in London who feared that the loss of Tobruk signalled the collapse of the Allied position in the Middle East, Auchinleck (understanding much better than they the tactics of desert warfare) was prepared to fall back, and back again. The retreat from Tobruk towards El Alamein was sometimes in terrible disarray, but in Auchinleck's mind at least it was not a rout.

Not knowing of the conflict between London and Cairo, it did not cross Dimbleby's mind that his account of the war, based on information which could only come from his own observations and his access 'to the highest sources' at GHQ, could be causing acute embarrassment at the BBC. But he was by no means Auchinleck's mouthpiece. Throughout his time in the Middle East he had been fiercely critical of the inconsistent and frequently petty censorship by the Army High Command in Cairo. By June it had become much more serious. In the middle of the month, when he was supposed to be the voice of the Middle East Command, he was complaining bitterly about his despatches: 'Nothing seems to have got to London and I've sent a note to Cairo which will have no effect I suppose! It really is disgraceful to deceive the public to cover up failures and I really believe that's what Cairo is doing.'

Moreover, he himself was just as anxious about 'the over-optimistic reports from the Middle East' as Sir Stafford Cripps was to be. For this, he did not blame the Army but the BBC in

London. It was the habit at Broadcasting House to combine his
reports with those of the news agencies. For a long time Dimbleby
had resented this—not least because he was suspicious and frequently contemptuous of agency reporters. In one diary entry
for the spring of 1942 he recorded an example of what irritated
him most:

> A long story on Reuter's board: how naive they are! Dateline—
> 'No Man's Land'—in this war! And as usual, 'I was one of the
> first correspondents to go with a patrol' etc. etc. They are so
> bloody proud of this and so trivial. Reuters, I think, are the
> worst of the bunch for making something out of nothing.
> 'No Man's Land' indeed.

On another occasion he had been offended by a news agency
'tribute' to two war correspondents lost at sea: 'Wish Reuters
hadn't put out *such* a long splurge . . . saying "There is something
in the courage of a war correspondent that transcends the courage
of a soldier!" For God's sake!'

By June his irritation with the news agencies was replaced by
a profound concern. His anxiety arose from a problem which
no-one in Broadcasting House had yet considered but which was
about to become critical. The nightly news bulletins of the BBC
were not only heard in the living rooms of Britain, they were
picked up on shortwave radios by the troops at the front line,
where the reports from the desert were received with the critical
obsession of men whose lives hung on the course of the battle. A
slight error by the BBC became a massive mistake; a report of
victory one day which became defeat the next turned the soldiers
against the 'lies' of the Corporation—and in the Middle East that
meant Richard Dimbleby. Newspaper reports of the war did not
reach the soldiers in the desert until weeks after the battle was
over and forgotten but the BBC news arrived while the battle
was fresh in the mind or even still underway. Some of this was
inevitable. On the 6th June (a day after a heavy British reverse)
Dimbleby had recorded in his diary: 'I suffered the horror of
hearing myself (or my stuff rather) lead thè 7.00 p.m. bulletin
with glowing news of our attack which was justified at the time
it was sent off! The two-day time lag is horrible . . .' The embarrassment was made needlessly more acute when the Cairo
censors held up despatches. It was worse still when the BBC
News included agency reports from the Middle East along with

his own: the agencies knew less than he did, they were frequently inaccurate, and they were much more optimistic. Early in June he asked the Cairo office to contact London on his behalf: 'May we plead with you not repeat not mix Dimbleby cum agency pollyana stop downplaying urgently necessary.' A few days later, when it was plain his pleas had been ignored, he cabled the BBC himself: 'Grateful if all News would make clear when quoting me and when some other source stop realise this not easy (but) recently had to stand racket pro several quotations ex agencies of which believe you know already my opinion.' Yet again the BBC ignored him. It was some relief therefore that he heard of GHQ's cable to the War Office 'suggesting that BBC in all Libyan stuff follow tone of my stuff ex 8th Army'. The BBC had seen in that cable evidence that Richard Dimbleby was a mouthpiece for an over-optimistic General; for Richard Dimbleby it held out the chance: 'to rehabilitate BBC at least in eyes of Army here who have lost a lot of faith in it because of *faulty and over-optimistic reporting of events in desert*'—the confusion was now complete.

Dimbleby's position had become impossible. He was a victim of a conflict between the War Cabinet and the Middle East Command of which he knew nothing; of the BBC's erroneous view that he was a mouthpiece for Auchinleck; of 'over-optimistic' reports for which he was unfairly blamed and for which he was not responsible; of a BBC which at no stage saw fit to explain the problems of Broadcasting House to him. It was now desirable (in the BBC's mind) that he should be removed. The corporate mind did not take much persuasion: old prejudices still rankled—he was too independent and too important. Moreover, the most ludicrous charge of all, he was too extravagant. He therefore became a scapegoat whose sacrifice did not unduly disturb Broadcasting House.

Ryan's letter to the Ministry of Information had continued:

Dimbleby went out at the beginning of the war—I gather rather accidentally—and has not the necessary background to do so difficult a job. Talbot [Godfrey Talbot, who was soon to leave for the Middle East] has been inside the BBC until he sailed, was carefully coached before he left as to what was wanted, and how careful he should be of getting into the pockets of the high military (while of course remaining on easy and friendly terms with them). He is a reliable, experienced newsman . . .

So, in a way which would seem incredible to those not versed in the ways of bureaucracy, Richard Dimbleby, who nearly three years before had left Broadcasting House proudly labelled as the Corporation's senior news observer, who had travelled more than fifty thousand miles in fourteen different countries, who for much of that time had been the BBC's only correspondent outside Britain, who had recorded hundreds of despatches which had been given great prominence night after night in Britain and all over the world, was, suddenly, for reasons of state, to be dispensed with.

On 16th July 1942, Richard Dimbleby received his last cable from London: 'Talbot due Cairo shortly relieve you stop Director-General decides you after two strenuous years abroad return home stop please hand over Talbot return quickest route Ryan BBC.' Dimbleby ignorant of his offence, protested vigorously but to no avail. On the same day Tony Philpott, a close friend of Auchinleck, wrote furiously to the War Office protesting against the BBC's coverage of the Middle East War:

> The BBC should know that by now their name stinks in all British circles, civil and military throughout the Middle East, and towards the end of the third year of the war it is time that they stopped being 'stiff and awkward' and tried to help with the war effort . . . The cruel fact is that Dimbleby is blamed locally for their stupidities and no-one could take more trouble to help them than he has done . . .

And a few weeks later, in a remarkable gesture, the Director of the Ministry of Information's Middle East Section, Owen Tweedy, wrote to the Ministry in London to protest against the 'pretty tough deal' that Dimbleby had suffered. The rank and file of the Army had 'come to loathe him personally' as a consequence of editorial decisions taken at Broadcasting House for which he was not responsible. He wrote: 'You have had umpteen "rocket" telegrams from the Middle East protesting against the BBC presentation of our news . . . it has only been editorial padding from the BBC which has really got people's goat.'

It was not in Dimbleby's nature to complain publicly and he mentioned his humiliation to no-one. But it was not in his nature either, to go quietly. He entered on a round of farewells which, according to Godfrey Talbot (who arrived at this moment to replace him), 'must have been unrivalled in the history of British journalism'. He was fêted throughout Cairo by friends and officials, Government ministers, ambassadors and Army commanders. Talbot was astonished by the affection and respect in which Dimbleby was held. 'I was a journalist succeeding a personality. There were war correspondents and there was Richard Dimbleby. He had made a quite extraordinary impression in the Middle East.'

Afterwards Dimbleby wrote not of his humiliation but of his faith in the certainty of the coming victory in the desert:

We lifted our eyes above the dust and the noise of Alamein and there in the far west we saw the green hills and wet valleys of Tunisia and the grey breakers of the Atlantic ocean. There, we knew, could be the greatest battle of Africa and the victory that would open the road to Europe and the salvation of her people. We were not to see that victory. Our work had been done in the sweating battles of Eritrea and Abyssinia, the dust and heat of Syria and Iraq and the mountains of Iran. It had been done in the icy cold of Greece and little Albania, where men died in their thousands to help the last victory. It had been done in the great plains of Egypt and Italian North Africa, in places which will live in our hearts and memories for ever—Sollum, Tobruk, Bardia, Capuzzo and Benghazi, names that ring in our minds as the Arabs' camel bells ring across the parched scrub and down in the southern oases.

We did our work, though it was only to watch and report, and we knew the hardships of heat and cold, of fear and chills, of the sweating rash and the unhealing desert sore. From the first day to the last we kept our eyes on the far distant frontiers to which our men were fighting, for we knew, as they knew in their grousing and cursing, that somewhere beyond those green frontiers they would win their great reward.

In the middle of August 1942, a few days after General Auchinleck had been relieved of his Command, Dimbleby took a flying boat for Britain. In London, lesser men in Broadcasting House huddled together to conjecture on his return. Was it his high living? Or his laziness? Or his 'disobedience'? Had he 'gone astray on policy'? Was it true that the soldiers had come to hate him? They would never receive an answer from him because he would never know and would never speak of it.

When he got back to London he at once sought to see Ryan who chose to be too busy. R. T. Clarke suggested that he take a short holiday. A memo drifted around Broadcasting House wondering whether he would stay or leave the Corporation. And the BBC Handbook for 1943 announced:

The need for fuller representation in the Middle East became increasingly apparent in 1942. The eyes of the public had become more than ever focussed in this area . . . The BBC had had a single war correspondent in the Egyptian theatre for some time past. Early in 1942 it sent out a small party, including a number of recording experts. These were followed some few months later by two war correspondents, Denis Johnston and Godfrey Talbot.

Not once in nearly three years had Richard Dimbleby received a word of gratitude or praise or sympathy from the BBC. Now the Handbook did not even mention his name. So far as Broadcasting House was concerned he had become a non-person.

7

Germany Bombed

Whatever people will tell you, the bomber will always get through.
The only defence is offence, which means that you have to kill more
women and children than the enemy, if you want to save yourselves.

STANLEY BALDWIN

'SAFE HOME, GLAD TO SEE YOU BACK!' SAID THE COM-
missionaire at Broadcasting House. It was almost exactly three
years since his departure for France, and Dimbleby felt tired and
much older. He sat down at his desk in an empty office and
looked out of the window into Langham Place. He wrote (rather
self-consciously in the third person):

> Suddenly, for no clear reason and with an intensity that shocked
> him, he wanted to cry. He held back the tears. It was indeed
> a homecoming, and for the first time he realised how much
> he loved this country, how much the hundreds of thousands
> of men with whom he had lived in the deserts and in the
> mountains must love it too. Perhaps they still did not realise it;
> they fought inarticulately and certainly they would have been
> embarrassed at the discovery of the depth of their affection.

He reported his arrival back, and then with Ryan's reluctance
to see him, took a train to Aylesbury where Dilys met him.
Within half an hour he was in the small cottage in Cuddington
which he had rented for her and their baby son David just before
the war began. Though he resented the gossip about his return
at Broadcasting House, he was glad to be back with the woman
he loved and the child he had hardly seen. His Middle East Diary
had been peppered with reminders of anniversaries, birthdays,

food parcels to send and money to mail; with anxious notes after heavy German raids on England, and delighted exclamation marks when letters arrived in Dilys's hand with the Buckinghamshire postmark. He had written too, constantly and lovingly, day-to-day accounts of his life, of old family friends suddenly arrived in Cairo or Ankara, of sore feet and fevers, of good meals and bully beef—but never of the war or the BBC.

Once in 1942, Dilys had taken it upon herself to travel up to London to Broadcasting House where she walked up and down nervously for half an hour, then summoned the courage to present herself before R. T. Clarke, and demand that the BBC's Senior News Observer should be paid more. 'I think,' she said, sounding more formidable than she felt, 'that my husband should have another £100 a year. He's been away for two years and his salary is still only £600.'

'I quite agree, my dear' said the Senior News Editor kindly, 'but you must see Mr. Ryan.' The Controller (News Co-ordination)—as he was now titled—was less immediately obliging. He was, though she did not know it, engaged in a considerable contretemps with her 'Master Richard'; but Dilys had her blood up. She gave a brief but vivid account of the dangers her husband must be facing in the desert, which by implication Mr. Ryan and others at the BBC did not face, and asked for her £100 once more. Ryan, defeated, agreed.

When Richard heard of it he was astounded at his wife's bravado. Such matters in the BBC of those days were sacrosanct; a mystique surrounded the salary. It was a trifle indecent to earn money at all at the BBC. To ask for more was vulgar. For a *wife* to ask for more was unheard of. 'What a woman!' he wrote admiringly in his diary.

Now in Cuddington he enjoyed a fortnight's rest. At first he did not fret. Not by nature an adventurer, he liked home and he had 'hated' the desert, though when he turned out his pockets for the cleaners and emptied some sand onto the bedroom floor he felt a sudden regret—his 'desert sickness'. He was away from the front, knowing that the British were about to start the greatest battle in the Middle East, the Second Battle of Alamein while he was in England with nothing to do. He read and he wrote and he waited. But he heard nothing from the BBC. Soon he began to feel as he later told his friend Cecilia Gillie: 'a forgotten man'. It would have been easy to give up and try another career. He was not overly proud of being a war correspondent, it was a job 'of very small importance', and he sometimes felt 'ashamed of having such interesting and independent work, when so many of his friends were doing such humdrum and dirty jobs in the services'. On his return, feeling that he ought to fight, he had registered for 'call-up' (though he need not have done), and it would be easy to push his way into Army service. But he believed the war correspondent did have some part to play as 'a link between the men fighting at the front and the men and women working in the factories and at home throughout the Empire'. 'It is useless [he thought] to ask for greater effort from the factory workers unless they have a direct connection with their husbands, sons and sweethearts abroad...only the war correspondent could bridge the gap between them.' That the job had some modest value kept him 'from unreasoning shame at being so free when others were so tied'.

He was also resilient: whatever the BBC view of him, he had returned from the Middle East 'confident and assured' and determined that it would take more than petty-minded bureaucrats (as he had now come to view some of his superiors) to force his departure from Broadcasting. When he returned to London it was made clear to him that the BBC would not seek to have him deferred from military service. The News Department debated whether to return his correspondent's pass to the War Office, 'if he is not going to be employed any further as a war correspondent', but decided to wait until a replacement for him was found. On his first day back at work he was offered a story: a demonstration by the Army of new techniques of military cooking on Salisbury Plain. The offer was not calculated malice but it was the only event happening that day. There was a mumbled apology, 'We're afraid it's not very interesting, Richard', but according to his colleague, Frank Gillard, he just smiled, nodded cheerfully to the room, and went off undismayed to cover it.

But there was little work for him; and though he would not show his disappointment, he did sometimes allow a note of rather unconvincing joviality to creep into his correspondence. He wrote, to G. R. Barnes, who was Director of Talks: 'I'd be grateful if your team would remember an at least practised broadcaster who appears to be "going spare"!' Talks, however, like News, failed to come to his assistance.

He was rescued from boredom and oblivion by the Ministry of Information which, apart from battling with the BBC, had since the outbreak of war been clumsily planting what it hoped were the seeds of high morale among the British public. Its campaigns had been notably unsuccessful and were treated by the people they sought to influence with laudable contempt. From the start it had been anxious to subdue 'five menaces to public calm'—fear, confusion, suspicion, class feeling and defeatism. To defeat such threats there had been established a Home Morale Emergency Committee. It was (as its title indicates) a clumsy body devoted to a questionable exercise of dubious necessity. Its campaigns ranged from the harmless (like attempts to encourage 'the value of neighbourliness') to the distasteful: in June 1940 the Committee prepared an 'Anger Campaign' designed 'to heighten the intensity of the personal anger felt by the individual British citizen against the German people and Germany ... we want the people to feel that it is their anger which is growing of their own accord'. Fortunately, in Britain, such absurdities had no chance of success.

The BBC, at least, had realised for a long time that the best way to stiffen morale was to use broadcasters like J. B. Priestley. His famous Postscripts, delivered to a vast audience in a soft Yorkshire accent, were dazzlingly successful—eloquent and patently honest. In fact he was too honest for the Ministry. In 1940 his fireside chats were brought to an untimely end because his undoubted and passionate patriotism was found to have a dangerously socialist tinge.

By 1942 the Ministry's irrelevant crudities were less in evidence. But by the autumn the Government was much disturbed by the growing chorus demanding a Second Front in Europe. The clamour was led by the most gifted politician outside the Cabinet, Aneurin Bevan. A few months earlier, bowing for once to the advice of his military advisers, Churchill had agreed that there should be no Second Front in 1942. But a natural desire for action and a powerful sympathy for the suffering of the Russians had created a groundswell of public opinion in favour of immediate action. It was the task of the Ministry to turn back the tide of popular feeling. Among other weapons they decided to use Richard Dimbleby.

In the autumn, with permission from the BBC, he began a speaking tour of the Midlands, Wales and the West Country. Ostensibly the talks were to be about his experiences in the Middle

East, but he was briefed to incorporate into his reminiscences the belief (which he held with conviction) that the Second Front activists were dangerously misguided.

One of the very first talks arranged for him was in South Wales at Tredegar, the home territory of Aneurin Bevan. He was unused to speaking to a mass audience and approached this talk with much trepidation. He travelled down on the train to Cardiff with Dilys, reading and re-reading his notes. Every so often he would look up, shut his eyes, and try to force the facts into his resistant head. It was hopeless. As soon as his eyes left the notes, a 'host of other stories' swept into his mind, obliterating the careful structure of his lecture.

In the hall at Tredegar he disguised his anxiety. The building filled with 'row after row of miners and their wives'. He had intended to talk for half an hour but he was told they had expected more. Then he was introduced: 'Richard Dimbleby, the famous war correspondent...' and he stood up, dry-mouthed, to speak. To his surprise the audience began to clap and then cheer. He was taken aback, forgot his notes, and began to speak: 'of Tobruk and its fleas and vermin, of ruined tanks rusting and blistering in the sun, the great heat by day and the cold, clear nights when men slept in their blankets under a deep blue sky... of the great battles... of the men who fought in them... of their patience and their courage'.

The audience was silent and motionless. He turned to the Second Front. He knew that there were plans for the invasion of Europe and 'he had read with intense irritation of meetings held at which the Government had been pressed to start the news campaign quickly'. Most of the clamour came from men who would not have to go themselves. Slogans like 'OPEN SECOND FRONT NOW!' infuriated him; and fiery speeches made by those 'without knowledge of our strength in men and material and the favourable array of the enemy' were, to him, irresponsible and unpatriotic. His judgment of Bevan was naive, but he knew better than to express himself in such critical terms before men and women who revered the man. Dimbleby sensed that many of those in front of him 'had themselves been urging the launching of the new front', so he restrained himself, arguing that the time would come, that it was not yet, we should stay our hand, and trust our leaders. He sat down: 'for a second time there was silence and then, like a great warmth enveloping him', he wrote, 'a burst of cheering, clapping and stamping that rocked the stage'. Elated, he walked out of the hall to back-slapping, hand-shaking and auto-graphs. It was, after that, the same wherever he went—a barn-storming success. At Woolwich, where he gave three talks, he noted: '800 or 1,000 women and men at each, and hundreds of autographs'; at Hendon: 'loud ovation on entering canteen'; at Cardiff: 'biggest audience ever'; at Newport: 'a packed audience again'; and at Swansea: 'we were clapped and waved on our way by crowd at gate'.

It was more than speeches that did it. He discovered for the first time at these factory talks that he had the ability to communication to a mass audience, to gauge the mood, and touch it to perfection. More than that, he realised that he was a famous man, that his voice was known to everyone. If he drew the further conclusion that his rapturous receptions were a popular statement, an acknowledgment, that his broadcasting had touched the people, he kept the thought to himself. Almost certainly he did not pause to consider that it was this—the blend of intimacy, patriotic fervour, and romantic grandeur that made his broadcasts so distinctive—which, winning an audience, so offended his masters at the BBC.

In November 1942, when it became plain that Dimbleby would not be leaving the BBC of his own volition, he was warned that the Corporation would not be sending him abroad. 'We all realise that this decision will be a disappointment to you, since it is likely to keep you out of active service (in the military sense) for some little time to come.' However, he would be staying to help build up the BBC teams for the coverage of the European Front where his experience as a war correspondent, he was informed, would be 'of great value'.

The letter was a sign that the BBC was about to wake from a long slumber. In 1942, when there were no despatches from the Russian front, or from the Far East, and when Dimbleby was the only correspondent abroad, the BBC felt able to congratulate itself publicly upon the News Talks, which gave listeners a per-sonal first-hand story of something that had happened, to explain a situation, or to describe a place, in a more human, leisurely way than could be managed in the news bulletin itself'. A more honest appraisal was made by Michael Standing (the Director of Outside Broadcasting) in an internal BBC memo. He did not mince his words: 'The Corporation has so far failed almost dismally to exploit the unique broadcasting possibilities of the war ... None of its few war correspondents has really established himself as a notable broadcasting figure.' The explanation was simple: the BBC had not given the matter 'proper priority', and nothing like the full radio resources of the Corporation had been employed; the Armed Services had been unhelpful; and in any case the news bulletins offered too little scope for radio's unique potential. Standing demanded 'drastic action' to 'put right these three basic troubles'. He suggested that the BBC should create six self-contained reporting teams, each with a reporter, a commentator, a recording engineer, recording van and 'if obtainable a portable recorder'.

Since 1936 Richard Dimbleby had been startling and sometimes irritating his colleagues with his 'wild plans' for teams of correspondents 'ready to go anywhere at any time'. In 1941, when the war had become a world war and he had urged it to be covered 'broadcast scale', he was ignored. But he was before his time. Michael Standing had chosen the right moment. By the end of 1942, A. P. Ryan had time to emerge from his confrontation with the Ministry of Information (though the struggle was by no means over) and to consider fully the proper function of radio as a reporting weapon.

We are able [he wrote] to give people remote from battle fronts two things that were impossible before this war. First the *voice* of a man with the forces in action can be heard. Sometimes it is not heard as distinctly as we should like, but there is a vivid quality about hearing a man speak, which does not come through in even the very best written prose. Secondly we can give some of the sound effects heard by those on the spot.

'Full use,' he continued, in superb understatement, 'has not yet been made of these two advantages, for war reporting is still in its infancy.' But by 1943, instead of one reporter in the Middle East, the BBC had no less than five. For the first time, the reports of Godfrey Talbot, Denis Johnston, Frank Gillard, Robert Dunnett and Howard Marshall began to combine (in one day) the mixture of colour, explanation, and analysis that had been impossible before. It was not merely that the BBC was beginning to wake up to the potential of radio. Equally important the Army in the Middle East was commanded by Generals who appreciated

F

publicity, and moreover were fighting a victorious, and obviously victorious, campaign. Facilities—travel, aeroplanes, co-operation over censorship problems—were no longer in grudging or inadequate supply but freely and enthusiastically available.

The special techniques of radio—'actuality' sound and recordings—about which the BBC had been so suspicious were becoming respectable journalistic tools. On those 'very rare' occasions when 'actuality' had been tried it had 'made a very great impression upon the listeners, and has done more to impress upon them the conditions in which these men are serving than any other form of broadcasting...' Both John Snagge, the BBC announcer, and Standing bolstered their arguments for more extensive coverage of the war by reference to some 'unique broadcasting material' produced by Richard Dimbleby at the beginning of January 1943. 'It was,' wrote Standing, 'a good example, I think, of a missed broadcasting, as opposed to purely news, news opportunity...I feel convinced that the public would have welcomed a more generous reflection of Dimbleby's exploit.'

The 'exploit' in question was a historic broadcast—made only four months after he had returned from the Middle East in apparent disgrace. On January 6th he became the first BBC war correspondent to go on an RAF bombing raid. He looked forward to the mission with Bomber Command with no excitement and considerable fear. He was to fly with Guy Gibson in a Lancaster bomber and their destination was Berlin. It was a night raid, and as they roared along the runway and took off, he counted around him between thirty and forty bombers: 'seemingly suspended in the evening air'. As they climbed up over the south coast, above the cloud, he switched on his oxygen supply. He felt nervous and tired. And then drowsy. He fell asleep. The next moment he was lying semi-conscious on the floor of the plane, with the co-pilot bending anxiously over him, fiddling with his oxygen mask. He had nipped the tube of oxygen supply and knocked himself out. It did not seem an auspicious beginning.

As they crossed over the enemy coast he saw signs of the German ack-ack for the first time:

It was bursting away from us and much lower. I didn't see any long streams of it soaring into the air as the pictures suggest: it burst in little yellow winking flashes and you couldn't hear it above the roar of the engines. Sometimes it closes in on you, and the mid—or tail—gunner will call up calmly and report its position to the Captain so that he can dodge it . . .

As they approached Berlin he saw the pattern of the endlessly criss-crossing searchlights lighting the sky—'a tracery of sparkling silver spread across the face of Berlin'. The flak was intense—'as we turned in for our first run across the city, it closed right round us. For a moment it seemed impossible that we could miss it, and one burst lifted us in the air as though a giant hand had pushed up the belly of the machine.' The other Lancasters were lost from sight. He could see only searchlights and flak. And then he saw below and behind them an explosion of light: 'white, and yellow and red'. The first of thousands of incendiary bombs had hit the ground: 'all over the dark face of the German capital these great incandescent flower-beds spread themselves'. He had taken a cine-camera with him, and now he tried to film the burning city. But it was too cold and the film jammed in the gate. They flew out into the safety of darkness, and then turned to run in again. They had one large three-and-a-half-ton 'dustbin' bomb to drop. The bomb-aimer chanted as they came in: 'Right—right—steady—left a little—left a little—steady—steady,' and then, 'hold it—BOMB GONE.' Dimbleby watched as below them the incendiaries turned 'to a dull, ugly red as the fires of bricks and mortar and wood spread from the chemical fires . . .' And he reported wondering if Hitler, Goering, Himmler or Goebbels were cowering down there in a shelter beneath them. 'This shimmering mass of flares and bombs and gun-flashes was their stronghold . . . [I was filled with] a great exultation.'

It did not last long. A few moments later as they turned back towards England, exhausted by his thirty minutes over the city, he succumbed to the twisting and turning and jolting of the bomber and to his fear. Turning away from Gibson he vomited on the floor missing the bomb-aimer beneath him by a few inches.

Later that night he caught the train back to London. It was crowded but he managed to find an empty seat and sat down. As they pulled out of the station some uniformed soldiers looked into the compartment. Seeing it was full they stood outside. Dimbleby was the only civilian in the carriage apart from an elderly woman sitting opposite him. She looked up at him sharply: 'I should have thought that a lucky young man like you would have the good manners to give up his seat to one of our fighting men.' He was too tired to reply.

The broadcast was a success; the first time that the public had heard a first-hand account by a reporter of an air raid. The Air Ministry (which had cautiously help up its transmission for two days) was delighted; and Bomber Command sent him a telegram: 'Good work'. He had been obsessed with the need to please the RAF who were suspicious and not a little contemptuous of journalism. When he got the telegram he was delighted, writing back to Guy Gibson: 'I was paralysed with fright, but it was an unforgettable experience, and it gave me a unique chance to see for myself what is being done week after week in the name of Freedom . . . I've just had the telegram—one of the best things I've received in years.' One of the consequences of his achievement was that the Air Ministry sought in future to deal with the BBC only through Richard Dimbleby. And, which was less gratifying, he became, in effect, the BBC's air correspondent as well. He was to fly another twenty missions with the RAF before the end of the war.

The momentum for change within the BBC was gathering force. Immediately after Michael Standing's demand for 'drastic action' (which a year earlier would have fallen on deaf ears) A. P. Ryan wrote a detailed memorandum for the Director-General, entitled: 'BBC Reporting of the Second Front'. It dealt with ways in which Ryan thought the BBC could:

> bring home to listeners in this country and all over the world what happens at the front or fronts in 1943. The assumption is made that 1943 will be a year of military action *in which the Government will put the highest importance on everything that is being done to keep up civilian morale*—which means keeping everybody not out in the battlefield as fully aware of and stirred by military operations as is compatible with security.

It was no accident that this dramatic new approach to the role of broadcasting coincided with the turning of the tide in Britain's favour. The United States had now joined the Allies; in the Middle East the British and Americans were moving towards the conquest of the Germans; and on the Russian front the enemy was hard pressed. For the first time in three years it seemed that the Allies were certain to win the war. The problems of propaganda, of reporting a losing campaign, were no longer pressing—

if not at an end. In future BBC reporters would be covering the victorious advance of the Allied Armies. If the invasion of Europe fulfilled expectations, then there would be no dearth of exploits to stir the hearts left at home; no conflict between propaganda and truth.

Until 1943, according to Ryan, the BBC had been treated as: 'a new troublesome kind of newspaper. In fact the BBC is something of a newspaper, something of a cinema, and something of its own.' Borrowing almost exactly Dimbleby's words of seven years before, Ryan avowed that what the BBC now needed was 'a team of men' to be 'on the spot' to report the war. By this means the BBC should seek to convince the Government and the Armed Forces that the BBC should 'keep the exploits of the British fighting services vividly and justly before the civil publics in this country, in the Dominions, in the United States, and Russia, and elsewhere in the world'. At last the BBC was speaking in a new language with a new confidence.

Soon afterwards it got permission to send two reporting teams to cover the secret exercises (codenamed *Spartan*) to be held in Oxfordshire as a full dress-rehearsal for the invasion of Europe. It was the most important news operation which the BBC had ever undertaken, and it was approached with the greatest care. It was also the means by which the BBC would prove to the Government and to the Armed Forces that in broadcasting the country had the most powerful weapon devised for mass communication in the field of news.

Perhaps appropriately, Richard Dimbleby found himself restored to favour as suddenly as he had been discarded six months before. He was deputed to lead the 'British' reporting team in the coverage of the mock battle across Oxfordshire between the Allied and Aix forces. Not surprisingly S. J. de Lotbinière who was in charge of the exercise recorded: 'I am more and more impressed with Dimbleby's competence as a reporter and with the value he is to a team.'

Spartan was excessively difficult to report since the BBC was under the same restrictions as in a real campaign and there was little of the fear and excitement and noise of battle. The campaign which lasted six days took place over an eighty-mile front, and the 'Allies' advanced through sixty miles of Oxfordshire in the process. The BBC's 'war commandos' (as the reporters were called in a flush of Administrative excitement) made over ninety

despatches, reports, features and interviews. A few days later it was
assembled into an hour long 'War Report' and at a crucial meeting
in the Director-General's office at Broadcasting House, it was
played back to various senior Government officials, including the
Secretary of State for War and the Commander-in-Chief Home
Forces. The BBC had consciously mortgaged its future to the
success of *Spartan*. Broadcasting House waited anxiously for the
verdict. It was unanimous: the BBC should be given the right to
report the war in full—three-and-a-half years after it had
started.

Richard Dimbleby was asked to prepare his own report on the
Spartan exercise—the first time he had been asked (though not the
first time he had offered) his opinion formally since he had been
at the BBC. He made use of it to the full. *Spartan* had borne out
many of the ideas and beliefs that he had held and expressed earlier
in the war. It was the first detailed report on the practical
problems of radio war reporting that the BBC had seen.

> *Spartan* has shown that the news observer with the team has
> his hands full with his own job; it is most unlikely that he
> will have any great length of time to co-operate with the
> Outside Broadcast or Features man. [As Standing had originally
> suggested, the teams each contained a reporter, a feature writer,
> and an outside broadcast commentator.] The *will* to do so
> should be there, of course, but I do not believe that the speed
> of battle will give the observer any time for anything much
> beyond his own despatches . . .
>
> In the past there has been criticism of observers in battle
> areas because they provide too much 'situation' material and not
> enough eye-witness descriptions (it had been a charge fre-
> quently laid against him). *Spartan* has shown that a combination
> of the two techniques is no longer possible. In this exercise,
> which was a close approximation to expected battle conditions,
> Force Headquarters was generally seventy miles from the
> forward area . . . Hence it is not possible for the observer to visit
> Force Headquarters daily or even twice weekly for a basic
> general picture of events; he must concentrate on the forward
> Headquarters. This means that his daily picture can be fully
> representative of one or perhaps two Corps sections but not,
> except in unusual circumstances, representative of the entire
> battle front. At the same time he can concentrate on the sector

where the most important, and, in the eyes of the world, the most 'newsworthy' battle is being fought ...

The pure local colour, the reporting of the incident [which Ryan had tried to force out of Dimbleby without success in the Middle East] should be handled adequately by the Outside Broadcasts man, who should not attempt to give any general picture even of a battalion front. It seems to be important that the Outside Broadcast's approach should be of the: 'here I am in a ditch' type; his report will be found to spring naturally from the more general despatch given by the observer.

His coverage of the Middle East war had been bedevilled by poor communications. Changes and improvements after were required 'urgently'.

The Austin saloon which I had during *Spartan* was grossly overloaded and rendered top-heavy by a wire mattress spread over its roof. I doubt if its springs would hold more than a week or two on the roads of Europe (such was our French experience with the Wolseley in 1939–40). However, a vehicle of the type (i.e. a fast car or utility) is essential for the observer ... The observer also needs a Jeep (for which I urge that application should be made). These fast little vehicles—ample for conducting officer and observer—are ideal for use well forward ...

He also raised again the question of propriety which had so concerned him in France and the Middle East. He confessed that it was 'a delicate point' but he felt 'that the senior engineers of the Corporation should be asked to choose only with the greatest care the recording engineers who are to wear war correspondent's uniform.

I have learnt how to conduct myself in the field and at formation Headquarters [he wrote a trifle pompously] by three years of hard practice. Last week I was given as engineer and travelling companion a young man who had never worn a uniform in his life until two days before, and who most certainly would never have passed the eliminating tests of officer cadetship. He wore his field cap at a rakish angle and had a cigarette drooping from his lips from early morning until he went to sleep at night. He addressed private soldiers, military policemen and sentries as 'old boy'. At least on one occasion, in my presence, he addressed an elderly War Office General by calling at him 'I say', again with the cigarette dangling. He kept it there while he talked, and when he had finished he gave a friendly wave and turned away.

Buried not very deep in Dimbleby's personality was a touch of that almost inevitable snobbery which afflicts most of those born into his background. Dimbleby was conscious of class (although not quite certain *where* he stood on the social ladder). But he had spent long periods in the desert with engineers from a very different background in great harmony. Above all else he could not abide behaviour which was unseemly or inappropriate. And perhaps fearing that he would be misunderstood he went on:

I hope you will not suspect me of being a 'Colonel Blimp'. No-one hates more than I do the unnecessary mannerisms of, for example, the Household troops. I am interested only in doing the war-reporting job efficiently ... We simply must fit ourselves into the landscape and conduct ourselves in accordance with the rank whose privileges we enjoy ...

Two months later, in May 1943, the War Reporting Unit was formed. It was charged, a little ponderously, with 'the responsibility for getting active service war material in any theatre of war and for meeting the demands of all consumers with sure regard for the interests of programmes as a whole'.

To put the plan into action the BBC needed three commodities which were in short supply—reporters, materials, and facilities. In Broadcasting House a 'Warcasts Room' was established to handle all 'traffic' between reporters at the front-line and the programmes for which they would broadcast. The 'traffic' would include discs, tapes, despatches, cables and telephone calls. The office would be staffed twenty-four hours a day. A 'copytaster' (to select and 'place' incoming reports) would be on duty all the time; and the officer-in-charge of the Warcasts Room would act as a link between his men at the front and the editors of the programmes for which the unit would be reporting.

For the first time in the history of the BBC, the reporter was to be treated with respect and even awe. It was suddenly recognised that the most important person in the operation was the man at the front-line without whom there would be no news programmes. The Warcasts Room would handle all messages to the reporters at the front so that 'instructions do not conflict' and to ensure 'that awareness is shown of the conditions under which war reporters are working'. Messages from the front (how Dimbleby must have smiled at this) should be dealt with quickly 'and sympathetically'; and 'approval of good despatches should be signified'.

A fistful of shibboleths were to be discarded: 'The war reporter,' announced an important internal document, 'is the BBC's *observer*. He is a named person who must exploit his opportunities for personal observation by vivid and accurate description...' Moreover, for the first time the BBC was prepared to see him in competition with the press.

> The first need is for *quick, accurate, concise news*... Communiqués and hand-outs will reach consumers via the agencies. The war reporter should therefore be more concerned with giving his own gloss on the communiqués and hand-outs than with giving the actual texts—unless he is ahead of the news agencies.

Even more, the war reporter should provide 'a general picture of the news of the past few hours—of *The Times* double column intro to the lead story—which tells the news, weighs every word and puts things in their right perspective'. The BBC was not only to compete against the press in speed but also in 'authority'. For the first time a BBC reporter was to be encouraged to do what Dimbleby had been castigated for doing in the Middle East, providing as he had put it, 'the broad canvas'. The BBC had broken away from its self-imposed shackles—its fear of the press, of Government, of failure.

Inevitably the creation of a new department, and one which moreover was to be in the vanguard of the most important undertaking the BBC had ever attempted, was not easy. There soon began a struggle over the infant body of the War Reporting Unit which almost destroyed it before it could crawl. For a time it seemed as if every department in the BBC felt that it had exclusive right to the control of the revolution in broadcasting. The new unit broke with tradition in that it summoned people from all other departments—feature-writers, reporters, commentators, editors, secretaries, engineers and producers. It was going to report the war 'on a gigantic scale' and it needed the best of the BBC to do it. The departments most affected fought and wrangled, as only bureaucracies can, to have the unit in their control. At one stage Laurence Gilliam (who was to become one of the editors of War Report) felt bound to write anxiously to the Controller of Programmes (Sir Richard Maconachie): 'The BBC is in danger of losing the really great chance that the war has given it of becoming a worldwide source of really accurate, up-to-the-minute vivid reporting of war news'; but the wrangles and delays continued— it did not end until William Haley, the BBC's new Editor in Chief, issued a rebuke to the warring parties:

> The reporting of the invasion will be one of the biggest and most responsible undertakings the BBC has ever faced. We shall be judged by our success or failure for years to come... If we attempt to meet anything so full of unexpectedness with an uncompromising rigidity, we shall fail ...

When that issue was resolved, another one arose: there were not enough war correspondents. As late as December 1943, Howard Marshall (who had returned from North Africa to become Head of the Unit) was lamenting that the BBC had only two 'star' reporters. William Haley was equally worried: 'The only two news observers of the required standard are Godfrey Talbot and Richard Dimbleby...we must strengthen our reserves. Once the BBC case for proper representation has been won, we must be in a position to be adequately represented.'

It was good luck as much as good planning which gave the BBC, by the time D-day arrived, a corps of correspondents some of whose names would be distinguished in the annals of war reporting. A search was instigated for suitable candidates; they came from Outside Broadcasting, the Features Department, and the News Room. Some of them had only commentated on sports fixtures, some had never broadcast before, others were happier writing plays. The 'commandos' as they were called went on special courses learning to map read, to interpret signals, understand weapons, and negotiate rough country. They were also instructed (much to Richard Dimbleby's approval) in good behaviour. 'A war reporter is given the courtesy rank of Captain,' they were told by Broadcasting House, 'the amount of saluting he will do must depend on his own judgment...' In general he should 'return all salutes' and 'in a group of war reporters, one should be delegated to return salutes'. In the street he should 'salute full colonels and upwards' and (here the BBC entered the realms of fantasy) at a General Salute, he must 'salute on the third and last movement of the "present" and drop the salute on the second and last movement of the "slope"'. If a war correspondent were to visit a general he might be 'invited to sit down', continued the BBC manual. Under these circumstances it would be 'in order for him to remove his cap' but this 'should be replaced and a parting salute given before going out of the room'.

Now that the BBC had decided that the war correspondent was more than an administrative inconvenience, his every need was to be met with tender care.

'War reporting is a strenuous job,' announced one solicitous memorandum, 'and a war reporter is entitled to make himself as comfortable as he can.' He could take with him to the war a 'Houndsfield bed, a quilted sleeping bag, military and civilian clothes, a tin hat, gas mask, gas cape, anti-gas ointment and eye-shields, toilet paper, razor blades, shaving soap and health salts, matches, a torch, a darning set, a tin and bottle opener, a Bible and/or a pack of cards'.

And the Administration which was enjoying a field day with lists, instructions, and memos piling deeper and deeper in the Warcasts Room, had also been forced to realise that a war correspondent needed to spend money. It had come to realise, not altogether happily, that the words of S. J. de Lotbinière could not be ignored. 'We have got to expect fairly heavy expenses', he wrote:

> A war reporter's life is a trying one. He is making new contacts all the time, and he is always on the stretch. If he seeks relaxation, it cannot be the sort of relaxation that he would get at home. He is living in hotels with other reporters—so that drinks and a good dinner are almost inevitable. I realise that there must be a constant watch against extravagance, but I do believe that the teams must be given the benefit of the doubt when they run up expenses beyond the normal.

Such thoughts, distasteful as they were to the Administration, were swallowed in mute acceptance.

It had been a slow awakening. In April 1944, a little over a month before D-day, and four and a half years since the outbreak of war, it was still possible for Tom Harrison (who had created Mass Observation) to write in the *Observer*: 'The BBC teams are conspicuously few and quiet. Their output has been, at least until recently, almost negligible...' And he called for 'a real radio service out of war's tumult, as newspapermen and cameramen do... There are some signs that of a new will to fight for BBC news. May it be multiplied!'

But at last the War Reporting Unit was ready: nineteen correspondents to cover the Western Front, six more in Italy and North Africa, others in the Far East, the Middle East, Ceylon, India, Russia, the United States and the Pacific. Apart from Richard Dimbleby, they included such names as Howard Marshall, Frank Gillard, Chester Wilmot, Guy Byam, Stanley Maxted, Stewart MacPherson, Robin Duff, Godfrey Talbot, Wynford Vaughan-Thomas, Richard Sharp, Edward Ward, Robert Barr, Michael Reynolds and Robert Reid. It was at last a team to rival any in Fleet Street. As D-day approached A. P. Ryan wrote each of them their final instructions. It is possible to sense the excitement that even Ryan allowed himself to express, knowing that BBC history was about to be written.

> We have a world audience and we mean to give it the fullest and the most vivid and alive account of coming operations that we can... Never forget that from the point of view of the listener as well as of the men in the field this will be a grimly dramatic time... Describe events of which you are eye-witness as accurately as you can. Give credit of course to gallantry and to generalship. Let pride in the achievement of our armies come through. But never seek to 'jazz up' a plain story. Events will contain their own drama.
>
> You will meet practical difficulties in the field... Field service is no picnic... Finally, good luck... you handful of men have been chosen to undertake the most important assignment so far known to broadcasting. Good luck.

A little before the invasion of Europe, Richard Dimbleby went down to Dover to an observation post on the edge of the cliffs. In the evening he sat alone listening to the sea as he had ten years ago when he was a local reporter in Lymington. He allowed his memories, of childhood, of boat trips to Boulogne, of a holiday in Ambleteuse, of 'thousands of happy people [who] once came and went on their missions and holidays' sailing across what had now become 'an empty, dangerous strip of forbidden water'. And he wrote that he was overwhelmed by a sense of tragedy and nostalgia. Writing in the third person (as he always did when expressing private thoughts for public consumption), he showed that romantic, almost sentimental, quality which each year of the war had strengthened:

> He was sighing for the happiness and excitement and the sorrow that belonged to the past, and in dwelling among them he prevented himself thinking about the future. He knew, as thousands of others knew, that his life might end before the summer was out... There was hope and strength in the knowledge that he was only one of hundreds of thousands. His feeling was not of fear; rather it was regret and a great sadness, and this longing for the things that had gone.

At midnight on June 5th, 1944 he was at Harwell, to report the beginning of the invasion of Europe: the departure of the first airborne assault troops for France. On the next evening, fifteen million people heard John Snagge introduce the first edition of War Report, completed from the despatch of nineteen BBC reporters from the air, the sea, and on the coast of Normandy.

From Harwell, Dimbleby's precise, clipped, excited voice, urgent against the roar of aircraft taking off, spoke of the troops taking with them:

> the hopes and fears and prayers of millions of people in this country who sleep tonight not knowing whether this mighty operation is taking place... There she goes now [he raises his voice against the Lancaster's roar, and the sound is momentarily drowned]... even as the first machine to go, climbs into the sky, her white tail lights lifting and lifting against the clouds, and the second one disappears below the hill to follow her, so the third machine begins revving up her engine...

And Guy Byam was with them:

> Their faces blackened with cocoa, sheathed knives were strapped to their ankles; tommy guns strapped to their waists;

bandoliers and hand grenades, coils of rope, pick handles, spades, rubber dinghies hung around them . . . like some strange creatures from another world.

From a Mitchell bomber over the Channel, Air Commodore W. Helmore reported a raid on a railway bridge on the Normandy coast:

> We're in a colossal static storm at the moment which is rattling in my ears like mad . . . There's something ahead of us there—do you see—do you see the light? Oh! I thought I was talking to the pilot. I recorded that—instead of talking into the intercom I talked into the record—we're just going in to bomb . . . Hold it! My God there's some bloody nasty flak around this place—very nasty flak, blast it!
> . . . Oh! there they go—my God, what a good lift, what a good lift up into the air! We feel much lighter now. The best thing is to get out of here . . .

From a studio on the south coast 'sitting in soaked through clothes with no notes at all' Howard Marshall who had 'hitch-hiked' back across the Channel from Normandy where he had landed on one of the first assault crafts:

> I'm just going to try and tell you very briefly the story of what our boys had to do on the beaches today as I saw it myself . . . As we drove in we could see shell-bursts in the water along the beach, and just behind the beach, and we could see the craft in a certain amount of difficulty because the wind was driving the sea in with long rollers . . . And suddenly our craft swung, we touched a mine, there was a very large explosion, a thundering shudder of the whole craft, and water began pouring in . . .

From Normandy, Guy Byam again, landing with the para-chutists:

> One minute, thirty seconds. Red light—green and out, get on, out, out, out fast into the cool night air, out over France . . . We're jumping into fields covered with poles . . . And the ground comes up to hit me. And I find myself in the middle

of a corn field. I look round ... and overhead hundreds of parachutes and containers are coming down.

Chester Wilmot landed in a glider:

With grinding brakes and creaking timbers we jolted, lurched and crashed our way to a landing in Northern France early this morning ... We shouted with joy—and relief ... and bundled out into the field. All around us we could see silhouettes of other gliders, twisted and wrecked—making grotesque patterns against the sky. Some had buried their noses in the soil; others had lost a wheel or a wing; one had crashed into a house; two had crashed into each other ... We could hear Germans shouting excitedly at a church nearby, starting a car and driving off furiously. A quarter of a mile away a German battery was firing out to sea ...

On the evening of D-day, eighteen hours after he had watched the assault troops leave Harwell, Richard Dimbleby in different mood, broadcast from a bomber flying low over enemy-occupied France:

Long stretches of empty roads, shining with rain, deserted, dripping woods, and damp fields—static, quiet—perhaps uncannily quiet, and possibly not to remain quiet. But here and there a movement catches the eye, as our aircraft on reconnaissance roars over a large and suspicious wood: three German soldiers running like mad across the main road to fling themselves into cover. And, nearer the battle area, much nearer the battle area than they, a solitary peasant harrowing his field, up and down behind the horses, looking nowhere but before him and at the soil.

The D-day programme was broadcast in the United States where the *New York Times* judged: '...you had a feeling that radio, in its capacity as an informant, had grown up ... The service of the British Broadcasting Corporation, as D-day listeners know, was not less than superb.' And a few days later, Glasgow's *Evening Citizen* reported that the British public 'has been entertained to a display of war reporting on a scale unprecedented in the history either of war or reporting ...'

George Blake, the author of the article, continued: 'We listen
avidly, marvelling that this is the voice of a man just back from
a flight over the beaches.' And he singled out Richard Dimbleby's
broadcast:

He brought back a picture of Normandy that I, for one, shall
always count as one of the best bits of descriptive reporting in
this war . . . Probably a faculty like this is inborn and unaccount-
able. You can do something with any cub reporter but no
amount of teaching and experience will turn the wrong sort
of man into the right sort of reporter.

The differing styles and personalities of the War Report team
soon became well known. Listeners, who numbered between ten
and fifteen million every night for nearly a year, would compare and debate the merits of Marshall or Gillard or Wilmot. John
Snagge's 'and now over to Normandy' became as famous as Stuart
Hibberd's 'This—is London'.

Richard Dimbleby, who had never fitted easily into the strait-
jacket with which the BBC had tried to restrain him in the Middle
East, now felt free to be as partisan and patriotic as good broadcasting would allow. With victory ahead, and no dispute between
War Cabinet and British generals, he could be himself—and the
BBC would not protest. On D-day he no longer felt himself to be
an 'observer' but 'deeply involved in the operation'. His own style
of broadcasting flourished only in these conditions. His broadcasting confidence now grew fast. His voice became perhaps the
most distinctive of all war reporters; always cadenced, always
flowing, seeming only just to contain his passion; instinctively
sharing the mood of his audience, but just a little heightened,
slightly mannered. Others, feeling no less powerfully, allowed
their phrases to collapse into incoherent jumbles of much-felt but
ill-expressed emotion; or, seeking to stay cool, straining after
detachment, they were accurate but lifeless. It was soon understood that Richard Dimbleby would cover the 'great occasions'—
the first crossing of the Rhine, the surrender of Paris, the entry
into Berlin, and the Victory parades.

A few weeks after D-day he was in Normandy listening to
Montgomery address the invasion troops. He did not broadcast,
but wrote—with vulnerable sentiment—of the first years of the

war: when he had reported alone for a BBC which was remote
and frequently hostile:

How many battles, how many bitter campaigns, how many
insubstantial triumphs, how much sacrifice and endeavour
would be forgotten for ever in this last and most vital operation.
Yet the liberation of Europe would have been impossible but
for the painful labours of those men who died in Eritrea,
Abyssinia and Greece and the deserts of Asia Minor...they
had no reward for the sacrifice. No glory and meagre praise.
Most of them died alone, and those that lived, fought in small
and scattered bodies throughout the vast expanse of the Middle
East... Sad, brave ghosts of the people: not soldiers, but
simple men who lived and died in the unutterable loneliness of
desert places that other men might fight in France, and live in
Freedom.

Just before D-day, Malcolm Frost had succeeded Howard
Marshall as Director of the War Reporting Unit. Now only a
few days after the invasion, Malcolm Frost collapsed and was
rushed to hospital, where he advised Richard Dimbleby should
succeed him; 'Richard was the only man who knew enough
about the job to take it over—there was no-one else who could
do it.' So for the next few months, as the Allies fought their way
across France, Dimbleby sat in the Warcasts Room in Broadcasting House, directing reporters in the field—sending advice and
instructions, praise and criticism, and responding to requests and
anxieties at the front. Howard Marshall cabled about the dangers
at the front-line, wondering whether the reports were worth the
risks:

I spent five—literally five happy hours on my nose in a ditch at
Div. H.Q. the other evening being shelled continuously by
88's ... every time the boys go forward they get shot at from all
directions. We've had some very lucky escapes here and there...
it does add to the strain—even the fire-eaters like Chester
[Chester Wilmot] show signs of it when they come in.

Dimbleby was always solicitous: 'I, for one, would never
suggest that a correspondent should risk his neck in a forward area
to get a half-minute piece on what a soldier looks like ...' But

he was anxious for more 'human' and 'detailed' reports—
descriptions of 'tired and dusty men making their way in single
file up the road, the deploying number of tanks across a wood and
into some trees or something so intimate even as one man sitting
on the ground writing a letter in his dirt-stained clothes, with
the wind ruffling the scrap of paper he is writing on...dammit
I could go on for ever.' He was anxious that, if the reporters
at the front-line did not record their commentaries against a background of tanks moving or planes flying, the public would begin
to regard the 'situation report' almost as though it were being
relayed from the M.O.I. (Ministry of Information) in London:
'That is why we must concentrate more and more on producing
the life and colour of the battle itself.'

It could not have escaped Richard Dimbleby's notice that the
success of War Report, from which the BBC had gained overnight prestige, depended entirely on the methods and techniques
that he had pioneered, and which he had argued with such passion
would give the BBC a 'vital part' in national emergencies. If he
felt any satisfaction he was careful not to display it. Instead he
chafed at his forced sojourn in Broadcasting House. Whenever he
could be spared, he left London for an RAF base (somewhere in
Britain) to fly with Bomber Command.

At the best of times he was frightened of flying; he always felt
ill and was frequently sick. Flying with Bomber Command was
statistically by far the most dangerous form of battle that the
Second World War could offer; casualties on some missions
numbered ten per cent; more than 150,000 airmen died; to survive
a run of twenty missions was to have luck on your side; two of
the BBC's three air correspondents (Dimbleby was the third) were
killed—the only casualties of the War Reporting Unit. After the
drama of early raids had worn off it was quite possible (and, given
the risks, permissible) to compile a despatch without leaving the
ground, from interviews with pilots and gunners. Yet Dimbleby
insisted on flying, completing twenty operational missions by the
end of the war.

Neither death wish nor bravado made him take such avoidable
risk; Dudley Perkins, who worked with him as Manager of the
War Reporting Unit, remembers that he left Broadcasting House
for an RAF base to go on a bombing mission with hardly a
mention of his destination, as if he were leaving to have lunch with
a friend. The compulsion of guilt—at being an 'observer' when his

country was at war—played its part: he believed that if he was to report the exploits he was bound to share the danger. More important, however, was that he was by nature incapable of detaching himself from the events he reported. 'I only wish,' he had once said, 'that there were some way of telling people in Britain what all these men are doing for them ... You hear people discussing the losses and being so complacent about them ... they've no idea what it means for men to take the strain of these operations day after day and night after night, always wondering what's going to happen to them.'

Once he had become assigned to the RAF, he became immersed in the bombing, a passionate apostle for Bomber Command, blindly loyal to 'Bomber Harris', an unquestioning advocate of the air war. When he felt that the BBC did not pay due regard to the achievements of the RAF he was outraged. On one occasion he wrote to A. P. Ryan:

> I feel honour bound to set before you my own point of view ... up to long after D-day the Command's casualties were higher than all the British Armies put together, and the list of young men whose nerves and morale have been shattered by the strain of the work runs into thousands ... we must surely not allow ourselves to believe that people are 'tired' of hearing about Bomber Command. I cannot imagine a more cynical or callous suggestion; nor in my opinion does it hold water.
>
> I do not believe that the public *is* tired of the air story. Certainly the several million people who are connected with the bombers are not. Even if they were, however, would it not remain our duty to report the work of a Command making such a notable contribution to the war effort—that is, if War Report is what its title suggests, and not an entertainment programme ... !

Taking careful (and prescient) note of the moral susceptibilities that might otherwise be aroused, William Haley had laid down firm guidelines about the way the BBC should report what would later be recognised as the 'terror' bombing of Germany: '... it is a scientific operation, not to be stunted, to be gloated over, or to be dealt with in any other way than the most factual reporting arising from the communiqués and from material obtained from Air Headquarters of Bomber Stations.'

Richard Dimbleby was incapable of such Reithian detachment. Had he been on the ground to witness the destruction of a half million German civilians, he would not have failed to imagine the bodies beneath, the burning flesh of little children, to recoil from the desperate, mindless, amoral devastation. He would have been appalled by Sir Arthur Harris, who was once held to have said, 'In Bomber Command we have always worked on the principle that bombing anything in Germany is better than bombing nothing'; and as the evidence mounted for the conclusion that saturation bombing had not even achieved its object of destroying the German military, industrial and economic system and undermining the morale of its people 'to a point where their capacity to armed resistance is fatally weakened', he would have cried 'mass murder!' As it was, like most of his fellow countrymen, he felt no moral scruples about deeds which were in no way 'scientific operations'. He did not reach for a phoney neutrality; he was unashamedly and proudly partisan. Like the aircrews with whom he flew, he insulated himself from the horrors below, by accepting and then preaching the propaganda of Bomber Command.

I think that not only in the smoke and rubble of Duisberg [he recorded after a mission over the Ruhr] but deeper in the heart of Germany, there must be men charged with the defence of the Reich whose hearts tonight are filled with dread and despair. For the unbelievable has come to pass—the RAF has delivered its greatest single attack against a German industrial target since the start of the war—more than a thousand heavy bombers, more than 4,500 tons of bombs—and it did it, this morning, in broad daylight.

I saw the grey patchwork of houses and factories, roads, railways and the dirty, dark waters of the great river ... then target indicators, and bombs, high explosive and incendiary, nearly 5,000 tons of them, went shooting down; and the German flak, and a good deal of it, came shooting up. Duisberg the arsenal disappeared under a filthy, billowing, brown bulge of smoke ... Duisberg lay underneath the shroud; and shroud, I think, is the right word.

As well as Berlin and the Ruhr, he went on missions over Holland and Belgium, to Cologne, to Munich and over the

Rhine. On the first day of the Rhine crossing in March 1945 six thousand British and Allied aircraft took part in the assault. Dimbleby flew in a Mitchell bomber towing a glider in which Stanley Maxted had found himself a place. As they roared down the runway Dimbleby shouted into the microphone clamped against his mouth against the noise of the engines:

'We are off, full boost now, flat out, as fast as we can go...we are climbing gently into the air, the glider floating steadily behind us...we are in the air and on our way.' As they approached the Rhine, Stanley Maxted took up the commentary his voice shaking with the excitement and the glory: 'It must soon be time to cast off... So Richard Dimbleby tell them when you get back about these guys and how they went into battle... Tell Britain, Richard, tell the world... There is not much time now.' And as his glider cast off, Dimbleby reported another going down, hit by German flak, which 'paused a second as though surprised and then reared up and fell somersaulting—there are no parachutes in gliders'.

On the second day of the landings he flew across the Rhine again:

> The whole of this mighty airborne army is now crossing and filling the whole sky...on our right hand a Dakota has just gone down in flames... Ahead of us, another pillar of black smoke marks the spot where an aircraft has gone down and yet another one; it's a Stirling—a British Stirling; it's going down with flames coming out from under its belly—four parachutes are coming out—one, two—three, four—four parachutes have come out of the Stirling; it goes on its way to the ground... There's only a minute or two to go; we cross the Rhine— we're on the east bank of the river...in just a moment we shall have let go...here comes the voice—Now!—the glider has gone: we've cast off our glider. We've let her go. There she goes down behind us. We've turned hard away, hard away in a tight circle to port to get out of this area. I'm sorry if I'm shouting—it is a very tremendous sight.

That was his last operational flight. A few days later he was on the ground himself in Germany.

8

From Belsen to Berlin

Such contradictory permanent horrors . . .

TED HUGHES

THE ADVANCE ACROSS EUROPE WAS RAPID. THE ALLIED
Armies overran towns and villages in its path without resistance,
watched by a bemused civilian population that had been taught
to believe that Germany could not lose. Now their main streets
and their country lanes were filled with the troops and tanks and
trucks of the enemy.

Richard Dimbleby, who was with the Second Army under
General Montgomery, reported some of the experience of the
advance. In one town he walked into a small hotel to hear the
nine o'clock news. In the kitchen he found an old man and his
family. They seemed ready to talk, but Dimbleby adhered strictly
to the rules; he 'had not come into the German kitchen to
fraternise, that strictly forbidden practice . . .' When the news
started the German family spoke no English, listened intently to
the long list of captured German towns, as Freddy Grisewood
read them out, and the tanks lumbered by outside as proof. With
a pencil the old man carefully marked each fallen town as it was
mentioned. It was a dramatic and pathetic scene. But Dimbleby
added to it the little insight which turned a colourful report into a
memorable one:

> As I watched them, a thought struck me. This was a recital from
> London of our success, of the growing and spreading defeat of
> their country, and yet there was not one sound or sign of regret

on their faces, no shock, no despair, no alarm. They picked up what was said, checked it on the map and noted it just as if they were a bunch of neutrals hearing all about somebody else. And, indeed, I believe that's what many of these front-line German people are: neutrals in their own country. They seem to have lost the power of passion or sorrow. They show no sympathy for their Army, for their Government, or for their country.

In London the News Department had already decided that Dimbleby should cover the Allied entry into Berlin (he had already broadcast from Paris nine months earlier as General de Gaulle made his triumphant return to the city up the Champs Elysées). One of Richard Dimbleby's severest critics in Broadcasting House, Donald Boyd, an astringent judge of others, had been bitterly irritated by his reporting from the Middle East: he had been passionate where he should have been dry, fulsome where he should have been spare, involved where he should have been detached. In the Middle East the weakness of the BBC's senior observer had been, in Boyd's words, 'his inability to detach himself from the social context in which he was reporting'. Now in Germany, the weakness was his strength. It was judged that Dimbleby was the BBC reporter who would best be able to reflect the mood of the British public on the eve of the coming victory. Even so, no-one in the BBC could have known at the beginning of April 1945 that the last weeks of the war were to allow Dimbleby to witness horror and suffering of a kind and on a scale which would demand moral and spiritual responses far above those required to reflect the sombre joy of victory.

Three weeks after the Rhine crossing he was at the Advance Headquarters of the Second Army, along with Wynford Vaughan-Thomas and Chester Wilmot. A large group of correspondents were relaxing at the Press Centre, when a report came in that there was a German camp a few miles away up the road. It was under the control of the SS, and the camp commander had offered to surrender so that the Allies could take in medical supplies for some prisoners who were unwell. There was a rumour too that there had been an outbreak of typhus in the camp. According to Wynford Vaughan-Thomas most of the correspondents, imagining that it would be little different from any of the other prisoner-of-war camps that they had liberated on their way through Germany, took little notice of the reports.

Richard Dimbleby, however, decided to go up to the camp with the small platoon of soldiers and a military doctor who were to take it over from the Germans. They drove fast because there were still German snipers on the road. Through a wet pine forest, across some heathland, through a village, and into the forest again, until they reached the camp. It was called Belsen.

At the gates to meet them was a small group of German soldiers and the camp commander, Joseph Kramer, immaculately dressed, politely at attention to salute the British officers and surrender the camp. He held out his hand and the British officers, ignoring the gesture, walked inside.

The broadcast that Dimbleby made a few hours later was to become an unforgettable, definitive statement about human atrocity. He was the first reporter into Belsen, which was the first German concentration camp to be discovered by the British. This is what he sent back to London:

I passed through the barrier and found myself in the world of a nightmare. Dead bodies, some of them in decay, lay strewn about the road and along the rutted track. On each side of the road were brown wooden huts. There were faces at the windows, the bony emaciated faces of starving women too weak to come outside, propping themselves against the glass to see the light before they died. And they *were* dying, every hour, every minute. I *saw* a man, wandering dazedly along the road, stagger and fall. Someone else looked down at him, took him by the heels and dragged him to the side of the road to join the other bodies lying unburied there. No-one else took the slightest notice—they didn't even trouble to turn their heads. Behind the huts two youths and two girls who had found a morsel of food were sitting together in the grass in picnic fashion, sharing it. They were not six feet from a pile of decomposing bodies.

Inside the huts it was even worse. I have seen many terrible sights in the last five years, but *nothing, nothing* approaching the dreadful interior of this hut at Belsen. The dead and dying lay close together. I picked my way over corpse after corpse in the gloom, until I heard one voice that rose above the undulating moaning. I found a girl—she was a living skeleton— impossible to gauge her age, for she had practically no hair left on her head and her face was only a yellow parchment sheet with two holes in it for eyes. She was stretching out her stick of an arm and gasping something. It was 'Englisch—Englisch—medicine—medicine' and she was trying to cry, but had not enough strength. And beyond her, down the passage and in the hut, there were the convulsive movements of dying people too weak to raise themselves from the floor. They were crawling with lice and smeared with filth. They had had no food for days, for the Germans sent it into the camp en bloc and only those strong enough to come out of the huts could get it. The rest of them lay there in the shadows growing weaker and weaker. There was no-one to take the bodies when they died and I had to look hard to see who was alive and who was dead. It was the same outside, in the compounds and between the huts. Men and women lying about the ground with the rest of the procession of ghosts wandering aimlessly about them.

In the shade of some trees lay a great collection of bodies. I walked round them, trying to count—there were perhaps 150, flung down on each other. All naked, all so thin that their yellow skins glistened like stretched rubber on their bones. Some of the poor, starved creatures whose bodies were there looked so utterly unreal and inhuman that I could have imagined they had never lived. They were like polished skeletons—the skeletons that medical students like to play practical jokes with. At one end of the pile a cluster of men and women were gathered round a fire. They were using rags and old shoes taken from the bodies to keep it alight and were heating soup on it. Close by was the enclosure where five hundred children between the ages of five and twelve had been kept. They were not so hungry as the rest, for the women had sacrificed themselves to keep them alive.

Babies were born at Belsen—some of them shrunken wizened little things that could not live because their mothers could not feed them. One woman, distraught to the point of madness, flung herself at a British soldier who was on guard in the camp on the night it was reached by the 11th Armoured Division. She begged him to give her some milk for the tiny baby she held in her arms. She laid the mite on the ground, threw herself at the sentry's feet and kissed his boots. When in his distress, he asked her to get up, she put the baby in his arms and ran off crying that she would find milk for it because there was no milk in her breast. When the soldier opened the bundle of rags to look at the child he found it had been dead for days...

As we went deeper into the camp, further from the main gate we saw more and more of the horrors of the place, and I realised that what is so ghastly is not so much the individual acts of barbarism that take place in SS camps but the gradual breakdown of civilisation that happens when humans are herded like animals behind barbed wire. Here in Belsen, we were seeing people, many of them lawyers, doctors, chemists, musicians, authors, who had long since ceased to care about the conventions or the customs of normal life. There had been no privacy of any kind. Women stood naked at the side of the truck washing in cupfuls of water taken from British Army watertrucks—others squatted while they searched themselves for lice and examined each other's hair. Sufferers from dysentery leaned against the huts, straining helplessly and all around and about them was this awful drifting tide of exhausted people, neither caring nor watching. Just a few held out their withered hands to us as we passed by and blessed the doctor whom they knew had become the camp commander in the place of the brutal Kramer.

We were on our way down to the crematorium where the Germans burned alive thousands of men and women in a single fire. The furnace was in a hut, about the size of a single garage, and the hut was surrounded by a small stockade. A little Pole, whose prison number was tattooed on the inside of his forearm as it was on all the others, told me how they burned the people. They brought them into the stockade, walked them in. Then an SS guard hit them on the back of the neck with a club and stunned them. Then they were fed straight into the fire, three at a time—two men and one woman; the opening was not big enough for three men ... They burned ten thousand people in this fire in reprisal for the murder of two SS guards— and back in the hut by the main gate of the camp, I questioned the sergeant who had been in charge of one SS squad. He was a fairheaded, gangling creature, with tiny crooked ears—rather like Goebbels—and big hands. His SS uniform was undone and dirty. He was writing out his confession while a young North-country anti-tank gunner of the 11th Armoured Division kept watch on him with a tommy-gun that never moved. I asked him how many people *he* had killed. He looked vacant for a moment—and then replied 'Oh! I don't remember'.

I have set down these facts at length because in common with all of us who have been to the camp, I feel that you should be told without reserve exactly what has been happening there. Every fact I have so far given you has been verified, but there is one more awful than the others, that I have kept to end. Far away in the corner of Belsen camp there is a pit the size of a tennis court. It is fifteen feet deep and it is piled to the very top with naked bodies that have been tumbled in one on top of the other. Like this must have been the plague pits in England three hundred years ago, only nowadays we can help by digging them quicker with bulldozers and already there's a bulldozer at work in Belsen. Our Army doctors, examining some of the bodies, found in their sides a long slit, apparently made by someone with surgical knowledge. They made enquiries and established beyond doubt that in the frenzy of their starvation, the people of Belsen had taken the wasted bodies of their fellow prisoners and removed from them the only remaining flesh— the liver and kidneys—to eat.

May I add to this story only the assurance that everything that an army can do to save these men and women and children is being done and that those officers and men who have seen these things have gone back to the Second Army moved to an anger such as I have never seen in them before.

Soon after he left the camp he met Wynford Vaughan-Thomas who was shocked by his dreadful appearance: 'He was a changed man . . . I had never seen Richard so moved. Until then I had always regarded Richard as a man who would never let his feelings show through his utterly professional surface efficiency. But here was a new Dimbleby.' For the first time in his life he broke down as he began to record his despatch with the BBC's recording engineer Harvey Sarney. He told Vaughan-Thomas: 'I must tell the exact truth, every detail of it, even if people don't believe me, even if they feel these things should not be told.' Now when the recording reached London the BBC, at first unbelieving, refused to broadcast it until it had been verified by newspaper reports. In anguish and outrage, Dimbleby telephoned Broadcasting House and told the News Room that if it were not transmitted at once, he would never make another broadcast in his life. When it was broadcast (in abbreviated, but still horrifying form) the British public heard for the first time the voice of someone who had been inside a German concentration camp. Some of them never forgot it. Many years later, he would be stopped in the streets while people told him of their shock and outrage and misery when they heard his voice speaking from Belsen. A few weeks later, with the images of that horror engrained permanently on him he broadcast again for the programme 'The World Goes By', reminding his audience of what had happened and then adding this statement, his own conclusion:

> When I began this talk [about the relief operation in the camp] I was going to try and divorce sentiment and practical measure of relief. But, of course, you can't, the two go hand in hand. With water and food, there must be the grain of hope, there must be a smile and a wave—things unknown for five years at Belsen. You must spread the news that help and love are coming, and as the word goes round, you will see tired heads lifting and withered hands twitching in salute, and people weakly crying with joy. Then you know, as the 2nd Army Brigadier said, 'that the spark of life is returning'. [And, with all the passion, that it is possible to convey in a quiet voice on radio:] There is one other thing that you must do—something without which all the measures of relief and succour would be but temporary remedies—and that is to vow with all your heart that such things will *never* happen again.

From Belsen, Dimbleby went on with the Allies towards Berlin. At the beginning of July he entered the city before the first Allied troops, becoming the first Allied war correspondent to witness the devastation that the bombing had wrought. He stayed in Berlin for six weeks, sending back more than one hundred and forty despatches only six of which were not used. He broadcast from Hitler's study in the Chancellery: 'Here by the window, where Hitler sat and Hitler worked, I found his chair and I am sitting in that chair now . . . in the filth and the rubble that is found in every corner of this huge building.' In the same triumphant mood he took a ride in Admiral Doenitz's Mercedes: 'Doenitz's chauffeur told me that the Grand Admiral did not like going too fast . . . only once was the chauffeur ordered to drive flat out—when Doenitz was on his way to Fleusberg as Fuehrer.

He might have saved himself the journey . . .' From the Chancellery he retrieved a set of silver knives and forks embossed with the initials A.H., was entertained by Russian officers, and two days later was arrested by Soviet troops in the Russian sector of the city—only being released when he claimed that he was one of the Churchill family and that there would be an international incident if he were not freed at once. When Sir Winston Churchill went on a tour of the ruined city he followed close behind— and at one point (to his great delight) the Prime Minister turned to him saying: 'I seem to see you everywhere, keep thinking you're Randolph, what are you doing here?'; and from the bunker where Hitler was supposed to have spent his last hours with Frau Braun, he picked a symbolic stub of a Churchill cigar for his study shelf at home. At the formal occupation of the city by the four battalions of the 7th Armoured Division— the Desert Rats—on behalf of the British Army, he broadcast simply as the National flag was unfurled: 'The Union Jack is flying in Berlin.'

But the triumph was shortlived. Between the British entry into the city at the start of July and the Victory Parade, with Montgomery and Churchill and an array of great soldiers and politicians, at the end of the month, from which he also broadcast, Dimbleby discovered the tragedy of Berlin.

The city—that part of it which was not rubble—was in chaos: desperate shortages of food and water, the threat of mass epidemics, no communications, a dazed and demoralised people. Dimbleby was much affected by what he saw. It upset the simple balance of right and wrong, of victor and vanquished. But it was not easy to find the right tone to convey his feelings for the people of Berlin to a British audience which for the last five years had been assiduously invited to abhor not merely Hitler but the German people.

Berlin [he began his first broadcast] has had it. As a clean, solid, efficient city, it has ceased to exist. In its place is a broken-down, evil-smelling rabbit warren of craters, and hulks of buildings, and everywhere dust and dirt and squalor . . . The spirit of the people has been shattered . . . these Berliners are the first completely cowed and submissive people I've met. They've no spirit at all, only an instinctive urge to live. And that's not very easy for the Berliner today.

I'm not asking for sympathy for them but there are certain hard-and-fast conclusions we can and must draw . . . Great quantities of food and drugs are needed now before the winter, not necessarily because we have pity for these people who are slowly starving, but because if we let them get any weaker there will be epidemics of disease later in the year, and we cannot allow epidemics where we have allied troops stationed. There are already enough dead bodies . . .

The city's water supply was polluted, the hospitals lacked even basic necessities, and there was no refuse collection. If cholera or typhus were to break out, most of the population was in such a weak state that many would join the thousands still buried 'in great heaps of rubble in this city and never to be rescued'.

The citizens of Berlin who were used to travelling far from their homes to buy fresh food no longer had the energy to do so: 'the exhaustion of the journey and the wear and tear on their shoe leather—people's toes are visible everywhere, and it has been pouring with rain for ten days—these things make the trip no longer worthwhile.' Slowly he built up a picture of Berlin, pathetic in defeat. He noticed too the bizarre—the police inspector 'aged and distraught. He waved to a heap of paper and cardboard blackened and dripping in his outer office. "All my files," he said, "all my files burned black, no check on anyone now, no check." And to him the fact that the citizens of Berlin were no longer under the iron rule of the police was the ultimate disaster.' The sight of a young Jew on the steps of the Chancellery touched and astonished him. The man came up to him offering a tour of Berlin:

to see the ruins, the Reich Chancellery, Goebbel's Palace, Gestapo Headquarters . . . and as I looked at him, I thought how for ten years in this city the Nazis had been insulting him and beating him, and how for ten long years they'd deported him and tortured him and starved him and gassed him, and here he was on Hitler's doorstep in 1945 when all his persecutors were dead or captured, and I wondered how on earth he'd stayed alive.

After he had been in Berlin for some weeks he felt more able to reveal his sympathy for the people of the city.

Always keep in your minds [he told his American audience] the picture of street after street of weed-covered ruins, of smashed water-mains flowing into the heaps of rubble and keeping them dripping and slimy, of foul-smelling canals . . . Keep in your minds the image of thousands of families broken up and lost, with father in Bavaria and mother in Prussia and all the children missing, perhaps dead . . . The collapse of the economic and social structure of this European capital is nothing short of disaster for its people . . . in fairness to these conquered and beaten people I must say that they're showing now considerable courage and resource . . . The German engineers have worked hard and well, with the result that there are now 400,000 people being carried every day on the subway, and a quarter of a million by the trolley cars. There are fifty buses running packed to the roof . . . The Americans and British authorities have begun to feed the 1,650,000 people for whom they are responsible, and train loads of fats, sugar and flour are on their way in from the west and south-west of Germany . . . Allied Government is beginning to work and I think it will work well.

By now Dimbleby had developed that rare confidence which allowed him to jump from the particular to the general and back again; from the smallest detail (that the buses 'will only last three months unless more tyres are found') to the bold assertion:

From all this, the disaster, the coma, the first faint movements of life, we have a great lesson to learn. What is happening here in Berlin is happening all over Germany . . . So it is here that we can see how the German people react to our treatment of them, how they are planning for the future, and how they intend to behave . . . This city is the key to the future of Germany and if, as it comes to life again, we recognise those first traces of a desire for something better, for democracy as we know it and for individual freedom, and if we can develop those desires under our Allied control, we shall have achieved something that will rank even with the decisions of Potsdam as a contribution to the future peace and happiness of Europe and the world.

Taken sentence by sentence, Dimbleby's thoughts about

Germany were without sophistication and even naive. His emotions were not profound, though they were deeply felt. But he broadcast with such authority (more in the manner of a statesman than a reporter) and he alighted with such unerring instinct on the right tone, that he evoked a response in the listener of much greater intensity than the bare words might have deserved. Faced by the humiliation of the enemy, by Berlin in defeat, it would have been easy to get it wrong, to gloat, to dramatise, to strive for heightened effect. Richard Dimbleby's art was that he never had to think to get it right. When he wrote scripts, he did not ponder them for long hours, they flowed from his pen at great speed, and hardly ever required alteration. His responses were those of Everyman, speaking from as well as to the people. And, like Everyman, he conveyed the truths that mattered to him with much greater effect than those, who searching after greater truths, lost themselves on the way. Like Everyman too, he could be guided to insights hidden from more sophisticated minds.

It happened—with dramatic effect—while the Allies were preparing for the Potsdam Conference which was to settle the future of Europe. The talks between the British, Americans and Russians were shrouded in secrecy. Apart from the details of the culinary arrangements at Potsdam (which, a frustrated Dimbleby informed Broadcasting House, could be reported by any competent woman columnist) the Governments' spokesmen confined themselves to ritual expressions of mutual respect and affection at the start of what everyone hoped would be a new era of co-operation reaped from a lasting peace.

Into this public relations euphoria Richard Dimbleby suddenly sounded a chilling note. He chose to broadcast on 'the question of our relations with the Russians', an issue which 'isn't easy to bring up, though no-one will be an honest correspondent if he ignores it'. In the course of his broadcast, he used an image which was uncannily prescient.

We must get on good terms [he began], without co-operation and some degree of trust we can hope nothing for the future. At the moment that trust is lacking. Somewhere between us and the Russians there's a barrier of suspicion and reserve. It's rather like trying to make friends with a fellow that you can't see over the other side of a high wall.

And as if to make the point even clearer, he continued:

At present passing through the Brandenburg Gate, which marks the boundary between the British and Soviet zones of occupation in Berlin, is like crossing a frontier. There are no barriers at all, but you can sense a different atmosphere on the Eastern side. You get the feeling that while you're tolerated you're not welcome.

It was the first time that anyone had spoken in such terms. That it should have been said by a correspondent of the BBC caused consternation. Richard Dimbleby—of all people—was flatly denying the official position of all three Governments—that there was much good will and trust, and that enduring peace was around the corner. The Soviet paper *Red Star* was the first to denounce him—the 'pessimistic oracle,' of the BBC, who 'has said so many clumsy things that now, when inter-Allied administration in Berlin has been successfully organised, he himself and those who trust him are feeling quite awkward.' (In fact in a separate broadcast he had said: 'I have nothing but admiration for the way the Russians have fought . . . Nor is anyone keener than I am for lasting understanding and friendship with the Russian people. Those things we must have or there is no hope of enduring peace for the world . . .' .) The Russians were soon followed by the Americans, in the person of Major-General Parks, the U.S. Military Commander in Berlin who avowed: 'there has been no friction between British and Americans on the one side and Russians on the other—no difficulty at all.' In Britain, *The Daily Express* (of all papers) led the attack on him for his 'astonishing broadcast', and under a heading 'Eden to Tackle BBC' reported that Dimbleby's report had been put before the Foreign Secretary as a matter of urgency. In Berlin the British negotiators were furious, and arranged for the Director-General of the BBC to be informed of how unhelpful his correspondent Richard Dimbleby had been to the cause of Allied co-operation, reminding Haley that it would be 'disastrous if our efforts to build a firm foundation of Allied unity to ensure the future peace of the world were impaired by criticism in the BBC'.

It was a measure of Dimbleby's stature in the BBC that the report was broadcast at all. Now, revealing a new BBC confidence, William Haley came to Dimbleby's support: 'I cannot feel,' he informed the Foreign Office, 'that they [the reports] have

G

overstepped the mark that a sense of responsibility and public duty would dictate.' And, as a final accolade, from the man who had so nearly brought his broadcasting career to a premature end, Dimbleby received a telegram from Broadcasting House; 'Ryan sends personal compliments your splendid work—endorsed by us all stop Good man stop.' It was the first formal praise that he had been given since the outbreak of the war. He replied coolly: 'Thank you for your pleasant message, which was comforting.' Sixteen years later almost to the day, he stood by the Brandenburg Gate, pointing out the nailheads which marked the 1945 boundary between East and West. A fortnight after that the Berlin Wall was built.

He had one last pilgrimage to make before his war would come to an end. He travelled to Luneberg to witness the trial of Joseph Kramer, the Camp Commandant at Belsen. He did not go to gloat. He hated the ugliness of Europe that summer: 'the recrimination, the revenge, and judgment . . . It's necessary I know. The heads must roll, but I wish they would roll without hysterical trials, poison and stomach pumps.' At Luneberg he was reassured by the careful, measured process of conviction. It was an unreal experience. At Belsen he had felt no qualms when Joseph Kramer was locked in a refrigerator on the night of his capture. Now part of him again cried out for his immediate execution. The big, white, clean courtroom where the 'Beast of Belsen' was treated with the courtesies reserved for those presumed innocent until proved guilty, seemed to mock his anger and outrage. Yet, the tortuous but proper process of justice being immaculately completed before him had a great purpose: 'the whole world will have been able to know not in passion but in cold, proven legal detail, exactly what happens behind the frontiers of a country that surrenders its soul to a dictator'.

The flight back to London was without incident except that, as usual, he felt sick and gave up the work on the broadcast he was preparing. Then they flew up the Thames Estuary towards London, and he forgot his sickness: 'I saw one of those sights that goes straight to your heart,' he wrote, 'that you only see or understand, perhaps, once in a lifetime.' It was London, at peace for the first time in six years—a late afternoon, slanting sunlight, the docks still battered and burned, Tower Bridge still closed, and 'a thousand tiny gleaming roof-tops of a thousand brave and simple people'.

In Whitehall a few days later, he broadcast on the State Opening of Parliament, the beginning of the return to peacetime Government. Whitehall was crowded. Montgomery drove by, and Churchill, and Attlee and Ernest Bevin, and the King and Queen, and a lone unknown M.P. on a bicycle, his morning tailcoat flapping in the wet wind. That evening on the balcony of the Ministry of Health, the new Prime Minister and his Foreign Secretary had a mixed reception from a crowd which shouted and sang, while they raised their hands for silence. In the end Bevin (finding a conveniently unifying theme) yelled above the noise 'Three cheers for Victory'. And the crowd was on his side.

Richard Dimbleby watching and reporting from a perch in Whitehall thought then of the man who had been the architect of victory:

He was not a member of the Government, but he stood up in the car with his top hat firmly on his head and a big cigar in his teeth . . . The crowd smashed through the handful of police by the car and surged round it. Six mounted police in front strove to clear a way . . . I could not help thinking as I watched Churchill make his triumphant way up Whitehall, what a bitter-sweet day it must be for him, and a wonderfully illogical, British day too. Thrown out of office at the very height of his personal triumph, and now rapturously cheered by the very people who voted against him.

Later the same night he broadcast again as the people danced in the street under the yellow lamp lights of Whitehall, surrounded by the buildings which were, 'the great bulwarks of our freedom'. And as the bells of Westminster Abbey echoed up towards Trafalgar Square he reported, as always quietly passionate, 'This is the beginning of a new era in the history of the world, and those of us here should be thankful that we've been in Whitehall to see it.'

But the joy did not last long. When the crowds gathered in Piccadilly on the day of the official outbreak of peace he felt no elation: 'When I look back tonight on the horrors and the misery and the cruelty and the death that I have seen in the last six years, of the unforgettable experiences I've had and how much older and tired they've made me, I just want to go and sit in a corner and thank God it's all ending.'

On holiday at Hope Cove in Devon he relaxed. He walked on the sand, swam and took cine films of his family. The pictures, grainy and grey, still exist: his eldest son David, now aged seven, is trying to teach his naked baby brother (the author) to crawl out to sea; his wife caught smiling proudly at them, turns self-consciously away from the camera; some friends in the background, dressed in grey flannel trousers rolled up to the knees look on, amused. It was a very ordinary family holiday. They went to Salcombe and watched the first yachts begin to race again. They went to the cinema to see the *White Cliffs of Dover*, and she wept, and he denied feeling a lump in his throat. He made a speech at Victory Tea at the local Women's Institute, where the average age of the audience, two hundred strong, was only seven and where there were cakes and jam scones piled high. He kept the speech short. One evening in Hope Cove there was a fireworks display. The local people had constructed an effigy of Hitler, with a lick of mock hair and moustache. He burned fast, and so did the fireworks. They were supposed to be lit one at a time but a squib jumped into the box and they went up in twenty seconds. There were bonfires all along the coast and Richard Dimbleby felt comforted:

> I looked out over the heads of the crowd to the dark sea, and across it to the headland where the next beacon glowed hot and fiery in the night, and I thought that this was how it must have been when we saw the Spanish Armada coming, from the top of Plymouth Hoe, and again when we waited for Napoleon to come, and yet again—and how little time ago—when we waited with fire for another invader to come, with fire not to give the alram, but to burn and repel him. Now on this summer night, all round the dark coast of Britain, the fires were burning in villages and coves, not because an invader was coming, but as a bright and warm and comforting signal that no ship but a friendly ship should ever again come to the shores of this island.

It was a time for reflection and thought about the future. His upbringing had been sheltered, secure and without adventure. His school had confirmed the values which his parents held. His first jobs had been untaxing; his instinctive love of ease and order had remained unprovoked. The country had satisfied a lazy romanticism, and in London he carefully shaded his eyes from too much reality. Through his own inclination and the requirements of a timorous BBC, he never saw the misery and humiliation of the poor, the jobless and those without homes. His first experience of human suffering was in war. It had an accumulative effect. He had set off to France excited, and a little touched with glamour. He had been bored. In the Middle East he had watched the futility of desert battle. In Greece he had witnessed the desperate struggle for national survival, he had seen blood and frozen corpses. In Eritrea, he had seen men kill each other in hand-to-hand fighting to win a mountain peak. He had seen the destruction of Germany from the air, the horror of Belsen and the downfall of Berlin. In six years he had seen more human misery, courage and atrocity than most men would ever see. He had felt deeply committed to the cause for which the war was fought; the defence of values and assumptions to which he gave unquestioning allegiance: 'democracy', 'freedom' and the British 'way of life'. He had never had cause or inclination before the war to doubt or even question the merits of Britain's social and political structures, and now he had seen men die to defend the country which he loved. The shattering experience of war, which touched him probably more than he was ever aware, transformed a natural allegiance to the British system into a crusade for its preservation. He had started the war innocently accepting the values by which Britain was governed; he ended it as an apostle for the system by which they appeared to be guaranteed. Richard Dimbleby's vision (whatever its other frailties) was clear and honest. He could express it in a way which touched and spoke for a huge majority of his fellow countrymen.

By September 1945, Richard Dimbleby had been in the BBC for nine years. He had become a broadcaster of distinction, at the top of his profession, probably better known than any other war correspondent in Britain. Even Broadcasting House, which had so often regarded him with a jaundiced eye, now judged him a brilliant reporter. He was about to be rewarded for his services to broadcasting with an O.B.E. It was at this moment that the BBC chose to decide, as they had twice already, that his services to the Corporation were not indispensable. On the 30th September, after nights of worried talk with Dilys, he resigned from the BBC. He was thirty-two.

9

Down Your Way

No people are uninteresting.
Their fate is like the chronicle of planets.

YEVTUSHENKO

'I AM NOW A FREE MAN,' WROTE DIMBLEBY IN THE autumn of 1945, 'and in some ways not awfully happy about it. It's rather a wrench after nearly ten years.' He had left the Corporation reluctantly—driven out by a combination of myopia and meanness.

By September, the BBC had begun a quickmarch backwards into the cautious, unimaginative ways of the Thirties. The War Reporting Unit, which had made the BBC the envy of every other broadcasting organisation in the world, had broken up. Its reporters—men like Chester Wilmot, Stanley Maxted, Frank Gillard, Wynford Vaughan-Thomas—had drifted away to other parts of the BBC or out of broadcasting altogether.

> Now that the war is over and party politics have begun again the importance of objectivity in BBC News becomes more than ever apparent [proclaimed the BBC with ominous severity]; the objectivity of BBC News involves a most rigid and absolute avoidance of expressions of editorial opinion, combined with an equally rigid refusal to omit or bowdlerise any news that is of sober public interest.

Those austere words proclaimed a doctrine of broadcasting which was to terrorise a young, enthusiastic and energetic News Room into petrified immobility; they ushered in a decade which was to be remembered with great bitterness by nearly all those who lived through it; and they were to have a profound effect on the future of broadcasting.

When Dimbleby strode back into Broadcasting House on his return from Berlin he expected a warm welcome, and an exciting future in the BBC: 'I had hoped—because I was reasonably well known by then, to put it pretty bluntly—I had hoped they would offer me something which was interesting.' Instead he was told that either he could return to his old job in the News Room (with no increase in salary) or he could leave the microphone, and join the Corporation's bureaucratic hierarchy. It was plain to him that the BBC had made him an offer that they knew he would refuse, and eventually (as he said many years later) 'I just thought to hell with that and said "No, nothing doing".'

However, he did not know why the Corporation had forced his hand; he was not aware that in a News Department which was about to retrench into drab orthodoxy, Richard Dimbleby was a liability. According to his colleague, Frank Gillard (who would later become Managing Director of BBC Radio) Dimbleby was 'too powerful, too famous, and too popular. In short he was too big for the BBC. He was an administrative inconvenience.'

It was still conceivable, however, that he would have accepted his old job back if the BBC had been prepared to raise his salary from £1,000 a year to £1,100. But with a dismissive wave of the hand, those who administered the News Department declared that it was out of the question. Some of his colleagues remember the unsavoury glee with which some Administration officials boasted that at last Richard Dimbleby had been put in his place. It was petty and shameful behaviour, and Dimbleby, who soon heard of it, made his decision at once. It must have been particularly galling for him that the man chosen by the BBC to write and thank him officially for his services to the Corporation, was the News Division's Administrative Officer, George Allport, whom Dimbleby was sure had played a major part in securing his departure, and for whom he held a deep and long-lasting contempt. Dimbleby's resignation, wrote Allport, 'is accepted with considerable regret and I am directed to thank you very warmly for the services you have rendered to the Corporation during your period of service.' Dimbleby threw the letter away.

He had never been tempted by the vicissitudes of a freelance

career and the first few months outside the BBC seemed to confirm his doubts. He signed a not very remunerative contract to
write film scripts for Alexander Korda (but wrote nothing); he
recorded a weekly fifteen-minute news letter called 'Off the
Record' for the North American Service (which paid him a guinea
a minute); and he did a few talks for schools programmes. He
was saved from acute discomfort by his Uncle Percy who offered
him (unwillingly and only after much persuasion) the post of
Editor-in-Chief of the family newspapers (his father, Fred, had
died in 1943). Gradually there was more work: he did a weekly
book review for the Light Programme, he became one of the
question-masters of a new quiz called 'Top of the Form', and,
most important, the Home Service started to demand his regular
services for its major 'outside broadcasts'.

None of it banished financial anxiety. To bring up his family
as he would wish required a large regular income. His ideas about
family life were born out of his own upbringing; it was a duty
(not merely a desire) to provide his wife and children with
stability, security and comfort. To be a freelance satisfied no
creative or independent urge in him—it was an unfortunate
necessity. If he did not crave a steady income, he derived no
satisfaction from one that was haphazard and therefore jeopardised
his aspirations for the family. He and Dilys had bought a large
house on Barnes Common, and were expecting their third child,
Nicholas, who was born in August 1946 (Sally, their fourth would
be born the following year). In addition he was in little doubt
that he had not yet made his final contribution to the art of
broadcasting. The schools programmes and quizzes were amusing,
even taxing, but they did not begin to fulfil him. So for family
and professional reasons he wanted a programme, with a large
audience, in which he, Richard Dimbleby, was the dominating
personality. Although he never expressed himself so crudely, he
let it be known he was confident that he could 'be of some use'
(one of his favourite phrases) to a wise producer.

The first producer to recognise that his talents were underused
was the new Head of the Light Programme, Michael Standing.
BBC radio was starting a new panel game called 'Twenty Questions'. 'Money for old rope,' said Dimbleby disparagingly. A
week later the BBC phoned him. Would he like to take over the
programme? He accepted at once. A few weeks later he was given
a new programme to be called 'Down Your Way'. The two

programmes gave him a guaranteed weekly income of £35—already twice as much as he earned as a member of the BBC staff.

The two programmes were typical products of the post-war BBC. The new Light Programme (which had replaced the Forces Programme) had many hours of silent airtime to fill. The demand for new—and cheap—programmes was insatiable. The audience was huge and uncritical. Within a few months Twenty Questions, with an audience which rarely fell below 15 million, was the most popular programme on radio. Down Your Way had a devoted following of at least ten million people.

The idea for Twenty Questions had been borrowed from American radio where it proved highly successful, though its origins (appropriately in a BBC which was fast consolidating what would later become known as its 'Auntie' image) lay deep in the Victorian drawing rooms of the British upper classes. Its resurrection by the BBC was greeted with uncritical acclaim. The team of Richard Dimbleby, Daphne Padel (though she was soon replaced by Joy Adamson), Jack Train and Anona Winn, with Stewart MacPherson in the Chair, and Norman Hackforth as the Mystery Voice, soon became famous radio 'personalities'. Critics chose to regard the programme as the rightful successor to ITMA, which had been brought to an untimely end by the death of Tommy Handley. Newspapers and magazines devoted thousands of words to the particular and differing skills of each panellist. Hard-pressed producers spent much time denying that the programme was rigged; that question-master and team were in league to provide faked drama; that Anona Winn (who talked much more than the others) did not know the answers in advance. 'I pledge my plighted troth,' explained one harassed producer falling over himself to put the record straight 'that everything about this programme is perfectly genuine.' When the panellists scored their first outright victory over Stewart MacPherson, it was considered to be an event of enough moment to find its way into prominence on the news pages of nearly every popular newspaper in Fleet Street. When Dimbleby once failed to turn up for a recording session, he had to give a public apology, and the BBC award him public forgiveness. People queued outside the BBC's theatre in Shepherd's Bush to watch the programme. Autograph hunters waited in small crowds to capture a Twenty Questions signature.

In a major feature devoted to the programme, *Picture Post* observed: 'Some say the British are an unserious people. Some say we would play games while the world burns. So while statesmen snarl and economists break their heads, half the country is wondering whether the problem is Animal, Vegetable or Mineral.'

In *The Spectator* Harold Nicolson devoted a whole page to an analysis of the programme's success, in which he managed to invoke the names of Herbert Spencer, Bergsen, and Hobbes to illuminate his argument. Twenty Questions, he avowed, was not (as the BBC described it) a 'parlour game' at all. 'No parlour game I have ever known contains a stage complete with actresses and journalists, or a numerous audience, who follow the proceedings with loud clappings and exhortations such as in old days echoed across the circus at Byzantium.' Its panellists were alert and erudite, the question-master had compelling charm, the Mystery Voice was a masterly blend 'of the surruptitious and the trustworthy, of the sinister and the confiding, of the mystic and the humane'. It was a moment of high excitement for an audience which inevitably sides with the 'underdog' panellists, when a few minutes before the end of the programme it was still unclear which side would win. Then there was the 'element of incongruity'—when

> We have a simultaneous perception of the thing as we, being in on the secret, know it to be, and of the successive unrealities in which the platform indulge. So when the object is the Forth Bridge, the question 'Can you put it in your pocket?' makes us laugh. Even beyond that, there was the moment of 'sudden glory' when possessing certainty ourselves we observe others floundering in the marshes of conjecture.

Even if Harold Nicolson wrote a little with tongue in cheek, he was, like the readers of *Picture Post*, a devoted listener. With his customary elegance he had dissected the mechanics of the programme but that alone could not explain its huge popular appeal at that moment, or why it entered so lastingly into the national psyche.

The British people were tired, drably readjusting to a future where the Churchillian rhetoric of war had yielded to the prosaic reality of ration cards and coupons. Instead of the peacetime plenty the people had been led to expect, they found themselves gripped by an age of austerity. By 1948, rations were tighter than in the war. It was a world of queues and shortages. There was no chocolate, little meat or butter; even worse, the Government once even ran out of dried eggs. There were bread famines and fuel crises. The British scraped and pinched; and darned thread-bare utility clothes. Their baths were never full and rarely hot. A shortage of soap permitted shiny faces and ensured grubby clothes. Yet if there was discontent, there was no rebellion. The new Labour Government, which had been voted into office on the rebound, had not yet been seen to betray the social revolution its campaign promises had implied. Aneurin Bevan was master-minding the beginnings of the Welfare State, there were great schemes to end squalor in the slums and provide homes for all. When the British raised their eyes beyond the coupon embers in the grate and a diminishing pile of ration books on the kitchen table towards the world beyond, they saw, not the promise of eternal peace, or the power and the glory which Britain had shown in war, but the chill of the approaching cold war and the start of the arms race but they did not complain.

Into this drab uncertainty, the BBC beamed a message of universal goodwill, reassurance and comfort. Twenty Questions was family entertainment, in which all, high and low, could share. Its humour was innocent (if limited), remorselessly cheerful, and cosily embracing. It crackled from clumsy Bakelite radios into drawing room and kitchen alike—where most were imprisoned by petrol rationing—persuading its listeners over their un-sweetened coffee that while it was still possible to play harmless family games, all was not lost.

Down Your Way flourished in the same fertile soil. Like Twenty Questions it was to survive for more than a quarter of a century, into an age when it could come to seem as out of place as a maiden aunt in a discotheque. By its last days it had become suffocatingly jocular, patronising, and remorselessly bland, and it was hard to imagine the part it had played in the British Sunday afternoon twenty-five years earlier.

Down Your Way's origins were humble. The Musicians' Union had imposed stringent limitations on 'needle time'. With so many hours to fill and so little music to fill them, the Light Programme hit on the idea of stretching music programmes by filling the gaps between the songs with words so that in any one hour of air time, only half an hour of precious 'needle time' would be used up. Down Your Way was the product of this imaginative policy.

The first Down Your Way had been introduced by Stewart MacPherson. When he returned to Canada, his place was taken by Lionel Gamlin, who was not a success. It then came to Dimbleby. At once he set about changing it from a record programme with interviews, into an interview programme with records. In the process he consolidated his reputation and ensured his fame. With the benefit of astringent hindsight it is not hard to lay similar charges against the Down Your Way of 1947 to those which convicted its successor of twenty-five years later. It too was bland and unadventurous (though it was never jocular or patronising). It too asked superficial questions of solid citizens; sedulously avoided any matter of political, social or economic moment; turned aside from controversy as if, in the words of one of its producers, 'it was the plague'. Week after week, year in, year out, it portrayed a country in which suffering and oppression were absent; in which all men were wrapped in a blanket of snug goodwill. Journalistically, if it was not a lie, it was a half truth.

But to criticise it in that vein is to miss the point. Like Twenty Questions, Down Your Way belonged to the Forties. Each week throughout the year, ten million fervent followers stayed indoors on Sunday afternoon to hear Richard Dimbleby— take them Down Your Way all over Britain. There can be no better illustration of the decline of the BBC after the war than the fact that Down Your Way was the only regular programme on the radio to make use of the techniques that Dimbleby had pioneered in the Thirties and which had been developed with such style and authority in War Report. Once Dimbleby had ensured that the interviews were to matter more than the music, Down Your Way was the nearest the BBC came to providing a radio magazine current affairs programme. It was not, of course, current affairs. It set itself a modest target: to paint a weekly word portrait of a city, town, or village of Britain through the voice of its inhabitants. At the time Richard Dimbleby and his producer, John Shuter, regarded themselves as pioneers in radio. When they arrived in town it was a public occasion. The local paper would splash the front page with the news; Richard Dimbleby would be fêted at civic lunches and in works canteens; and in private houses housewives would give up valuable coupons to press on him a piece of steak. Frequently the police would close off streets to traffic to give the recording engineers the silence their craft has always sought. Local reporters would be sent to interview Dimbleby, and to follow him through the day. Afterwards the local press would record the town's reactions to the programme: 'Mixed Reception for Down Your Way; Flawless Production; Omissions Cause Controversy.' They would quote at length the interviews, and list the record choices each participant had made. Since elsewhere in the BBC the unscripted, unrehearsed interview was almost unknown, Down Your Way seemed charged with vitality. Nowhere else on radio was the voice of 'the man in the street' regularly heard at some length (each interview lasted three minutes): to hear different accents talking about different jobs in different parts of the country was obsessively fascinating. Within a few months the programme became a broadcasting institution. More than ten years after Dimbleby had given it up, listeners would still write to him at Down Your Way, and his poor successor, Franklin Engelmann, had to suffer the indignity (which he bore with typical generosity) of being asked by local journalists 'What time does Richard Dimbleby arrive?'

In six years, Dimbleby, missed only two programmes (and it ran for fifty-two weeks a year); he had interviewed three thousand people and heard three thousand record requests; he had been to three hundred towns in every nook and cranny of the British Isles. He loved the travelling, though he often affected to be exhausted by it (not least when he was demanding that his fee for each week's programme should be raised from £20). He never lost the romantic thrill that gives an edge to every journey. If he went by car, setting off in the early morning, he was a character out of Buchan, driving fast along empty roads to an unknown destination; by air (even when he was scared) he was joining an élite who were not pinned down by humdrum nine-to-five lives; by rail—usually on a first-class sleeper across the country—he was setting out aboard a British Orient Express, on which the steward, who always knew him, would, to his lasting satisfaction always bring him a late-night Ovaltine and an early-morning tea. He took a childlike pleasure in memorising the departure times of all the main line trains out of London. He knew their routes and their destinations. On a quiet evening he would suddenly go to his study to look up his Cooks to see 'where we would be now if we were on the Rome Express'. When friends or family went on holiday, he would sit for hours surrounded by timetables pondering the quickest or the most beautiful or the cheapest route to their destination. If a member of the family was away (he was adept at sending his mother to South America by banana boat, even when she was in her late seventies) he would pin maps to the wall to chart their journey across the world.

Dimbleby delighted in Down Your Way. He wrote:

> On every Wednesday of every week, all the year round (and for three years or more, solid so far) I have to go to a different town or village in Great Britain to interrogate ten citizens on whom I have never set eyes before . . . I have met and talked to not less than 5,000 different men, women and children and interviewed 1,700 of them at the microphone. Whether that's a broadcasting record for a non-stop programme I'm not sure, though I rather think it is . . .

He never got bored. Those who saw him with strangers never doubted:

> I'm intensely interested in people and their ways of life. If I am watching a pretty girl operating an oily machine I *want* to know how she gets her hands clean and white when she goes out at the end of the day. When I see a woman packing goods at flying speeds, I am curious to know if she is quick and deft when she works in the home, or whether she learns speed and dexterity in the operation only by constant repetition . . . I can [on Down Your Way] indulge my curiosity . . . For example, I know why a signalman always looks out of the cabin window as a train goes by, what a 'fluffer' and a 'flapper' are, how they lift the bascules of Tower Bridge, how a golf ball is made, what makes a kipper golden brown, what a bus conductor does if he runs out of change, how a girl is sworn into the WRAC, how a criminal is executed, who does it and how long it takes, how rennet is made, and how the letters are put into a stick of rock . . .

He was curious about details with a child's pertinacity, never satisfied until he had a complete answer. Once he knew he never forgot, and loved to display his store of knowledge to those who expected his concerns to dwell on higher matters. There was nothing false about his interest either in the jobs or the people who did them. It was not unusual for people to approach him, long after he had left the programme, rather timidly in restaurant, shop or street with the words: 'You won't remember me Mr. Dimbleby but I'm . . .'—to be stopped by him, carefully scrutinised in silence, and finally answered: 'Now let me see, yes, you come from Grantham . . . and didn't you work in the bakery where they make the stone ground loaves . . . and your name is . . . let me see [he enjoyed extracting the maximum from the encounter] yes . . . Tom Smith.' And in yet another British household his name would become hallowed.

The microphone was still a rare sight. The mobile recording van was rarer. It was still widely regarded as an intrusion into privacy to push a microphone into someone's face and expect him to speak into it. Stagefright was common. Dimbleby approached each interview like a surgical operation. He wrote in the *Radio Times*:

> We are sometimes, though rarely, accused of staging the whole thing and working from a prepared script [as nearly every other branch of radio did]. There is no script of any kind, nor any rehearsal. My experience has always been that interviews are much better when they are impromptu. What happens is that Shuter . . . [the producer] chooses the ten men and women to be interviewed and, of course, calls on them to ask their co-operation. He does not discuss with them what they should say. When I arrive the following morning I go with him from one house or factory to another, meet each person, have five minutes' talk with them privately [during which time, very often, the actual broadcast is not mentioned] and then proceed immediately with the interview, using a microphone which is produced at the psychological moment.

Since Dimbleby was virtually the only BBC interviewer his views on the new craft were constantly solicited. Inside the BBC it was still a matter for wonder that 'they' should have anything to say. Outside the Corporation the 'impromptu' interview became an issue for public discussion.

> I am often asked [wrote Dimbleby] whether it is difficult to interview people for broadcasting and 'how do you make them

talk?' Of course it's difficult—by far the most ticklish form of broadcasting—but there's no such thing as *making* a person talk. You can encourage, cajole, lure, egg on, even trap, but you can't make a person talk who doesn't want to.

In 1947, it was not thought that the interview had any intrinsic merit or purpose. It was necessary, according to Dimbleby, because most people '*cannot* make a small speech, particularly in the friendly, informal manner so essential to broadcasting'. The job of the interviewer was to ease the way for the would-be broadcaster. The interview was not yet a means of extracting painful or revealing information; it did not test or challenge ideas, beliefs, attitudes, and assumptions. The interviewer had not yet become an unofficial tribune of the people, or prosecuting counsel, or chat-show host. His job was to discover some very simple facts: if he did more than that, it was chance, not design. It was not thought proper to enquire (even gently) into private lives, or social problems; to ask about money, or industrial relations, or politics. But the qualities Dimbleby identified as necessary to the good interviewer were timeless. He should be quick-thinking, curious, and sympathetic not only towards those who were in trouble but the person 'who suffers no obvious handicaps, but who leads a humdrum life with no material prospects. An understanding of other people's worries and problems—you cannot cultivate this, it must be there . . .'

Dimbleby took a great pride in his ability to complete an interview within the three minutes. The possibility of talking to someone for much more than his allotted three minutes and then editing the interview down to the time required did not occur to him or his producer; if suggested it would almost certainly have been regarded as unprofessional and of dubious morality. Dimbleby's conception of the interview gave him a distinctly limited role. But at the time he was breaking new ground simply by recording 'impromptu': for him and millions of listeners, it was enough to hear the people speak.

In the late Forties too, the subjects of Down Your Way had a special (if temporary) charm. When ten million people sat down every Sunday afternoon to listen to other people talk about their job, or their hobby, or their family, or their town, it was not an abrasive analysis of rural or urban life that they wanted, but the comfort of discovering that all over England people like them, in other towns and other villages, shared their hopes and interests, and overcame problems and anxieties with a similar commonsense and phlegmatic optimism. As the programme's guide Richard Dimbleby soon became a beloved figure with a huge fan-mail. If anyone were to suggest that the subject matter of Down Your Way was trivial, he was incensed: 'Not a bit of it. Add all these things together, and a thousand more as well, and you have the very pattern of our life in this island . . . it all adds up to something that I cannot define. Is it pride, admiration, wonder, satisfaction? I don't know but it's a good feeling.'

With the success of Down Your Way and Twenty Questions, Richard Dimbleby was now a national celebrity, a winner of radio awards; but at the end of 1952, after much heart-searching, he gave up Down Your Way, arguing in a letter to Kenneth Adam that although it was still unusually popular: 'it seems to me to be better to take it off while people still like it,' explaining:

From my own point of view, taking off Down Your Way will mean the loss of valuable provincial publicity and a closer contact with the public that no other programme has ever given me. Down Your Way seems to have something about it that endears it to people and wherever I go in Great Britain I am hailed with cries of 'Hullo . . . Down Our Way today?' For this I am grateful, of course, and I like to think that the programme and I have come to be thought of as one and the same thing . . .

But he had now travelled at least 150,000 miles for the programme:

I know every sleeping car conductor in the land, nearly all the main railway timetables, guards and ticket inspectors, all the good and bad hotels, the roads and internal airways, and I am beginning to find them all rather exhausting. The strain of regular journeys, week in, week out, has been pretty heavy, and I feel I simply must have a rest.

There was a more pressing reason which he did not mention: the Coronation of Her Majesty Queen Elizabeth II was only six months away. It was to be a turning point in the history of broadcasting: almost overnight, television was to supersede radio as the main means of mass communication. It was a prospect which Dimbleby had relished for a long time, having already established himself as the BBC's best-known television and radio personality in the years since the war.

Television had flickered unobtrusively into a few London drawing rooms for the first time a month after Richard Dimbleby joined the BBC in 1936. The new service had immediately enthralled him. When most broadcasters thought the new medium an amusing irrelevance, Dimbleby was convinced that it would replace radio. At least fifteen years before the BBC began to take television seriously he had submitted a plan for the 'televising of news and current events' to the pre-war Controller of Television, Gerald Cock. He had been thrilled to cover (for television as well as sound) the return of Chamberlain from Munich when 'viewers were among the first to see him holding aloft the fluttering piece of paper (the writing was visible) being his own signature and that of Hitler'. He had been gratified when the *News Chronicle* noted that the BBC's 'F. R. Dimbleby [was] as good a commentator as any at Broadcasting House'. And when television started again in 1946 (it had been closed down for the war) he was determined to be in it from the beginning.

He had heard that the opening of the service was to coincide with Victory Day, on June 8th 1946. At once he wrote, in typically breezy fashion, to the new Head of Television, Maurice Gorham. 'Have you a vacancy for a commentator on Victory Day?... You'll know that I've done a good many commentary jobs for sound O.B.'s and I think I understand the different technique for your medium.' Impressed at least by Dimbleby's assurance, Gorham appointed him number two to Freddy Grisewood who was to be the senior commentator for the Parade. 'I think it should be made clear to Dimbleby,' noted the Manager of Television Outside Broadcasts, Ian Orr-Ewing, 'that Grisewood would have to be responsible for leading, and stopping any tendency of Dimbleby's to lapse into "sound" commentary.'

The re-opening of television was a moment for intense public curiosity. Few people had seen it before the war, and every memory was hazy. No-one was quite certain what it could do, or what should be done with it. There was however an almost universal assumption that, intrinsically, it was a frivolous medium.

When the BBC introduced its new Head of Television to the public, it tried rather dismally to set the light-hearted tone that was presumably thought appropriate for the medium:

He works in his shirt-sleeves at the BBC and his scanty leisure is spent studying that characteristic English Institution, the public house. His only published book to date is entitled *The Local*. Mr. Gorham is a boxing fan, an amateur criminologist and has walked from London to Brighton.

If TV was to be jolly, then the poor Mr. Gorham would have to be too.

Yet the first major test of television was to show that the medium was potentially much more powerful than most in the BBC wished it to be. The Victory Parade, on the first full day of post-war television, was greeted in ecstatic terms by the entire press.

If this column is a trifle incoherent [wrote Jonah Barrington in the *News Chronicle*] forgive me for I have just witnessed an outstanding and historic BBC triumph—the televising of the Victory Parade in its entirety—and the thrill is still upon me. I saw it in a darkened private drawing room, together with some twenty other enthralled viewers, in Guildford, 35 miles from London . . . and I saw it, I swear, better than many people in the Mall. On a steady brightly-lit screen, ten-and-a-half by eight-and-a-half inches wide, we twenty viewers, without craning our necks could rubber-neck for whole minutes on end the famous personages who crowded the saluting base.

Even *The Times* was moved to a semblance of excitement.

Some of those who had grandstand views of the procession in the Mall were not in London at all [began its report], they sat at home with the blinds down and saw it all by television. Privileged even beyond prime ministers, they had no waiting. At ten to eleven, just as the Royal carriage drew up before the saluting base, the magic eye opened . . . With the band playing and the crowd cheering . . . it was like being there: this was the real thing. The small silvery screen became in effect a window on the Mall.

The Times thought that Dimbleby and Grisewood had performed 'excellently' but (like the *News Chronicle*) added the mild
reproof that 'having at last its own window on the world, one
eye went ahead of the commentary. "Oh! there are the Duchess
of Kent and Princess Alexandra" said the people at home, and
then noticed complacently a few minutes later that either Mr.
Grisewood or Mr. Dimbleby was still wondering who they could
be . . .' Dimbleby himself was aware of the shortcomings:

> How we fumbled and groped after the right technique [he
> wrote later] I had to unlearn most of what I knew from pre-war
> and war-time experience. The commentator in sound radio
> must create almost the entire picture for his 'blind' listener;
> and at first we tended to deliver sound-style commentaries on
> TV, doubling up on the picture and talking a great deal too
> much. [He found the Victory Parade so fascinating—his pro-
> gramme, 40 pages long, is covered with detailed notes—that]
> for the first few minutes I fought a furious battle with time,
> striving to get in a description of the units as they passed our
> cameras . . . suddenly I realised what I should have grasped
> before—that viewers can see it all for themselves. All they
> needed were facts that were not self-evident, dropped in at the
> psychological moment . . . At the end of this massive outside
> broadcast, feeling like a squeezed orange and quite exhausted,
> I realised that I had found the right technique. The com-
> mentator was no more; in television he was the *annotator*, the
> man who puts helpful notes in the margin. Thenceforth on all
> great occasions I tried to fulfil this role . . .

So few broadcasters or producers were excited by television
that Alexandra Palace (the headquarters of the service) resembled
one of those exclusive clubs whose members talk with fervent
enthusiasm in incomprehensible terms about their shared obsession. Everyone knew everyone else; every new programme
was an experiment; there were some disasters (which never
mattered) and a few triumphs. All those who were in television
in the Forties look back on those days with the nostalgia of
pioneers who have lived to see their discoveries and conquests,
which were then so momentous, disappear into the footnotes of
history.

The excitement at Alexandra Palace was shared, not by Broadcasting House (where 'radiomen' frowned in disapproving dismay) but by the public. As television aerials began to sprout further and further from London (by 1953, there were two million licence holders) the new 'lookers-in' were besieged by a fanfare of publicity about the new medium. 'Welcome Stranger' shouted the northern edition of the *News Chronicle* (in 1951). 'Tonight thousands of Northerners will turn the knobs of their shiny new television sets at 8.00 p.m. and focus into view their first peep of television.' Richard Dimbleby, Sylvia Peters, Macdonald Hobley, Mary Malcolm and Joan Gilbert, became overnight celebrities, the strangers 'who will be part of the family circle this winter'. 'The principal family gift in many York homes this Christmas,' reported the *Evening Press*, 'will be a television receiver . . . In several thousand British homes the first person to cross the threshold will be Richard Dimbleby. . .' When the new transmitter reached Newcastle in April 1953, the *Sunday Sun* summoned the new 'viewers' ('looker-in' was quickly discarded) to

> take stock of the family you're joining and get into the picture on your programmes . . . when the bread-winner returns home it's almost time to switch on for the evening's viewing. During the honeymoon period you will probably find yourself regulating your meal time to suit TV. Later there'll be programmes not to be missed.

Merely to have your face on the screen regularly was to be a 'celebrity'; the most popular stars were, therefore, the announcers. Dimbleby shared their status in the public mind (at first to his intense surprise) not for his commentaries but for a programme called 'London Town'. Now long forgotten and unlamented, London Town was one of those experiments conjured up one enthusiastic evening at Alexandra Palace. In 1949 when it first appeared, it was hailed as a miracle of television invention. Technically, it was one of the most complicated programmes that television has ever devised. Editorially it was unpretentious—a kind of television Down Your Way without the music—but it was the first magazine programme of what was to become a famous type. Tonight and Nationwide had their origins in the programme devised by Stephen McCormack and Richard Dimbleby at Alexandra Palace. London Town was the first magazine programme to use a mixture of film and studio; to interview ordinary men and women without scripts; to be presented by a 'reporter'; to inform as well as entertain; to have any journalistic pretensions.

'Good evening to you all and welcome to London Town' were Dimbleby's opening words, each month. A typical programme (on June 2nd 1950) promised

> a visit behind the scenes of a newspaper, to see tomorrow's issue being prepared; we shall take a stroll in St. James's Park; drop in on some diamond merchants; pay a visit to a place which has been a nerve centre of London's defence for hundreds of years, and still is; and in case you haven't been able to get to Kenwood House, which was re-opened this month, we shall take a glimpse inside. But before all that, the other day . . .

—at which point the producer 'mixed' to a film of Dimbleby walking in the Strand and the programme began.

The ambition of both McCormack and Dimbleby was to fill most of the programme with 'on the spot' interviews. But since the Features Department had no mobile sound camera, it was an urge they could not fulfil. Instead they set about the creation of an elaborate illusion whereby the viewer would be led to believe that the interview was being conducted on film when in reality it was taking place 'live' in the studio. So, in this case, as Dimbleby walked (on film) along the Strand, and then turned down an alley towards the Embankment he would give a commentary: 'From the endless traffic of the Strand bustling around St. Clement's Church, I turned out of the Strand into this quiet backwater.' At which point the recording engineer rapidly turned down the volume of his 'traffic noise' sound effects. The film then cut to Dimbleby entering a little doorway and climbing into a Roman Bath, and approaching the Bath attendant. At that moment, the producer 'mixed' back into the studio, where a near perfect replica of a corner of a Roman Bath had been constructed, and the interview, with both men in the studio, began. The viewer was led to believe—and all but the initiated were fooled—that Dimbleby was still in the Bath. At the end of the elaborately rehearsed interview, on a cue from Dimbleby, Steve McCormack mixed back to film of the outside of the Roman Bath, while Dimbleby, from the bowels of Alexandra Palace, completed the illusion with the words: 'But just imagine, as we're talking here so quietly, the traffic roars past in the Strand'. At which point

Dimbleby hurried across the studio to introduce the next item. 'You crossed the street; went into a building, walked along a corridor; through a door; into a room; sat down and chatted with another man. Then you retraced your steps,' wrote one perplexed viewer, 'the sequence was completely unbroken and I wondered how on earth it was done.' As McCormack mixed from film to studio, Dimbleby would stand on the set marking time so that as the film gave way to 'actuality' he could walk across the stage in perfect time with his 'film' self.

It was a cumbersome and complex formula. The programme needed twelve different studio sets (the detailed instructions for which filled twelve closely typed foolscap pages). Dimbleby had eighteen studio 'links' which he had to remember or 'ad lib' (since he had no 'teleprompter') and time perfectly since they led into film sequences for which he had to give a ten second cue (usually by rubbing his hands lightly down the side of his nose); he had to deliver sixteen snippets of 'live' commentary over film; he conducted ten interviews; and he had to memorise twenty-five important moves across the studio, in and out of different sets. The details of the complete forty-five-minute programme had to be firmly in his head: if he made a mistake 'on the night' there would be chaos. As it was, according to Stephen McCormack (with whom he had an almost telepathic relationship—which was fortunate since no other was possible) he never made a mistake. It was in London Town that he earned for the first time the reputation of unflappable infallibility. Other performers marvelled at his skill; other producers coveted his services.

Richard Dimbleby was fond of saying that he had 'a constitution like an ox': his appetite for work was insatiable. By the early Fifties he was on radio or television every night of the week. His diary for one typical week in 1952 gives some indication of the schedule he set himself:

MONDAY   *AM*   Filming London Town at Chiswick Bus Works. Driving on skid pan.

                PM   Filming London Town, House of Commons. Sits in PM's chair. Feels like Churchill. Then to Albany Club—three 'future ideas' meetings. Then theatre [with Dilys] and home to Sussex [where they had bought Danley farm], arriving 1.00 a.m.

TUESDAY   AM   To *Richmond and Twickenham Times* Office.
Meetings/discussion—advertising policy,
readers' letters, new plant; writes leader on
Richmond as tourist resort; hires new
reporter. Then to London. Lunch with
Laurence Pollinger, literary agent, pressing
for new novel.

PM   Returns Richmond. Approves page proofs
for *Thames Valley Times*. The King's Cross
7.00 p.m. train for Aberdeen. Dinner on
train. Then bed with Friday's London
Town script to learn.

WEDNESDAY AM   Meets Down Your Way producer John
Shuter. Breakfast in Caledonian Hotel.
Begins interviews: trawler-skipper, har-
bour master, stone quarrier, housewife,
Lord Provost.

PM   Continues Down Your Way interviews.
6.20 Aberdonian to Kings Cross. London
Town script again.

THURSDAY AM   Breakfast National Liberal Club. Two
London Town rehearsals. Different locations. Then to Richmond.

PM   Newspaper meetings. Discussion with local
Mayor. Letters. Then to London Editing
session London Town. Ends 7.45 p.m. Taxi
to Paris Cinema, Lower Regent Street, for
Twenty Questions. Afterwards to Jermyn
Street Turkish Baths. Sleeps all night in
cubicle.

FRIDAY   AM   Early interview at club with woman's
magazine. Richmond 10.00 a.m. over-
seeing tomorrow's paper. Then to
Alexandra Palace, London Town rehearsal.

PM   Rehearsal. Timing, script-reciting in dressing room; more rehearsal, marking
positions on studio floor, trying out movement with cameras, checking films again,
fiddling with the script, getting a suit
pressed by 'wardrobe', arranging make-up.
Phones Richmond, checking all well with

paper. Gives interview to journalist 'trailing' him for day. 9.30 on air. 10.15 Red Light out, perspiration, exhaustion. Phone rings. When able to shoot sound-film for National Children's Homes? Arrives home 1.20 a.m.

SATURDAY AM Domestic conference. Costs, income tax, no solution. Shopping.

PM Family visit to Frensham Ponds. Then to local farm to see animals. Then home to letters (twelve invitations to open functions, address meetings, etc.). Three articles to write. The first to be in post tomorrow.

Colleagues wondered at his stamina and enthusiasm. But it was not merely an appetite for action, nor was it merely a deeply engrained protestant ethic (though that played its part); he had a powerful ambition, not merely to succeed, but to do more and be better than anyone else. Although he had much greater modesty than many lesser talents, he was not unaware of his growing pre-eminence in radio and television. No-one else worked with success in both media, and no-one else ranged across the spectrum from Twenty Questions to London Town to the State Visit of President Aureole of France. He was now the 'first choice' for all kinds of different programmes in radio and television. He guarded his pre-eminence with some jealousy (though later he took immense pains to help younger colleagues and junior rivals). In 1949, in a letter to Arthur Phillips (who occasionally produced Down Your Way) he added a note praising a commentary by Wynford Vaughan-Thomas but adding (with heavy joviality), 'I hope you'll remember that I normally do these things!'

When Stewart MacPherson left Twenty Questions, the question of his successor as Chairman became a gossip-columnist's delight. For a time Dimbleby took the Chair, which he much enjoyed. The BBC, however, wanted him back on the panel. To Dimbleby it seemed that he had been found wanting, and his pride being wounded, he imagined that his reputation had been damaged. Michael Standing, a master of tact, hastened to soothe him:

Nobody has any complaint to make about you or your

performance...very much the reverse, but you have made it
difficult to choose you for the simple reason that you have
become indispensible to the team...without you the team
seemed to lack body—I mean intellectually rather than
physically... I hope that you will now appreciate that we
intend to you anything but 'a very passed-over appearance'.

Dimbleby had a childlike susceptibility, acutely sensitive to
apparent slight, instantly mollified by gentle praise—though it was
a point of honour with him always to disguise such human
frailty, a public demonstration of which in others, he much
despised. However, his reply to Standing would have deceived
no-one.

> I hope you won't think I was being pernickety about this
> business...[he wrote to Standing] but you know how easily the
> public can get the wrong impression. I have discovered in my
> travels around the country with Down Your Way that people
> feel Twenty Questions very closely and take an extraordinarily
> personal interest in each one of us. For the reason I am most
> anxious that they shouldn't start gossiping about the choice of
> the new question-master.
>
> I wonder if it might be possible, when any announcement is
> made, for a note to appear in the gossip columns of the Radio
> Times hinting that you want to preserve the team intact?

The mild attacks of self-esteem which occasionally afflicted
Richard Dimbleby at this time were frequently prompted by a not
quite acrimonious correspondence with the BBC over his fees.
From the start he was convinced—with some justification—that
the BBC was not paying him enough. At first he accepted it,
but as demand for his services grew, he became—with genuine
reluctance—more aggressive. He hated the discussion of money,
finding it embarrassing and vulgar—but he knew his worth.
Resenting the BBC's tendency to regard him for financial purposes as a walk-on extra but having little taste for confrontation,
he at first attempted to shame the BBC into sharing his own
evaluation of his worth. However, the BBC being brazen in
such matters, his success was limited. He adopted a sterner line,
accompanying his demands for higher fees with a less than modest,
but not overly exaggerated account of his contribution to broadcasting.

In the case of Down Your Way he told the BBC:

The plain fact is that I do not receive, I feel, an adequate reward for the tremendous amount of work that goes into the programme... I have to be a kind of BBC ambassador in nearly one hundred and fifty cities, towns and villages of the United Kingdom... I attribute to the popularity of Down Your Way the fact that I was only .01 behind MacPherson for top place in one branch of the National Radio Award. I wonder if you can perhaps put the thing on more realistic basis. I do not want to state a higher fee and then haggle over it—I always hate that—but I do feel that a front-rank national programme, which is, frankly, held together and put over by only *one* paid artist, does merit a better reward after three years.

As a last resort (to which he retreated frequently) he simply refused the fee—which caused consternation in the Contracts Department, which was forbidden to accept unpaid contributions. 'I am returning the enclosed contract... as I am anxious—for the sake of professional standards—to adhere to the understanding that my minimum fee is five guineas... It's not the money in this case, rather the principal,' he explained on one occasion. On another:

I really cannot accept a fee of ten guineas... that is the bare minimum that the BBC would have to pay if they were asking a novice would-be broadcaster to try his hand for the first time... One can scarcely measure these things by the number of words spoken... if the BBC is unable to increase it, I will do the broadcast for nothing—at least as a demonstration of goodwill!—but *not* for ten guineas.

Occasionally producers—who were forbidden to negotiate fees—came to his rescue.

There is no question that Dimbleby is entitled to be regarded as a first-class commentator for fee assessment purposes [one of the luminaries from the Contracts Department had written] at the same time he is inclined to be rather grasping over fees. But I am glad to say that for two forthcoming broadcasts he has accepted the fifteen guineas and eighteen guineas... in lieu of twenty guineas.

His pleasure was shortlived. The two programmes in question were Outside Broadcasts from the Cenotaph Service and British Legion Festival. The Head of Outside Broadcasts, S. J. de Lotbinière, reacted sharply, 'I would not have suggested twenty guineas for these two jobs had I not thought it the right fee. They are both royal occasions of considerable importance...' And Dimbleby got the full fee.

Dimbleby's sense of grievance against the BBC for what he called 'its quite unreasonable parsimony' was given edge by his now publicly recognised pre-eminence in broadcasting. By 1952 he was taking part in more than two hundred programmes each year; he had been voted Radio Personality of the Year once and runner-up—twice; and in the National Television Awards he had been elected personality of the year three times in succession. So ubiquitous was his presence, so popular his programmes, that Dimbleby was in danger of becoming a public hero. Unlikely as it may now seem, when television is aged and battered, and its performers are in their proper place, he was treated to a deluge of public acclaim which would normally have been reserved for a much-loved statesman, monarch or film star. It became impossible for him to walk freely in the streets, to go on a bus, or travel in the tube. He had become a piece of public property to be smiled at, stopped, spoken to, and touched. If he stood still in public, a crowd would gather to stare; if he walked through a crowd, people would pull his sleeve—'just touching you for luck, sir! that's all'. At first he found it disconcerting and embarrassing. In one Northern town, where television had newly arrived, a woman stopped him and said: 'Mr. Dimbleby, do you mind, I just want to say that I have touched your coat.' Others sought autographs or to shake his hand. He smiled uncertainly, and did as he was bid.

It was an innocent and spontaneous identification with the star of a new medium which was having a greater impact than anyone had imagined. The mood was infectious. His programmes were treated to wholly uncritical acclaim by the press. It was miracle enough that programmes on television actually appeared; it was a mark of genius in a man to stand and talk to the camera with such eloquent aplomb. Dimbleby was 'TV's number one', the 'BBC's ace reporter', the 'star of television', and 'Mr. TV'.

Gossip columnists followed his every move: when he fell off his horse, caught chicken pox, bought a new car, went to the theatre or a restaurant, made a joke, spoke a harsh word, caught a cold, or lost his voice. His life became public property. He was wax-worked in Madame Tussaud's; Jackie, the heroine of a strip cartoon in *Girl Magazine*, went 'down Dimbleby's way'; his picture, suitably colour-tinted, appeared on the cover of *Everybody's Illustrated*, and *Tit-Bits*. Profile-writers sharpened eulogistic pencils. In 1951, the year in which he was voted both Radio and Television Personality of the Year, he became a subject for constant and repetitive study in the following vein.

> Richard Dimbleby looks 'authoritative'. His bulk gives a comfortable sense of infallibility. His clothes are well tailored and country-squirish, his smile is employed only when amused, his sincerity and boyish glee in what he is doing are obvious... He is a technician, perhaps the greatest in TV. He is quick-witted. He is never caught on the hop. In an emergency he fills the gap with fascinating and—apparently—impromptu talk...

The *World Digest* discovered: 'He has an enthusiastic zest for living, and retains those boyish spirits that cause him in the midst of a stroll round the garden, for instance, to swing his sixteen stone from the branch of a tree...' Only the most sophisticated judges allowed a hint of criticism to creep into their copy.

> Mr. Dimbleby is incomparably the best of commentators [observed *The Listener's* Critic on the Hearth]. His manner is pleasant, in appearance he has an agreeable, well-fed air, he leans forward eagerly to the microphone and camera as if he were really interested in what he is saying, and his voice is well-tuned and fluent. It flows on and on, inexhaustibly, as if he were never at a loss for words. He does not repeat himself, he never takes refuge in false or outlandish phrases, he has no broken sentences, the grammar is always correct, his predicates agree with his nominatives, he is perfect. Now that is an intimidating thing. Thomas Hardy used to say that he deliberately split his infinitives because too uniform a perfection is bad art. There must be relief, contrast, variation of tension. In other words, Mr. Dimbleby would be even better if he were sometimes less good.

More often critics adopted a tone of bewildered wonderment.

A journalist allowed to watch the preparation of one of Dimbleby's programmes in Bath reported:

> There is no red tape, no shouted commands, just a quiet orderly co-operation that gets things done...so natural is the whole procedure that one can hardly realise that a really big national TV feature is being fashioned into shape before one's eyes... I was shown the complexities of the whole set-up and how picture taken on one film at the same time that the sound track—synchronised by the use of 'clappers'—is being recorded on another film in a nearby BBC recording van...

Watching Dimbleby at the start of the boat race, the *Glasgow Herald* reported: 'Ah! there's Richard Dimbleby', the knowing word goes round: autograph books are thrust forward, eyes follow, ears strain to hear, for he is the interpreter, the go-between, the man, who himself human, can approach the heart of the mystery and explain it to mortals...'

The attention, the praise, and the flattery—all of which Dimbleby enjoyed—had no discernable effect on his behaviour at all. He had no inclination to bask in the glory thrust on him, in adulation he received; nor did he have the time. The pace and pressure of life to which he had committed himself continued. So did his ideas.

Early in 1951 he suggested that London Town should be replaced or at least complemented by a more adventurous programme. He suggested for it the sentimental but significant title 'This Land of Ours'. 'I would like to emphasise my strong feelings on the subject,' wrote Dimbleby, of the importance of his projected programme. It would provide the BBC with an opportunity

> at this critical stage in our history to emphasise people, things, and places that are British and try to further the message of the Festival [1951 was the year of the Festival of Britain] that Britain is still strong and flourishing. This theme will give the programme its panoramic quality, the implication being that much of the strength of character of the British people— particularly the strength that shows itself in emergency— springs from the long unbroken history and tradition of the land of which so much remains today.

It was a theme to which he returned again and again—that Britain was free, democratic, still a power in the world, a force for good, peopled by men and women united by more than what divided them; Britain was a beautiful country, with great traditions to be preserved not merely because they enshrined old values, but because they also protected those that were new and good.

It was not an original view; nor was it profound. On the lips of most public men, the sentiments would have echoed with the hollowness of insincerity. But from Dimbleby, implied, not stated, they reflected a very real public mood. There was a powerful feeling—which ran across the classes—that this little island of Britain, battered by war and the hard times which followed it, was once again on the verge of standing powerful, upright and noble in the council chambers of the world. It was at best a romantic, at worst a sentimental, illusion: Dimbleby, like his public, held it, however, with absolute sincerity.

In 1952 This Land of Ours emerged on the screen rather less romantically as About Britain. Produced again by Steve McCormack, it was virtually a national London Town. Like that programme it was greeted with almost uncritical acclaim by the critics—as a breakthrough in television reportage. As he had been the first radio reporter, now he was the first reporter in television.

By virtue of his immense broadcasting output on radio and television he was able, not by direct expression, but more usually by implication, to propagate his views. Moreover, since they were not out of tune with the times, they were acceptable to, even welcomed by, the BBC. Imperceptibly, he became the embodiment of those values for which the Corporation stood, but which, by reason of its vow of editorial silence, it could not express. Broadcasting House affected to watch the public adulation for Dimbleby with dry detachment. In fact it was a matter for ceaseless and gratifying wonder—no-one quite knew why it was, and no-one really sought to know: it was enough that it was there. Most in the BBC were forbidden to speak their minds, to hold public opinions. Dimbleby could say what he liked. In the controversy which surrounded the Festival of Britain in 1951, Dimbleby made no attempt to stand in the middle. For years afterwards, the garden at home displayed the tattered remnants of the spirit of the Festival, brought back from the South Bank

in triumph: six plain garden chairs, their once bright yellow faded
to off-white, their sprung metal seats collapsed, their legs bent.

Dimbleby broadcast in the month before the Festival, at its
opening, while it was on, at its closing, and after it. (In rousing
patriotic fashion he even gave the first public performance on the
organ in the Festival Hall.) In his weekly column in the *Sunday
Chronicle* he declared his faith in the Festival:

> I am earnestly, sincerely and vitally interested—and so must
> you be—in Britain. In a Britain knee-deep in care and trouble,
> in debt, hung round with every handicap a malevolent world
> can devise, and still looking upward and onward, still believing
> that she can offer moral, if not physical leadership and set an
> example that many countries of the world would be glad to
> follow. That Britain is staging a festival in the middle of its
> tribulations, collecting its strength and skills to produce positive
> proof to the world that it still has something real and valuable to
> give—is not that an inspiration? I think so—and what is more I
> believe that is what most of the rest of the world will think.

The Festival had been devised by the Labour Party. Its affairs
were under the guidance of the Party Chairman, Herbert
Morrison. Its Director-General, Gerald Barry, had been editor of
the *News Chronicle*. The Festival had been created, wrote Barry
afterwards: '... on hilltops, in gardens, round a log fire, wherever
half a dozen people could forgather and talk. It was made
clambering among rubble and cement mixers, amid the uproar of
cranes and pile-drivers, overheated railway carriages and under-
heated motor cars...' What Barry meant was that the Festival
was an expression of popular feeling, that it was the People's
Festival. He was not quite correct. A majority—nearly sixty per
cent according to a contemporary Gallup Poll—were in favour,
but there were some strident voices in opposition. Much of the
aristocracy, the upper classes, the City, and the right-wing of the
Conservative Party were against it. To them it was a waste of
limited resources on the one hand and the celebration of the
miserably second-rate on the other; it smacked of soft-headed,
wishy-washy Liberalism. It was a shade vulgar and rather 'wet'.

Richard Dimbleby's outspoken advocacy of the Festival put
him firmly on the side of the romantics against the realists, and,
insofar as the split took this form, of the left against the right.

He was attacked from two quarters: some said he was commending wasteful expenditure when so many were living 'in want and squalor'; others suggested simply that he was 'a softy'. Most, however, said he had echoed their own thoughts.

Herbert Morrison judged that the Festival was 'the people giving themselves a pat on the back'; Barry thought that it would show 'what the Land has made of the People, and what the People have made of the Land'. For Dimbleby it symbolised progress and humanity:

> it is a wonderful opportunity, at a crucial moment in history when the democratic nations need trust and confidence in each other, for Great Britain (and let's keep that word Great) to remind the world of her enormous contribution to civilisation. Whatever the state of things at home, however difficult life may be, it is vital that we should show a brave and proud face to the rest of the world. We are still a first-class power imbued with nothing but good intentions towards the rest of mankind. We still have resourcefulness, invention, justice, humanity and wisdom, and now is the time to say so.

Words which now seem simplistic were then an expression of middle-brow high-mindedness. They were not the product of sophisticated thought but of deep liberal and patriotic sentiment. It was at this time that Dimbleby's politics (insofar as that term can be applied to the general and vague principals to which he adhered) crystallised. Within a few months of each other, the three major political parties asked him if he would care to represent them in the House of Commons. Though they hoped to cash in on his popularity, he could without difficulty have stood for any of them. He was a Liberal by instinct, but would have accepted most of what the right of the Labour party and left of the Tory party then had to say. His politics were never based on class (which is what helps distinguish the real politician in any party from the rest); he did not even understand what the term implied. The concept of a 'class-ridden society' or 'class-war' was incomprehensible to him. His political education was negligible; his view of politicians naive: 'if only someone banged their heads together then perhaps we would get some sense out of them', was his solution to most political dilemmas. He regarded most politicians with distrust and even contempt.

H

He clung fiercely to his political principles, standing tenaciously in the centre, his politics the politics of instinct. He loathed the extremes. He abhorred: 'the detestable, arrogant, dangerous nationalism' which racialist South Africa nurtured, and which grew 'as quickly as the rankest weed in my garden'. He was outraged by General Peron in Argentina who was: 'fighting against freedom of speech, personal liberty, indeed democracy itself...' He was no less aroused by the attitude of Britain towards Peron's regime:

I sometimes wonder if our industrialists led by the Exchequer and the Board of Trade are not deliberately blind to everything but the lure of exports. In their dealings with Argentina they overlook such monstrous events as the suppression of one of the world's leading newspapers, La Prensa, the hounding of its proprietor, the persecution of its courageous editorial staff, simply because they dared to criticise a regime that like all dictatorships, cannot face criticism ... how long are we to gulp down our pride and have dealings with these goose-stepping imitators of Hitler?

At the same time he deplored the way Communism in Britain was 'spreading in mysterious ways and deceptive guises'. He wanted a national referendum to decide whether or not a Communist was ipso facto a traitor: 'We cannot afford to have people living with us and working with the enemy. They should be proscribed.' He could hardly bring himself to speak to a Communist. On one Down Your Way occasion a local reporter was introduced to him as 'a member of the Communist party'. Dimbleby, refusing to speak to him, turned on his heel and walked away. A hatred of fascism and totalitarianism of all kinds, and a love of Britain's form of democracy was the core of his political being. Subtler men, those more astute in the ways of the political world would have been more circumspect, more cynical. He had no such inhibitions, expressing himself bluntly, simply and with disconcerting passion. Though he had put his war experiences firmly at the back of his mind after 1945—he did not once trade on that horror—he retained an everlasting hatred not merely of what he called the 'German spirit' but a fundamental suspicion of all Germans. When it was rumoured in 1951 that

West Germany planned to open an information office in Pretoria he warned his readers darkly:

> Believe me, a bureau of this kind will never stick to information; it is not in the German make-up to miss any opportunity of furthering Germanism . . . for all I know there may be perfectly friendly democratic Germans (there are a few) but they are bound to be tempted, not least by those who believe that we must encourage the German spirit all over again so that we can use it against Russia in war. If war should come, we must defeat Russia and Communism, but not by using the very people and the very spirit that we defeated, or thought we had defeated, at such frightful cost only six years ago.
>
> Should I apologise, I wonder, for the fact that I cannot accept the Germans? My memories are too new and too vivid . . . Though we may have to re-arm Western Germany for our protection, though American policy dictates that war criminals shall be released, for heaven's sake let us not condone the terrible thing that has been done in the name of Germany because of our proper hatred of all the terrible things that have been done in the name of Soviet Russia.

If Dimbleby's perspective was limited, his values were clear, and the passion with which he held them remained with him for the rest of his life. The broadcasting career, for which he would be most remembered, was about to start. From being a 'personality' and a 'celebrity' he was about to become an 'institution'.

IO

The Coronation
and the Commentator

How but in custom and in ceremony
Are innocence and beauty born?

W. B. YEATS

VABEL MOVED MAJESTICALLY UP THE THAMES, UNDER TOWER
Bridge and London Bridge, past St. Paul's, under Westminster
Bridge, until it reached a point midway between St. Thomas's
Hospital on the left bank and the House of Commons on the
right. There, Richard Dimbleby's new possession, a dutch sailing
barge, picked up a mooring. It was a week before the most
important event of 1953, the Coronation of Queen Elizabeth II.
Dimbleby could have stayed in a hotel, or at his club or even with
friends. A boat on the river was not an ideal base from which to
work; his clothes got damp when it rained; his typewriter
stuttered every time a trip boat went by; he could not have a bath;
and the current was too strong to row ashore—so that he had to
hail a friendly police launch every time he wished to reach the
Abbey. Yet he insisted to incredulous friends and colleagues that
he had brought the yacht round from Chichester (where ke kept
her moored) as a matter of convenience: from the river he could
reach the Abbey much quicker than they, who would have to
find their way through huge crowds, police barriers, and roads
sealed off to ordinary traffic. So Richard Dimbleby, the BBC's
principal commentator for what would prove to be the most
important single day in the history of British television, sat in
lordly isolation on the Thames and prepared the last details of his
broadcast. The decision to live afloat filled him with glee, spicing

the romance of the occasion with adventure. It was fitting, too, that he should 'be in attendance' (one of his favourite understatements) upon the Coronation in some style; he relished the police launch escort to the steps of Westminster Pier; the isolation of the river filled him with a gratifying sense of distinction. More important he had settled down for the duration at the symbolic centre of Britain: the buildings which he saw through the portholes were the outward forms of the institutions which the monarchy blessed and protected. The Coronation was an affirmation after troubled times of the nation's faith in that system. On the river, after the meetings, the briefings and the rehearsals, the six months of preparation, Richard Dimbleby could immerse himself in the glory of the occasion.

Seventeen years before, in 1936, he had been in the News Room of the BBC, while his colleagues (with his support) had voted to strike if the Corporation continued to censor news of the abdication crisis. Fortunately the King had settled the matter by deciding to announce his renunciation of the throne in public the same evening. In 1939 he had been sent by the BBC to cover the royal tour of Canada by the new King and Queen. It had been the first occasion on which a BBC reporter had accompanied the Royal Family on such a trip—and he regarded his selection as a great honour.

In those days there was no more important news than the doings of royalty. From the beginning the BBC had revered the Crown. Sir John Reith had established the habit by which no royal event could pass unnoticed by the BBC; regarding the monarchy with awe and devotion, he sought to stimulate and perpetuate similar feelings in the BBC's public. But the Corporation's obeisance before royalty was not merely a Reithian foible. Between the most senior and the most junior institution of the Establishment, there was a natural affinity. The BBC was always under threat of criticism, rebuke and punishment from Government and the other institutions of state; only the monarchy was above playing the part of the bully, only the monarchy was exempt from criticism. Out of politics, usually above controversy, stable and permanent—it embodied every quality of virtue to which the BBC most aspired. The BBC could give unswerving and uncritical allegiance to the Crown yet maintain its integrity and independence. In the process, by its open devotion to the system which worship of the Crown implied, the Corporation was able to establish itself the more securely as a mature and responsible if junior pillar of the state.

The first royal tour accompanied by the BBC was a matter of great moment. In Canada Dimbleby reported with enough distinction to earn a tribute from the Board of Governors for his 'outstanding' coverage of the tour. To his delight he met the King and Queen. On one occasion he played the piano in front of them and they sang songs together. At Banff Springs he had a twenty-five minute conversation with the King: 'he and the Queen had had dinner privately upstairs,' he wrote gleefully to Dilys, 'and between you and me and the Rockies, he dined rather too well. That and the mountain air made him, shall we say rather "excitable". Anyway he came suddenly into the lobby, looked around, and then came over to me, to my confusion . . .' The King was plainly in expansive mood for he discoursed on a wide range of topics from radio to Hitler to democracy, declaring 'don't talk a lot of twaddle about the end of democracy'. In Britain, he informed Dimbleby, both it and the monarchy would survive. Despite the fact that his King was 'not quite normal' (even in a letter Dimbleby could not quite bring himself to use the word 'drunk') the meeting was a proud moment. The only jarring note came from a reporter from the *New York Daily News*, whose sense of propriety was less highly developed than Dimbleby's.

> He pushed his way in and began talking very loudly to the Queen. They were both amused by his accent and remarks but after a while we all began to get uncomfortable . . . He kept calling her Queen, and once when they were talking about a 'goddam milk train' he had had to ride on the previous evening he tapped her on the front of the shoulder to emphasise some point he was making!

In 1939 he had been in France when the Duke of Gloucester arrived to inspect the troops. Three years later, when an M.P. made the unfortunate suggestion that the good Duke should be put at the head of Britain's armed forces, the House of Commons had erupted in spontaneous mirth. In France Dimbleby was irritated that the monarchy should send such a symbol to greet its fighting men. He was embarrassed by the regularity with which the Duke insisted on referring to the Allies in booming tones as the 'Froggies'.

By the Coronation Dimbleby's instinctive respect for the institution of monarchy had developed into an absolute but considered devotion. He had no doubt that his job was to preserve and enhance its prestige, writing:

> The truth is that monarchy has long since become our way of life. For us, it means justice, respect for the rights of the individual, and freedom . . . Parliamentary democracy, the system of Government which guarantees protection for each and every one of us, flourishes best, it seems, where there is a monarchy, where there is at the head of affairs, one person willing to sacrifice herself entirely to the good of her people.

In Elizabeth Our Queen (which was published just before the Coronation) he wrote of the 'tremendous strain' that the throne imposed—

> a whole public life must be lived in front of crowds, troops, dignitaries and cameras. The spontaneous applause that rises and falls as she passes is an unbroken sound in her ears . . . wherever she goes the music of the anthem is with her; troops are always motionless and at attention; people about her always formal and correct. Everything she does is watched, everything she wears is noted, everything she says is treasured and remembered.

His eulogy sprang not from sycophancy, but from romantic necessity: the Queen had to be in reality what she was in his mythology:

> She has a great sense of humour that lies just below the surface, waiting to break through solemnity whenever it can. Photographs rarely do her justice; she is smaller, slimmer, and altogether more lively than they make her. She has a flashing smile that can cut right through the barrier of formality, and a clear incisive voice . . .

He was filled with reverential admiration when at a Royal Maundy Distribution Service, she took hold of the hand of a blind woman and pressed the money into her palm 'without prompting'—almost as if anyone else would have behaved with less sensitivity.

Merely to enjoy the pageantry of royal ceremony was, for

Dimbleby, to be a spectator at 'an impressive but meaningless ritual'. The lives and deaths of monarchs, the manner of their coming and going, the trappings with which their lives were embellished, the formalities which they had to endure, the customs and traditions which imprisoned them, were for Dimbleby part of that 'sacrifice' which guaranteed the survival of those freedoms which the war had led him to cherish. It was an uncomplicated view of the monarchy, untouched by doubt, and informed by detailed understanding of the rituals—which gave them their meaning. But the little boy who had taken his first unaided steps at the sound of a town band was still—in maturity—moved by ceremony. His belief in the monarchy was not dispassionate; it was to partake in an emotional experience in which his whole being was involved. To the non-believer such passion can be absurd, irritating and even offensive; for those who share the passion, blindly or inarticulately, the man who has the capacity to express their feelings, giving incoherent thoughts and emotions shape and dignity, earns undying affection.

By the Coronation Dimbleby had perfected his broadcasting techniques. His war reports, the victory parades, a royal wedding, a royal anniversary, state visits, several trooping the colours, and memorial services, had made his royal tones familiar, respected and admired. If Down your Way, Twenty Questions and London Town had between them ensured his fame, his royal commentaries had secured his reputation. His manner and style were unique—and in the view of every critic beyond compare.

By 1953 he had already reported the funeral of Queen Mary for television; her lying-in-state for radio; the funeral of King George VI for television; then again on radio his lying-in-state. This broadcast, his last major radio commentary, was his finest— the apotheosis of his technique. The voice was quiet, gentle and sombre; almost conversational but never lacking emotion. The words were simple, the style alternately plain and rhetorical. The language had its echo in the orthodox version of the Old Testament. The phrases, by turns ornate and simple, followed each other with the assurance of a hand that has an instinctive feel for rhythm and cadence. The meaning, without which all else would have been hollow charade, was plain. The faith, conviction and devotion shown without shame:

It is dark in New Palace Yard at Westminster tonight. As I

look down from this old, leaded window I can see the ancient courtyard dappled with little pools of light where the lamps of London try to pierce the biting, wintry gloom and fail. And moving through the darkness of the night is an even darker stream of human beings, coming, almost noiselessly, from under a long, white canopy that crosses the pavement and ends at the great doors of Westminster Hall. They speak very little, these people, but their footsteps sound faintly as they cross the yard and go out through the gates, back into the night from which they came.

They are passing, in their thousands, through the hall of history while history is being made. No-one knows from where they come or where they go, but they are the people, and to watch them pass is to see the nation pass.

It is very simple, this Lying-in-State of a dead King, and of incomparable beauty. High above all light and shadow and rich in carving, is the massive roof of chestnut, that Richard the Second put over the great Hall. From that roof the light slants down in clear, straight beams, unclouded by any dust and gathers in a pool at one place. There lies the coffin of the King.

The oak of Sandringham, hidden beneath the rich golden folds of the Standard; the slow flicker of the candles touches gently the gems of the Imperial Crown, even that ruby that King Henry wore at Agincourt. It touches the deep purple of the velvet cushion and the cool, white flowers of the only wreath that lies upon the flag. How moving can such simplicity be? How real the tears of those who pass and see it, and come out again, as they do at this moment in unbroken stream, to the cold, dark night and a little privacy for their thoughts.

Who can know what they are thinking? Does that blind man whom they lead so carefully down the thick carpet, sense around him the presence of history? Does he know that Kings and Queens have feasted here and stood their trial and gone to their death? And that little woman, with the airman by her side— does she feel the ghosts that must be here in the shadows of the Hall? The men and the women of those tumultuous days of long ago, of Chaucer, Essex, Anne Boleyn, Charles and Cromwell, Warren Hastings and those early Georges? Or does she, and do all those other seventy thousand of the nation, who will have passed through this day alone, think only of the sixth George . . . ?

I thought when I watched the Bearers take the coffin into this Hall yesterday that I had never seen a sight so touching. The clasped arms of the Grenadiers, the reverent care with which they lifted and carried their King. But I was wrong. For in the silent tableau of this Lying-in-State there is a beauty that no movement can ever bring. He would be forgiven who believed that these Yeomen of the Bodyguard, facing outwards from the corners of the catafalque, were carven statues of the Yeoman of the Tudor Henry's day. Could any living man, let alone a white, bearded man of eighty, be frozen into this immobility? The faces of the two Gentlemen at Arms are hidden by the long, white helmet plumes that have fallen about them like a curtain as they bowed their heads. Are they real, those faces, or do the plumes conceal two images of stone? And the slim, straight figures of the officers of the Household Brigade, hands poised lightly on their arms reversed—what sense of pride and honour holds their sword so still that not one gleam of light shall be reflected from a trembling blade? Never safer, better guarded, lay a sleeping King than this, with a golden light to warm his resting place and the muffled tread of his devoted people to keep him company. They come from a mile away in the night, moving pace by pace in hours of waiting, come into the silent majesty of the scene and as silently leave again . . .

For Dimbleby the Coronation was a reaffirmation of the nation's devotion to the Crown. For the BBC it was the biggest broadcasting operation in its history. At the 1937 Coronation (the BBC's biggest operation until then) there had been seventeen sound commentary positions along the route (ten of which were from the overseas services); television had three cameras, all at Hyde Park Corner. In 1953 there were to be ninety-five sound commentary positions (of which eighty four were for overseas services); television was to use twenty-one cameras, of which five were to be in Westminster Abbey. The preparations took more than twelve months and involved long and detailed discussion between the BBC and the Palace.

The talks started badly. The Palace was deeply suspicious of television, regarding it as a potentially vulgar intruder whose uncouth cameras and cables would destroy the dignity of the day. Most of the peerage felt likewise. The Duke of Norfolk, who in his capacity as Earl Marshall of the Realm had a powerful voice, was uncertain. He could be crotchety and difficult, and he was never unaware of the 'vulgar' instincts of those who ran television. But he recognised that broadcasting, in particular the new medium of television, could help present the Royal Family to the people: 'if it was properly controlled'. In 1953, he also had the feeling that whether he, or the Royal Family liked it or not, television had arrived to stay. In addition, behind his crusty exterior, there lurked a showman—an audience of 20,000,000 people for the spectacle he was to prepare was an enticing prospect.

Meanwhile the press was perpetuating a debate about who would be the royal commentator. John Snagge, Howard Marshall, Frank Gillard, Wynford Vaughan-Thomas, and Richard Dimbleby were presented as competitors in the broadcasting equivalent of a beauty contest. The *Sunday Graphic* published an opinion poll nine months before the Coronation. It showed that by an embarrassingly large margin, Dimbleby had seventy-two per cent of the vote—'an outstanding triumph'. He was the first choice for the job of television commentator. At the BBC, both radio and television, meeting for the first time in serious competition, fought for Dimbleby's services. Radio was unquestionably the senior service, but Dimbleby was the only commentator who had mastered the craft of television outside broadcasts; the future of television, it was felt, would hang on the success of its Coronation coverage. Dimbleby was persuaded without much difficulty by his friend de Lotbinière, Head of Outside Broadcasts, that he should do the television job.

Then came an announcement from the Palace: a blunt statement to the effect that the BBC would not be permitted to televise in the Abbey. It was tantamount to informing the Corporation that the monarchy neither wanted nor required the attendance of television upon its affairs. By now (October 1952) the televising of the Coronation had assumed great importance to the Corporation; both its own prestige and the future of the medium were at stake. It had invested much time, energy and money in the preparations for the ceremony and privately it was 'damned' if a stupid, short-sighted decision was to be allowed to ruin its plans. So while Fleet Street now tipped Dimbleby as the sound commentator, the Duke of Norfolk and the Archbishop of Canterbury were lobbied fiercely by Broadcasting House. Three months later, after protracted argument and even a demonstration in the Abbey of how unobtrusive the cameras could be, the Palace at last relented. Soon afterwards, to his great relief, the BBC announced that Richard Dimbleby would be the television commentator in the Abbey, while John Snagge would report for radio.

Coronation Day, June 2nd 1953, was blustery and cold, storm clouds threatened heavy rain. The route from Buckingham Palace to the Abbey was lined ten, sometimes twenty, deep with crowds who had arrived from all over Britain and the rest of the world. They huddled under black umbrellas while hawkers and vendors found a ready sale for Coronation momentos, Union Jacks, balloons and cups of 'lovely Coronation tea'. It was an excited crowd, ready to laugh, cheer, smile, and clap in that crowd unison which suggests an unseen conductor. They laughed when a peer dropped his coronet; they clapped big Daimlers decanting red-faced lords and fat ladies; they cheered gold, silver and scarlet coaches, drawn by silky, gleaming horses. They smiled and tapped their feet as military bands played. Unknown Heads of State from all over the world were greeted with the effusion normally reserved for old heroes; and when the Queen of Tonga, waving her huge arms, and smiling in joy came by, they cheered, sharing her delight.

The timing, the order, the drama of pageantry is superb; each moment greater than the last. The British Royal Family arrives, the glass coach with Princess Margaret. The crowd wave and cheer. Near the Abbey they sing the National Anthem; and then the white doors of the Abbey open. Her Majesty's procession arrives: 'All of us surrender completely to our eyes, and to the art of pageantry, and to colour, to the music, to the crash of bells, to a species of ultimate earthly splendour some of us have never expected or suspected' wrote Geoffrey Grigson. The Coronation coach, the six greys pulling it, the grooms beside, the postillions aloft—and inside a small, gently smiling woman, almost lost amidst the encrusted gold and silver splendour of the massive four-and-a-half-ton vehicle in which she has travelled past her cheering and devoted subjects. She leaves the coach and enters the Abbey; she knows that whatever doubts she may have had about the public's feeling for her and the Crown can be banished. The people lining the streets have witnessed a pageant and shared an experience that they will never forget.

But the people on the route were not the whole nation. Inside the Abbey Richard Dimbleby waited to deliver his commentary. For six months he had prepared for this moment. He knew every detail of the service, the history of every ritual, the symbolic point of every movement, he had written numerous articles for newspapers and magazines about the significance of the Coronation, he had broadcast, and written a book about it—he was immersed in the ceremony.

'Your voice, and the things you say in the Abbey on Coronation Day, are of great importance to us,' the Controller of Programmes, Cecil McGivern, had written to him, 'I have full confidence in the fact that in no way will you let us down . . .' Dimbleby had never been in any doubt about the importance of the day either for the nation or for the BBC.

Dimbleby had been sitting in the Abbey since 5.30 a.m. that morning, in his commentary position high up in the Triforium, looking down on the Coronation Chair. He sat in a little glass, sound-proofed box, feeling acutely nervous:

I felt profoundly conscious that I was seeing history in the making, and indeed the whole pageant on the floor of the Abbey moved with a slow irresistible rhythm that seemed to lift it out of time altogether. I thought at one moment as I half closed my eyes and watched the measured ceremony being carried through that I might be watching something that had happened a thousand years before.

For him the success of the broadcast would not merely be measured by the numbers of viewers, the absence of technical breakdown, or the extent to which he could accurately and elegantly convey the detail of the Coronation service. It would only succeed for him if those who saw it were to feel that they shared in a profoundly important ceremony—'a service of deep religious significance . . . I was deeply conscious not only of the responsibility upon my own shoulders, but of the tremendous duty that rests upon the television service as a whole . . . it is a mirror held up to the life of the nation.'

At 10.15 a.m. in the morning Sylvia Peters opened the proceedings for television:

Today is the Coronation Day of Her Majesty Queen Elizabeth II. It is a day of rejoicing for the Queen's subjects wherever they may be. But it is a day too of deep significance—for beneath the splendid pageantry of all the processions and of the Abbey ceremony there is the simple fact that the Queen is today dedicating herself before God to the service of her subjects . . . It is surely the greatest moment in television history as we take you out into the heart of London to these memorable events.

As the BBC team of seven commentators watched the Coronation procession on its way to the Abbey, Dimbleby looked over his notes. They still survive: pages of carefully prepared commentary, phrases and sentences worked at again and again, words crossed out and reinserted, and crossed out again. The days of rehearsal, exact notes about the precise length of each section of the ceremony, allowed him (for the first and last time) to write much of his commentary beforehand, and then deliver it, with only minor variations, at the proper moment. He saw himself as an 'annotator'—providing background notes for the viewer, and explaining each act in the ritual. But no mere annotator expressed himself in Dimbleby's terms: his voice, slow and reverential, wove a pattern around the echoing tones of the Archbishop of Canterbury, Geoffrey Fisher, so that it seemed to some watching it on television, as if the Coronation were being conducted, not by the Archbishop, but by Richard Dimbleby. His words, written at home, rewritten on the river, blended in style and tone with the words of a ceremony derived from Old Testament references to the anointing of kings, and Samuel's crowning of Saul, and almost unchanged since the crowning of King Edgar at Bath a thousand years before. Yet the words that Dimbleby chose, came from no rubric or order of service. It was his identification with, almost sublimation in, the ceremony that framed the sentences he spoke. The art of the commentary (and he was never in any doubt, as he frequently insisted, that it was 'an art') on this occasion was for it to become in essence part of the ceremony:

Richard Dimbleby: 'Her Majesty returns the orb and the Archbishop now places upon the fourth finger of her right hand the ring, the ring whereupon is set a sapphire and on it a ruby cross, this is often called the ring of England.'
Archbishop: 'Receive the ring of kingly dignity and the seal of catholic faith and as thou art this day consecrated head and prince so may you continue steadfastly as the defender of Christ's religion that being rich in faith and blessed in all good works you

may reign with him who is the king of kings to whom be the glory for ever and ever. Amen.'
Richard Dimbleby: 'Now the Dean of Westminster brings to the Archbishop the sceptre with the cross and the rod with the diamond while the Chancellor of the Duchy of Lancaster offers to the Queen the traditional glove of white kid lined with silk embroidered with thistles, shamrocks and English oak leaves and acorns.'
Archbishop: 'Receive the royal sceptre, the ensign of kingly power and justice, receive the rod of equity.'

It was impossible to be objective, to stand emotionally outside the event, to watch the procession of quaintly dressed figures, some fat, some lame, some red with much whisky, some bowed with age as if they formed part of a pantomime. He was much moved by the ceremony: by the incantations—'Vivat Regina Elizabetha! Vivat! Vivat! Vivat!'; by the anthems—'And Zadok the priest took an horn of oil out of the tabernacle, and anointed Solomon. And they blew the trumpet; and all the people said God Save King Solomon'; by sudden shouts—'God Save the Queen'; by the injunction: 'God crown you with a crown of Glory and Righteousness, that by the Ministry of this our benediction, having a right faith and manifold fount of good works, you may obtain the Crown of an everlasting Kingdom by the Gift of Him whose Kingdom endureth for ever'; and by the obeisance of the Nobility—'I swear to be your Liege man of Life and Limb, and of earthly worship; and Faith and Trust I will bear unto you, to live and die, against all manner of Folks.'

His Coronation commentary was heard all over the world. RAF helicopters took film of the ceremony to waiting Canberras which flew in relays across the Atlantic to Canada and the United States. In New Zealand, the *Auckland Star* reflecting a world-wide sentiment spoke of: 'Dimbleby's genius for rising to the event his words flowed out in subdued but dramatic torrents. At times he approached almost Churchillian rhetoric . . . his accounts were models of finally edited description, and fully deserved the tremendous world-wide audience he was accorded.'

On the afternoon of the Coronation the BBC decided that Dimbleby should go back into the silent Abbey later that evening for a reflective postscript to the great day. So he finished his day's broadcasting in the Abbey after midnight—seventeen hours after he had entered it that morning. 'I shall never forget those hours in the Abbey,' he wrote afterwards, 'when the whole nation was swept by the same sense of love and pride that filled those of us standing so near the Queen.' He wrote too that he had: 'never felt so acutely the strain of describing a public event . . . but I have never been so proud or so glad that I was able to contribute in a small way to history...' The experience had been momentarily—but revealingly—marred for him when he finally left the triforium and saw around him the litter left by the peers. He was greatly distressed:

> It seemed to me amazing that even on this occasion we could not break ourselves of one of our worst national habits. Tiers and tiers of stalls on which the peers had been sitting were covered with sandwich wrappings, sandwiches, morning newspapers, fruit peel, sweets and even a few empty miniature bottles . . .

Sometimes Dimbleby could be as prim about the behaviour of his social betters as a below-stairs-butler about drawing-room improprieties. The pompous outrage with which he expressed himself on this occasion was as rare but as real as the inverted snobbery which caused it. He believed that peers should live up to the image that ordinary people had of them; on a state occasion they should behave with fitting solemnity. To leave litter was to let the side down, to bring the peerage into disrepute. That the nobility might have looked upon the Coronation with rather less awe than he, as an amusing diversion for the masses, did not occur to him.

The Coronation produced a public euphoria which has not since been recaptured. The young Queen in her Coronation vestments seemed for a moment to embody the hopes of the people. In the public mind Richard Dimbleby became inextricably associated with the event. For the rest of the decade the entire nation (insofar as its view is reflected in Fleet Street) had an apparently insatiable appetite for Dimbleby's views on royalty. Year after year in the popular press and periodicals he repeated his theme—in devoted terms—that the existence of the Crown was a guarantor of the British 'way of life'.

> It is not easy to express the feelings that we have for the Queen or the part that the monarchy plays in our daily lives. Love,

Richard Dimbleby

(Observer)

(B

In the West Gallery of St. Paul's
Cathedral commentating on Sir
Winston Churchill's funeral,
January 1964

His view of the Coronation of
Queen Elizabeth II, June 2 1953
(Topix)

By 1960, for the wedding of Princess
Alexandra, Dimbleby commentated
from a bank of monitors covering every
stage of the occasion

(1

July 1962, broadcasting via Telstar from New York
to London

Richard Dimbleby leading the BBC team at the start of a general election marathon

Doing his 'homework'

His main relaxation

'He much disliked
real agricultural
activity'

The family home at Danley Farm—'to escape the trappings of suburbia
had become his most important earthly ambition'

Dilys crossing the lock-cut to the island on the Thames to which
they moved from Danley Farm

With the author

With David on board *Vabel*

With the rest of the family—(from left to right) Sally, Dilys,
Nicholas, Richard, the author

Dilys' favourite portrait

On holiday in Devon on the Dart where he
wished to spend his old age

With his doctor, Ian Churchill-Davidson, at 'Picnic Point' on the
edge of the Dart in August 1965. His last holiday

admiration, loyalty, respect; these are the obvious emotions shared by us all. But behind them there is something deeper and more mysterious that it is difficult to put into words . . . The realisation that we of Britain and the Commonwealth have preserved our security and freedom throughout the centuries under Royal Government. When we look at the Queen, we see, in part, the Sovereign who in changing human form has guided and guarded our affairs for nine hundred years.

It was at the very least, a rose-tinted view of the monarchy's part in British history—but it was widely shared. The extent of public euphoria can perhaps be glimpsed from the fact that the *Daily Herald*, the most radical Fleet Street paper, thought it fitting, a few days before the Coronation, to run a strip cartoon feature written by Dimbleby called 'The Cavalcade of the Crown'—the last instalment of which proclaimed 'The Nation Shouts Its Joy: . . . another page in the story of our island has been written . . . a young and fair Queen has been crowned. GOD SAVE THE QUEEN.' Caught up in the prevailing mood, the BBC waxed unusually lyrical:

> The power of broadcasting to enrich the spirit as well as the mind of man has never been more clearly shown than in the year under review, dominated as it was by an event which produced in the British peoples a mood of spiritual exhortation and an awareness of their traditions. The upsurge of emotion, which none who experienced it will ever forget, could not have been so widespread and so overwhelming without the massive efforts of the BBC, which on the day of the Coronation of Her Majesty Queen Elizabeth II successfully carried out the biggest broadcasting operation in its history.

The Corporation's Director-General, Sir Ian Jacob, formally conveyed his appreciation to Dimbleby: 'Sincere congratulations . . . it could not have been better, and I send you my grateful thanks.' The Head of Outside Broadcasting felt more free:

> I always thought that Richard Dimbleby and our cameras ought to be there, but I never imagined that the impact of their being there would be anything like what it has been. It was a long road that led to the Coronation theatre, but we got there,

and then a miracle happened and we seem to have achieved
something beyond most people's dreams. Thank you so much
for playing such a conspicuous part so faultlessly.

And from the Duke of Norfolk he received a tribute, which he
interpreted as a missive from the monarch herself: 'you had a great
triumph everywhere. I am so glad. May we meet again soon and
so many thanks.'

The press was no less moved. Peter Black, by no means the
most starry-eyed of critics, informed his *Daily Mail* readers that
the Coronation in the Abbey was 'a sublime experience'. He felt
certain

> that not one person of the millions who watched the solitary,
> dedicated young Queen moving so composedly throughout
> the ritual of the service will easily forget those one hundred
> and fifty minutes in which they seemed to share her dedication.
> It took the significance of the Coronation into twenty-five
> million hearts. At the end of the service, when at last the Queen
> moved towards the west door of the Abbey, crowned and
> carrying the Orb and Sceptre it was in a spontaneous, un-
> selfconscious gesture that in millions of homes in Britain
> viewers rose to salute her.

The Times added its majesterial voice to the chorus of acclaim:
Yesterday, for the first time, in perhaps a thousand years, the
Sovereign was crowned in the sight of many thousands [*The Times*
presumably meant millions] of the humblest of her subjects . . .'
To Dimbleby's delight *The Times* emphasised the one point that
for him had been the whole purpose of the broadcast:

> Yesterday, by penetrating at last, even vicariously into the
> solemn mysteriousness of the Abbey scene, multitudes who had
> hoped merely to see for themselves the splendour and the pomp,
> found themselves comprehending for the first time the true
> nature of the occasion. No mere report could have impressed so
> strongly on those who now looked on the scene that this was a
> deed of dedication, in which they, too, silently and reverently
> participated . . . more tremendous yet, was the sense,
> intellectually accepted before but only now vividly appre-
> hended, of the rate of responsibility being laid upon the young

spirit with the addition of each significant historic jewel. And here one must remark on the debt the television audience owed to Mr. Richard Dimbleby's quiet, lucid and dignified explanation of much that might otherwise have perplexed them.

In *The Sunday Times*, Maurice Wiggin reiterated much of *The Times*' sentiment, but, in one of the first serious articles written about television, he took the argument a stage forward. Of the opposition that had nearly robbed television of the right to cover the Coronation he commented:

> [it] was symptomatic of an attitude towards television by no means confined to a few officials deeply concerned with protocol; an attitude, which, after Tuesday's magnificent broadcast, becomes an historical oddity, as anachronistic as the man with the red flag who walked before the motor-car.

He went on to analyse (almost for the first time) the prodigious and unique power of television outside broadcasts:

> Television introduces a new and revolutionary element into the art or craft of reporting. Even now one has not fully apprehended the nature of this element, which is often called 'actuality'. On Tuesday it was possible to catch myself wondering if this deeply significant ceremonial were *really* taking place as one watched, or if it were just a film. Almost too good to be true. The power of 'being' in two places at once is the newest that man has rested from reluctant nature . . . The social implications of the miracle are endlessly debatable. No doubt it is possible to have too much of a good thing: but although a nation of onlookers would be a bad consummation, against that danger must be balanced the advantage of a vastly heightened awareness of other people's ways of life . . . The influence of the new reporting on the older journalism is likely to be wholly good. I am not aware of any conclusive evidence that television supplants the printed word: on the contrary, it seems to stimulate a demand for it: in this matter of the word, television is challenged by its own cameras. Its choice of commentators must be judicious. The outstanding excellence of Mr. Dimbleby's work in the Abbey made the shortcomings of his colleagues on the processional route more obvious . . . The BBC has magnificently vindicated the noble

idea of a public service. It has behaved with impeccable tact and
dignity and has undoubtedly made innumerable new friends . . .
After last Tuesday there can be no looking back.

In one day, television had come of age. It was still strange,
exciting, and potentially a little dangerous—but it was now for the
first time to be taken seriously as a means of communication. The
most valued jewel in the BBC television crown was the Outside
Broadcast. It was the 'O.B.' that made television a unique force
in communications; O.B.s were able to show you events 'as they
happened'; there could be no faking, no exaggerating, they told
the ungarnished truth. Television—by means of the Outside
Broadcast—would be (as Dimbleby saw it) a mirror held up to
society to reflect reality. In the BBC mind there was no limit to
what the Outside Broadcast could accomplish; its potential was
limited only by the capacity of men to make use of it. As land
and spacelinks developed so nation would be able to meet nation
'live' via television. It was not only romantics like Dimbleby who
believed that through the medium of the outside broadcast the
BBC's motto 'Nation shall speak peace unto nation' could at last
be realised.

The Coronation seemed to be the public vindication of that
ambition which more modestly had sprung to life three years
before in 1950. On the 100th Anniversary of the first transmission
of a telegram from England to France by underwater cable, the
announcer at Alexandra Palace introduced the first cross-channel
television programme which would 'not only mark the centenary
of that historic achievement of the last century, but herald in a new
and important era in international communication'. The screen
flickered. A fuzzy human form appeared. Then a voice: Richard
Dimbleby was in Calais, calmly describing the town's Clock
Tower and the Rodin statue of the Burghers of Calais. Calais
was 'en fête'—as Dimbleby described the vague visions before the
viewers—'in its own merry haphazard way—and we're privileged
to see it—a great mélange of sideshows and roundabouts and
lights, music, entertainments . . .' At the end of the broadcast,
the Mayor of Calais sent municipal greetings to the Mayor of
Dover and congratulations to the Director-General of the BBC.
A band played the two national anthems, and an era of international goodwill and understanding—it was thought—was about
to begin.

Two years later in July 1952 Richard Dimbleby was again in France, for a 'Grande Semaine de Paris' organised jointly by the BBC and the new French television service (ORTF)—the first time in the history of the medium. The promise of two years before seemed to be holding good. The *News of the World* reminded its readers: 'It's not often that you and I have a chance of making history.' And one BBC executive who took part in the programmes wrote soon afterwards: 'I believe I have taken part in a new chapter in the history of communication.' Only *The Star* sounded a less euphoric note, reporting sourly that the Paris week began 'with the slickness and good fortune of an elderly tortoise on an escalator'.

The purpose of the programmes from Paris was to show the glories of the city, fostering good relations between the citizens of the two countries in the process—or at least those few million that possessed television sets. Unfortunately co-operation between the two television services—admirably disguised from the public—proved more difficult than had been expected, not least because the French attained a level of enthusiastic incompetence and chauvinistic arrogance that their BBC guests had not thought possible. There were programmes from Montmartre night-clubs, the Louvre, the Eiffel Tower; an obligatory military parade with a band down the Champs Elysées, a visit to the opera, to the Left Bank, and to sundry street markets. On the first night a ferocious thunder storm all but obliterated the carefully rehearsed shots of the Eiffel Tower; the usually solid form of Richard Dimbleby was transformed into a frenzied, crackling, blur, reminding his public that 'the combined forces of the BBC and the French Television Service can't beat the weather'.

The two services had planned a televisual glossy night out for their viewers two evenings later. The French suggested that a bâteau-mouche be metamorphised into an open-air night-club—giving the British an opportunity to taste vicariously a little of Paris's elegant night life, whilst gently drifting down the Seine with the famous skyline as a slowly changing backdrop. The British, more prosaic in such matters, reminded the French that since all three O.B. cameras would be needed for the floor-show, the Paris skyline would be invisible. They suggested that the boat be tied up at the bank, which without spoiling the moonlit river romance, they suggested discreetly, would solve otherwise alarming technical problems. Reluctantly the French agreed (it

was a notable breakthrough for the BBC as until then the French
had insisted on controlling, producing and directing everything
themselves—while the British picked up the pieces).

The programme began well—even startlingly—with a diver
emerging (for what reason was never made clear) from the depths
of the river. Some mannequins gave a show on the towpath,
and then the night-club evening began. Sitting at a candlelit table
Richard Dimbleby talked with a group of singers and cabaret
artists until the moment arrived for one of them, Monsieur Liné
Renou, a vocalist of renown, to do his turn. To ensure his usual
standard of excellence, Monsieur Renou had insisted that his
voice be pre-recorded, and he would mime to himself 'on air'. At
Dimbleby's cue he stood up, assumed a stance of soulful passion,
opened his mouth, framed the words of the opening line—and
there was silence. Frantically the French director signalled to
Dimbleby that the play-back machine had broken down. With
his usual aplomb, Dimbleby invited the singer to sit down and
continue their conversation. A few moments later on another
signal from the agitated director, Monsieur Renou began again—
but at that moment, as if on cue, one camera, and then a second,
went 'dead'. A cry of 'Mon Dieu' echoed feebly across the
Channel as the French director gave vent to his anguish, rushed
across the set, issued a stream of incomprehensible instruction to
the English camera crew. At this point he was virtually arrested
by the floor-manager and Stephen McCormack took control.
With the one remaining camera which worked, he and Dimbleby
began an impromptu picture tour around the boat, Dimbleby
grabbing a pair of headphones and a microphone began to describe
the towpath, the Eiffel Tower, and a train crossing a distant bridge.
In London, recognising that irredeemable technical chaos had
broken out, the Controller of Television, Cecil McGivern,
ordered that the plugs be pulled.

The critics, still wonderingly innocent before the miracle of
international television, seemed to notice nothing—though the
Glasgow Herald did observe that 'the programme finished with
unexpected abruptness, but not before shots of a stray yacht or two
and an inevitable Seine bridge had added to the inconsequential
pleasures of the evening.'

For once, knowing that if the director had not panicked, the
programme could have continued, Dimbleby was furious. He
stalked past his hosts towards the gangway, stopped by a table,

picked up a bottle of champagne, held it in the air, walked to the edge of the boat and let it fall deliberately into the water. Watched by his incredulous colleagues he returned for a second bottle and then a chair, throwing them into the Seine as well. That done, he walked coolly down the gangplank, rubbing his hands in satisfaction, announcing to his perturbed producer: 'I will never, God help me, work with those clots again'—all of which being 'off air' went unnoticed. But the BBC producers were so alarmed by his unexpected outburst that they at once cabled Dilys asking her to fly out to join them in mollifying him. She arrived the next day.

Richard Dimbleby's uncharacteristic display of temperament had immediate effect: the French decided that the British should be allowed to make a larger contribution to the Great Week; Dimbleby reverted to his usual charming self, and afterwards, one of the British producers, Berkeley Smith, wrote that 'in those most difficult programmes, involving co-operation between two headstrong and highly nationalistic television services, it was always Richard who best survived the heat of the day . . .'

A few days later his own favourite disaster occurred. He was in a shopping boulevarde opposite the Louvre. The plan was that he should describe the scene 'out of vision' and then walking into picture, advance up the street towards camera, and engage some Parisian matrons in genial conversation. However, when the moment arrived for him to appear in vision, he saw, to his alarm that there was no camera in sight. As he pondered imminent disaster, it suddenly appeared from round a corner, being pushed by a group of shouting and gesticulating Frenchmen: 'It went right *past* me at a rate of knots and disappeared into the distance,' he recorded later, 'As it went by the cameraman screamed at me, "Ils sont fous, monsieur! Complètement fous!" '

In the fifteen years between 1950 and 1965, Richard Dimbleby covered more than five hundred outside broadcasts for radio and television and one hundred and fifty major Royal, State or National occasions—Royal comings and goings from London Airport or Westminster pier, Royal visits abroad, State visits to Britain, Royal celebrations, Royal marriages (Princess Elizabeth to Prince Philip, Princess Margaret to Anthony Armstrong-Jones, Princess Alexandra to Mr. Angus Ogilvy, the Duke of Kent to Anne Worsley), royal funerals and lying-in-states, papal funerals, coronations and visits, Presidential celebrations, elections and deaths, a Moscow May day parade, numerous remembrance services, trooping the colours, and state openings of parliament.

He approached each one of them with meticulous care and an obsessive attention to detail, representing, as they did for him, the essential distinctive purpose of broadcasting. A letter he wrote to the Head of Outside Broadcasts, in 1947, during the preparations for the Wedding of Princess Elizabeth to Prince Philip gives an indication of his devotion: 'I managed to join the Palace Party this morning (all with blue noses!) and do some careful timing,' he wrote a few days before the ceremony. 'As a result, I suggest one small alteration to the commentators' timetable . . .' He then detailed the exact times at which the various coaches in the procession drew up at the west door of the Abbey. Although other commentators (Peter Scott and Wynford Vaughan-Thomas) were to cover the route to Westminster, while he would wait at the Abbey, he decided to follow the whole way to 'get a feel' of what it would be like:

> . . . the advance points [of the procession] entered Parliament Square, just before 11.25. In spite of this the coach did not draw up until exactly 11.28 at the west door. I suggest that Wynford should cue to Peter Scott at 11.25 instead of 11.26 . . . He will probably need to come to me at 11.27 instead of 11.28 but he can judge that, of course, as he sees it . . .
>
> One other point, for guidance. The bride *departed* on the dot at 12.30. The Irish Coach for the King and Queen drew up at 12.31.45., and stood until 12.34, exactly—when it left. That should give Scott about two minutes—possibly a shade less before he comes back to me.

In 1947, for an early and important outside broadcast, such painstaking concern was perhaps not surprising. But eighteen years later, after he had covered at least fifteen trooping the colours, his notes for the 1965 edition of that ceremony, are as closely and lovingly detailed as they were for the first.

His 'homework' which others more portentously called his 'associative material' was not only extensive: it was invaluable. The history of major outside broadcasts is littered with the frayed nerves of producers and engineers, just avoiding, and sometimes accepting disaster. Yet Richard Dimbleby (who could not abide clumsy or incompetent production) came to relish the prospect of crisis. When he alone stood between order and chaos, he was able to demonstrate his supremacy at his craft. To O.B. producers he became known, affectionately but only half-jokingly, as 'the Master'. In some notes for a lecture on 'The Art of the Commentary' he jotted down 'Homework—the vital ingredient—no matter how small or easy the job'. Sometimes near-disasters emerged from what should have been the most straightforward occasion. In 1954 the Queen Mother visited the Royal Needlework School at St. James's Palace to open an exhibition. Before her arrival Dimbleby was to introduce the items on display, give a brief history of the school, and then, at a fanfare of trumpets, announce the Queen Mother. He completed his brief tour on time and awaited the trumpets: there was silence. Unperturbed, though not knowing why royal protocol had failed, he conducted another tour around the exhibition, recounting the history of the craft as practised in China, Japan, Persia and Europe, explaining different stitches with the precision of a man who had spent the night before among their mysteries. He went on, talking fluently and expertly for twenty-five minutes, when at last the trumpets sounded. As the Queen Mother entered the gallery, instead of starting her tour, she walked up to him. Instinctively sensitive to the proprieties Dimbleby at once stuffed his microphone inside his jacket behind his back. The next day Fleet Street wondered aloud what the Queen Mother had mouthed silently to him on the television screen. Unmindful of the medium, but ever gracious, she in fact expressed herself grateful for the tour of the exhibition which she had watched him conduct on her television; it had been so fascinating that she had quite forgotten the time. She was sorry she was late, and hoped it had not proved inconvenient for him.

Some of the delays became famous. The President of France thirty-seven minutes late at Covent Garden; Prince Rainier and Princess Grace forty minutes late on the balcony at Monaco after their wedding; the Queen twenty minutes late at the French Opera and delayed forty-five minutes on a motorcade in Bonn. There were others too but the most famous was the fifty minutes' delay at the Wedding of Princess Margaret in 1960. The ceremony had been watched by an international audience of some 300 million people; it was the most glittering Royal occasion since the Coronation. In the Abbey, Dimbleby had delivered another of his distinctive commentaries in the soft, gentle phrases which so moved those who shared his feelings. Margaret entered the

Abbey with cheering crowds outside, and a swelling, majestic anthem inside:

> ...and the processional choir moves off with the bride's procession behind. For one moment we see the bride now as she looks about her at the Abbey in this lovely gown of white silk organza, with the glittering diadem on her head, the orchids in her hand, and the comforting, tall, friendly alert figure of the Duke of Edinburgh on whose right arm she can rely...

After the service he had hurried to Westminster pier to watch the departure of the happy couple on their honeymoon aboard the Royal Yacht. Together with Anthony Craxton (the producer with whom he worked on nearly all major occasions) he had already prepared a twenty minute sequence to guard against their late arrival. When Dimbleby had worked through his twenty minute sequence, with no sign of the couple, they had to begin again. Craxton's cameras followed Dimbleby's words onto the Tower, the Royal Yacht, the London skyline, the wharfs, Tower Bridge, even the helicopters which droned infuriatingly above his head—and he talked and talked and talked, smoothly, calmly, and elegantly for another thirty minutes.

> The most remarkable aspect of this unexpected marathon [wrote Craxton] was that Richard wove his commentary into a masterpiece of continuity; so that few people realised that what was being seen and said had not been planned in great detail beforehand. Unrelated subjects and objects were somehow, by Richard's description, made into a pattern that at once seemed natural and flowing.

By the end, for the first time, he had not merely run out of words, but had exhausted every last comma of his 'associative material'.

Before the wedding, one or two newspapers had reported the dismissive remark attributed to ITV's commentator, Brian Connell, that the wedding was 'something any competent senior reporter in Fleet Street could handle'; afterwards when it was embarrassingly plain that competence was not enough, the *Sunday Despatch* editorialised:

> Whose voice dominated the broadcast of the royal wedding?

Not Tony's or Princess Margaret's —they were barely audible. Not even the Archbishop of Canterbury's—movingly though he uttered the words of the service. The voice we're thinking of belongs to Richard Dimbleby. Once again this fine reporter rose to the occasion and won the respect of his fellow journalists as well as the affection of millions. When will he be honoured with the Knighthood he so well deserves?

And the *Daily Mirror*, which had not always been so generous had an editorial praising the bride, the Duke of Edinburgh and Richard Dimbleby who: 'never put a foot wrong...here's a bouquet for his performance yesterday'.

The BBC was delighted and warm in its praise. The Director of Television, Gerald Beadle, thanking Dimbleby for his 'superb and masterly performance', judged that the wedding was 'one of the most brilliantly successful broadcasts ever undertaken'. Leonard Miall (the Head of Talks) wrote simply of his 'magnificence'—'How extraordinarily lucky we are to have you'. And Kenneth Adam (Controller of Programmes, Television) wrote:

> I hope that the number of times that I have written to congratulate you and thank you for jobs you have done has not made you feel that this is now no more than a formality. I assure you this is not so, and on this occasion I am writing not only on my behalf but also on behalf of the Programme Committee, representing the most senior people on the programme side, to say that we are certain you surpassed even your own best last Friday. I was myself particularly pleased to see that the ranks of Tuscany, in the shape of the *Daily Mirror*, not only 'could scarce forbear to cheer' but did, in fact, cheer.

The universal acclaim prompted a rather different response from the BBC's Head of Outside Broadcasts, Peter Dimmock. For ten years the BBC had worried about the fact that the BBC relied exclusively on Dimbleby for every major occasion. Now Dimmock wondered 'whether it might not be wise to establish one or two commentator posts in the Television O.B. Department so that we can train some new voices in O.B. techniques... Dimbleby could walk under a bus or transfer his allegiance.'

It was not the first time that Peter Dimmock (and others) had expressed their anxieties about the lack of a substitute for Dimbleby. Five years before, in November 1955, Dimmock had noted:

> We have not yet been able to find a commentator to measure up to Dimbleby on royal occasions... The television O.B. from Covent Garden suffered considerably because Dimbleby had to give preference to a Twenty Questions Sound programme. Now that we are in competition with ITA I feel the Corporation would be wise to use Dimbleby whenever possible on Royal occasions...

And in 1964, the BBC's senior executives were still sending worried memos to each other about the problem; senior BBC men (like Ian Trethowan) were deputed to 'sit-in' on his commentaries to learn the craft; but there were no substitutes to be found.

Dimbleby had no doubt, as he once said, that 'great commentators are born not made'. It was partly a question of fluency—'the ability to translate instantly thoughts, colours and unexpected incidents into words; and to give form and shape to his sentences'. But there was more than that. Dimbleby derived great satisfaction from the particular skills required by television, which he knew (though he never mentioned it) that he possessed to a greater degree than anyone else. He delighted in the idea that the great commentator had to be a 'schizo-phrenic'—able to deliver 'well-chosen, harmonious phrases, balanced and delicately delivered to match the picture' in the most uncongenial circumstances. Those who imagined that his commentaries were spoken from a remote vantage point, where in lordly isolation he could concentrate on his flow of fine phrases, were reminded that he had sat on draughty rostrums, on roofs in the rain and the snow, inside crowded offices and dark crumpled cubicles:

> Once in position, the commentator, looks out of the corner of his eye at the scene before him, but otherwise concentrates only on his little monitor—which shows the same picture that the viewers are receiving at home. He holds a 'lip-microphone' to his mouth. Over his ears he wears a pair of headphones.

Through one he hears the sounds of the Occasion picked up by the microphones: the music, the military orders, the marching feet and the rattling hooves. In the other, he listens to his producer, talking not only to him but to cameramen, directors and production assistants—a cacophony of advice and instructions: 'On you Two! Hold it there. Pan up a bit. Three, I'm coming to you in a moment. Hold it... Mix to Three. O.K. Richard, ready for the identification. Not too fast. I'm getting behind you... watch it One, keep the Queen in the centre of your picture. Thank you. Richard, what's going on in the corner there? Lead me to it if you want to... No wait, they're starting the anthem...'

He hated mistakes, being much irritated even when he made the smallest slip (though he did smile when it was brought to his attention that he married off Edward Heath on one occasion, and transformed the Dean of Westminster into the elegant wife of an elderly British peer on another).

His sensitivity to criticism (which he had displayed so formidably in the war) was nevertheless acute; when taken even mildly to task, he reacted with the fiercely defensive arrogance of insecurity: behind every word of his rejoiner to some criticism of his coverage of the Trooping the Colour in 1962, was the implied question to the BBC executives 'Well, could you have done any better? On this occasion he was charged with giving the wrong time (11.45 a.m. instead of 10.45 a.m.)—'This must have been a slip of the tongue,' he replied, 'and I would have thought an entirely unimportant one. However, I apologise'. He identified Princess Margaret as Princess Anne—'This was the type of corrected error which is part and parcel of every commentary on such occasions. I was looking at two tiny figures far away, and casually changed Princess Margaret back to Princess Anne as soon as I was sure. This, again, strikes me as trivial.' He 'tended to fumble the identification of the members of the Royal posse' during the inspection—'Perhaps we might arrange for a playback of the O.B. to check my "fumbling" of the members of the Royal procession? While this is always an extremely difficult one to identify, as it passes so quickly, I was under the impression that I had done it rather neatly...' He was alleged to have identified Princess Margaret, on the balcony, as the Duchess of Kent. 'This is incorrect. The Duchess of Kent *was* standing behind the Queen Mother on the balcony with her mother-in-law and Princess Margaret.' In general, Peter Dimmock (who had made these points) thought that Dimbleby had 'seemed less sure of himself than usual'—'How this impression was given,' reported Dimbleby, 'I do not understand; I felt perfectly sure of myself.' He did not pause to consider that the fact that the BBC was prepared to make such detailed criticism (and in fifteen years it occurred on no more than a handful of occasions) was an indication of the importance the Corporation attached to such occasions, and of his own mastery of the craft.

In a period where the technical complexity of an expanding medium dominated the television mind, Richard Dimbleby complained repeatedly of the way in which the commentators (without whom the electronic wizardry was a waste of money) were not treated with the respect their pre-eminence demanded; that they were not given proper facilities: tables to work at, chairs to sit on, quiet rooms to rest and think in, good positions to see from, monitors that were not fuzzy. He sensed early (and with some prescience) that the machines were beginning to run the men, that the electronic toys of the medium could soon become more important than the message they were supposed to transmit, and he did his best to resist the inevitable. The foreigners were the worst offenders: in a letter to Cecil McGivern he asked that the BBC raise the matter at a forthcoming meeting of the European Broadcasting Union:

> There is a steadily growing tendency among the television services abroad to divorce commentators from the scene of action by grouping them at a convenient point to deliver their commentaries from monitors... I am sure the first consideration now among these television services is not whether it is feasible to give the commentator a direct view of the proceedings, but simply whether it is not much easier technically to group everyone together in a big room.

The irritations of this were great:

> a commentator who is limited to one monitor set out for his vision might just as well be doing the job from his home broadcasting centre without being abroad at all. He loses all his preview, has no idea what the producer is likely to do next

(and the Continentals, as you know, have a pretty habit of changing their minds in mid-stream), and cannot use that part of the scene before him which is temporarily out of camera shot to deepen and reinforce his commentary. Furthermore if anything goes wrong, he is completely out on a limb... when Churchill received the Cross of Liberation from de Gaulle, I was cooped up in an office with no view of the proceedings with all sorts of odd people strolling around and coming in and out throughout... I notice with misgivings that more and more often it is accepted automatically that the commentator will be miles away from the event... I am quite certain that general acceptance of this commentary off the monitor is going to lead to a very serious decline in the quality of the work that we do...

His anxieties were justified. Within a few years (in 1963) he was to commentate on the wedding of Princess Alexandra from a sound-proofed booth in the BBC's central control room in the Abbey. He had before him eighteen monitors on which he could see at the same time what was happening at at least six different locations between Buckingham Palace and the High Altar. Where ITV had at least six different commentators the BBC relied solely on him. It made for great smoothness and easy transitions, as he switched from inside the Abbey to the procession outside with a gentle guiding phrase—but he did not enjoy the divorce from reality. Anthony Craxton, always sensitive to his needs, was equally apprehensive about the principle, but preferred one Dimbleby to half a dozen others. Craxton's judgment proved right. However, respecting Dimbleby's urge to be 'on the scene', he arranged on the next great State occasion in St. Paul's Cathedral that Dimbleby should have two booths— one filled with monitors showing the processional route, the other, overlooking the nave, at the service below him.

Fluency, technical skill, obsession with detail, an ability to stay calm in emergency; these qualities made him the most professional man in the medium. Other qualities—more subtle—made him 'irreplaceable'. In some notes he prepared for a lecture, he underlined the importance of 'the quality of the emotion'—'he [the commentator] must *feel* without letting his emotions run away with him.' He believed absolutely, and unquestioningly, in what he did. It was his uncanny ability not only to observe the event, but to enter completely into its mood that lifted his commentaries above the expert or the eloquent and made him, as *The Sunday Times* said: 'Our Public Orator'. The 'our' was significant. The tones in which Dimbleby rehearsed the rituals of state (tones much criticised by those more sceptical or more cynical) precisely reflected public attitudes towards them. It is tempting to dismiss the State Occasion as an insignificant or irrelevant charade—a sham, jingoistic rite designed to blind the people to reality. Yet every State presents a ceremonial front to its own people and to other nations. Behind the expensive formalities of a Trooping the Colour, or a Moscow Day Parade, or an American Presidential motorcade, lies propaganda, of course—but also traditions, customs, and attitudes which have their roots deep in the national psyche. Though distrusted by some, such public statements of national identity cannot easily be dismissed: that they are made, and the way in which they are made, are an expression of a particular social need. In the Fifties these ceremonies were rarely ever criticised. They were expressions of national self-esteem in which the treasured institutions were displayed for the first time, through the medium of television, to a huge audience.

Dimbleby's patriotic pride, his devotion to the values which the ceremonies seemed to symbolise was shared by most people; it was the very ordinariness of his emotions which contributed to his extraordinary success. One Controller of Programmes, Stuart Hood (who later became a radical critic of the BBC) once described Dimbleby as 'a kind of Everyman, the voice and personification of thoughts and emotions no less deeply felt for being either mute or inadequately formulated'. Though Dimbleby's views and sentiments were inimicable to him, Hood recognised the truth that they 'were echoed by the generality of the citizens of this country'. His art, his conscious purpose, was to make the essentially meaningless appear significant; his words were to make sense of a succession of otherwise incomprehensible pictures. In the process he created that sense of moment, of history, and mystique which, as the Controller of Television had intimated, made his words matter.

It was in the sense that he spoke *for*, as well as *to* the people that during the Fifties he became, in the words of Huw Weldon, 'the voice of the nation . . . the voice of our generation, and probably the most telling voice on BBC radio or television in this country so far'. Richard Dimbleby's voice, interpreting solemn events, crystallising national self-esteem, was loved by millions of people; it pleased the Establishment; and it was also invaluable to the BBC's own status. In this sense, 'the voice of the BBC' was not only 'irreplaceable' but invaluable. After the Coronation, as television began in earnest to take hold of the public imagination (in the following year the number of television licences doubled), more and more State occasions were covered. It was through its brilliant coverage of these events in the Fifties and Sixties that BBC television secured its place in the public mind as the *national* service. And Richard Dimbleby's own personal following was so great that much of the Corporation's public prestige was embodied in him. On this level the BBC and Richard Dimbleby became synonymous. In the process the BBC entrenched itself firmly in the Establishment which had once been suspicious of the new medium—respected and even welcomed by other institutions of state. It is probable that, during this period Richard Dimbleby did more than any other individual to secure the position of the monarch in the affections of the British people; he certainly did more than anyone else to secure the reputation of the Broadcasting Corporation.

Dimbleby was not merely moved by ceremony. The human content of formal occasions touched him too. So when he went to cover solemn moments in other countries, he reacted, not with the mannered precision of the diplomat or statesman, but in ordinary, universal terms. Like the rest of ordinary mankind, he was shocked by the death of President Kennedy in 1963, disturbed by its implications, but most of all upset by the intimate human tragedy for his family. Much moved, his voice once half-breaking, Dimbleby reflected the world's grief in his commentary that day:

> The two children join their mother, little Caroline and little John, such poignant figures. And everyone about them in black... All the time Mrs. Kennedy preserves this quiet silent dignity. Many people ask how long can she continue. And the family follow behind. The President, his face lined with sorrow and indeed with strain which has shown in the three days since he took office, follows slowly behind in his place... President de Gaulle follows up the steep steps, Queen Frederika, King Baudoin, the Chancellor of Austria, the President and the Chancellor of West Germany—two by

two—they enter from the brilliant sunshine, through the west door of the Cathedral, and inside to where the Low Pontifical Requiem begins, the choir chanting as they come in...

And after the services, as they left, he continued in the same quiet slow terms, no word scripted beforehand, against the rustle of leaves, the faint sound of birds, the murmur of voices, the distant noise of traffic, and one funeral bell tolling:

And so outside to the sunshine where the bearer party, some of them coloured servicemen, drawn from all the services, proudly—reverently—carefully—bear their dead President and Commander-in-Chief down the steep steps back to the gun carriage which waits for them at the bottom. [He paused while the bell still tolled, then continued:] Cardinal Cushing sprinkles holy water on the coffin—and kisses it. Somewhere high above a single bell is tolling and the slow, careful party moves on to the gun carriage. Mrs. Kennedy, the children, the other mourners, follow down the steps behind. The Presidential flag, the American Eagle between the Arrow of War and the Dove of Peace—but facing the Dove of Peace—is borne away to take its place in the procession—for the journey—to begin—to the National Cemetery—at Arlington... And thus here in the United States, the official events of a sad and bitter day have come to an end. They leave behind, burning like the eternal flame that lit his graveside an hour ago, a thousand memories of the man lost to this nation and to the world.

II

Birth of Panorama

He who moulds public sentiment goes deeper than he
who enacts statutes or pronounces decisions.

ABRAHAM LINCOLN

WHEN RICHARD DIMBLEBY DREW UP OUTSIDE THE
gloomy back-street main entrance of Lime Grove on Monday,
September 19th 1955, he found no expectant cluster of schoolboys
hunting autographs waiting to greet him. Later, when Panorama
had become a national institution, a small crowd would always be
there to welcome him. The first opening of the BBC's Window
on the World was a distinctly modest occasion. No Corporation
heralds trumpeted; no public soothsayers pronounced upon its
future. The *Manchester Guardian*, it is true, reported rather limply
that Panorama would be a weekly programme every Monday
night: 'bringing illustrated reports, personalities and comments on
affairs at home and abroad' in which Richard Dimbleby would be
'the chief commentator', but inside the BBC the only certainty
about the programme was the role to be played by Dimbleby. 'He
will be the central figure in this important new weekly programme,' wrote Panorama's guiding spirit, Grace Wyndham-
Goldie (a most formidable and influential intellect), urging that he
should be paid between 75 and 100 guineas for each programme—
'I don't want to lose him...he is to be a key figure in this
forthcoming new series.'

It was ten years since the collapse of War Report, and ten
years to the week since a reluctant Richard Dimbleby had been
forced out of the Corporation. In the intervening years he had

become the foremost figure in radio and television in Britain, the dominating voice of the BBC. Yet he had never lost the journalistic obsession which had led him to batter at the doors of Broadcasting House in 1936; to become the first BBC war correspondent; to fly again and again in bombers over Germany; and to stay in Berlin to the very end of the war. From the beginning he had produced an increasing flow of ideas. As well as his plans for radio, he had before the war submitted a scheme for the televising of news and current affairs to the first Director of Television, Gerald Cock—while nearly everyone else still regarded the new medium as a frivolous 'magic box' to amuse the populace. In 1943, he had urged that, at the end of the war the Corporation should station BBC reporters in Europe ready 'to fly anywhere at a moment's notice to "be on the spot" to cover the news'. In 1946, he had transformed Down Your Way from a 'record' into a 'feature' programme and he had helped to devise London Town. About Britain, which followed, was his own idea, and he had urged that it should cover 'hard news' so that its effect would not just be to tell viewers 'this is beautiful' but also 'this is important'.

By the early Fifties he was feeling intense frustration at the limitations of both programmes. Although they were popular (and he was publicly judged to be 'the Number One Personality' of the Documentary department) he knew that their days were numbered, that they were cumbersome and in important ways, phoney. When at the end of 1954, Maurice Wiggin in the *Sunday Times* made the first public complaint about London Town, he was voicing doubts that Dimbleby had nursed for four years.

> We have had too much fact-based fiction cooked up in the studio [complained Wiggin] ... No matter how painstaking the research nor how honest the intention, it is still less than the truth... Television is an unbeatable reporter: it should go straight to its sources. Agreed the camera must select as the human eye selects: but selection is very different from 'reconstruction'.

London Town and About Britain had their critics within the BBC, and in the summer of 1954 it was rumoured that Cecil McGivern was planning to drop both programmes. At once the press reported that 'if the television chiefs get their way, Richard Dimbleby, one of the most famous of TV figures, will virtually disappear from the screen'. And Dimbleby was quoted as saying, 'If I were dependent on television, this means I would be ruined.' 'Don't let him go' implored one anguished critic—though most guessed correctly that the BBC had no such intention.

Amongst those in the BBC who saw London Town's faults was Grace Wyndham-Goldie, who thought it 'quite beneath Richard's intellectual stature'. Wyndham-Goldie was a producer in the television Talks Department where she had developed the radio 'talk' into the television 'illustrated talk', by using pictures, prints, photographs and film to accompany the arguments of her speaker. The 'illustrated talk', had its origins in the didactic tradition of radio; and Grace Wyndham-Goldie (who was more of a teacher than a journalist by nature) found the intellectual sloppiness of programmes like London Town wasteful of talent and resources. The original idea for Dimbleby's programme had been borrowed from the 'soft' feature pages of Fleet Street; it invited ordinary people to speak but not to air their views; it did not enquire, or analyse, or explain, but like Down Your Way, held up a rose-tinted mirror to the sunny side of life. It was from an unlikely fusion of the form of Dimbleby's London Town and the content of Wyndham-Goldie's Talks that Panorama was born.

In 1950, five years before the birth of what was to become the most important regular programme ever produced by the BBC, both Wyndham-Goldie and Dimbleby, in different departments, and unknown to each other, were discovering a new type of television. Wyndham-Goldie saw television moving towards 'something quite new, for which no name has yet been found; whose form is only just beginning to emerge; which has to be shaped, to be invented, to be created; and which is going to be of the greatest importance'. At the same time, pursuing his undying obsession with the potential of the young medium, Dimbleby wrote to Philip Dorté, who was Head of the Film Department: 'I have in mind,' he wrote, 'the coverage of a field which I submit television has not yet tackled. It is the big and vital field of topical but non-immediate news.' He went on to distinguish between three types of news: 'immediate' news, which was covered by the Newsreel; 'permanent' news which was the responsibility of the Documentary; and 'current' news—'which does not demand coverage "tomorrow" but which cannot be left for three months'. This field, he argued, had not yet been dealt with by television.

He thought that the programme should confine itself to the coverage of events in Britain to begin with, though there was no reason why it 'should not go as much further afield as it likes'. It would report either those events which were not dramatic enough for inclusion in a news bulletin, or which started as 'immediate' news but were worthy of treatment in greater depth. He suggested that 'a well-known observer, accepted by the viewer, should be the central figure of each report, rather in the manner of the special and named correspondent sent to an event by a news-paper'—though he forbore to add that he thought he might be of some service in this connection.

The programme would be made on location on film. There would be no need for 'reconstruction' or 'mixing' between film and studio; the whole story, he wrote:

> should be complete when the unit returns to the studio, and no dubbing or studio sequences will be needed, except, of course, technical editing. In a sense the production might be described as a filmed television O.B. inasmuch as it all takes place in, say, twenty minutes. A major difference, however, lies in the fact that, although the action of the report is continuous, it does not need to be in one place...

And—an indication of how revolutionary his idea was—he continued,

> The fact that the inclusion of three locations in twenty minutes of a continual story must, *ipso facto*, be a 'cheat' does not matter. What does matter is that each section of the report comes from the authentic spot. The mix or dissolve from one point to another is a technical trick to be worked out by the producer...

At the end of his proposal, he summarised:

> It is an on-the-spot investigation, presented as a connected whole... It must come back to the studio complete and ready, but for the trimming. Most important of all, the observer must lead, point and explain throughout. He is guiding the viewer's eye in his capacity as a trained news man; he is *NOT* a commentator talking to suit the requirements of a cut and tailored picture.

I believe that this scheme ... offers something that television does not yet have—a regular, authoritative report on news of common interest in which the viewers can be made to feel that they have gone out from their firesides to see and hear for themselves.

His proposal for a 'current news' programme in 1950 was as remarkable as his plans for radio had been in 1936; both were far-reaching in their implications for the BBC; both defined a new journalistic craft; both were precise and detailed; both were carried out; and both came before the Corporation was ready for them. In 1950, Philip Dorté was much taken with Dimbleby's scheme, submitting it at once to Cecil McGivern, and writing back to Dimbleby a few days later to say that the Controller of Television liked it very much too. They wished him to prepare six programmes for the series but regretted that it would be impossible to draw up a contract at once because of the shortage, among other things, 'of certain pieces of film equipment'. It was the old story: although sound cameras were available, television was not important enough to be given the money to buy them. Without a sound camera Dimbleby's proposal was impracticable. So Dimbleby's programme—he thought of calling it 'Eye-witness'—disappeared into a file, never to be removed again. Those who came later would be credited with the creation of 'current affairs' television. His blueprint came five years too soon.

It may seem curious that Richard Dimbleby did not submit his plan to the BBC's huge and prestigious News Division instead of the Documentary Department. It was, after all, to be a 'news' and not a 'documentary' programme. But the history of the BBC is littered with the limbs of those who have torn each other apart in pointless internecine warfare—in 1950, BBC News and BBC Documentaries were engaged in bloody, profitless hostilities, which had a profound effect on the future of radio and television.

The doctrine of broadcasting which had driven Dimbleby out of the BBC in 1945 had forced BBC News to retreat, humiliatingly, into the cautious old ways of the Thirties. (See Chapter 9, page 204.) On the eve of victory in 1945, when War Report had won for the BBC a reputation for flair, accuracy and courage, which it had never before enjoyed, the new Director-General, William Haley, made an extraordinary, and on the face of it, inexplicable decision. Two years after judging that the reputation of the BBC 'for years to come' would hang on the way its war correspondents covered the invasion of Europe, he calmly accepted that in peace there was no reason why the BBC should form its own news collecting service in the United Kingdom. That decision, taken despite the furious opposition of A. P. Ryan (the Controller of News), was tantamount to a decree that after the war the Corporation should rely yet again on the News Agencies for its coverage of 'home' news.

In BBC mythology, the man blamed for much of the bitterness which followed was a New Zealander, unknown outside the BBC but of immense authority within the Corporation, called Tahu Hole. His influence had been felt in the News Room since before the end of the war. Made News Editor in 1948, he imposed rules and restraints on the staff of the News Room which stifled talent and strangled enthusiasm. Under him the search for truth was destroyed by the demand for accuracy; the slogan 'if in doubt, leave out' was elevated to the status of a divine commandment. An obsession for political 'balance' made a mockery of proper journalism; investigation was impossible; 'scoops' were forbidden; the authority of the News Agencies was absolute; and no report by a BBC foreign correspondent could appear in a bulletin unless it had been first confirmed by at least two Agencies. As a result radio ceased to be a serious journalistic medium. By the time it had recovered, 'steam' radio had been superseded by television.

It is too simple to blame Tahu Hole alone. He was a faithful servant of the BBC, an honest interpreter of the Corporation's will. In the Twenties and Thirties Sir John Reith had sedulously stunted the growth of news so that he should not be exposed to the cold winds of controversy, or felled (as he had so nearly been in 1926) by Government displeasure. In the war years it was only when victory was assured, when controversy was absent, when politics was dead, that the war reporters were free fully to practise their craft. Even then for all their brilliance, they spoke on behalf of a BBC which was a weapon of war, a servant of Government. At the end of the war, with the victory of democracy over fascism, the BBC still lacked the courage to test its independence. For the first time in twenty years, it had the techniques, the equipment, the talent and the reputation to exploit radio in peace as in war. Instead the Corporation squandered the lot. Like Sir John Reith before him, free to let news flourish, Tahu Hole allowed it to wither.

It did not go unnoticed by the listeners. In March 1947, after Britain had been gripped by the longest and coldest winter in memory the *Spectator's* critic spoke the weary refrain of a constant complaint:

> The news bulletins and news talks of course dealt with the country's plight in a bald and colourless way, but surely something more imaginative should have been forthcoming. There was an abundance of material for background and 'documentary' programmes which might have helped people to understand the crisis and appreciate what it means to the country. Such lack of imagination and enterprise is, I suppose, only to be expected from a bureaucracy.

It was ten years to the week since Richard Dimbleby's reports from the Fen Floods had been acclaimed as ushering in a new form of journalism: now it was as if none of it had ever happened.

Tahu Hole's formidable influence was not confined to Broadcasting House. Like other senior BBC executives he appeared to regard television with contempt. For many years the only concession the News Division made to the existence of the upstart young medium was to 'pipe' the Home Service bulletin across from Broadcasting House to Alexandra Palace where it was transmitted late at night over a blank screen.

The Television Newsreel which was started in 1948 by Philip Dorté's department was regarded with abhorrence by the News Division—which fortunately lacked the bureaucratic might to destroy television's vulgar little journalistic venture. The Newsreel, famous and popular as it was, had limited journalistic pretensions; it was slickly produced, entertainingly written (by young talents like Richard Cawston and Paul Fox) but most of its 'news' was several days old, and all of it had the timeless quality of the cinema newsreels from which the idea for the programme had been borrowed. If television journalism was to advance there would have to be a marriage between the techniques of the Newsreel and the facilities of the News Division. Such a union, given Hole's hostility to television and a violent clash of temperament between him and Dorté, was out of the question. In that sterile atmosphere, no ideas could flourish, no advance could be made.

By the end of the struggle the 'old men' of radio were to find themselves despised and rejected by the 'brash young men' of television; and, more important, an artificial wedge would have been driven between 'news' (controlled by BBC Radio) and 'current affairs' (created by BBC Television). For whilst the sorry struggle over news between the old and the new medium exhausted the energies of both protagonists, neither noticed that the restless talents of the Television Talks Department (untouched by the dispute) were quietly creating that 'something quite new' of which Grace Wyndham-Goldie had written in 1950 and which Richard Dimbleby had identified as 'current news'.

The birth of Panorama was a momentous event in the history of the BBC. In September 1955 spurred on by the imminent threat of commercial television, the Corporation took the first tentative steps into the mud of the real world from which it had flinched for more than thirty years: where people endured hardship and poverty; where there was ignorance and prejudice; where the powerful in one country would overrun the weak in another; and where the mass of mankind was threatened by extinction as a result of a confrontation between two incompatible and obnoxious ideologies. Panorama became the first BBC programme to tread in the political minefields that competent reporters always have to cross. For the first time the BBC allowed the people to be heard, on topics which mattered, in ways which were memorable.

It was for these reasons that the Talks Department required the presence of Dimbleby in the Panorama 'Chair'. 'I can put it no other way,' Grace Wyndham-Goldie has since said: 'he was quite simply the only person who could do it. His knowledge and authority were unique; he had an understanding of life which was based on his own experience, not on what he had read in the newspapers or seen on television.' The decision to ask Dimbleby was quickly approved; not least because the Corporation, fearful that he would leave to join the new independent television service, was anxious to give him a regular television commitment to replace the outmoded London Town and About Britain. But they were also frightened that he would refuse the offer: by 1955 men like Peter Dimmock, who was in charge of Outside Broadcasts, referred openly to him as 'the prince of commentators' or the 'master', and producers of radio and television 'O.B.'s' fought for his services. He was also very busy. On the face of it, the new Window on the World, produced by the tiny Talks Department, might not seem a very tempting proposition. Not knowing of his obsession with 'current news' the BBC was delighted when he accepted the invitation with alacrity. No-one, least of all Dimbleby, had any idea how extraordinarily significant his decision would be; that, in the words of Sir Hugh Greene, 'Panorama with Richard Dimbleby, would become the embodiment of the BBC, so that it would be impossible to conceive of the BBC without them.'

Panorama derived its name but little else from a programme which had been running every fortnight for the previous two years under the chairmanship of Max Robertson. The original Panorama had consisted of a mish-mash of disconnected and frequently frivolous items that had won commendation from no-one. It had been chiefly distinguished by the idiosyncratic presence of Malcolm Muggeridge who had enlivened one programme by enquiring of a celebrated brain surgeon, who had just completed the separation of Siamese twins, whether, if called upon to do so, he could join them together again.

By the summer of 1955 Cecil McGivern had decided that the viewers should be spared any more of the programme. He invited Leonard Miall (who had become Head of Talks) and his assistant, Grace Wyndham-Goldie, to rejuvenate or replace it. Wyndham-Goldie at once said that if she could have the freedom to hire and fire whomsoever she wished, she would take it on—but she had insisted that Richard Dimbleby should be 'anchor-man'.

Panorama's first producer, under the guidance of Wyndham-Goldie, was a young graduate, aged twenty-five, called Michael Peacock. He was one of the clever young men (Donald Baverstock who created 'Tonight', was another) whom BBC mythology has turned into a genius of the medium. In fact Peacock (who was one of several future television executives discovered and trained by Grace Wyndham-Goldie) was able, tough, and not a little arrogant. He had first met Dimbleby five months earlier, on the eve of the Queen's return from a triumphant and much publicised Commonwealth tour, when he had been put in charge of a television 'special' (in last-minute rivalry with radio) to celebrate her return. Despite the disapproval of the Documentary Department (which was jealous of its 'star') Peacock asked Dimbleby to be the anchor-man for an extremely complicated half-hour round-up—Peacock's first major studio programme. It was a success: 'When radio circuits failed he switched faultlessly to the standby routines worked out the night before,' wrote Peacock, 'he produced immaculate unscripted documentaries to the edited telerecordings he had not seen before. He hit cue after cue as he promised he would.' And afterwards he wrote admiringly to Dimbleby: 'As I told you repeatedly after the programme, no-one else but you could have done it... I do hope that we can work together again sometime.'

The fact that Richard Dimbleby seemed the only man capable of holding a programme together in the face of catastrophe, led Wyndham-Goldie to suggest him as 'anchor-man' for the 1955 General Election programme. At first the Director-General, Sir Ian Jacob (who had replaced Haley), was reluctant, preferring a neutral political figure from outside the BBC for a programme which would demand great political sensitivity if the BBC's impartiality was not to be damaged. He thought that Dimbleby lacked the necessary expertise. Like so many in Broadcasting House he had little understanding of television, and certainly no comprehension of the technical complexity of a General Election studio. Grace Wyndham-Goldie insisted on Dimbleby, and eventually Jacob relented. More than anyone else in television, she recognised that Dimbleby's contribution would be much more than professional. With that flair which enabled her to hire most of television's ablest practitioners, it was her intuitive, though tentative understanding of the extraordinary rapport which Dimbleby could establish with his audience that made him her first and final choice.

Like all its successors the 1955 Election programme was a marathon; Dimbleby was 'on air' throughout Thursday night, took a shower, had a shave and ate an apple at five o'clock on Friday morning, was on again at 7 a.m., and did not finish broadcasting that day until late that night. He revelled in it. The 1955 Election night was the first of what were to become famous national occasions: with David Butler the enthusiastic psephologist (though no-one yet called him that) on one side and Robert Mackenzie (not yet swingometered) excitedly charting the state of the parties on the other; and sitting in the middle, dominating events, Richard Dimbleby. A critic, describing his part in such proceedings, noticed his extraordinary role:

As always there is Dimbleby, adding to the general proceedings by his very presence a tremendous sense of occasion. Dimbleby places his finger-tips gently but firmly together, and looks thoughtfully for a moment up to the right-hand corner of the studio ceiling, before telling us that it might be a good moment now to hear what Bob Mackenzie has to say about the situation. And so smoothly does Dimbleby do it that Mackenzie takes on a kind of oracular significance even before he gets the first word out.

Before the programme, Dimbleby asked that a detailed card index of every constituency be prepared for him. At home he learned the details, turned them into his own material with extensive hieroglyphical notes on each card, and then 'on the night' having memorised most of it, he provided an extensive flow of information about the candidates, as if he had been a political correspondent all his life. In addition, his Down Your Way experience gave him knowledge of so many of the constituencies that he was able to throw in small asides which transformed a statistical occasion into a human event. (In the 1959 Election, when the card-index system collapsed, he stayed up until five o'clock in the morning on the previous day to make his own index, and then worked without flagging throughout Election night.) On every Election occasion, one or other of his colleagues would be astonished to see him at six o'clock on the Friday morning, when everyone else had gone for an hour's sleep, walking backwards and forwards across the studio in slippers, rehearsing his moves and preparing his words for the opening of that day's proceedings.

After the 1955 Election Grace Wyndham-Goldie, who was not given to over-statement, was overwhelmed by his performance:

> I appreciate your whole approach more than I can tell you [she wrote afterwards]. It was not so much your immense skill and the professional ease of your approach, for which I was grateful, since I had expected and counted upon these; but I was more delighted that I can say by your unfailing good humour in circumstances that were often, I know, very trying, and the confidence which your professionalism and ease gave us all. You were generosity itself in your help to everybody who worked with you and not least to myself... Thank you very much and I hope that we may work together again some day. Yours ever, Grace Wyndham-Goldie.

At the end of that first 'tele' marathon in the BBC's history, Ed Murrow, America's most distinguished broadcaster, appeared on the screen to pay tribute to the BBC and to Dimbleby; it had been a triumph for the young medium, and praise which might have seemed mawkish a few years later (such was the speed of television's growth) was universally regarded as an appropriate flourish.

The tone of unanimous delight in a generous British press was set by Peter Black in the *Daily Mail*, who recorded that

> In the history of TV, this election will become a significant date ranking with the Coronation, which of course it greatly exceeded in complexity and duration. The operation lasted nearly twenty-four hours; ranged in distance over almost every area where there was a television transmitter and came over without any serious hitch. From all the hours that I was watching I recall only one unrehearsed incident; the extremely gratifying sight of Richard Dimbleby eating a biscuit. I congratulate Dimbleby on the most impressive performance of his career, as much a test of character as stamina, and one which could only have been achieved by a clear, keen and flexible brain. For over eighteen hours Dimbleby held the visual part of the broadcast together; and at the end his eye and voice were as vigorous as ever . . .

Only Alan Brien in the *Observer* noticed the film *See It Now* which Ed Murrow had prepared for American viewers about the British campaign. While the BBC had been paralysed by the strait-jacket imposed on it by the political parties at elections, Ed Murrow had been around the country filming the campaign. Once the polls were closed, the BBC was free to show it.

> This was a brilliant piece of journalism [wrote Brien]. What has Murrow got (apart from audacity and imagination) which the BBC couldn't buy with our money? *See It Now* was, perhaps, too good. It had more argument, passion and excitement than the whole of the Election campaign. The people in it talked with a racy vehemence that was slightly shocking. The earthy candour of the muscular slum housewife, the lady-like reasonableness of the suburban shopper, the cynical distrust of the two slightly drunk men in the pub; this, one suddenly realised, was what the television camera was meant to capture.

It was precisely the absence of this real world from British television that Panorama would have to rectify if it were to cross the
twin barriers from the didactic to the journalistic, and the 'soft' to
the 'hard'—and so become the 'something quite new' which Grace
Wyndham-Goldie had visualised.

The first Panorama, reflecting the uncertainty as to what precise
form the 'important new weekly programme' should take,
startled no-one. There was film from Moscow of some Japanese
Kabuki dancers; an interview with Lord Harewood and another
with the Reverend Marcus Morris; Max Robertson reported on
foreign visitors to Britain; Patrick O'Donovan spoke from the
United Nations General Assembly; Woodrow Wyatt reported
from Malta; and Richard Dimbleby helped John Cherington
demonstrate a radio-controlled tractor in the studio. Each item
lasted about seven minutes, and, although the programme was
lively and slick, it contained nothing which would ruffle any
British political feathers: it lacked investigative or controversial
bite. Later Michael Peacock was privately to judge that the early
Panoramas were no more than 'disconnected jottings in the
marginalia of our times'.

Gradually, however, the programme stepped forward. In the
fourth edition, alongside a film on myxamatosis and a reconstruction of the Battle of Trafalgar, there was a film on unemployment
in Northern Ireland. Three weeks later Woodrow Wyatt produced a report on the housing shortage in Britain, and two weeks
after that conducted a rehearsal on the debate about Capital
Punishment. At the beginning of 1956, while Malcolm
Muggeridge reported improbably from a Hunt Ball, Wyatt sent
back the first of many despatches from the Middle East, standing
pugnaciously in the desert pointing first towards Israel and then
towards Egypt, with all the aplomb of a seasoned tour operator.
By later standards his techniques (though not his journalistic
skills) were primitive, but when it was still a novelty to rush film
back to London the day before transmission, hustle it through
editing and onto the air, not only Lime Grove (where the Talks
Department had its headquarters), but the critics and the public
were entranced by the drama. Panorama soon had an audience
of over eight million people, which far outstripped 'Wagon
Train'—the opposition chosen by the programme planners of
ITV.

The bizarre cocktail of the trivial and the significant which marked the new programme soon gave way to a more consistently serious approach. In the early summer of 1956 Christopher Chataway was lured away from ITN (where with Robin Day he had become one of television's first 'newscasters') to join Panorama's reporting team. At once he started to make a series of sharp reports which for the first time clearly defined the distinctive character of 'Current Affairs' television. In May he reported on the mood of the Welsh coalminers, and a month later on unemployment in the car industry. But in September, on Panorama's first birthday, he made the most memorable report of the year—which showed for the first time how television could strip away comfortable British clichés in a style and with an impact that Fleet Street could never match. His subject was the 'colour-bar' at British Railways. His technique was the dramatic intercutting of contrasting points of view. First he interviewed some unemployed Jamaicans who told him they had tried to get work at the Smithfield depot, and had been refused, despite a long list of vacancies on British Railways' books. Then he spoke to Management, producing a memorable exchange with the Goods Agent at Smithfield: Why had the men been turned away? 'Well, there is a general reluctance by men to work with these coloured chaps,' replied the Agent (with more candour than more wily interviewees would permit themselves in later years). Chataway persisted: 'But you have vacancies now and you would take a white man now, and yet these coloured men were told that there were no vacancies at all.'

'Well, you see, we're dependent, as I say on the nature of the chap as to his ability to undertake . . .'

'. . . but these men weren't tested at all; in fact there is really no denying that in this depot there is a colour bar.'

Impatiently, Chataway questioned an NUR representative:

'But now, not every coloured man surely is much slower than every Englishman; you *can't* judge a whole race like that.'

'No, I'm talking now of the majority of the particular type of coloured man that I've contacted . . .'

It was a new type of reporting, in which the interviewer assumed the right, and the duty, to inquire, investigate and cross-examine. As one reviewer observed: 'That official tried to get round the question . . . But Chataway kept pestering him like a dog with a bone.' And Richard Dimbleby, whose journalistic antennae were always more acute than some of his colleagues chose to imagine, said later with proprietal pride, that Chataway was 'the chap who never takes no for an answer'. It was Dimbleby's presence in the studio which made such aggression acceptable.

Another symptom of Panorama's growing confidence was that its reporters were allowed to editorialise with impunity. Thus Chataway ended his report with the words:

> What is disturbing, I think, is that the men at Smithfield, and at depots like it, should deprive West Indians of any chance to prove themselves simply because of their colour . . . If this colour prejudice persists, then there's going to be a great deal of un-employment of coloured men. The only other alternative is to ban West Indians from coming into this country, and if we ever decided to do that we should certainly have forfeited our right for good and all to criticise South Africa or the extremists in the Southern States of America. Good night.

It is inconceivable that the BBC would have allowed one of its own men to broadcast such a statement before the advent of Panorama (and equally inconceivable, incidentally, once that 'only other alternative' had become Government policy).

In the public mind, Panorama soon became identified with Richard Dimbleby; others might make fine films or conduct sharp studio discussions; others might plan, edit and organise but Dimbleby *was* Panorama. When Panorama reported the crises of Suez and Hungary in the autumn of 1956, Richard Dimbleby's air of reassuring authority turned Panorama from a magazine programme into a national institution. The absurdity of Suez and the tragedy of Hungary, destroying futile dreams about Britain, and confirming nightmares about Russia, was baffling, disconcerting and frightening. Panorama returned again and again to the subjects, with Dimbleby guiding his public through the military complexities and human miseries with a mixture of professional detachment, common man's perplexity, and paternal wisdom.

At the end of October, as the Soviet army crushed all resistance before it, and refugees poured out of Budapest towards Austria, he introduced the first film of Hungary in sombre language:

> Good evening. This is the Hungarian frontier—as near as any

film camera has yet got to the centre of the violent and heart-rending events which may prove to be the turning point in the history of post-war Europe ... you can only pray that something worthwhile will emerge from all this courage and sacrifice.

In Panorama, even when he had few words, he spoke in the sweeping and supra-journalistic terms that had been so effective in the war; and gradually the Panorama audience began to base their judgments upon his attitude. The following week, when he leaned across his desk and picked up the studio phone to ask, 'Have you got Vienna ... you have? Thank you,' it was almost as if he were conducting not merely Panorama, but the event itself. 'It does appear tonight,' he observed with measured (but unfeigned) sadness, 'as if events in Hungary, the revolution in Hungary, is moving to a tragic end ...' And from Vienna, on cue, the refugees appeared to tell the pathetic story of the collapse before the Russian tanks.

In the same programme, when he conducted Rear Admiral Angus Nicholl around two huge relief maps of Egypt and the Suez Canal, it again seemed as if Dimbleby (and not the Admiral) were explaining what had happened that morning after the British troops had landed on Egyptian soil. From Nicholl, Dimbleby elicited the opinion that the British troops had control of the sea and the air; that the canal (which the Egyptians had blocked) would soon be cleared; that Egyptian resistance was negligible; that no other Arab states would intervene; that 'negotiations' would soon persuade other Governments in the area to 'carry out the will of—er—that we have decided on imposing'. And, typically, at a point when some of the viewers might have been feeling a little lost, he interjected an unscripted comment: 'You know, it's difficult to comprehend, isn't it, that both these crises and all the events of them that have developed both in Hungary and in the Middle East, have all virtually happened in the last fortnight'—imperceptibly bringing the chaos under control and into perspective, tacitly inviting his audience to relax.

If he offered comfort, he could also, unintentionally, create illusion. According to Michael Peacock, Panorama was forced to cover the Suez crisis with a degree of neutrality which denied the proper function of journalism. Yet so massive was the assurance with which Richard Dimbleby conducted the programme that no-one noticed. One critic, reflecting a common view, wrote:

> The historic and tragic events of the last two weeks have been confused and chaotic. That they are gradually becoming clearer and their probable results are becoming more apparent is largely due, in my case at any rate, to television—and particularly to Panorama. Last night, once again, Richard Dimbleby and the Panorama team . . . put the world picture into its right perspective.

It was a new voice, reflecting a new reality: people were starting to rely not on newspapers, or on radio, but on television as their main source of information. The viewer and the medium were growing up, graduating from the days when announcers were stars.

Yet none of Panorama's followers noticed that Suez—the most controversial action of any British Government since the war—was explained and interpreted with virtually no reference to the fact that it *was* controversial. For this remarkable omission, the BBC was not wholly to blame. At the end of July, at the start of the crisis, Richard Dimbleby had opened Panorama thus: 'Good evening. The Suez Canal. Not much reason, I think, to tell you why it's the first item in Panorama . . .' but he went on, 'because of the fourteen-day rule of which you will have heard before we can't tonight discuss the rights and wrongs of the situation . . .' The fourteen-day rule stipulated that no discussion of any subject due for debate in Parliament should take place on BBC radio or television in the fourteen days before the debate started—a Government-imposed gag on the airing of all topical controversy. So while the 'rights and wrongs' of Suez were debated savagely in the House of Commons, and loudly aired in the press, they were ignored by the BBC. It might have mattered less had someone noticed or complained on the BBC's behalf—but no sound was heard, save a chorus of praise for television's Window on the World.

It is true that early in the crisis a pugnacious but long-winded Hugh Cudlipp did interview the Foreign Secretary, Selwyn Lloyd, but apart from denying that the British public had been 'kept in the dark' over Suez the Minister said very little at great length. And at the end of the interview, in the manner of one whose doubts have been dispelled, a proprietorial Richard Dimbleby thanked the Foreign Secretary 'for his appearance in our programme tonight'. And that was that. It was not Panorama's (or Dimbleby's) fault. Fourteen-day rule apart, the long-standing ambiguity of the relationship between the Government and the BBC, had not been resolved since 1945—largely because the BBC had never tested its own strength. Suddenly in the middle of Suez, the BBC was plunged into its greatest constitutional crisis since the General Strike thirty years before. Masterminding the last stand of the British Empire like Custer at Little Bighorn, Sir Anthony Eden was outraged when the BBC offered the Labour Party the right of reply to his Prime Ministerial Broadcast, and it was promptly made clear to Broadcasting House that the Corporation was in imminent danger of Government take-over. However, for the first time in thirty years the BBC was resolute. Harmon Grisewood, the Assistant to the Director-General, made it equally plain to Downing Street that the BBC would fight to preserve its independence, avowing that 'Suez was a Parliamentary issue. It was not a national war; the BBC should not and would not be manoeuvered into acting as though it were.' So for the first time, the BBC served notice on Government that, even if its independence were not sacred, it would not be yielded without a struggle—and the Government gave way.

But the BBC was cautious in victory. Even when the fourteen-day rule did not apply, Michael Peacock was forbidden to treat Suez as a party-political issue. At the height of the crisis the BBC's Board of Management refused to allow him to approach the Foreign Secretary for an interview. The pressure on the Corporation was intense. On November 12th, Panorama was reduced to reporting world reaction to the Government's threat to bomb the Egyptians into surrender. Since the world was highly critical, the programme aroused the ire of the beleaguered Conservative Party—with Peter Rawlinson and Ian Orr-Ewing raising a barrage of hostile questions in the House. The BBC was able to dismiss this political hysteria with elegant assurance; the Window on the World was unshattered. But in the aftermath no-one outside the BBC noticed that the whole fiasco had still been reported without a single critical British voice being heard; not once was the massive authority of Richard Dimbleby's Panorama challenged.

The public faith in the programme could have bizarre consequences. On April 1st, 1957, at the end of Panorama, he introduced a film of the 'Swiss Spaghetti Harvest' made by a BBC cameraman called Charles de Jaeger. It showed healthy young girls carefully picking long strips of spaghetti from large bushes and placing them tenderly in a suitable basket. The film was accompanied by romantic music and a commentary written by one of the programme's producers, David Wheeler, which was spoken by Dimbleby in his most matter-of-fact but serious voice.

It isn't only in Britain this year that spring has taken everyone by surprise. Here in the Ticino, on the borders of Switzerland and Italy, the slopes overlooking Lake Lugano have already burst into flower, at least a fortnight earlier than usual.

But what, you may ask, has the early and welcome arrival of bees and blossoms to do with food? Well, it's simply that last winter, one of the mildest in living memory, has had its effect in other ways as well. Most important of all, it's resulted in an exceptionally heavy spaghetti crop. The last two weeks of March are an anxious time for spaghetti farmers. There's always the chance of a late frost which—while not entirely ruining the crop—generally impairs the flavour, and makes it difficult for him to obtain top prices in world markets . . .

Spaghetti cultivation here in Switzerland is not, of course, carried out on anything like the tremendous scale of the Italian industry. Many of you, I'm sure, will have seen pictures of the spaghetti plantations in the Po Valley. For the Swiss, however, it tends to be more of a family affair.

After picking, the spaghetti is laid out to dry in the warm Alpine sun. Many people are often puzzled by the fact that spaghetti is produced at such uniform lengths, but this is the result of many years of patient endeavour by plant breeders who have succeeded in producing the perfect spaghetti.

At the end of the film, Richard Dimbleby bid his public 'good night'—'on this the first day of April'—and half the nation was taken in: Panorama had told a lie and thousands thought it was the truth. The BBC switchboard was jammed with quizzical and even angry phone calls. Letters followed. The newspapers were filled with the hoax: some approving and some (like the

Daily Telegraph—'BBC fools about with spaghetti') affecting disdain. One teacher wrote to Dimbleby to inform him that she had always encouraged her children to watch his programme, but that his hoax had unforgivably let her down; a couple in Bristol wanted him to resolve a family quarrel (husband: 'but Dimbleby *said* it grew on trees'; wife: 'but I *know* its flour and water'); others wrote to ask if it were possible to grow spaghetti plants in England, and if so, where they could be purchased? Thinking it wise to inform the Director-General in advance of Panorama's spoof, Leonard Miall, the Head of Talks had sent a message about the item to him. But it never arrived; and Sir Ian Jacob was as perplexed as the rest of the country—until a nagging doubt drove him to his encyclopaedia and the truth.

Thereafter Panorama would sometimes be judiciously frivolous. But Suez and Hungary had given the programme its reputation. For the next ten years, sometimes glib and occasionally ponderous, Panorama would lead its huge audience from crisis to catastrophe with a flair and authority that its rivals could rarely match.

12

Home

Home is where one starts from ...
There is a time for the evening under starlight,
A time for the evening under lamplight
(The evening with the photograph album)

                                        T. S. ELIOT

MY PARENTS BOUGHT DANLEY FARM IN 1952. IT STOOD
in a valley surrounded by thousands of acres of wood and heath;
twenty-five acres of grassland neatly divided into four fields. The
house was at the bottom of a steep hill leading up to the village
of Lynchmere, in a corner of Sussex which borders Hampshire
and Surrey, about fifty miles from London. It was built in the
sixteenth century for a yeoman farmer, with old beams, low
ceilings and small leaded windows. There was a large barn, a
granary, a stable block and a row of pig-sties. The buildings, old
red-brick and brown tiles with moss on them, were clumped
round the house.

My father's dream as a young man to escape the drabness of
suburbia had become his most important earthly ambition.
Danley Farm was the apotheosis of the romantic idyll that he had
sketched for himself and my mother twenty years before in
Lymington: the England where he could live a rural life, where
his children could be brought up to the sound of the birds and
the sight of cattle, away from the dirt and noise of the city; where
he could lean on gates and gaze into the distance, surveying his
land, watching the pattern of the seasons, and dreaming of the
unchanging values of the country man.

There had been much doubt about the purchase, which would
cost £12,000. The house was too small, and for my mother it

seemed far out in the country and isolated. But my father was determined; and she never seriously tried to block his will for long. He knew that it would work: the granary could be turned into bedrooms; the barn could become a massive playroom; if necessary the house could be extended; the loft over the stables could be a studio for David—there was nothing that was impossible if you really wanted to do it. The fields would have cows, there would be pigs and hens in the yard, and the stables would be filled with horses.

My father had that rare gift of convincing others that his romances would come true—and he was invariably right. Nothing would stand in his way, least of all the lack of money. In 1952 he was not rich as good businessmen are rich: he had no money stored up in city shares and although he had just started to earn £10,000 a year from the BBC, he lived consistently above his post-tax means. He was in constant debt to the bank manager and the Inland Revenue—much to the distress of his lawyer and sister-in-law, Myfanwy Howell, who combined a strong belief that to be in debt was to be half way to ruin, with the knowledge that her opinions were worth hearing. Her devotion to him was absolute but not uncritical; and she had a formidable intelligence. As when they had been young lovers, my parents were a little nervous of her strictures: 'Don't worry, Myffy dear, we'll find the money somehow,' was my father's constant and unconvincing rejoinder to her pleas for restraint. My mother, admiring his disregard for caution, enjoyed his extravagance. They were both imperviously optimistic. Between them they set about the transformation of Danley Farm and within a few years, under his expansive guidance, and her practical inspiration, it was done.

When Richard's enthusiasm was up he was unstoppable. He took up farming at a moment when the BBC was making more demands on his time and energy than on any other broadcaster; when he was writing one and frequently two articles each week; and when he was in the process of taking control of a family newspaper which required much attention. He knew nothing about farming except that it seemed congenial. Yet he was determined that if he were to farm, it would be done properly. So he went to the local branch of the National Farmers' Union, bought books and sought all manner of advice. Then he bought the animals. First came the pigs—or rather a heavily pregnant, bad-tempered sow called Myfanwy (named with no disrespect, and to her amusement, after his sister-in-law). Myfanwy produced, not as might have been expected, nine or ten piglets, but twenty-two (and on the next occasion it was twenty-eight). Some died quickly, and as there were not enough teats to go round, the others weakened. The local vet was called, and on his breezy advice, my mother took the weakest into the house and (since it was now late at night) into the warmest place, their bed. None of them survived, my parents had a sleepness night, and the next day my father left for the BBC determined that they should pig-farm more professionally in future. Advice was taken again. Soon a row of six new wooden sties were erected at the top of the hill far from the house. They were of the latest design, with automatic feeders and drinking troughs. Then came six sows, much younger than Myfanwy, and much smaller. And they began to produce. Soon the farm was surrounded by the running, squealing, and grunting of young pigs.

Next came the cows. At first my father was determined to begin a herd of Dexters (a breed of diminutive cattle, notorious for its bad temper, low milk yield and tough meat), thinking that small cows would look better on a small farm. When it proved impossible to discover any suitable Dexters, he settled for a less exotic mixture of Friesians, Ayrshires, and Herefords—which the local farmer kindly supplied. My father regarded this motley crowd with the same affection that he had prepared for the Dexters, leaning over a gate on a summer evening by the drinking trough, his stick in his hand, while the gnats buzzed round his head, watching his herd benignly as if he had farmed all his life. He much disliked real agricultural activity: when the Hereford bull once escaped early on a Sunday morning, he called from their beds Dilys, his sister and some friends who were staying and ordered them out to drive the marauding creature—who had already done much damage to the front lawn—back where he belonged. While his family and guests ran back and forth (in some fear, and with nightdresses soaked from the morning dew of the long grass) he sat himself behind the steering wheel of the Jeep, explaining to them: 'Someone has to keep control of the operation and drive the vehicle.'

It was unwise, my father thought, to buy a flock of poultry to run wild. They should have a proper house, their eggs properly packaged and collected each week. So the hen-house was built to the latest design, and the first two hundred chickens went inside. For a time all worked well. They produced their eggs, and the lorry took them away. Then remorse set in: it was no life for a hen, to exist forever in a dull, deep-litter house, producing little white eggs for the Marketing Board. They should be allowed to range freely. So the expensive purpose-built, temperature controlled, automatic feed-and-water-distributing hen house opened its doors, and the chickens started living—and stopped laying. (Their successors were finally removed from the farm altogether after the automatic water system went wrong. The drinking troughs overflowed, the water rose overnight to the depth of a foot, and, though most of the birds stayed on their perches, a few panicked, and leapt into the rising water. There, immobilised by terror, they allowed themselves to be drowned. At that point my father decided that they were too stupid to be tolerated.)

So there were the cows and the pigs and the chickens and the geese. There were only ponies to buy. By this time the children (or the three youngest, the author, Nicholas and Sally) had conceived a passion for riding. First the local farmer lent a little old mare and then my father 'rescued' a Shetland pony from some pits in the West Country. Then there were more ponies, two, three and four more; then, as we got older, came the horses: two, three, four, then five. It was always hard to discard unwanted animals, so the collection grew and grew—at one time the farm had no less than ten horses and ponies.

The building was done too. The granary, which soon became 'The Ship', was divided into four small bedrooms, with bunks and porthole lights, and a 'baby alarm' to connect the children to the house on those evenings when Nicholas thought that the 'Fieldy-ghosties' were coming. My father told us bedtime stories which invariably centred around the doings of Lottie Teapot and Charlie Staircase. Charlie had a nasty habit of putting Lottie on the hotplate, and burning her backside; then in remorse, rushing her into the fridge to cool her off, where she froze and had once more to be rushed to the hotplate. My father wove a series of endlessly riveting adventures around this central theme, while we, knowing all the time that Lottie was being forgotten (either burnt or frozen) demanded in loud chorus but to no effect, that Charlie should *do* something.

The barn became a playroom, with wall-bars, a rope to climb, a slide, an ancient grand piano and a huge old television set. The loft of the stables became David's study. And the house was extended: walls were knocked down, rooms were added—even a public right of way was re-routed so that the one or two who walked by at the weekend did not have to pass through the new cloakroom on their way.

An estate of such proportions could not be run by my mother and father alone: it required a staff. After the war they had moved from Buckinghamshire to London, where they had bought one of a cluster of houses in the middle of Barnes Common. There they had hired a butler and a cook. The butler was a very strange individual whose mental stability—always in some doubt—was severely affected by thunderstorms, new moons and alcohol. When afflicted he returned home convinced that he had fallen passionately in love with my mother. Once, presumably thus aroused he tried to punch my father in the face. He missed, but smashed his fist into the wall, crushing the plaster. My father was not a man of violence; he had never hit a man before in his life. But now he drew himself up to his full height, and threw a powerful punch in the general direction of his butler. It connected with his chin, and the man collapsed to the ground, unconscious. The next day he was invited to look for a job elsewhere. A few months later they met again quite cheerfully in Whitehall: Richard Dimbleby's would-be assassin had found himself a job at the War Office as a messenger. It delighted my father to imagine that inside the O.H.M.S. briefcase that he was carrying were a host of Government secrets waiting for the next new moon.

From London, intent still on escaping the dreary round which his imagination had imposed on suburban life, they had moved in 1950 to a village in Surrey called Greyshott just off the A3, about forty miles from London. The new home—Greyshott House— was built in the Thirties in nondescript style. It was huge (twenty years later being turned into four 'residential town houses') and despite the experience of the butler, required a larger staff: a cook, a nanny, a daily help, a gardener and an odd-job man. When, two years later they moved to Danley Farm, the daily help, Winnie Howick, moved with them, and so did her husband, Arthur, as chauffeur. Winnie and Arthur, who had never lived out of a town in their lives, and had never wanted to, found themselves convinced by my father that there was nothing they desired more in life than to live in a new bungalow (which he had built) fifty yards from a chicken house, in the depths of rural Sussex. But more staff were needed. First there was Tom who looked after the pigs, and with whom my father held long discussions about the state of the piglets (and sometimes the world). Then there was Freddie, son of the local farmer who came at weekends to trim trees and mend fences; he had a huge old diesel tractor, which being one of the very first of its kind, bounced and thumped so much (even on level ground) that we were jolted into near-concussion when we rode on the back. Will came later. He was the gardener and odd-job man; he wrote poetry, some of it erotic, which he presented to Olga, one of the grooms, as a token of esteem. In charge of the horses was Kath, who had run a riding stable but was lured into selling it by my father to work for him instead. Inside the house there was a slowly changing procession of staff. First Marie-Jean and Micheline, who were French and volatile. Marie-Jean was small and thin and Micheline was tall and fat. They were inseparable and had a habit of disappearing to bed in the early evening, leaving the supper they were preparing to cook itself. My mother thinking they must be prone to tiredness, was indulgent. It was not for several months that it was borne in upon her innocent soul, that the frequent need to retire to bed had more to do with appetite than exhaustion. After them, for a long time, there were Antonio and Patheta; Antonio was butler, Patheta, his wife, was cook. She had a baby after two years, and the house had to be extended again to accommodate the new arrival. Later, when they returned to Spain, Tess the groom's mother replaced them. Once a week, Mrs. Reynolds from a village three miles away would come in to cook. Later, when we children moved from the granary to the house, which was newly extended to find room for us, my mother's eldest sister, Olwen, who had lived with us for many years moved into 'The Ship'. On two days a week, my father's sister, Pat arrived; my mother was his planner and agent, Pat was his secretary.

In the middle of the week during the holidays there were eight members of the family, seven or eight members of the staff, and (since everything was always being expanded) usually four or five builders as well. The egg van would arrive, the lorry to collect the manure, the vet, and the farrier, the dogs' meat man (there were three dogs), the butcher, the lorry with the Calor-Gas, the grocer, the surveyor and the architect, the man from the

Ministry of Agriculture, the vicar who was a close friend and wondered if the middle field could be used for a gymkhana to raise funds for the church, and at least in the early days, a nice young lady from any one of a dozen woman's magazines, who was to write a profile on 'Richard Dimbleby's country retreat'.

By the mid-Fifties, Richard Dimbleby had surrounded himself with an entourage which would have done justice to feudal England. It was not for the show, and it was not out of greed for the material excesses that success could bring. After the first flush of newspaper articles about his home life, and the photographs of him with his offspring, by his house, by his horse, in his jeep, holding his gun (it did not work), or at his desk or piano, he decided that his public life should no longer intrude upon his private. Thereafter photographers and reporters were politely kept at bay, and the gossip-columnists took to saying that Richard Dimbleby lived at a secret and unknown address 'somewhere in the South of England'.

He was never burdened by his possessions or responsibilities. The more of both he acquired the happier he became. The possessions were not ostentatious: he hated, with the snobbery of the established middle class, displays of vulgar opulence. Nor did he aspire to an elegant style of life. Had they wished to both he and Dilys could have spent every weekend in the country houses of the titled and the notable. They never did so, and the great or the famous were never invited to the farm. He did not like leaving home in any case, and when he was there, he wanted to be alone with his family, or with his handful of close friends. He was sometimes disconcerted by those whom he thought were better born than he. Once when he went alone to stay on a country estate, he came back naively appalled. He had left his packed suitcase in the bedroom when he went down to dinner. On his return he was embarrassed to find his case unpacked, his clothes put away, his pyjamas on his bed—it seemed to him an unwarranted, and slightly prurient, invasion of his privacy. Worse, they were given *shepherd's pie* as a main course—'served by a butler in a white coat!' he reported back in perturbed surprise. Not that there was anything wrong with shepherd's pie, or with the butler, but the conjunction of the two at a nobleman's table did not fit his conception of how matters should have been arranged by the aristocracy. Though he hid it well, his social insecurity was profound.

It was imagined by many that he had intimate knowledge of the Royal Family, that he spent several weekends a year with one or other of them. In fact his contacts with royalty were, almost without exception, confined to frequent but brief pleasantries exchanged at public functions. Even these cursory meetings caused him immense delight. He would return home afterwards with undiluted joy to recount the occasion, with the enthusiasm of a schoolboy cricket fan who had just shaken hands with Donald Bradman. Once, for ten minutes, he was left in sole charge of Prince Charles and Princess Anne, at Windsor Castle, and he was able to talk to them of ponies and riding. For a long time afterwards he and my mother remembered the exact conversation that had been held. Once in Malta, the Queen had smiled directly up at his commentary position in a silent 'hello', and Prince Philip had joked afterwards: 'Fancy seeing you here!' He had danced with the Queen at Windsor Castle and before that, to his much greater delight, with the Queen Mother. 'Would it be in order for me to dance with Her Majesty?' he had asked her Equerry, observing the proprieties. Her Majesty would be delighted, he was informed—and he had two dances. When members of the Royal Family made awkward formal visits to the BBC to watch a television programme or to see round the television centre, the Corporation always asked him to be present to act as an informal co-host. He did not however count as a friend—the Royal Family was as remote from him as from all others beyond its closed circle. Of course he knew that he was highly regarded by them: the Queen Mother had told him that his Coronation commentary was beautiful; the Queen let it be known that she much admired his work, waved when she saw him and made enquiries of producers whether Mr. Dimbleby would be covering her next big engagement.

Although signs of royal favour were infrequent and slight, he was never unduly offended by the omission. It is almost certainly true that he did more than any other individual to show the place of the monarchy in British life during the Fifties and early Sixties, yet when newspapers, reflecting their (and his) post bag urged that he be given a knighthood for his services to the nation, he was embarrassed that the Queen should be exposed to such pressure.

However his friends, and many of his colleagues, were much irritated by the Royal Family's show of indifference towards him; by their unimaginative failure to express their regard for him

until he was too ill to be warmed by it. In 1958 he was awarded
the C.B.E. but almost certainly on the advice of the then Prime
Minister, Harold Macmillan, who had been much impressed by
his reverential handling of the State Opening of Parliament.
Although protocol made it difficult, if not impossible, for the
monarch to award a knighthood on her own account, his friends
felt that it should not have been beyond the bounds of Her
Majesty's imagination to make it clear in the proper quarters that
she would be gratified by the opportunity to honour him in this
way. Even those who regarded the monarchy as irrelevant, and
the Honours system as marginally absurd, thought it quaint that
the Queen did not see fit to honour her most devoted and
invaluable servant with a knighthood. It never occurred to
Dimbleby that his was a bizarre omission from the Honours list,
or that the monarchy had failed either in its duty or (according to
another standpoint) in its public relations. The one royal dis-
courtesy which he *did* notice did not irritate, but hurt: on no
occasion was he invited to attend one of the Queen's regular
Friday gatherings which she used to make informal contact with
those of her subjects who had made a distinctive contribution in
one field or another to British life. But his omission from such
gatherings was, for Dimbleby, only a passing pain. For most of
the time he felt proud to serve the monarchy, and he did not
expect his Sovereign to feel bound to pay homage to him for that.

Our life at home was unpretentious. My father had fled
suburbia, but he had not escaped his background. Nor did he
wish to; his father had been a Victorian who lived the ritual of
family life to the full, and his son was no different. By nature
Richard was no adventurer; his delight was to be: 'with my little
ones and my lovely wife around me' as he half-jokingly expressed
it. Under my mother's guidance, the house looked pretty,
welcoming and lived-in. The once-fine velvet curtains looked as
if they had been in another house before; the stair carpet was
worn nearly to the underfelt in places (it was removed suddenly
a few days before David was due to bring home for the weekend
the daughter of a rich businessman, who my father feared, would
be dismayed by such a display of tattiness); the furniture—chairs
and chests and tables of old oak, elegant but battered. The house
had few objects of great antique value, but much, greatly loved,
bric-à-brac. Invariably those pieces of china which were supposed
to have some worth were soon laced with a network of lines

where a painstaking hand had glued together the shattered pieces. The house was once summed-up perfectly by the notoriously tactless wife of a colleague who took a long and searching look around the drawing room and then turned to my mother, saying: 'Well, Dilys you've got quite a collection, haven't you— of *little* things.' For an instant, thus patronised, my mother would sigh after the elegance of *Vogue* or *Country Life*. But the designs for 'gracious living' depicted in the glossy magazines were a family joke: there were too many dirty gum boots, wet children's sweaters and jeans, mud-spattered dachshunds, and dripping mackintoshes (all tinged with the faint odour of horse manure) which spread far beyond the confines of the cloakroom, for any delusions of grandeur.

My father's tastes were simple. His greatest pleasure was to sit at the piano, which he played with more panache than elegance, favouring loud ringing chords and long ralentandos. He was more gifted than he pretended to be, mocking himself with exaggerated gestures, lifting his hands delicately high into the air after each resounding blast. Nearly always he played by ear; we could hum a tune to him and at once he could reproduce it in full harmony. He played pop and jazz but much preferred his own mock classical compositions. He played for a little after dinner every evening, with my mother looking on and the children in bed. His favourite composer was Mahler, being loud and romantic, though he knew the Schubert symphonies well. Sometimes, when his friend Norman Hackforth, the 'mystery voice' of Twenty Questions, was down for the weekend, they would sit together playing Noel Coward duets (Hackforth had been Coward's accompanist), and Gilbert and Sullivan. His bookshelves were not extensive. He liked Dickens, Churchill and biographies. He read Agatha Christie, and reread C. S. Forrester again and again. Although he did not care for poetry, he delighted in indulging my mother's taste with a carefully chosen volume of Dylan Thomas. Most of his time was spent satisfying an insatiable appetite for the daily papers, which he 'gutted' like any journalist. Year after year he faithfully stored *The Times* 'because it could be a very useful reference in time to come' he would explain. He never looked at them again.

Much more of his time than he would have anyone believe was spent watching television. Although the hours each week which we children were permitted to watch television were rationed, and although he wrote and spoke much about the damage to family life which the 'magic box in the corner' could cause, he allowed his own addiction full rein, explaining unconvincingly that his viewing was a professional obligation. But his devotion went far beyond the call of duty. He never missed Dixon of Dock Green, Phil Silvers, or Perry Mason. He liked the Black and White Minstrel Show, and watched engrossing soap-operas, explaining to those who disturbed him or mocked him: 'I have to watch it—because I need to know who the director was!' As the credits rolled he would say, with the air of a man whose expectations had been fulfilled—'Oh! yes, it's old...(and he would read off the name of the unknown American as if he were an old family friend), I thought so.' It became such a habit with him, that the family would wait for the end of any programme to point out to him with much eagerness: 'Oh! yes, Papa, it's old Joe Smith on Sound—you can always tell his work, can't you?'.

When he watched the news, current affairs, or outside broadcasts, he kept up a barrage of critical comment like a football manager barracking the opposing team, all but destroying the possibility of watching the programme. 'Will they never learn!' 'Who's that nincompoop masquerading as an interviewer?', 'Get camera one in close, for God's sake'; 'For Christ's sake stop talking so much'; 'Will they never learn!'; 'That's right, miss the point again!' Although there was no malice in his observations, he could never resist expressing his awareness of others' professional limitations.

His family upbringing had instilled in him the belief that it was mildly improper, and certainly embarrassing to discuss 'one's feelings': they were not for public or even family consumption. If you were upset, frustrated, bored or sad, you kept it to yourself. Although by nature he was sensitive to the sufferings of others, and unfailingly sympathetic to the childhood woes of his offspring, displays of emotion embarrassed him. At moments of televisual passion, of anger or romance or love (bland as they all were) he felt bound to distract his family from the screen; not because he disapproved of emotions (his were easily aroused) but because he found the concentrated silence of shared emotion disconcerting. On such occasions his jokey asides, revealing his own discomfort only too plainly, were more embarrassing than irritating. Although he hugged his children readily, he found it impossible

K

to embrace my mother naturally in front of us, without going
through an elaborate performance designed to show that he was
under attack from her, his hands frantically waving behind her
back as if she were squeezing the life out of him. He did not like
their love to be on display before us.

Gossipy colleagues, seeking to dent his image of perfect un-
corruptibility, created an enduring myth that he was obsessed
with pornography, and maintained a massive secret collection of
the stuff. They misunderstood the mixture of bravura and shame
with which normal adults of his generation and background,
reared in innocence of sex, regarded the improbable fantasies of
girly magazines. In fact he took a disarming schoolboy delight in
mild erotica, believing it quite daring to buy *Playboy* on a railway
station, showing his purchase to friends, who had seen much
harder stuff in their time, as if he had just committed a wicked
but delightful sin. Once he bought in Paris a book of bawdy and
mildly indecent cartoons, which he showed surreptitiously to
Norman Hackforth, saying: 'Your last look, dear boy'. 'Oh!,
why?' asked Hackforth, and was astonished to receive the reply:
'I'm going to burn it tonight, in case the children get their hands
on it.'

His sense of propriety clashed with a powerful liberation
instinct. He never condemned sexual frailties in others, although
being the product of a generation which regarded homosexuality
as a vice or at least an illness, he was quite willing to hear and
sometimes tell disparaging 'queer' jokes. But he was not offended
or revolted as some of his less emancipated peers were—reacting
to adolescent public school peccadillos with, 'My dear boy, don't
worry, it's quite natural—but try not to be found out, it makes
everyone's life so much easier.' If one of us had a girlfriend to
stay and spent too long in her room, saying an endless intimate
goodnight, he did not charge to the bedroom door in outrage.
Instead as he went to bed (at least two hours after us) he would
walk, coughing conspicuously, to the room, tap on the door and
in almost apologetic fashion say: 'Well, I think it's time we were
all going to bed now, don't you? Goodnight.'

He found it hard to discard his natural reticence about sex
even when he wrote fiction. His agent, Laurence Pollinger, who
handled some of his country's most distinguished novelists was
convinced that 'if Richard had stuck to writing, he would have
been another John Buchan.' Pollinger spent frequent fruitless

lunches at Madame Prunier's attempting to persuade his author to write more books (his only published novel, though not ambitious, sold more than 10,000 copies). But his putative Buchan never seemed to find the time. In the early Fifties he did begin a draft for a novel, and casting off all restraint, decided to include a love scene between his hero and heroine which took place on a sitting-room floor in front of the fire. When he had completed the chapter, he showed it nervously to Dilys and his sister Pat, who finding it a little complicated, decided to enact his description of the scene to see if the act he described were possible. Finding themselves locked in an improbable embrace, which made the natural fulfilment of passion quite impossible they extricated themselves in a state of hysterical laughter; my father concluding that he should confine his writing to the factual word.

Weekends at home followed a traditional pattern, breakfast at nine o'clock was attended by my father in shirt, collar and tie, shaved, his hair washed and neatly brushed but wearing an old dressing-gown and slippers. After breakfast he retired to his dressing room to prepare for the day. Most of the morning he spent with the newspapers, letters and bills, and sometimes a book. In winter he enjoyed cold and wet afternoons, for then Dilys would not force him outside in gum boots and mackintosh. His youthful abhorrence of physical exertion had endured (though he rode his horse regularly until in an inevitably heavy fall, he broke two ribs) and he looked forward with dismay to those fine afternoons when my mother would insist on 'a family walk'. Although he did not mind a brief amble around his 'estate', his delight was to sit inside in front of a log fire in his high-backed armchair, his feet up smoking a long cigar watching the racing. On these winter afternoons he made his only concession to the existence of commercial television, when he swopped frantically between Sandown on the BBC and Redcar 'on the other side'. He kept a telephone on the floor beside him and dialled constantly, furiously, to lay a pound here, ten shillings there on his 'certainties'. He took his betting as seriously as a Coronation commentary. The room was wreathed in smoke; newspapers, carefully annotated, littered the floor; and strict silence was ordained. Never escaping his family's moral tradition, he regarded gambling as a wicked pleasure. In all his betting (on the horses, on the pools, or at occasional casinos in France) he claimed unique access to infallible systems—which invariably failed. We laughed at him, not because they failed, but because they failed so boringly: so cautious was he, so complex were his methods, so carefully did he cover himself, that he could neither win nor lose with panache. On those rare occasions when he won convincingly, he treated the money as a windfall, and spent it at once.

Meals were always full but simple. My father's favourite food was roast beef and Yorkshire pudding, with well-cooked vegetables. Wine he regarded as a luxury; the cellar under the stairs was never well-stocked. Weekends, when we would have a decanted bottle of very ordinary wine for Sunday lunch, were special occasions. My father's instinct told him that one bottle was probably enough for six people, though when their thirsts determined otherwise, he was never ungenerous. He preserved an old low-church distaste for those who drank more than a little. We had an old, long, narrow refectory table, and he sat always at the top, frequently saying little but listening always to our noisy argument. If it became too much for him he would say: 'That's enough, men' or 'steady the buffs' (in mock military sternness) and we were quiet. He rarely raised his voice in irritation. He was only angered if my mother was upset by us: to be rude to her was an offence he did not easily forgive. On those occasions when we offended, he would readily and at great speed march us to our bedrooms. He could not bear to hit us; but had a way of making us think that if we had behaved badly we were not angering, but disappointing him, and the shame was much greater.

His presence dominated the household and our lives: although he was never obtrusive, never noisy, rarely volunteered his opinions or prejudices, when he spoke we were always silent. He had a magical way of drawing others into his circle and into his mood. It was not only with the family: when friends came, tired or tense or over-talkative, he soon had them at ease—enveloped in his own relaxation. He was never dull: the days when he was at home were special, not just for his presence, but for the prospect of surprise. Rarely flustered by work into irritation or depression, my father was always filled with ideas for the family: a picnic, a treasure hunt, or a 'mystery drive'. He wrote plays for us to act; he performed one-man puppet shows; and when we were older and had our horses, he wanted to be at gymkhanas, and horse shows, even refusing broadcasts which clashed with his Saturday outing in the horsebox. Then, in gum boots, in an old mackintosh missing buttons, sitting upright behind the wheel of the lorry,

labouring noisily up the long twisting climb of the A3 towards
the Devil's Punchbowl at Hindhead on a Saturday in summer, he
was content. A long procession of over-loaded family cars heading
for the sea would gather behind him. He would look in his mirror
slowly counting them: 'Twenty, twenty-one, that's right, now
just wait ... No, no' (as one would pull out in a dismal attempt
to overtake), and then triumphantly bellowing to us, cramped on
the front seat beside him: 'I've got nearly forty of 'em; where
shall we take my public today?' and as we reached the top of the
hill and they started to struggle by one or two of them would
look up at their tormentor, and, amazed to see Richard Dimbleby
behind the wheel of a lorry, would point up at him in fascination.
He, treasuring his privacy, would grin back maniacally, and, in
the voice of a gossipy old crone, exclaim: 'Yes, yes, that's him,
no it isn't, yes it is, yes that's right ...'

He took our riding exploits as seriously as we did. Like a
caricature of a Thelwell parent he stood by the ringside with
critical concern watching us perform. If we hit fences he wanted
to know the reason why. If we performed well, he wanted to
know what had nearly gone wrong. If the BBC had kept him
away, he pressed us for the exact details of the day in the evening.
How long had it taken us to get there? By which route? Who
else was there? Who had won? Why had not we? What had the
judge said to us? Had our instructor been pleased? He was never
content until he had a full and exact picture of the occasion in his
head. When we were unhelpful (monosyllabic or self-pitying if
we had failed) he did not rebuke but gently pressed on with his
questions. He was irrepressibly generous. So Jonathan required a
better horse? 'Well, let's see, there's the bank ... Oh! I know, we
can get one on a mortgage. Don't tell Myffy!' Later, when the
author took show-jumping with extreme seriousness, giving up all
else in the elusive pursuit of international honours, he accepted
it without a murmur: if his son wished to be a full-time professional horseman, working at training stables, it was his right to
do so. His only concern was 'that you should do it well'. His
equanimity was much tested. Two of his sons, in late adolescence,
had between them a serious commitment in rapid succession to
the Army, the stage, the Navy, agriculture, professional show-
jumping, sculpture and journalism. He took each obsession with
the same seriousness, discussing each at great length, buying books
on the subject, finding out the best places to study, and promising

his full moral support as each 'vocation' came to the fore. The only profession he advised against, with great earnestness, was broadcasting or television. As a young man he had promised his wife, 'something better than journalism'; for his sons he now wished 'something better than television'. He was never quite clear what was wrong with television but it was as if he felt that the medium was not quite serious enough for able people. There were better (and though he did not quite say it, more gentlemanly) ways of earning a living and serving the community. He never forgot the irritation and even humiliation, when television began, of people asking him: 'Do you think you'll ever be an announcer?' He sensed acutely the indignity behind the fact that to be a Face was to be a Name, feeling, quite wrongly, that his sons despised the medium, and were ashamed of some of the 'show-biz' aspects of their father's work. He believed that somewhere at the heart of television there was a deep emptiness and he did not wish his sons to spend long years finding their way there.

He rarely brought his work home, and had to be pressed to talk of it. Although, in the twenty years between 1945 and 1965 he never took a holiday of more than three weeks, and outside that summer break, and some weekends, he devoted himself obsessively to work, he had the rare ability to seem wholly untouched by it. It is hard for some men to escape the pressure of public life, to discard the public persona for the private, public concerns for private worries. For them, the isolation of the public life destroys the intimacy of the private. My father hardly recognised, and certainly never experienced, the distinction. When he moved from a State occasion to the fireside armchair he did so without suffering any psychological jolt. He never needed to 'wind down' or relocate himself, because he was never wound up or disorientated. He never seemed tired, or run-down; when he was depressed, he confided it only to my mother. To us he was always the same: the only gloom that descended upon Danley Farm was when a beloved animal had grown too old and was to be destroyed. On that day there were tears from us and comfort from him for the mourners. Then Panorama and state occasions were matters of no moment.

The only time that we were aware of, and even took interest in, his work for the BBC was when he was preparing for a major occasion. Then, like most journalists, he could only work when pressed into a deadline. Kenneth Adam once called him 'the master of associative material'; and his first outside broadcast producer, S. J. de Lotbinière, a critical mentor in the early days, had impressed upon him that 'homework was the touchstone of success'. The BBC assumed that he spent long painstaking days at his desk. In fact his days at home were spent postponing his homework. Once he had forced himself to begin, he worked at great speed and, having a rare memory, was able to retain every detail on the page, for so long as it was required, discarding what he would not need again as soon as its purpose had been realised. He sat in his study until two or three in the morning, night after night, smoking cigars and drinking glasses of milk, dressed in pyjamas and dressing gown, surrounded by maps, charts, encyclo-paedias, reference books, camera scripts, producer's notes, formal 'orders of the day', and page after page of his own hand-written notes, which when he had finished this frenetic study, would be compressed on to small cards, into neat hieroglyphics, com-prehensible only to himself. When any of us walked into his study, we were never made to feel that we were in his way; and since his was a magnetic presence for us, it was only the firmness of my mother and his sister Pat, which kept us away. He enjoyed the interruptions—not least because they gave him an excuse to stop work.

My mother organised my father's life entirely. She discussed every detail of his work, made all his plans, all his bookings, negotiated all his contracts, and was, as he said, 'my severest critic'. It was no chance that once she had begun to deal with the BBC on his behalf early in the Fifties, the wrangles had all but ceased and the fees all but doubled. Frequently she went with him (at his own expense) on royal visits, helping him with commentary details—like the precise colours and materials of regal dresses, which was a matter of great concern to his critical female viewers —and protecting his privacy. He trusted her judgment absolutely, and, though he dominated the house, was a little in awe of her. She had been a good writer: in the Thirties, at a time when women did not easily work in Fleet Street, she was offered jobs on at least three papers. More important, her range of sensibilities was wider than his, her judgments more subtle, her critical faculties more highly developed, her emotions more clear.

And although she devoted very nearly thirty years to his needs and his children (as she would say: 'In that order') she never lost her independence of character. By friends and colleagues she was never regarded as his appendage, his 'little woman'. She adored him—seeing, but loving, his faults; he worshipped her—seeing no fault in her. Neither would countenance criticism of the other. His life with her was a constant wooing. He lavished little signs of love upon her: buying flowers every Friday for twenty-five years before he came home; buying new perfumes and pretty soaps; buying books each with a freshly thought inscription. We never saw him angry with her; she never raised her voice at him. The only occassion on which I heard him shout at her was once before a major royal broadcast. There were no clean shirts or socks in his wardrobe. 'What am I meant to do, go there in my underpants?' he bellowed from the dressing room. 'I know it's not very important, just a bit of old broadcasting, but it does pay the bills, you know!' To my twelve-year-old ears, it sounded so harsh that afterwards I crept anxiously into the bedroom to ask my mother: 'You're not getting divorced are you?' Their marriage was completely and deeply happy. My father embraced my mother's whole life: in her eyes he was the gayest, most exciting man she had ever met. His personality—so untarnished by the world, so generous, so gently powerful— simply made all others lesser men.

The most exuberant days—those which the participants remembered long afterwards with joy but no sentimentality— were the Wednesdays on which Richard was supposed to devote himself to work. His beloved sister-cum-secretary, Pat Haines, arrived on Tuesday evenings, and despite her jokey prodding, Dilys and Richard resolutely refused to start work until nearly midnight. Then they would all disappear into the study, staying there until three in the morning, writing letters, doing expenses, completing articles, and paying bills—when the constant hum of voices and the muffled tick-tack of the typewriter was punctuated by the sudden clink of glass against bottle and an occasional shriek of laughter. Next morning they would try to start work early, but never got going until a little before eleven o'clock. Then Cath would arrive from the local riding stables with three horses—one each for Pat, Dilys, and Richard—and they would disappear into the country until lunchtime. That meal was the noisiest of the week—Cath crying with laughter at my father's risqué asides, Dilys feigning shocked innocence, Pat disguising her little-sister adoration with gentle, mocking banter ... In the afternoon they retired again dutifully to the study—and this time, since Pat had to return to Richmond in the evening, they would work hard and in near silence.

The ease with which my father moved from public to private world was partly a consequence of personality; it was also a matter of attitude. His home for him was not merely a cosy little cocoon where he could be pampered in front of a hot fire, his shelter from the blasting storms of the outside world. It was the centre of his life, the citadel from which he advanced upon the outside world. More than that, all that he said or implied about Britain, the State, the Monarchy, about peace, tolerance and justice, sprang from a romantic conviction about the ideal society. The purpose of the institutions of state, which the monarchy guarded (and in his imagination guided) was to preserve and secure his notion of family life. Like his outspoken commitment to British institutions, his commitment to the concept of 'family' was a little larger than life. His 'family' included not only a wife and children, mothers, sisters, aunts and uncles, but an entourage of cooks, butlers, cleaners, grooms and gardeners—for whom he felt responsible, and whose cares and worries he liked to consider as his own. By nature he was a patriarch, needing the dependency of others upon him and relishing the responsibilities thus imposed on him.

Characteristically, his beliefs about the family extended to Dimbleby and Sons Ltd, which was for him a 'family' business not only in name but in deed. The firm was far more to him than a cushion against hard times at the BBC—it was another state in his patriarchal domain. When he rejoined the family business in 1946, as Editor-in-Chief, he determined, not to restore its fortunes (which never suffered much) but its reputation. The company had not recovered from the Thirties, when the hostility between his father Fred and Uncle Percy, had made Dimbleby's a miserable place to work. The bitterness in the family had not ended with Fred's death in 1943. The circumstances of his sudden collapse (in the editorial office in which he had been born) are unknown; but it was believed by many of the workers, and some of the family, that his heart-attack had been brought on by a furious row with Percy, who was therefore held by some to have 'caused' Fred's death.

Richard arrived to take his father's place more than a little persuaded of his Uncle's 'guilt'. The auguries for the relationship between the old Managing Director and the young Editor-in-Chief were not good; they were made worse by Percy's utter distrust of his nephew, who had been gallivanting all over the world as some kind of 'star' reporter, and by Richard's obvious determination to batter at the citadel of his Uncle's parsimony. Percy's ways had changed little. The paper had come to reflect his penny-pinching attitude to life: it was thin, dreary, out-of-date, and devoid of 'style'. Moreover, his frugality had done little to improve the relations (as he saw them) 'between master and man'. Percy was not burdened by romantic illusions about the purpose of the business. He had been tough in the Twenties and Thirties, and in the Forties, when the print workers were not yet powerful, he exploited their weakness, paying poorly and offering little security and primitive conditions. In return he enjoyed the cordial dislike of nearly all the company's one hundred workers.

He spent much time scrutinising the expenses of his staff—his niggling reaching such proportions that the reporters in the Twickenham office (where he had refused to instal a lavatory) would include on their daily expense sheets 'One penny—for use of public lavatories', knowing that he would grumble at the editor: 'I bet they don't always do it in my time!' His frequent but irregular prowls around the works were notorious: his arrival would be signalled not by his footsteps but by a hand, and then an arm creeping around the door, searching for the light switch—to save electricity. Reporters and printers would have to grope in the half dark of the late afternoon until he was safely out of the way. He refused to spend money on typewriters, chairs, or new tables, let alone new machinery. Yet he was as frugal with himself as with others. Although he lived in modest comfort, he never drew more than £2,000 a year in salary, though he could easily have authorised himself four times as much; and the Directors' lavatory was equipped, not with soft toilet paper, but old copies of *The Richmond and Twickenham Times*.

He was the antithesis of his nephew and both men knew it. The eight years between 1946 and 1954 when Richard finally wrested the company out of his uncle's hands, were a source of great frustration—though unlike his father, he refused to become embroiled in family rows, preferring to avoid his uncle unless it was absolutely necessary to confront him. But he was determined to improve the three papers under his editorial command. He wanted to redesign the lay-out, buy new machines, use more photography, and hire more staff. He was unable to do any of it without spending money, which had to be sanctioned by Percy; and the Managing Director was resolutely stubborn. So Richard resorted to the memo, badgering his uncle in much the same way as he had the BBC, ten years before.

One of these—'a proposal to install a photo-engraving plant at the 'Times' Printing Works, Richmond', written in 1949 when he was doing much more work for the BBC than any other broadcaster, shows both his expert knowledge of the business, and his barely-controlled irritation with his uncle. 'We must have more pictures' he urged, 'For reasons of economy [by which he longed to say short-sighted meanness] we are using now only half (and often less than half) the number of pictures used by some of our contemporaries. It is an accepted fact in journalism that *good pictures sell papers*. I want more, and certainly a full page for each paper in the end . . .' At the end of a closely argued case for the expenditure of £1,500 on the photo-engraver, which he said would pay for itself within five years, he summarised his conclusions:

When I first mooted the idea of an engraving plant in July 1947, the total cost—for identically the same equipment—was £1,300, or £200 less. Delivery was promised in three months. Now in 1949, the price is £1,500 and delivery six months. I am certain that if we wait another two years, the price will be £2,000 and the delivery a year. The plant is something that we have got to have in the end, and I suggest that the sooner we order it, the better.

With his uncle still adamant, he did what he could with his own resources, hiring freelance contributors (since he could not have more staff), partially (but frequently) re-designing the front page, and often writing his own editorials. A stickler for perfection, he wrote a booklet introducing a new 'house style' for the papers. Nervous sub-editors and printers knew that he would unfailingly spot mistakes that they were supposed to have seen, and his subsequent memos from the editorial office were never gentle: if he could see the mistake, he suggested, then so should they. The 'house-style' book included a 'Chamber of Horrors'—of words or phrases that should on no account appear in his papers. On occasion, for safety's sake, these instructions were taken too literally. From a combination of proper hostility to journalistic mawkishness, and middle-class snobbery he had ordained that the term 'Lady' was never to appear in the paper. One junior reporter, forgetting the injunction, had sent back copy from a Council reception in Twickenham reporting the words of welcome made by the Mayor to 'The President of the Chamber of Commerce and his Lady'. The mistake was duly corrected by a sharp-eyed printer, and appeared in print as 'the President . . . and his woman'—which had to be followed the next week by a humble apology to the aggrieved worthy.

In Richmond, where Conservative councillors were returned to office with unswerving faith, the relationship between the *Times* and the community, and in particular the political establishment, was delicate. Local councillors, in the manner of those who have importance thrust upon them, frequently tried to cajole or threaten *Times* reporters into seeing matters their way. In the Thirties the Dimbleby newspaper had been known locally, with only a touch of irony, as the 'Thunderer'; from the beginning it had prided itself on an editorial policy of political independence, and it was jealous of that reputation. When nearly all council business was decided behind closed doors, and then presented to the public as a *fait accompli*, the only way the paper could ensure that issues of importance to the community were aired before being resolved in secret, was to prod dissident Tories into leaking their party's plan.

To the mass of obedient councillors it frequently seemed that *The Richmond and Twickenham Times* was pursuing a vendetta against the Conservative Party. One Tory even felt constrained to spread the rumour that Richard Dimbleby was a Communist 'plant'—campaigning with such enthusiasm that the Editor-in-Chief felt bound to summon the local Conservative agent to the office. Ironically, Richard had a quaint rule that Dimbleby and Sons Ltd should not accept advertisements from the British Communist Party, explaining to sceptical executives, 'We will not have *their* money making our profits'. He guarded his independence carefully. When the Leader of the Twickenham Council stormed into the office to complain about his treatment at the hands of a *Times* reporter (who had refused to accept a vow of silence which the politician had sought to impose on him) he was astonished to confront, not a genial fellow member of the Establishment, but an outraged editor, who dismissed him almost at once, with the warning that if he tried again to instruct 'one of my reporters' as to what should or should not go 'into my paper' he would regale the readership of *The Richmond and Twickenham Times* with the full story.

When the staff did transgress, he administered stern rebukes, summoning the offenders to his office for a partiarchal dressing down, or sending a stiff memorandum which usually ended with the injunction 'I never want to see anything like this in the paper again.' His sense of propriety was keenly developed. It was a rule of his that Court reports of matrimonial disputes should not be published in any of the Dimbleby newspapers, nor should wills— which, being private matters, it would be prurient to report. He did not readily distinguish between 'intrusion' and 'investigation', being prone to believe that in both cases the motives tended to be disreputable, and that both were best conducted by men in dirty macs who hung around sleazy nightclubs. Being acutely sensitive to what he regarded as malicious attack, and lacking that sharp edge which enjoys deflating other egos, he was easily aroused to anger by articles or paragraphs which could wound or even offend their subjects. He needed to know that the attack was necessary. Nor could he abide 'personalised' journalism. Once, when he had become proprietor of the paper, he was furious when the editor, Reg Ward, wrote a brief, amusing, but sharp account of the way he had been blackballed from a local Club (on account of the Establishment feathers that the *Times* had ruffled in the town). However absurdly the worthies of Twickenham may have behaved, the editors had been venting personal spleen— and that, in Dimbleby's book, was a misuse of the paper's privilege.

In a pamphlet he produced about the operation of his papers, which he called 'Democracy at Work', he wrote with boyish excitement of how a last-minute front page story—a big fire in Twickenham—found its way into print with minutes to spare:

Whatever happens, the paper must be in the hands of the newsagents over an area of a hundred square miles by dawn, so that you can have it by breakfast time, so that you can pick up this ingenious, complicated, delicate, intricate product of forty men and women and say, 'Ah! the local rag!'

and he added, under the cross-heading 'WHY WE ARE PROUD', a personal note:

> We Dimblebys are proud, as a family, to own a series of newspapers that for threequarters of a century have told the truth, and told it first and best. We believe absolutely that freedom of speech is sacred, and that in it lies the strength of our democracy. We believe also that, in the whole world of the press, there is no better standard-bearer of democracy than the local newspaper, unbiased, sincere and trustworthy.

The concept of the 'family business' was not for him an arcane device to snare the workers into the belief that the 'family' would always protect them, only to discover that when it suited the family, they, like their colleagues in the large corporations, would find themselves out of work as the business was bought up, and then closed down by 'rationalisation'. He believed that the family business formed the ideal framework for production in a free society, disliking large companies where unions seemed locked in constant conflict with bosses who ruled from a distance and treated men as units of production. Though he did not pause to consider the nature of that conflict, the atmosphere of distrust and even hatred that it created appalled him. With some naivety, but much sincerity, he wished to prove, at least to himself, that such tension was not inevitable. He could not do that, or improve the paper, while his ageing and increasingly difficult uncle remained in charge.

Richard spent much time plotting Percy's removal. But the old man clung on, as convinced that his nephew would ruin the business if he went, as Richard was that it would die on its feet if he stayed. Finally, by means of a complicated manoeuvre (which the Inland Revenue would now frown upon but which then was quite legal) Percy was persuaded to relinquish his Chair. As compensation he was to take into retirement a pension and £40,000 in cash. On the morning of the transaction, the family was on holiday in *Vabel* on the Thames. A cheque had to be posted to Percy to complete the deal. When my father had written it out (showing it to David in glee, saying: 'You've never seen so much money as that in all your life!'), he marched down with his eldest son into Cookham to post it. He always took delight in testing the efficiency of the Post Office, and whenever he had a really important letter to send, he would go out of his way to avoid a main Post Office and find some little-used and out of the way letter-box. It added to the excitement of this occasion to search Cookham for an old letter-box, which they eventually found in a back alley, and which to his immense satisfaction had been set in the wall in the reign of Queen Victoria. The letter duly arrived; and Richard became Managing Director of Dimbleby and Sons Ltd.

The paper soon improved: he bought new machines, expanded the staff, and transformed the look of each of the three papers. He also appointed his brother-in-law John Haines as Company Secretary. John, who was a much trusted friend, was soon given the nickname 'tight-wad', and for the next few years Richard spent long hours explaining to him, 'My dear boy, money is for spending.' He produced a series of plans for expanding the papers which alarmed the General Manager, Roy Annette, who thought they were a recipe for financial ruin, but as soon as he was talked out of one scheme he talked himself into another. He formed a film company called Puritan Films and then another called Film Partnership (making for the BBC the first ever 'holiday' films to appear on television, which he sold to the Corporation for no profit).

Ernest Marples once told him that a good businessman should invest in garages as more people were buying cars and they would always need petrol; but there were no garages immediately available and then he grew bored with the idea. He nearly invested in a company called Trans Europe Television which would record on video-tape circuses, football matches and operas on the Continent, using an EMI recording van, and then sell the programmes to television companies all over the world. But they had too little capital, no-one wanted the programmes, and the little he invested was lost. He nearly formed a company to make video-cassette machines but his anxious lieutenants persuaded him in time that the newspapers could not stand the risk. He almost invested in a company to bid for an ITV franchise, but he discovered that his putative partners seemed a little less than reliable, and he pulled out in time. He thought of buying new newspapers, and other print-works; but his enthusiasm waned as wiser business heads wore him down.

Though he dabbled in business my father was no entrepreneur: lacking dedication and the necessary ruthless edge. When Lord

Thomson once suggested mildly that he might care to sell the Dimbleby papers, Richard's 'over my dead body' reply sprang from a much deeper commitment: the business was prosperous, but there was more to protect than the money. As Managing Director, he was now in a position to re-create his vision of the 'family' business, and repair the damage done by Percy. For a long time 'Mr. Richard' had taken to going down into the works whenever he could. He knew the names of all the workers, and remembered the details of their family life, not caring if production slowed down as he stopped to talk to an older man who had looked after him as an apprentice. Those visits were without formality. Once he walked up to one of the compositors, Len Carter, who was going blind, but was still as fast as any at 'making up' a page. 'Len', said one of his colleagues, 'there's someone here to see you'. 'Is there?' said Len, deeply engrossed, 'Who is it, Mr. Annette?' 'No,' 'Well, then, tell whoever it is to fuck off—I'm busy!' 'Very well, then Len, I'll fuck off then,' said the Managing Director, quite unperturbed, and wandered on his way leaving Len Carter who recognised the voice, standing speechless with mortification.

My father had few egalitarian principles, and ideas of workers' participation or industrial democracy had not yet been noised abroad. Had anyone suggested to him that there was a lie at the heart of a paternalism in which some members of the 'family' had to work for their living, while others (the real family) reaped the benefit of that work, he would have been confused and distressed: his belief in the 'family' business was no less sincere for being unrevolutionary. The bonds between the workers and himself were personal and enduring; he was a true patriarch. On the rare occasions when it was necessary to sack someone, he shrank from the decision for days. Even when there were cogent reasons—in one case the alleged 'indecency' of a worker towards a succession of secretaries—he tried to forestall the inevitable by protracted argument with his senior staff, yielding only when he had been finally worn down by the irrefutable logic of their case. He was much happer when called upon to prepare pension plans, accident and life insurance policies, and new wage rates (all of which, in the Fifties, were unrivalled in the trade); when he could sign Christmas bonus cheques; send a worker who was ill to Harley Street and the family of another back home to Italy for a short holiday when the man was ill with cancer. He needed the affection of those who worked for him. If someone was off-hand, or cold when he walked through the plant, he was not angry but anxious, worrying for days about 'doing the right thing'; and he would be unhappy until good relations were restored. Then he failed to hide a beaming boyish elation. When men were ill, or got married, or their wives had children, he sent flowers and fruit, and letters in his own hand which were carefully preserved.

Until 1959 Dimbleby and Sons Ltd was a member of the Newspaper Society (which represented the interest of provincial newspapers, among other matters, in negotiations with the Unions). Over the years the Society had earned a justified reputation for clumsy and crusty negotiating tactics. Soon after he became Managing Director, Richard Dimbleby earned lasting disapproval by settling with his own workers above the level offered by the Society. In 1959, the Society (limbering up for yet another confrontation with the Unions) told its members at one stage in the negotiations to serve notice on their employees and put them on 'day-to-day' working—in effect threatening the Unions with a lock-out. The prospect filled my father with horror. He found it almost unbelievable that other 'family' businesses seemed quite prepared to put their men out of work; it had never occurred to him that his attitude was unusual, that others did not share his sense of obligation to his staff.

He reacted instinctively at once: within a few hours of the 'advice' the secretary of the Newspaper Society had a telegram on his desk, signed by Richard Dimbleby informing him that Dimbleby and Sons Ltd had that day resigned its membership. A few days later, the Managing Director wrote a 'leader' in *The Richmond and Twickenham Times* explaining his (by now much publicised) decision: the Society had been 'provocative and foolish'; it had been 'ponderous and unyielding'; and he was 'convinced that a settlement could have been reached if a sensible offer had been made when the Unions' first demands were delivered'. He went himself to negotiate at the headquarters of the Printing and Kindred Trades Federation, and settled on almost precisely the same terms as the Society was forced to concede after a fortnight's unnecessary dispute. Long afterwards Granville Eastwood, the General Secretary of the Federation, wrote of 'the example he set as an employer and the lead he gave to the industry'.

Richard's romantic faith in the family business shone most brightly on firm outings (to the seaside, to Boulogne for the day) and at the Annual Dinner. He launched himself into these occasions with an enthusiastic skill which brought a wry (but delighted) smile to the lips of some of his more cynical executives, who saw the effect that his personality had on industrial relations.

At dinner, he presided over the gathering from a top-table, flanked by his family—his mother (Chairman), his wife (Director), his sister, Pat Haines (Director), his brother-in-law, John Haines (Company Secretary), and, as they grew old enough, his sons and daughter, nephews and nieces. Before him, two hundred strong, sat the company: wives, sons, daughters, and sweethearts. There were many courses and much wine. There were presents for the wives: radios, deckchairs, food vouchers, and make-up kits. For their husbands there were raffles for fortnights in Majorca, seven days in Spain, a weekend in Paris. And at the end of the meal, silence would be called, and the Managing Director would make a speech. It provided one of those rare occasions when my father was seen to be nervous before he began, clearing his throat, fiddling with his cuff, trying too hard to seem to be at ease. Yet when he started, he showed the same gifts that had won his factory audiences in the war. First he would introduce and welcome his family, telling a joke about one, recording a success of another. Then he conducted a brief survey of the 'family' fortunes, with a sobering thought here, and some praise there. Then he told some stories about the business, remembering odd incidents in the year which others had forgotten but loved to recall; making references to his affection for them, and dotted with shared jokes which he and they but no-one else would understand. At the end, one by one the company would rise up to applaud him, and at the end of the evening, when most inhibitions had been released, he would be dragged into the centre of the dance floor with his mother, and his wife, and his sister, while the entire company stood round them bellowing: 'For he's a jolly good fellow'.

Afterwards, with his wife and children dozing beside him, he would drive home happily to Sussex, carefully and fast in his much treasured Rolls-Royce.

The Rolls-Royce was an important symbol. From 1959 when he acquired his first, he was always at the top of the buyers queue for the latest model—the Silver Cloud Marks I, II and III. As the time came for each replacement he would spend many hours discussing different colour schemes with the family around him.

Should it be grey, or silver and grey—or should we try maroon this time? Or would that be a shade vulgar? It never seemed to him a flamboyant or extravagant gesture to buy so luxurious a car. Instead he allowed himself to believe that it was a necessary accoutrement—giving him an appropriate flourish of distinction. Although he did not quite put it in such terms, he felt that his position in national life demanded that he be seen to have the best.

He enjoyed the luxury and style; when he drove in London, it did not offend him that people turned in the streets to stare; and, even, on some occasions when he drove to his commentary position for a state occasion, cheered as he went smoothly past. If we ever suggested that he did not really need a Rolls, he would reply, not quite seriously, 'Do you really expect me to attend upon my Monarch in a Morris Minor?'

When he went on state visits to Europe he frequently had the Rolls shipped over in advance—where, as a result, he was frequently mistaken by local dignitaries for the resident British Ambassador. His principal reason for such elaborate manoeuvres was his delight at driving fast and in silence on European motorways; he had never lost the thrill that made him chart the motoring details of his European honeymoon with such care. Occasionally, after a royal visit, he took a few days' holiday with my mother, deriving great pleasure from driving back to Britain across country, stopping in isolated villages where the people would crowd round the car in wonderment. Making no attempt to disguise his pride, he would open the doors and bonnet for them, and let them work the electric windows—an international salesman for a large, gleaming machine that they could never buy. That it gave a proper flourish to a state visit for the BBC's principal public figure to sweep into European capitals in 'the best car in the world' provided him with a gratifying but secondary justification.

It caused him pain that at least one of his children could not bear for him to arrive at school in the Rolls-Royce. So sensitive to slight was he that he interpreted schoolboy embarrassment at grandeur as a rebuke for his opulence—wrongly believing (as he had with his role in television) that a son thought his car vulgar. In fact our reticence, such as it was, was caused by the desire, if not the need, to appear as ordinary as possible. Schoolboys, and sometimes teachers, needed little prompting to remind us that 'just because you are Richard Dimbleby's son, it does not mean you can do that, you know'—and on occasion they could be much crueller than that. In any case, my father was tender enough towards the sentiments of his children always to arrive modestly at the author's school in Dilys's elderly saloon or the farm Land-Rover—parking it alongside the rows of Jaguars and the Rovers which the City had provided for most of the parents of Charterhouse pupils.

Against their own inclinations my parents sent all their sons to public school (though Sally was spared), in the erroneous, but prevalent belief that the more they paid for our education, the better educated we would be. It caused them much anguish. At the start of each term, we and my mother would part in tears; and afterwards, miserable himself, my father would spend long hours comforting her with the reminder that by sending us to public school, they were 'doing the best' for us, and that in any case the holidays would soon come round again. They were both incensed if they heard other couples rejoice that 'the children have gone back to school, thank God!' If they had not thought it faintly improper and certainly irresponsible, they would have much preferred to send us to a local day school when we could have lived all the time at home instead of less than half the year.

As it was, the school holidays assumed great significance in their and our lives, when my parents went out of their way to compensate for our term-time absence. All celebrations were observed with a great ritual according to long-standing family custom; chairs were prettily decorated with flowers; tables delicately and elaborately prepared; presents unwrapped, not quickly in private but with the rest of the family watching on, admiring the display; songs were sung and family games were played, not haphazardly but with the formality of much-loved habit.

Of all our celebrations Christmas was the greatest, and, because it symbolised so much that mattered to my father, the most carefully organised ritual of all.

The preparations began weeks in advance when the children and everyone else on the farm—Tom, Freddy, Cath, Olgar, Winnie, Arthur, Antonio and Pathita, and if they were there the builders as well—were required to stir the Christmas pudding. Later my father would find old silver sixpences to hide in it. In the middle of December, Tom and Freddy, the farm workers, would be despatched to collect trailerfuls of holly and ivy which were then hung in great clumps from the beams of the barn, so that the room took on the appearance almost of a woodland glade. Huge logs were cut, the open fire in the corner which always smoked devouring them like kindling wood. We pinned up hundreds of Christmas cards on the wall—those from Ambassadors and Heads of State, from Coco the Clown and Dixon of Dock Green, hung with that discreet prominence which ensured they would be noticed, but did not seem like name-dropping. Huge quantities of food were brought to the kitchen by an endless round of delivery men—turkeys, geese, ducks and chicken for each meal of the celebration.

In the early hours of Christmas morning my father went gently round the house, hanging stockings prepared by my mother at the end of every bed. At breakfast, already gorged on chocolate, we ate boiled eggs, each one hand-painted with a funny face—and then just after ten o'clock we went to church. My father was not a Christian of deep conviction but he believed strongly in the Christian ritual, strongly enough to insist that we attend church with him every Sunday, sitting in the pew which was unofficially reserved for us between the organ and the choir. He was never unmoved by St. Peter's Lynchmere: by the organ that wheezed, by the little fat man who puffed its bellows, by the organist, who was a family friend, and who cursed not too quietly at the choir which ignored her lead, by the Colonel, the Major and the newspaper tipster who week after week exchanged smiles of real pleasure to see him, by the vicar who tried unceasingly but to no avail to have him discard his low-church prejudice and be confirmed a full member of the Church of England. After we had sung Christmas hymns and psalms, and said prayers, not loudly but firmly, we hurried back to open presents, piled high in the drawing room, each person with his or her own chair full. Sometimes hidden as a surprise in the stable, or delivered while we were away at church, there would be a pony, and once a horse and trap. On one occasion, while we were at church, a dovecot was erected in front of the house, ready for the fantail pigeons which were waiting wrapped on top of the grand piano, a gift from husband to wife.

Christmas lunch lasted not too long—ending when Dilys organised her reluctant husband and children into a family walk. After tea we played old-fashioned games in the drawing room. We had supper and went late to bed. Early on Boxing Day relations began to arrive for the annual family party: grandmothers, aunts, uncles, nephews, nieces and cousins, some from far away with luggage for the night. At Boxing Day lunch we always ate goose and there were always at least fifteen of us, ranging across four generations. In the afternoon more family arrived, and some of the handful of close friends who came every year with their children. By the evening when the party began, there were more than thirty of us.

The Boxing Day party was enjoyed according to family tradition. We sang Christmas carols, we performed the nativity play, and each child had to sing or recite or play the piano. Each year, the Mystery Voice of Twenty Questions, Norman Hackforth, disappeared in the afternoon to 'visit an old aunt of mine'; and two hours later to the sound of sleigh bells my father would arrive down the hill in the Land-Rover with an immaculately clothed Father Christmas, who had been forced to leave his reindeer 'up at the top because the hill was too steep for them'. The custom only ended after one of us, detecting a familiar tone, shouted out in triumph, 'that's not Father Christmas, it's Uncle Norman'. Later, we played 'family coach', a game appropriately devised in Victorian England. We all sat in a large circle, while my father sat in the middle to tell us the story of the family coach, of the prince and the princess, and the king and the queen and the journey through the night, and the coachman, and the highwayman, and the hold-up, and the escape and the happiness ever after. Each of us had a part to play: one was the princess, another the coachman, a wheel or a whip or horse. Thus metamorphosed, whenever we were mentioned we had to stand up turn round and sit down again. At the mention of 'family coach' everyone had to perform the same manoeuvre. To forget was to incur a forfeit. My father told the story at such speed—'and the horses, the first, the second, the third and the fourth, all the horses, galloped and the coachman cracked his whip, and the wheels spun, and the princess smiled at the prince, and he smiled at the princess and the family coach rushed on its way'—that the room was filled with gyrating adults and children; and with the forfeited shoes and watches of those who had become so engrossed in the story that they had forgotten to move when their name was called. The game became more difficult as we grew older, when some of us—more extravert than others—deliberately forgot to stand up when summoned in order to enjoy redeeming our forfeit with an act or a song or the chance to kiss a cousin.

Later in the evening my father and Norman Hackforth sat down at the grand piano to thump out Sir Roger de Coverley while we danced. They started slowly but then played faster and faster, the sweat pouring from their faces for fifteen minutes at a time, forbidden by the rest of us to stop until each individual, from grandmother to grandchild had been through the entire barn-dance routine. The party went on and on into the morning.

To my father, Christmas was more than a feast, more than a celebration of the birth of Christ—though to him it was both those things. It was above all a celebration of the family, a reaffirmation of a romance with a way of life enshrined in a ritual which he had first observed in Richmond as a child of Edwardian England. As an adult he rejoiced that the whole family gathered at *his* house, that other families would choose to be in his home rather than their own, that he could give presents and food and drink, and most of all extend a gentle patriarchal goodwill which warmed everyone around him.

Yet it was not Boxing Day or Christmas Day which mattered most, but Christmas Eve, when each step in the simple ritual was a symbol of all that he valued. At midday the family and everyone who worked on the farm stood together in the barn to drink to each other and celebrate the arrival of the festival. At six o'clock in the evening, the family filed into the drawing room. The great family Bible was placed on a table in the centre of the room and opened at St. Luke chapter 2, verse 1, and each of us, starting with the youngest, read a verse of the story of the nativity. Then we checked that the light over the crib (which was repainted each year by Nicholas) still shone on Jesus, that the oxen and the asses, the kings and the wise men, had not fallen over in the straw. Then we sang carols, my father at the piano trying to orchestrate us, and affecting disapproval when we turned in mock innocent astonishment to listen to the deep contralto of my mother in 'Come All Ye Faithful'. (When we were older and stepped insensitively over the borders of propriety, threatening to destroy an essentially serious moment for him, my father was much upset, saying that if we could not behave he would give up our family rituals.) After the carols, the children stood round the single twenty-four-hour candle which had been placed in the window by the front door. Each of us lit a match, and one after the other helped set the candle alight.

Then my father would disappear into the kitchen to prepare a huge hot punch—pouring in gin, and orange, and wine and cloves and apples, while fumes of steaming alcohol soon seeped through the house. At ten o'clock that night we waited for the first sounds of the carol-singers coming down the long hill from the village. Danley Farm was their last and most favoured destination. Twenty-five or thirty people, their faces red, their hands raw, bellowing 'Hark the Herald Angels Sing' marching down the hill, crunching across the gravel, and into the barn. My father sat at the piano, and the village sang for its punch. For him this was the real village—not the commuters (who lived here because it was just close enough to London, and amongst whom he never numbered himself), nor the local gentry—but the people, whom when he had been in Lymington, he had thought were the 'soul of England'; country people, with Hampshire accents, whose fathers and fathers before them had never strayed far from the village.

Once the punch had begun to take effect, the carols gave way to songs, and the songs to bawdy songs, while my father still banged away. And then when the moment was right, he stopped and demanded 'one more carol please, men' before the choir trudged away up the hill, their shouts and laughter echoing back into the valley.

13

Critics and Controversy

> Shrieking voices
> Scolding, mocking, or merely chattering,
> Always assail . . .
>
> T. S. ELIOT

'WHAT'S EATING DIMBLEBY' WAS THE HEADLINE IN THE *DAILY MAIL* in November 1958. 'Nothing' would have been the short answer. However, since the paper was beginning a three-part 'intimate, revealing, close-up of one of the most successful and controversial figures ever to look out of a TV screen . . .' 'Nothing' was clearly not enough. As the writer of the article observed, Richard Dimbleby 'is at the top of his career at the dizzy top of the transmitter'.

There were no precedents in the new medium of television but Dimbleby had expected that he would be subjected to the same kind of treatment as radio and stage personalities: there would be complaints and criticisms; fellow journalists would want to know about his private life, and would feel free to make up what they could not discover. They might call him boring, or predictable— or even pompous, though that did rankle. Believing that, with one or two exceptions, the critics were ignorant of the medium they sought to report, he imagined that he would be only mildly pleased or rebuked by their judgments. It was to his alarm and consternation that in the Fifties he became a centre of controversy: the object of embarrassingly fulsome praise and cruel abuse. The praise pleased him but passed him by; he had seen nearly all those who had been 'stars' beside him ten years before fade into anonymity. The vituperation which was heaped on him for no reason he could understand came as a painful shock. No-one in the history of radio or television has suffered quite the intense personal hostility that was directed at him in the Fifties.

It started in 1951—as a mere murmur. Under the headline 'It's that Man Again', the *Evening Standard* columnist, George Campey, issued a mild rebuke to 'the owner of the voice that goes on and on...' Richard Dimbleby, avowed Campey, was doing too much radio and television. Within three days, he wrote, Dimbleby would be heard on no less than six major television and three radio programmes. The BBC was 'overworking their ace commentator'. He would earn 'a minimum of £500' for the programmes but 'what shall it profit the man if he loses public interest?' It was hardly scorching criticism: Dimbleby *was* over-working—in television he had no rivals and was in constant demand. It was, though, the first serious complaint laid publicly against him, and he thought it unfair. In addition it touched a tender spot. He would have much liked to earn £500 from the eight broadcasts. In fact he was paid £199 10s. He wrote to Campey complaining that the estimate was

> impertinent . . . God knows what sort of fees you think the BBC pays us . . . While I normally ignore criticism when it is unjust and inaccurate, I really cannot let it pass this time... You are good enough to say that I am the BBC's 'ace commentator'... if I *am* the ace commentator, who else would you expect the BBC to use on any great national occasion? . . . I seldom take offence at what is written about me [he concluded with more bravura than honesty], but I really draw the line at your damaging, unkind, inaccurate article.

Mr. Campey's article was a model of courtesy in comparison with those which followed. It was as if he had lifted a taboo. For years, Fleet Street had heaped dutiful praise on Dimbleby. Month after month a zealous reporter on one paper would look up the cuttings and reproduce, with the judicious shift of an adjective here and there, the same catalogue of 'outstanding' achievements of the BBC's 'ace commentator'; now, as if instructed by some unseen ventriloquist, the writers of Fleet Street, decided that the moment had arrived to destroy the image that they had created. The kindly Marshall Pugh in the *Mail*, who found it 'unreasonable' (but irresistable) to imagine Dimbleby 'suffering from insomnia in his four-poster Rolls, shamed by all the hems he ever kissed in public', thought the hostility was inevitable. It was part of 'the ancient English blood sport of tearing down the hero, something which has happened to almost every human piece of public property, excepting Nelson. It was not Dimbleby the family man the hounds were after. Dimbleby was also a public institution.' Dimbleby might protest, as he did to Pugh, 'no I am not, no I am not, I am *me*'—it would make no difference. In any case the venom of the onslaught was much more vindictive than was required by mere iconoclasm. It was given to a *Sunday Express* gossip columnist, called Logan Gourlay, to lead the attack. In December 1952 he informed his readers: 'no longer can I suffer in silence'; and he informed Dimbleby 'I am yawning . . . it is time someone told you that you're trite, tedious, and too pleased with yourself . . .'; and his readers again:

> I must shout out in protest against one of the major bores in the wide sphere of entertainment . . . even if his qualifications had been outstanding when he started—and I doubt that—they would have become blunted after all this time . . . I suggest he is now trite, tedious, repetitive, often fatuous, always faintly patronising and never stimulating . . .

The programme which roused Mr. Gourlay to such a convincing display of outrage was Down Your Way, and he told his readers 'how I have wished to crack one of those old gramophone records over his smug head . . .' But it was not only Down Your Way: 'his too-smooth voice has spoiled many an outside broadcast for me. He has loomed frequently on my television screen making me thankful for sightless radio. There has been altogether too much Dimbleby—a deluge of Dimbleby . . .' His parting advice to the broadcaster was as graceful as the rest of his article: 'take a rest Mr. Dimbleby. Go down your own way and stay there a while.'

It was the first time that any broadcaster had been attacked in such terms. Dimbleby was angry and wounded. He wanted to sue and to write letters to the *Express*, he wanted to meet Gourlay face to face—there was no limit to what he would then do. He had never imagined that his work could bring such calumny upon his head. He simply could not understand why someone should store up such malice against him. In vain his family, friends and colleagues told him that Gourlay was only a Fleet Street gossip columnist, while he, Richard Dimbleby, was the BBC's premier broadcaster. Only by persuading him that it would be unseemly to be seen to be mixing it with Gourlay was Dimbleby eventually soothed into inaction.

He received little consolation the following week when the *Express* (rather too obviously perhaps revealing the purpose of the original Gourlay article) announced in a headline: 'THAT ATTACK ON DIMBLEBY. It starts the hottest-ever argument on this page...Gourlay's assessment has provoked a cyclone. Never before has this page unleashed a controversy so passionately fought out...' An entire page was filled with letters 'for' and 'against' Richard Dimbleby.

Against him were readers who thought that he was variously: an arch-bore, pathetic, sneering, platitudinous, unctuous, self-satisfied, 'cat-been-at-the-cream', and a 'banana-oil exuding character'. One writer thought that the BBC might as well employ 'a member of the Luton Girls' Choir to broadcast the Coronation' as Dimbleby. Another complained of his failure to do any of the thousand and one things that would proclaim this automaton to be made of flesh and blood.

Those 'for' Richard Dimbleby found themselves 'seething at the drivel of Gourlay's attack'; Mr. Gourlay was to them 'a complete boor' his attack was 'wicked and slanderous'; one writer assumed 'that Gourlay used to write rude words on walls'. Richard Dimbleby was 'the finest BBC personality . . . clear, confident, polite, at ease'; he had 'brought excitement and colour into many lives'; he was supremely able to 'put people at their ease' and 'could paint beautiful word pictures'. 'May it be many years,' wrote one reader, 'before Richard Dimbleby's incomparable charm of manner, his outstanding inspiration, and his great personality are lost to us and his much-loved voice silent.'

Dimbleby was gratified by none of it. He intensely disliked the vulgarity of the *Express* in counting the 'fors' and 'againsts' and showing 'the running so far'—although this showed that by a margin of 65 per cent to 35 per cent, the *Express* readers supported him. It was not an accolade which he would have sought, any more than he relished becoming 'the most controversial figure in television'.

After Gourlay came a phalanx of other Fleet Street talents using much the same language to say much the same thing. Not until 1956 did anyone focus the attack on what was to become the main source of hostility to him—his attitude towards the monarchy. The writer responsible for the first of these articles was Cassandra (Bill Connor), the famous *Daily Mirror* columnist. His article was superior to Gourlay's: the invective was harsher, the prose purpler, the tone crueller. 'Richard Dimbleby,' said Cassandra:

> shimmers in his own unction. He swirls in glycerine respect for his subject that makes the Royal Family look like an advertisement for an immensely costly hair tonic—for which Mr. Dimbleby may sign up the advertising rights any moment . . .
>
> He is the royal radio Pussy Cat. He purrs from the Coronation to a polo match, from a Ducal Household to a County Fair. And still the result is the same—glossy pap soused with the mayonnaise of unlimited unction. You have only to hear half a dozen of his carefully modulated syllables to know that there is nothing more to learn. He stands to attention with cushioned respect. He is like Mr. Michelin, the symbol of French motor tyres—but even more confident that there are no punctures ahead. To listen to Mr. Dimbleby describing a royal occasion is like tuning in to an oily burial service . . . With his immense talent for the inevitable mental bow at the hips and with his genius of affability and condescension he moves around the Throne Room purring with more than accustomed ease. In his way, Richard Dimbleby is the greatest and most accomplished radio butler that Broadcasting House has ever seen . . .

And so Cassandra went on, mixing a myriad of metaphors, purpler and purpler and doubtless more and more sure that in debunking one of those 'who rule the House of Radio (and) dominate the Tower of TV' he was fulfilling a great national service.

Again, and inevitably, Dimbleby was much wounded and greatly angered. This time he consulted lawyers; they thought he had a case. Again, just in time, his sense of decorum overcame his outrage. He felt impotent, humiliated and misunderstood. He stood accused, openly or by implication, of some of the most despicable human traits—and he could say nothing. The anguish for him was that the charges were impossible to meet: he had not been misquoted, or quoted out of context—he had not been quoted at all. He was accused of no identifiable offence, no evidence had been marshalled against him. He was not a politician, attacked for speeches he had made, or decisions he had taken. The hostility which he had aroused, was for nothing that he had said or done but, much more woundingly, for what he *was*. It was impossible to counter-attack save by denying the charges, and then it would be said of him 'methinks he doth protest too much'. On this occasion he realised that henceforth he would have to suffer, if not in silence, at least with dignified reticence. So when a much cleverer and more eloquent pen found it impossible to resist this open target, he kept his counsel. The writer, Malcolm Muggeridge, who was at the time an iconoclast of no fixed abode, had written a series of articles in *Esquire* magazine attacking the Royal Family—or rather, the slavish awe with which all things royal were regarded. The articles, the first of their type, caused outrage, not least in the hierarchy of the BBC. He was at once banned from Panorama, where for four years he had been the most individualistic of the programme's reporting team. He thus became free to pin Richard Dimbleby with his merciless pen. The phrase he used to describe his former colleague (whom he regarded with a cordial dislike which was readily reciprocated) was 'Gold Microphone-in-Waiting'. The phrase was picked up by lesser pens, and tossed around Fleet Street newspaper columns for years. Dimbleby suffered in silence—though Muggeridge was not forgiven. (Richard's mother, a woman of fierce pride would not mention the man's name, until some years after her son's death, she met Muggeridge by chance at a Foyle's lunch, where she was so captivated by the famous Muggeridgean charm that he was at once forgiven.)

The attacks on Dimbleby were greatly outnumbered by the eulogies; although the latter (being less interesting) were soon forgotten. For a long time Gourlay, Cassandra and Muggeridge were not only on the Dimbleby blacklist, but notorious wherever his friends gathered together. To this day no serious commentator or reporter in radio or television (or in Fleet Street) has been treated to such a display of sustained invective. It cannot merely be explained by the fact that he was the only man in his profession to reach a position of national pre-eminence.

Inevitably much of the criticism became the common currency of the discussion about Dimbleby, both within and without the BBC. Even those who wished to show independence of mind felt compelled to offer obeisance to the prevailing clichés about him, before coming to his defence. So, a not unfriendly article about him had to be entitled 'Smoothy Talks'. Its opening words had to be 'Richard Dimbleby O.B.E. was anxious to prove that he was not (as critics suggest) solemn, suave, bland or pompous...' And when critics wished to praise him (at least in the popular press) they felt bound to remind viewers first that they were not instinctive fans: he had to be the 'Mr. Hush Reverence' or 'Mr. Regal Whisper' or 'Mr. Pregnant Pause'. In more serious papers, critics who wished to report his mastery of an occasion, dutifully noted that on the occasion in question he seemed to have 'discarded' the reverential solemnity of manner, which they had never even noticed in him before.

Questions about Dimbleby soon became assumptions. As a consequence, he spent much of the remainder of the Fifties being asked by interviewers to defend himself against the charges that he was obsequious, pompous or unctuous. He remained admirably courteous. What could he do? A refusal to answer, would be demonstrable evidence both of his guilt and his self-importance. If he took them seriously, he would seem portentous. His solution was to try to explain why the criticism arose, and then to laugh it off. It never really worked. The only occasions on which he seemed truly pompous to his friends was when he tried to make light of the charges against him. Once he started, he could never disguise how much he was stung by the criticism. The jollier he tried to be, the more ponderous he seemed.

One charge in particular touched him deeply. Sometimes openly, and always implicitly, the cruellest of his critics contrived to suggest in essence that he was not merely a pompous bore, but a greasy, *fat*—even grotesque—pompous bore. Dimbleby had always been excessively sensitive about his size. At school he had been 'Dropsy'; after school he had been 'Bumble' (because 'he was fat and he buzzed'). He would never, even to the innocent enquiries of his children, reveal his weight. The sight of really fat men in bathing costumes disgusted him. He would never—though he loved the water—swim where he could be seen by others. Even with his family he was self-conscious—wearing a huge bathrobe until he was at the water's edge and not leaving the sea until Dilys was there to wrap him in it again. He spent much of his adult life conspiring unsuccessfully with a succession of diets to cast off excess pounds. He walked very upright and fast, with quick, short strides; worried about appearing clumsy he moved with extreme delicacy and adroitness. Nor was he grotesquely fat. He was nearly six feet tall, immensely broad and solid and certainly not corrugated by excess rolls of flesh.

Yet, although his consciousness of size put him on his dignity, he would frequently play the fool in private and sometimes in public. In 1938 he had beautifully mocked his Nazi hosts; he had broadcast from a Turkish bath and from inside a diving suit; he had once arranged for a novelty joke 'fart' to be put under the cushion of his chair in a 'live' interview (allowing the audience to believe that the interviewee (who was the sailor, Uffa Fox) had played the noisy joke on him); he let himself be photographed sitting in a village stocks, in a clown's mask on the back of a Hereford bull, admiring his Madame Tussaud's torso. But once the attacks started, public fun stopped. He had never been loud or noisy; he had never sought to obtrude. Now he behaved with the decorum and dignity of a man who would avoid the risk of ridicule.

It deeply offended him to think that people could interpret his sense of dignity and propriety, which had deep roots, as shallow pomposity. 'Let them criticise me as a professional—as a broadcaster' he complained 'but not just for my person'—his size, his sensitive size, should not have been a matter for public discussion. Once, when he was stung into telling his critics publicly that most of them were 'reporters who have turned to television as a change from crime', he was much gratified by their outrage. It was not by chance that the two critics for whom he had the most respect (Maurice Wiggin of the *Sunday Times* and Peter Black of the *Daily Mail*) at no stage in their long careers drew unflattering attention to his shape or his alleged pomposity. They confined their criticism of him—which was occasionally stern—to those matters which he thought relevant.

Only once did he allow himself a public outburst. On the twenty-first anniversary of his broadcasting career, in September 1957, Panorama invited him to interview himself (by means of taping the questions and answers separately) about his career. He chose to answer the charge that he was pompous:

> well that's something that makes me livid. Look, I do not think that they know, half of 'em, the difference between pomp and weight. In all the years that I worked in radio and wasn't seen, nobody ever said I was pompous. The moment I appear on a television screen, they say—he's pompous. I know what it is, they see I am enormous—and I can't help that, I am—and because I am heavy and large they think heavy and large people are pompous . . .

So uncharacteristically vehement was he, that he seemed to be irritated even by the question which he had chosen to raise himself. Next day with a show of surprise, the press reported that he was not after all insensitive to criticism.

In the same 'interview' Dimbleby ascribed his alleged reverential attitude towards the monarchy to the technical limitations of his job: 'On a State occasion or a big occasion . . . if you are in a hushed hall during a solemn ceremony you can't shout in a Light Programme type of voice, or you would drown the ceremony and bring it to a standstill. That is the only reason why I ever whisper anywhere—it is not reverence, it is pure necessity'. So obsessed was he with the need to squash the charge of pomposity that Dimbleby was not fair to himself. He *was* reverential before monarchy; he was even unctuous—but only in the original meaning of the word, as someone possessing 'a fervent or sympathetic quality in words or tone caused by or causing deep religious emotion or other emotion.'

Some of his critics were irritated as much by his virtues as his vices. Why was he always so calm? Never at a loss for the right word? Always so faultless? —they complained. His mastery of the medium, so complete and so unrivalled, was a goad compelling them to envious protest. How could—why should—one man stand so apart and above the rest; so dominate the most powerful instrument of mass communications; seem so omnipotent, so omniscient, and—worst of all—so nice? Others seemed dimly to perceive that in attacking him they were attacking the Corporation. The BBC did arouse frustration in those who had no access to its microphones; who distrusted its cultural hegemony; who felt powerless before its impervious authority. Yet none of those who railed at Dimbleby made it clear that they were attacking the BBC.

There were serious questions to be asked. How was it that one man could hold such a unique position in so powerful a medium? Why was he so loyal a citizen? What effect did his words have? How healthy was it, that every state occasion should be treated through him, by the BBC, with such unquestioning devotion? Why should the public be openly enjoined to worship the Crown? Where in this adulation was the objectivity and impartiality upon the maintenance of which the BBC had so often laid the justification of its very existence? The Corporation might well have met the questions—but they were never even put. As time revealed, the attacks on Dimbleby were shallow and ill-conceived. They sprung up suddenly, they flourished for a season, and they withered overnight. By the early Sixties, when iconoclasm was common, when the BBC was infected (for a brief Indian summer) with a glorious sense of freedom, Richard Dimbleby had become beyond reproach. In 1954, the *Sunday Times* had described him as a 'national institution . . . our Public Orator; the custodian, not exactly of public morals, but of the public sense of conformity, decorum and propriety . . .' When he pronounced, he spoke 'for the majority and the majority is flattered to find itself so eloquent, so apt, so oratund . . .' By 1960 despite and perhaps because of his critics, he was all that and more: he had become a televisual father of the people, not only respected but loved in a way which has been accorded to very few other public men.

Throughout the Fifties the Management of the BBC was anxious that Dimbleby might leave the Corporation since he was still technically a freelance, with no permanent contract. Yet it adopted a curiously schizophrenic stance towards him: regarding it as essential that he should stay, it treated him in ways which seemed positively designed to make him leave. As early as 1951, as part of the BBC's 'anti-Luxembourg campaign', the Programme Contracts Department was instructed to 'endeavour to tie him up under the scheme approved by the D.G. (Director-General)'. The Department set about compiling statistics of his earnings from the Corporation, on the basis of which the BBC was to offer him a guarantee in return for his exclusive services. On the basis of a projection from his earnings for three months, the accountants concluded that his salary from the BBC for a year amounted to about £10,000 (for which he made about two hundred and fifty broadcasts, rarely earning more than £40 a programme). The BBC then offered him an exclusive guarantee of £4,000 a year— with the proviso that if he were offered work he did not think suitable, the money he would have earned for those programmes would be deducted from the guarantee.

When he received their offer he wrote back dryly:

While I am most grateful for the knowledge that the Corporation would like to retain my services, I feel that the minimum amount offered is somewhat inadequate. You will appreciate that . . . the minimum guarantee suggested in your letter is less than twice the fees that I receive for one programme alone, i.e. Down Your Way . . . I hope that I shall not be thought ungrateful if I say that I would prefer to continue on my present casual basis . . .

By 1954, the prospect of his departure was unthinkable. Already several able BBC staff had been lured away to the new independent companies by the promise of greater responsibility and much more money, and the Corporation had been forced to pay dramatic salary increases to those whom it could not afford to lose. Yet again the BBC, in the person of Michael Standing (Controller of Entertainment for Sound Radio) approached Dimbleby. It was no secret that Richard Dimbleby had been approached by several of the new ITV companies who were prepared to offer him huge fees to tempt him away from the BBC. Once more, the Corporation attempted to persuade Dimbleby to accept a long-term exclusive contract; and (though no precise figure was mentioned) it was presumed, a five-year guarantee of £10,000 a year. Once more Dimbleby declined, and Michael Standing reported back:

He does not wish to sign one but at the same time he has no intention of going to the opposite camp. He treasures his association with Royal occasions and, though he does not exactly say so, with the BBC generally . . . I have made it clear to him that though we naturally accept what he says about a personal loyalty to us and a distaste for commercial television, these circumstances might change and we cannot, without the assurance of a contract, feel absolutely certain of his permanent willingness or availability to us on the big occasion and he must therefore be ready to see us attempting to develop and groom others who might eventually succeed him . . .

As Dimbleby well knew, the blackmail was a hollow threat, and it did not unduly disturb him. He would continue to make it plain that he was always available for the big occasion; he would continue to help beginners, who were sent to sit in the commentary box with him to learn his techniques (complaining to Dilys 'What the bloody hell do they think I am, expecting me to train someone to take over my job'); and he would continue to be irreplaceable. Two months later, prompted by some press publicity about the contracts that Gilbert Harding and Wilfred Pickles had signed for the BBC (at sums which he knew to be much less than he could have commanded) he wrote to Michael Standing, explaining his position for the record:

> While I am grateful to the BBC for showing sufficient trust in me to want to place me under exclusive contract, I would prefer to keep my freedom . . . This does not mean I have any 'ITA' plans—I have none at all, nor any present intention of working for that body or its contractors. With the newspapers, my writing, my film company, which is now operating, and such work as the BBC may offer me in spite of my recalcitrance, I shall be fully occupied. I hope sincerely that my decision will not impair my long and happy relations with the BBC [he held no grudge from the war], for which I will always be prouder to work than being bought by somebody's soapflakes, and I trust that I may be allowed to continue the fairly substantial contribution that I have been able to make to the development of television since the war. I appreciate your reminder that the BBC, if it could not be sure of my exclusive services, might have to replace me. I shall have to rely on such professional ability as I possess to ward off that evil day!

No BBC executive could ever understand (nor did they trust) his unswerving devotion to the BBC. None of them seemed ever to realise that he had an almost pathological abhorrence and contempt for Independent Television (he once described ITV as 'an octopus whose tentacles are already reaching out through the length and breadth of the land'). He had the same reverence for the institution of the BBC, though not for those that worked within it, as for the Monarchy.

In 1957, when the BBC was losing viewers at an alarming rate, he wrote in the *Daily Herald* that the BBC was facing 'the biggest crisis in its existence', arguing that the Corporation should not fight back by lowering its standards to appeal to an audience which 'the Independent service so brutally calls the "Admass"', but by spending more on those areas where it excelled: plays, documentaries, features and outside broadcasts.' The BBC, he wrote, had

> traditions of public service of which it is rightly proud. It has fulfilled the terms of its charter correctly and wholeheartedly,

serving the whole public to the best of its ability . . . The kid
gloves are off now, and the big battle is beginning . . . I have
faith in the Corporation's integrity and ability. I would not miss
the fight for worlds.

Two years later he was forced, momentarily, to call that
integrity into question; the issue—a decision by someone in the
bureaucratic works of the BBC that his commentary on the arrival
of General Eisenhower at Balmoral at the end of August 1959
should be fed to Scottish (Independent) Television—provoked
him to write angrily to Peter Dimmock (the General Manager
of the Outside Broadcasting):

> I am so cross about it that I had decided to write straight to
> Cecil [Cecil McGivern the Controller of Television], but
> second thoughts told me that it was obviously your province
> directly. I feel so strongly about the matter that I hope you
> will not fail to send this letter on, if you cannot dispose of the
> question yourself . . . [This morning] I had a call from
> Programme Contracts to tell me, to my amazement, that not
> only were the pictures being given to Scottish Television Ltd,
> (which I knew) but that I was also doing the commentary for
> them. I was asked for my views—but what kind of view I could
> be expected to produce that had any practical meaning 24 hours
> before the event, I cannot imagine.
>
> Furthermore, when I expostulated, I was told politely but
> firmly that if I studied Clause 12 of the contract I would find
> that the BBC had the right to do this anyway. What worries
> me most of all about this is that the Corporation seems to be
> selling the fort quite cheerfully. This is a precedent. As far as I
> know, no artist—certainly no commentator—has been handed
> over by the Corporation before to the opposition, and
> confronted quite blandly with a 'fait accompli' . . . if it *is* true
> that the BBC has some value in its commentator, it seems little
> short of madness to give him away on a plate to the enemy.

In fact, since he had signed no contract, he was free to refuse the
broadcast altogether (which at this last moment would have
caused more than inconvenience), a fact which he did not hesitate
to point out ('If the Corporation really feels any of the regard
for me or my work that it frequently professes to do, it might

well be politer in its approach and less offensive in its attitude'). But his fundamental anger was reserved for the BBC's madness: 'After a good many years of being entirely faithful, I simply will not be given away by the Corporation to the very people whom I have so firmly eschewed, in the face of much temptation. I don't mind the Corporation having it all one way, but it can't have it both ways—not with me, anyway.'

Had he not been so passionately committed to the concept of 'public service' broadcasting he would almost certainly have been driven out of the BBC before the end of the Fifties. Between 1950 and 1960 when he became 'the voice of the BBC', when he was, in the BBC's mind, quite indispensable, he was frequently irritated, sometimes angered, and on occasions much wounded by the clumsiness, indifference, and neglect with which he felt the BBC treated him. Sometimes there were pinpricks: in 1951, the Corporation discovered that he was replying to the letters (up to two hundred a week) which he received from Down Your Way, on notepaper headed 'Richard Dimbleby c/o BBC'. According to the rules, only members of the BBC staff were entitled to use Corporation headed paper. An internal memo judged decisively: 'there really is an objection in principle to people who are not our staff using printed notepaper which associates them with the BBC in this way...' He was informed that he should cease the habit. In vain he protested that he was writing as a servant of the BBC for more than fifteen years, that he did not wish to publicise his home address, and that by replying to his letters himself (which he felt bound to do) he saved Broadcasting House time and money. A rule, he was informed, was a rule, and could not be bent.

Sometimes there were passing irritations: in 1957 after his return from covering the State Visit of the Queen to France, he received a letter from the BBC about his expenses. 'We are very much concerned' wrote the Television Booking Section 'to see that you are claiming £17 1s. 10d. over and above the currency allowance of £56 8s. 2d. (for eight days at £7 a day)'. It was profoundly irritating. It had been a week beset by technical disaster which almost single-handed he had managed to transform into triumph. At the end of the Queen's visit to the French Opera, with a crowd of 100,000 in the street outside, he had been about to describe her departure when the power failed in the small booth in which he was sitting in the bowels of the Opera House. His picture-monitor went dead, the lights went out, and his telephone did not work. He had no contact with the producer—no way of telling him what had happened. And he was 'on air'. So, listening to the distant cheers outside, he had described the departure 'blind', imagining the scene outside. No viewer complained, no critic noticed. His performance throughout the State Visit (which had been regarded as a symbolic re-aftermath of the bond between France and Britain) had been universally acclaimed as magnificent. He returned to London, to what he imagined would be a grateful BBC. On his return from Paris he had received letters from the Outside Broadcast Department praising his 'superb' performance, and from the Controller of Television, a telegram which read 'Many sincere congratulations on your excellent commentaries yesterday. You really are the daddy of them all'.

The letter complaining about his expenses, though not a surprise, was exasperating. However, he wrote back with as much weary reasonableness as he could muster:

I feel the Corporation does not appreciate the fact that I am in a difficult position, whether I like it or not. Fortunately, or unfortunately, I am quite well known in European countries . . . and am generally received 'en fête' [he did not mention that he was frequently welcomed to a State occasion abroad with a much greater show of enthusiasm than the British Ambassador]. This necessitates a degree of reciprocal entertainment which I cannot avoid. Also, although I may commit the Corporation to higher expenditure by reserving, for example, a sitting-room for working purposes, in addition to the customary bedroom . . . The fact is that when you are undertaking the lion's share of the commentary work as I had on these occasions, you simply cannot do the preparatory labour on the edge of a hotel bed or in the maelstrom of the BBC office which everyone is sharing.

It seems to me that I shall have to adopt one of two courses. Either very reluctantly to withdraw from these foreign visits altogether if the Corporation is unwilling to take a realistic view of my expenditure or to pay the excess out of my own pocket and claim only the £7 a day. This is something which I shall have to decide for myself when the next occasion arises. Meanwhile in the case of the Paris expenses, I think the matter will be most easily settled if you strike out the extra sum claimed of £17 1s. 10d. and pretend that I never claimed it at all.

RICHARD DIMBLEBY

The BBC's response to his plea (curiously the Corporation accepted without question 'the embarrassing position of knowing that he had used his own currency on BBC business', though they did not admit so to him) was to raise his daily allowance from £7 to £9 which, since newspaper correspondents, and every other television organisation in the world enjoyed almost unlimited expenses on such occasions, left him unmoved. None of them had to fulfil the ambassadorial role that he felt was forced on him. To make matters worse he earned less by going abroad for the BBC on major occasions than he did by staying at home and fulfilling his regular broadcasting commitments. Had the BBC and state occasions mattered less to him, the cumulative effect of these irritations would have made the flattery and the fees proffered by ITV irresistible.

The particular idiocies of the BBC's bureaucracy did not surprise him. What offended him was that no-one in the hierarchy saw fit to ensure that he was not burdened by them. The cavalier manner in which he felt the BBC so often treated him led him to the conclusion that the Corporation did not appreciate either his value or his loyalty, taking both for granted.

For a man who was generally so easy-going and who lacked most of the traits of the television prima donna (in the studio his one vanity was to insist that the bald back of his head should be hidden from the camera's scrutiny) he was easily ruffled by apparent slights. Thus aroused he could seem vain and self-important:

You will appreciate the importance of billing to a professional like myself, the more particularly as, having won two television awards this year, I now have an end to keep up [he wrote to the editor of *Radio Times* in March 1951]. For that reason I was surprised to see a newcomer to television (though a friend of mine)—Colin Wills—walking this week straight into star billing in the ex-Pickles programmes. It's a little galling if you have worked and studied very hard over five years to get near the top of the television tree.

Now that Wills has a 'name' billing over his programme, I would like to ask for the same privilege in future for my own name in connection with London Town. I hope that you will believe that I'm not writing in any conceited or pompous manner [he was always aware when he was at the edge] but simply as a sound and television professional who can't afford to seem the minor fry compared with a new boy! I have an uncomfortable feeling that a lot of people judge one's status by one's presentation in the *Radio Times*. Hence in the theatre and film world, the fearful strife over billings and credits.

As always, his anxiety sprang not from a love of publicity but a fear of its absence. He was continually insecure, not so much about his own ability, but about the BBC's appreciation of it. When some press reports had noted critically that a programme called Joan Gilbert's Diary was too much like his own London Town and About Britain in form, he wrote,

> I am told that there was even a marked similarity between the items in the two programmes on the last occasion and that by showing film on herself on location followed immediately by a studio interview, Joan seemed to be using practically the same technique as ourselves . . . I do assert a prior claim in this type of feature since we invented it and have been running it successfully for four or five years.

Dimbleby's main anxiety was that Gilbert's programme might replace his own, or that other people might snatch away the territory which he had conquered, or hoped to conquer. The entire edifice of his anxious argument was constructed on the flimsy base of a few press cuttings; at the time the BBC was terrified that he would leave, he had no confidence that the Corporation was confident in him.

Even in 1958, soon after he had celebrated twenty-one years in broadcasting, in a letter thanking Gerald Beadle (who had followed McGivern as Controller of Television) for a private BBC dinner given in his honour, he felt bound to return to the theme. Beadle had surprised him by asking 'how he felt' after so long a career. Dimbleby, who could not bear to be portentous in private speech, had shrugged. Now he thanked Beadle for an occasion

> that I shall remember for a long time . . . I think I should have summed up my feelings after twenty-one years with the BBC by saying that I have profound respect for the Corporation and complete loyalty in the face of some

temptation. I hope in return, that I may feel assured that the Corporation regards me as a useful servant as much today and in the future as it has done in the past.

He then continues, gratuitously, since the occasion of the dinner had been to celebrate his unique contribution to broadcasting:

> It may not be modest, but I think it is *true*, to say that my long association with 'great occasions' of every kind has given me a unique position and prestige with people of every rank and kind. I have always used this prestige to the BBC's advantage, I think with occasional effect.
>
> Sometimes I wonder if, when one works in the more serious side of the business, one is not a little overlooked by the BBC publicity people, and those who organise billings. This latter applies particularly to my type of O.B., in which one is apt to end up in the tiniest available type at the very bottom of the bill. In some solemn cases, of course, this is desirable, but there are times when the commentator's own prestige and following may attract viewers to the programme, and in such cases it seems to me a pity to 'waste' him.

Dimbleby did have a small point. There was no doubt that it was he, and not the BBC, which led the mass of the people on state occasions to watch the 'public service' rather than ITV; and he did not receive the same 'star' billing as those who worked in light entertainment. But, by 1958, he was acknowledged, not only in Britain but throughout Europe and the English-speaking world as the master of his craft; there was no-one to supersede him. But he always needed reassurance. He confided only to Dilys his fears that the BBC wished to find others—not merely to understudy him—but to replace him; 'they want new men, not an old man like me', he would say only half-jokingly, complaining when he was only in his mid-forties, 'Of course when I'm worn out, they'll forget me, I'm just their reliable old commentator.' His demand for his position in public life to be recognised by the BBC, was in fact a plea for the Corporation's good opinion. It was an important insecurity: though his painstaking, obsessive hard work had its roots in his commitment to his type of broadcasting, it was nurtured by this insecurity.

Despite numerous public protestations to the contrary, Dimbleby did not lack enemies within the BBC. The Corporation was no less, and no more, vicious than any other Institution. There were the envious and less talented who saw themselves as rivals. And there were the producers (and even senior executives) who resented his hold over the British public. One or two of them, who frequently professed their undying admiration for him—not least when he was no longer there—tried assiduously to destroy his position in the BBC, even on occasions discreetly inspiring their friends in Fleet Street to wonder in public whether he was as indispensable as he was assumed to be. Some of them resented his domination of the medium, and the way in which he seemed to speak for the BBC and so for them; others felt the common resentment of the executive for the 'performer'—or as he is called in American television (making the point harshly) the 'talent'. Dimbleby's insecurity was by no means paranoid.

Early in 1958, he was deeply wounded by an incident which on the face of it seemed slight enough but demonstrated to him that his own fears about the BBC were justified. In March, the Home Service programmes planners decided that Twenty Questions (of which he had been on the panel, with one short break, for twelve years) should be recorded on Monday nights—at precisely the same time as he was due to introduce Panorama. The Contracts Department rang Dilys to tell her about the clash, adding that the BBC therefore supposed that Dimbleby would have to leave the programme. It did not cross the BBC's corporate mind that although he no longer needed the money, Twenty Questions had become a part of his life. The programme belonged to the early days of radio, to which he looked back with some sentimentality and much affection. He felt loyal to it, and those who worked in it; one or two (like Norman Hackforth, the Mystery Voice) had become close friends. He believed—wrongly as it happened—that without him the programme would be taken off. When he heard of what had happened, and how his wife had been told, he was incensed at the Corporation's treatment of him:

It would not surprise me if the BBC said this to a Jugoslav juggler whom it did not want to use in a variety programme being recorded for the Overseas Service [he wrote to the Head of Programme Planning]. In my case, I regard it as off-hand to the point of calculated rudeness. At least, however, it gives me something by which to measure protestations of loyalty, affection and co-operation as far as the BBC is concerned, and

the strength of its attitude towards one who has been engaged in
broadcasting and television for twenty-one continuous years.'

And to John Snagge he wrote (as to an old colleague):

> I am under no contract to the BBC yet in spite of innumerable
> offers, have refused all broadcasting and television work offered
> from any other source. I feel bound to say the Corporation
> must now understand that I feel free to accept other engage-
> ments if the need arises. I shall very much dislike doing this . . .

In the BBC there was immediate panic. On one of the internal
memos which flew back and forth, a nervous hand wrote 'This
is the sort of thing that could easily reach D.G. [the Director-
General Sir Ian Jacob]'. The soothing letter which followed this
bureaucratic flap failed to mollify Dimbleby. He wrote again,
refusing to accept the BBC's explanations for the embarrassing
situation:

> My real feeling in this [he wrote to another old friend, Rooney
> Pelletier] is that, whatever the BBC's official arrangements
> are, one is entitled to some kind of 'personal friendship'
> treatment . . . If the Corporation has been willing to take me on
> trust for several years—and I, the Corporation—something
> better than a last-minute formal mention of a clash is called
> for.

Six months later, never understanding why he was so hurt, the
BBC wrote asking him to rejoin the programme, which was now
to be recorded at a time which would not clash with Panorama.
He wrote back declining the offer, informing the Twenty
Questions producer, 'To be quite honest, I am still smarting from
the impact of my abrupt dropping from the last series after so
many years . . . I still feel very strongly . . . I am sure the series
did very well without me this year and will not suffer in 1959'.
Only when the Home Service was forced to tell him that the
programme planners had carefully rearranged their schedules: 'in
order to obtain your services', did he unbend a little:

> I find this altogether a bit difficult. I will not ask you to agree
> with, or necessarily understand, my very strong feelings about

what happened last time. But I have been forced to the firm conclusion that not even the British Broadcasting Corporation can be allowed to run rough-shod over those who have worked for it in the public eye, as I have done, for twenty-two years . . . Nevertheless I am not really one for sulking in a corner and I certainly do not want to seem to be turning my back on old friends and colleagues by being pig-headed over the issue . . . I feel I ought to say that I am grateful to the Home Service for their consideration in re-arranging schedules to move the programme to Tuesday. How I wish this could have been done last time.

Dimbleby never really considered yielding to the 'temptations' of ITV. His commitment to the BBC, to the 'public service' sprang from a faith in that the true purpose of broadcasting could be fulfilled only by the Corporation. Had he (and others in the BBC) been told then that the Outside Broadcast would end its days transmitting nothing more than sport, 'It's a Knockout', and the occasional international spectacular, he would have been appalled. To him it was the O.B., helping to bring international co-operation and understanding, presenting the 'ungarnished' truth, which made television matter. The demise of the O.B. would be the end of the quest of the broadcaster. As he watched television begin to turn away from the art at which he was the undisputed master, he was saddened and frustrated. He never understood why it happened.

The recognition that the film team with light, portable sound-cameras, would supersede the clumsy, expensive, inflexible outside broadcast unit was gradual. The slowness of the awakening was due in part at least to an attitude towards broadcasting symbolised by Richard Dimbleby (although he was the first BBC television film reporter). In its most extreme form this view was that television was a medium by which at one level people would be entertained, and at another be informed, and enlightened. By means of the outside broadcast the public would be invited to witness, even—vicariously—partake in, the great national and international events of the age. They would not be invited to examine the meaning of such occasions, to put them in context, to question or criticise them, to see how they interposed themselves between those who held power and those who were ruled. The Outside Broadcast by its nature, was a purveyor of received opinion and unchallenged assumptions. But as the technology advanced and the BBC grew more confident so the limitations of the Outside Broadcast became more apparent. If one day can be picked out to symbolise the inevitable and irreversible awakening; the blossoming of a new attitude towards the function of television, it was October 28th 1958—the first televised State Opening of Parliament, and hailed as one of the great television triumphs in the history of the BBC.

In permitting the broadcast, Harold Macmillan's Government had made clear that the event was to be treated as a 'state' and not a 'political' occasion. The negotiations were protracted and delicate. For the BBC it was an opportunity to reveal to mistrustful (and usually ignorant) politicians that television could take a major annual state ritual into the nation's sitting rooms, enhancing and not demeaning it in the process. The Government's acceptance of the BBC's request to broadcast from Parliament for the first time in the history of radio or television was of great symbolic importance, an indication of respect for the BBC which imposed great responsibilities on the Corporation.

The occasion was given added spice by the fact that ITV, for the first time on a big occasion, had been permitted to 'take a feed' from the BBC cameras, and use its own commentator to describe the occasion. They chose Robin Day. The press immediately saw the obvious: 'Day versus Dimbleby', 'Dimbleby v. Robin Day', 'Richard v. Robin', 'Dimbleby v. Day' were the Fleet Street headlines. In the public mind (as dramatised in the press) the two men epitomised the opposite extremes in serious television. Dimbleby was the reassuring father-figure, the voice of reverence, the man with the silken flow of choice words, who brought dignity and authority to the affairs of the nation. Day was brash and aggressive. He was the boldest, and some thought the most dangerous exponent of a new form of television reportage—the interview. His admirers called him 'vigorous', his detractors found him 'hectoring and bullying'. In all ways his approach to television and his manner on the screen were in stark contrast to Dimbleby. Day approached the broadcast with trepidation:

> this was an assignment in which practically everything was against me. As the ITV commentator I was a novice competing with the master-craftsman . . . It was an exceedingly tricky business to form appropriate phrases with the roar of the crowds

and bands in one ear, and Dimmock [the BBC producer] shouting his control-room instructions in the other . . .

It had been made clear to Day that ITV expected him to adopt a different style from Richard Dimbleby but 'it was not made clear to me how this difference was to be achieved. This was left entirely to me. How *could* one be very different in tone from Dimbleby . . .? yet any attempt to imitate or outdo the master with majestic, flowing descriptions was doomed to failure . . .'

Robin Day's concern to find the right style was not merely a proper anxiety about his own reputation. It was a year in which the pre-eminence of the outside broadcast seemed assured—in which the BBC covered no less than twenty major royal or state occasions with Dimbleby as commentator. ITV was competing in what most people, and certainly the press, regarded as the most important form of television, and one which, it was assumed, was naturally and properly the BBC's function. ITV with Robin Day was seeking a foothold on the slopes from the top of which Dimbleby and the BBC ruled supreme. So the problem of competing with Dimbleby was both important and baffling. Suddenly, according to Day: 'I realised I was approaching it in entirely the wrong way. There was no need for me to consciously aim at a different style from Dimbleby, for we were different people with different approaches to the occasion . . .' It was the implication that lay behind Day's 'different approach' (which now seems much less marked than it did at the time) which signalled the beginning of the end of the O.B.'s supremacy.

In a (possibly unintentional) disparaging reference to Dimbleby's approach, Day wrote of the event: 'This was not just another ancient royal ceremony—it was a profoundly significant expression of modern political reality. Descriptions of ceremonial details were obviously necessary to assist the viewer, but I tried to give these without adding any unnecessary verbiage . . .'

Day's commentary was brisk, dry and efficient, and in his own view it was clearly successful. Dimbleby's style was unchanged.

'Well, it is a dull, damp morning,' began Robin Day.

'It is a grey, rather still, misty day,' said Dimbleby.

'And down there the clump of dirty grey from the wigs of the High Court Judges,' said ITV.

'Now the cluster of judges in scarlet and ermine and black and gold take their places . . .' observed the BBC.

'Lord Montgomery, who on this occasion has a silent role to play . . .' half-joked Robin Day.

'There is Viscount Montgomery, chosen this year to carry the great Sword of State,' said Dimbleby.

But it was in the closing passages of each commentary that the difference between the two was most sharply revealed.

'Later today, in the Commons, the debate and doubtless the argument over the Government's programme will begin. But for now, as Her Majesty returns to the Robing Room and thence to Buckingham Palace, she leaves behind in all of us, a memory of a State Occasion at its most magnificent . . .' were the words of Richard Dimbleby.

'The Queen will go back to Buckingham Palace. The crown will go back to the Tower of London. All the scarlet and ermine robes will go back to wherever they came from. And Parliament will go back to work . . .' said Robin Day.

And over the final shot of the empty Throne, Day's closing words were, 'everyone is wondering at Westminster what Government will write the next speech from this Throne. Before Her Majesty sits on it again there may be a General Election. That is when we have our say. And what Her Majesty reads from this Throne depends on what we put in the ballot box.'

Dimbleby ended his commentary thus: 'The Throne remains, rich, shining—near yet remote—the symbol of this rare meeting of the Queen, the Lords and the Commons—the Three Estates of Parliament. And so begins, with ceremony that springs from the very roots of our democratic history, the fourth session of the three hundredth Parliament of the Realm.'

The BBC was delighted with Dimbleby. In his most headmasterly fashion, the Director General, Sir Ian Jacob, wrote to him:

I should like to congratulate you most heartily on your commentary on the Opening of Parliament. It was right up to the high standard that we have all come to expect from you. I have had a letter from the Prime Minister expressing his great satisfaction, and he asks that his special congratulations should be sent to you . . .

And more warmly from Gerald Beadle, the controller of Television:

My dear Richard, your part on Tuesday was superb. I admired

everything about it immensely, especially the timing. How you achieved such precision in such complicated circumstances is quite beyond my comprehension. Thank you my dear Richard. You made us all proud.

The press, pursuing its alliteration to the bitter end, concluded almost unanimously that it had been 'Dimbleby's day'. The judgment sprang not least from the attitudes towards such occasions that still prevailed. Even Cassandra, who had before attacked Dimbleby so bitterly, judged in the *Daily Mirror* that on this occasion he was 'Excellent'; and reflecting the public euphoria, he found the coverage of the State Opening of Parliament 'magnificent... to millions of British subjects it was the wondrous revelation of a pageantry that has gone on for hundreds of years—totally unseen and unknown to the masses. The Queen was almost heartbreaking in her dignity and her frailty ...'

The difference between Dimbleby and Day was more than one of style. The critics—and the public who overwhelmingly watched the BBC for the occasion—might have preferred Dimbleby for his voice, his choice of words, his tone, and his approach; he heightened and romanticised the occasion, concentrating on its symbolic and historical significance. Robin Day played down the emotional, ceremonial content: briskly, sometimes dryly treating the occasion in the same terms as one might a school 'open day', when teachers and pupils are on show to curious outsiders. But underlying Day's commentary (and completely absent from Dimbleby's) was the recognition (now a commonplace), that it is what happens within the institutions of State, rather than the institutions themselves, which is significant; that content matters more than form.

Not surprisingly Dimbleby touched the public mood with greater sensitivity than Day: the ceremony impressed the people, and Dimbleby's commentaries—eloquent, moving avowals of simple beliefs—still reflected public awe; but the heyday of the outside broadcast, portraying the great, solemn, symbolic moments of an era, when television recorded an array of massive and memorable 'firsts', was a fleeting moment in history. As soon as sceptical men began to wonder *what* freedom, and *whose* justice the great institutions of Britain preserved, the portrayal of the state occasion in Richard Dimbleby's way would become a near anachronism. By 1958, if that time was approaching, it had not yet arrived.

14

The Window
of the World

With news of all the nations in your hand,
And all their sorrows in your face.

WILFRED OWEN

'BIRTH OF A BABY ON TV—PICTURES OF A BABY ACTUALLY BEING BORN will be shown on BBC television tonight—the first time that such scenes have been televised in Britain . . . Richard Dimbleby, who presents the programme, will warn viewers beforehand that the childbirth sequences may not be suitable for family viewing.' The reaction of Fleet Street (in this case the *Daily Mirror* in February 1957) to every tentative step forward taken by Panorama was seldom restrained. Yet it reflected a public sense of propriety which still saw television as a potential intruder into the privacy of the home; if the press was prurient it was because the public was prudish.

Panorama's audience—which was eighty per cent working class—had a deeply entrenched conservative morality; it was easily embarrassed and readily offended. It fell to Richard Dimbleby to take the television audience by the hand and guide it gently into more tolerant, liberal ways. Intuitively sensitive to public attitudes, frequently sharing them himself, he had an acute sense of what was felt to be proper. Sharing many of the doubts and anxieties of his audience, having discarded yesterday the prejudices they held today, he was the perfect television mentor. He knew he was trusted and he felt himself to be a guide. Although the accident of time, of television, and of personality had transformed a journalist into a national totem, his instinct was to inform and entertain, while gently pushing back the barriers of ignorance and intolerance. This was no crusade (like his obsession with the Monarchy) but the natural urge of a good journalist. But so accurately did he touch the public pulse that he soon attained the status of a televisual father of the people. 'You may not wish your children to watch', 'some of you may not want to see this' he would advise; and by a gentle inclination of the head and a look which seemed to say 'no, we don't talk about these things at home either, but we can't ignore them' he made the unmentionable acceptable. Panorama broke new ground the more easily because Richard Dimbleby never seemed to move at all.

In the case of the 'BIRTH OF THE BABY' which was a film about natural childbirth, some of the press (including the *Mirror*) having once raised their headlines in consternation, were not unsympathetic, quoting the film's maker as saying 'the mother is seen to be happy and contented in labour, and there is a complete absence of fear and discomfort. This is followed by the supreme happiness and joy when she holds the child in her arms . . .' But (an indication of the state of public morality at the time) the *Daily Sketch* filled an entire page with its outrage:

> Revolting. Beyond the pale. I condemn the BBC for the worst display of taste ever—last night in its 'Panorama' programme, [wrote a senior reporter]. They showed us a baby being born in all its stark, primitive detail. We saw the look of anguish on its mother's face as the birth spasms racked her body . . . It sickened me. It sickened my wife. If we had printed the pictures of the birth we should rightly have stood in the dock.

Inevitably Dimbleby was to blame: 'I suppose compère Richard Dimbleby, who prides himself on his tact when dealing with the moneyed and titled classes, will get away with it. I hope, in future, that he sticks to his smarming activities on the Stately Home and Purple Passage beats . . .' Yet despite this huffing and puffing, the BBC's phones were not jammed with protesting voices, and the letters which complained did so mildly. Most viewers, treated gently, had responded in kind.

Unwittingly, however, the *Sketch* reporter had stumbled upon an important point. The constant juxtaposition in the Fifties of state occasions with Panorama had not only vastly increased the prestige of the current affairs programme, but it had seemed to create two Richard Dimblebys. So in April 1957, the 'first' Dimbleby returned home from the Royal Visti to France, to an appreciative Maurice Wiggin in the *Sunday Times*:

> The whole business involved fifty-three French cameramen— but only one Dimbleby. For hours and hours he went on saying exactly the Right Thing. What a remarkable institution he is . . . never at a loss for a fluent turn of editorialising rhetoric precisely suited to the occasion . . . It is his lot and his gift, to respond to given stimuli with exactly the words that most of his hearers are groping for . . . He is irreplaceable.

And a few days later, after he had singed his eyebrows demonstrating the dangers of children's nightclothes, the 'second' Dimbleby was informed (under the headline 'Whoosh—and Dimbleby catches fire') that 'It's the common touch that wins'. The *Birmingham Mail* congratulated him for displaying, 'an understanding of domestic problems which must have put a good many husband viewers to shame'. In fact, of course, there was only one Dimbleby; he was simply not (as so many television performers were) one-dimensional. His rapport with the television audience sprang from this fact—that he responded to a wide range of circumstances just as they would have wished to react themselves. The man who was 'Britain's public orator', interpreting the great state occasions, could also talk on television about sex and baby clothes.

He also had few rivals as a reporter of simple human drama. Visiting (for radio and television) the refugee camps of Europe he broadcast

> For ten years, since the end of the Second World War, we of the free countries of the world have failed in our duty to succour and protect a third of a million innocent men, women, and children, who are slowly dying—not necessarily of disease, though there is disease enough, but of homelessness and hopelessness and apathy and resignation. Something that doctors can't cure, but you and I can . . .
>
> They come from a dozen different countries and speak a dozen different languages. They all know where they came from . . . They have told their stories so many times and have been interrogated so many times . . . but none of them know where they are going. No-one seems able to tell them that— and that, is all they want to know.

Between 1948 and 1965 he raised in appeals on radio and television just under a million pounds. In 1962, when an earthquake destroyed towns and villages in Western Persia, he raised over £400,000, informing his public, 'The need is enormous and the need is terribly urgent . . . I believe that you want to help. This is the quickest, best and most effective way to do it. I have never asked for anything more seriously than I am for this, at this moment.' And a year later when another earthquake destroyed the town of Skopje in Yugoslavia, he appealed again. This time, before he went on the air (but after the appeal had been announced) he said that he would not broadcast unless the Foreign Office promised to provide an aircraft to transport relief supplies to the stricken town. Thus cornered, the Foreign Office capitulated; and Dimbleby said simply 'The Foreign Office have agreed to find the planes if we can find the money, and I am wondering if among the ten million or so of you who are watching, we can find this amount of money now . . .' Again, the appeal raised more than £400,000. A few weeks later he went out to Skopje to report from the disaster for Panorama.

> The real tragedy of Skopje [he told his audience] hits you and hits you hard when you come to this cemetery just outside the city. Particularly when you come on a day like this with low cloud in the sky and driving rain. This is where they brought eleven hundred men, women and children and a lot of tiny babies and buried them all in these trenches, giving each one a simple spade-shaped red headboard . . . There are names. Some have no names at all. Some say: Unknown man aged fifty-five; others just say: A baby. Here they lie on the hillside. And if you look just across there, a bit further on, you'll see where they've dug the long, long, trenches in the clay to receive the other thousand bodies that they never did find in the rubble of Skopje.

In Skopje, he sploshed through the mud in mackintosh and gumboots, shared a tent on the edge of the floodwater which rushed through the town; and boiled coffee for everyone on the little spirit stove, which only he had remembered to bring. To those who had drawn their image of him from state occasions or sombre Panoramas, his presence was a refreshing surprise.

Afterwards Barto Stuart, who was in charge of the young British volunteer force of engineers working in the debris of Skopje (eighty per cent of which was under water) sent the BBC an unsolicited memory of him: 'There was Richard in his gum-boots . . . with spanner and screwdriver cheerfully engaged in making up his ex-Army bunk for the night . . . I still see him, cigar in mouth, and feet in water, brewing coffee . . . He was not an awe-inspiring figure but a dear friend.' As they left Skopje by train, Richard Dimbleby stood in the window clowning the absurdities of the television interviewer, and Stuart recorded, 'as the train finally departed Richard still stood framed in his screen . . . and his newly made friends had tears of non-stop laughter and affection running down their cheeks.'

However, television gave Dimbleby an aura it was impossible to shake off. The contrast between Dimbleby's public and private persona was so great that friends spent much time explaining to those who had never met him that in reality he was a delightful companion, amusing, earthy, outspoken, and filled with an inexhaustible zest for life; he was the kind of man, they would say, 'with whom you'd go anywhere'. The television studio before transmission offers a most explicit mirror of human frailty: when the performer reveals much that the audience never sees. Then he is ill-tempered or self-important; he sneaks admiring glances at himself in the monitor; he sits nervously fingering his notes; he speaks too sharply to a secretary or even throws a tantrum. Studio crews see it all, day after day: a series of egos, inflated by the small screen into instant importance. Perhaps sensing their disdain, many studio presenters and interviewers, lacking the inclination, say that they have no time to talk with technicians, thus widening the gulf.

Dimbleby *preferred* to talk with studio crews rather than with his professional colleagues. On Monday afternoons and in the evenings he wandered round the studio, knowing faces and remembering names, talking technicalities and telling dubious jokes. It was so rare in television that he endeared himself permanently to cameramen, lighting assistants, sound recordists, and call-boys: to them he was not only the most expert performer, he was also the most affable. There was always a cluster of technicians around his desk to talk to him, enjoying his earthiness. After a Panorama on the Pill, which he had introduced with much delicacy, he caused uproar immediately afterwards by calling out to the Floor Manager, Joan Marsden: 'Oh! God, Mother [his nick-name for her] stick to gin and jumping off the table.

When he returned from Germany after cursing in a crisis 'Jesus Wept'—not realising that he was being heard by a shocked British public—it was a studio crew, not his fellow reporters, who placed a specially made 'swear box' on his Panorama desk.* On his return (and before he had seen it) his first words as he entered the studio were: 'Jesus wept—you all still here then?'

'On location' abroad, Dimbleby always played the part of host, suggesting outings, ordering the meal, advising on the best night-club in town, always late to bed. Although his plans frequently went wrong, colleagues like Wynford Vaughan-Thomas, found him, 'the life-enhancer of them all'. In Sweden where he had been covering the Royal Visit (impressing his hosts by arriving in the Rolls-Royce), he persuaded most of the correspondents of Britain and Europe to join him on an SAS plane which had advertised a flight northwards 'to see the Midnight Sun'. On board Dimbleby virtually took over the plane, ordering champagne for everyone, while the stewards who had expected to offer rather more limited hospitality, found themselves agreeing with 'Mr. Dimbleby, sir' that of course SAS would be delighted to provide it free of charge. They landed at a small northern town, where at once Dimbleby promised to go and discover 'what goes on in this place'. He returned, like a successful tour guide, to inform the assembled correspondents that he had found a magnificent night-club which performed a decidedly risqué floor-show. Dutifully, his colleagues trooped behind him to the club, where, after more than an hour of waiting, they discovered that the exotic floor show was in fact a traditional Lapland dance performed at great and stately length by a troop of sturdy men and women very fully dressed in national costume. After twenty minutes he was so overcome with mirth that, tears streaming, he had to flee the club.

At Lime Grove, though, he always seemed a little apart. By the late Fifties, as the BBC expanded, he was one of only a few who had been in television since the beginning. There were many new young faces; few of them knew him, or his past and he sometimes felt a little lost among them. He distrusted those who pushed too hard or argued too well; who tumbled Governments and destroyed reputations with one *bon mot*. It was a shallow sharp world which he slightly feared and a little despised. Loathing

* See 'Giles' cartoon on p. 409.

argument, he avoided discussion. He kept his distance, affably aloof, stepping over the struggles of the cutting-room floor and the producer's office, ignoring mock battles won and lost, and interminably recounted in the club bar. Nor could he understand how it was that those whom the BBC had succoured, giving shelter and employment could turn against their benefactor. Though he was critical of the Corporation, of its clumsy bureaucracy, he believed absolutely that in a tortured world the BBC was a beacon of good sense and sound values. It offended him that others refused to lift up their eyes and see it.

Inevitably he was distrusted by the BBC's 'young Turks'. As Panorama matured, growing in both age and authority, they saw in it—and in Dimbleby—the embodiment of all that they disliked about the BBC: its subservient allegiance to the *status quo* and the Establishment; its pontifical airs; its self-imposed isolation from the people; its pervasive middle-class, middle-brow morality. The young avant-garde who arrived on training courses, to work as researchers and then producers, who saw the start of Tonight, and then Monitor, and then a host of late night satire shows, chose Dimbleby as their symbol of the Corporation's complacency.

Yet the best among them, complaining about him in corners, soon found that there was little to say. All criticism of him was soon reduced to complaints against the Corporation. Nor could they rid themselves of the awe with which he was regarded by those who knew much more about the medium than they. Men like Anthony Smith, who would later become one of the best BBC producers, remember the sense of occasion they felt when they exchanged their first words with 'the great man'. And when they saw him in action they understood: he knew so much about the medium; he was so flawlessly professional. James Mossman (who was perhaps the most eloquent film reporter produced by television) once wrote that Dimbleby was 'the most disciplined performer' that he had ever seen: 'He approached his job like an artist or an engineer, and to watch him...was to see technical perfection.' Even Malcolm Muggeridge (who despite his own skill has expressed scant respect for the medium wondered at Dimbleby's presence in the studio, at the natural ease of his control. Once though, unable to contain a sudden upsurge of irreverence, he 'handed over' to his colleague after a discussion of Orwell's *1984* with the words 'and now back to Big Brother'.

Richard Dimbleby played only a small part in the editorial

process. He occasionally wrote or telephoned with suggestions, but felt that the weekly choice of subjects could be decided only by those who were engaged on the programme with all their energies—*his* function was to set the tone and find the mood through which the ideas of others would be best transmitted to 'his public'. But he could not bear to find himself merely in the role of 'frontman' with no work to do. On those rare occasions when an innocent new researcher offered him a completed script to read as an introduction to an item, he was severe: '*I write*,' he would inform the timorous junior, 'I *always* write my own links'. On one occasion a researcher was saved by the quick-thinking of a colleague who snatched the offending script off Dimbleby's desk, and hastily restored it to note-form again before he had noticed.

He wrote his scripts at speed, and invariably committed the gist of them to memory before writing them out again in truncated form on huge 'crib' cards in capial letters which were then either pinned under the camera or held up by a long-suffering Joan Marsden. In the programme, he occasionally glanced at his crib, but more usually ad-libbed his way through his half-memorised script. He never used a 'teleprompter', regarding it as an infernal device designed for plastic men with no thought in their heads. Sensing that artificial aids threatened the authority of his position, while strengthening the power of the off-screen electronic whizz-kids who would play the puppet-master, he was scathing about those of his colleagues who required even their 'Goodnight' to be written up before their eyes before they could end a programme. More than that, he was convinced that the elusive contact between broadcaster and audience was destroyed by the fish-eyed rendering of prepared scripts. Believing that television was at its best when 'live' with 'live' people, he argued that recorded television and teleprompters produce 'dead' men in moribund programmes.

Richard Dimbleby's uncanny ability to break down the electronic barrier between the studio and the family living room was in part an accident of personality: it was also a conscious and careful professionalism. Although some of Dimbleby's gestures were unthought (he once introduced an item about Christmas with the words: 'I expect you have all got cards on the wall', pointing up instinctively to the bare studio wall behind him) he had a powerful sense of the dramatic. This studied glance at the palm of the hand, a gentle smoothing of retreating hair, a barely perceptible pause for a particularly significant phrase, were subtly calculated dramatic gestures designed to control the style, tone and pace of the programme.

As television technology advanced, so did the risk of technical chaos. New techniques permitted more complex programmes: a 'live' outside broadcast, a recorded studio interview; a film; a telephone call; a 'live' studio interview; a report via the Euro-vision link; another satellite. By the sixties there were few limits to the games that those more excited by the medium than the message could play. For a mercifully brief period in 1960, Panorama opened with a melodramatic flourish which at its best was disconcerting and when it failed was hilarious:

Richard Dimbleby: Your Window on the World
Robin Day: What next in South Africa?
    ROLL OF DRUMS
Robert Kee: Is there at last some hope for disarmament?
    ROLL OF DRUMS
Dimbleby: Good Evening. Four years ago the Government decided to set up a rocket testing range . . . they chose the island of South Uist . . . Let's go there now with Ludovic Kennedy and the Panorama unit . . .
    PAUSE AND VOICES THEN SILENCE THEN MORE VOICES IN AMERICAN ACCENTS THEN SILENCE
Dimbleby: Thank you—I'm sorry—that must be the most unusual visit to a rocket range on South Uist in the Hebrides that you ever did see. A slight confusion reigns because we seem to have got some film in the wrong order. But never mind . . .

On another occasion, with the drums put away, Dimbleby began the programme thus: 'Good evening. The Western Summit talks ended in Paris today; President Eisenhower is already in Spain; Mr. Macmillan comes home tomorrow. Now yesterday Robin Day flew to France and earlier this evening we recorded this report:

Day: Hullo, Good evening. This is Robin Day in Paris. Well, of the millions of messages delivered throughout the world this

	Christmastide, the most important of all lay on Mr. Krushchev's desk this morning . . .
Dimbleby:	I have to apologise for the fact that Mr. Robin Day has got cut in half, and the bottom half put on the top half—which is most unusual. But just you wait a moment, no doubt I'll be told what we're going to do to get him the right way up again. That was one of those electronic recordings of an interview which took place an hour ago between Paris and London. Now what shall we do, I wonder? Shall we go on or shall we re-place Mr. Day . . .

It was the aplomb with which Dimbleby handled constant near-disaster in the studio that made him so invaluable to directors and producers. He could master last-minute changes after the start of the programme with no outward show of alarm, without notes and usually without any 'talk-back' carphone to the producer's gallery. Refusing to be chained to the electronic gadgetry of the medium, he was never its servant.

If the 'golden age' of radio was in the Thirties, then the 'golden age' of television, which was much briefer, began at the end of the Fifties. By 1960, current affairs television dominated the medium in the way Outside Broadcasts had done in the early Fifties. With Tonight taking much of Panorama's local workload, and the News, particularly ITN, 'scooping' the 'hot' stories which had once been Panorama's preserve, the BBC's longest-running programme was left with a narrower field. It began to concentrate increasingly and almost exclusively on the major national and international events of the era; and it did so in ways which were to make the first years of the Sixties the heyday of serious television.

Already men like Woodrow Wyatt, John Freeman, Christopher Chataway, Malcolm Muggeridge and Francis Williams had brought distinction to Panorama. But by 1960, the programme had created a team of reporters who were to make their public reputations almost exclusively as a result of television. With Richard Dimbleby in the Chair, Panorama's team in 1960 consisted of James Mossman, Robert Kee, Ludovic Kennedy and Robin Day.

The programmes of that brief era were memorable for the scale of their ambition. It was a time of journalistic adventure, when politics was a moral and not merely an economic matter, when Britain still seemed (just) to be a force in the world, when America seemed to offer the 'free' world a new, young, liberal leadership, when Africa was in turmoil, when summit diplomacy seemed to have meaning, and when the H-bomb loomed as ominously threatening as ever. It was a time when Britain still cared about what happened beyond her own shores—and even if she did not, producers (like Michael Peacock) had the moral sense to believe that she should. It was not yet a time merely for the investigation of local ills, for the examination of industrial relations and the balance of payments, for the perpetual circling arguments about survival in affluence while the rest of the world starved—all of which would later come to pass for 'current affairs'.

In those simpler days, Panorama reported with assurance and individuality. It sought to unravel big issues and it assumed that the public cared. Typical of Panorama's self-confidence was Richard Dimbleby's introduction to the programme of February 26th 1962: 'Good evening. Four continents come within the scope of Panorama tonight: Asia, Europe, America, Africa—in that order . . .' And from a polling station in Bombay, the slightly raffish, eternally laconic figure of Ludovic Kennedy loomed into vision to begin an elegant political travelogue through India's elections, introducing the distinguished statesman Krishna Menon ('volatile, shrewd, witty, unpredictable, a scholar as well as a politician—his enemies say he looks like a cross between Machiavelli and Mephistopheles'), and assuming in his audience, if only a vague knowledge, at least an absolute interest. His questions were on the grand scale: 'Does the policy of non-alignment mean that you feel that there's nothing very much to choose between the communist way of life and the Western way of life?'; and his tone was liberal: 'Here in squalid one-room huts sleep families of five and six, existing on an income of about a pound a week.' With the freedom that reporters then assumed, he editorialised: 'When one sees these hovels for the first time and considers the affront they make to human dignity, one wonders how India has managed to avoid Communism for so long . . .'

Back in Europe, the most passionate of Panorama's liberals,

Robert Kee talked of the H-bomb with Hugh Gaitskell on the Leader of the Labour Party's return from Washington, where he had been considered important enough to discuss the matter with the American President. Again the questions were on the grand, simple scale: 'Mr. Gaitskell, have your conversations with the President of the United States affected your view as to whether or not nuclear tests should be resumed?' and, on receiving a cautiously affirmative reply: 'But doesn't this open up the most appalling prospect, because it means that every time one side has a series of tests which gives them a technological advance, the other side then has to have another series of tests to overcome the technological advance, and so on in a spiral *ad infinitum*?'

With India and the bomb despatched, Richard Dimbleby introduced James Mossman from Ecuador, where, standing on the site of a mountain, on the outskirts of the capital, seeming as always perturbed by the world's refusal to be moved by liberal reason, he spoke of the 'superb baroque architecture, raised by the sweated labour of the defeated Indians whom the ruling classes have exploited ever since' where the people 'poor and often illiterate' had been politically asleep for ages.

Back in the studio to finish the programme Richard Dimbleby turned 'to our fourth and last continent—that is, last tonight—Africa.' Sir Edgar Whitehead was in the studio to talk with him about the future of the Central African Federation. Dimbleby could be a very much sharper interviewer than some of his colleagues would allow. He was not aggressive, he did not accuse Whitehead of racialism (though he did ask how the Prime Minister could reconcile banning all nationalist groups with his declared policy of racial integration) but he neatly extracted the nub of Whitehead's disingenuous argument. Kenneth Kaunda (one of Dimbleby's warmest admirers) was the foremost African leader in the Federation. Dimbleby wanted to know how Whitehead would react if Kaunda emerged as the leader of what was then Northern Rhodesia. 'Our aim is this,' Whitehead replied, 'we want all Rhodesians to be able to feel that merit is the first consideration and race the second. And if they achieve that—if they can defeat the nationalists and racialists of all races, and really build a Rhodesian nationality, we shall have achieved our object.' 'Yes, but how do you class Kaunda?' Dimbleby asked. 'Kaunda has always been a nationalist.' 'Do you think he might change if he became Prime Minister.' 'I would think it unlikely,

I would think he's so deeply committed.' 'Then would you stay in the Federation if he was also in it. As a leader I mean, naturally?' 'As far as Northern Rhodesia's concerned, I'm quite certain that there is no constitution probable that would leave him as Prime Minister . . .'

The strength of those Panoramas was two-fold: they were glamorous and they assumed, almost in the manner of the Workers Educational Association, that the mass of the predominantly working-class audience sought to increase its knowledge of the world, and relied on the programme to help them. Reporters like Kee and Mossman, who had the instinctive authority of all good journalists, were given great freedom to say what they wished (even if, particularly in the case of Kee, it caused the Current Affairs Department much protective argument with Broadcasting House). Though none of the Panorama reporters strayed from the liberal consensus, the viewer sensed always that the films they made, and the words they spoke were theirs, and not the product of some orthodox corporate mind. The producers of Panorama at this period had the imagination and confidence to recognise the essential truism of journalism: that success or failure hangs in the end on the journalist. Though other talents play a crucial part, not least the film crew, one mind must define the standpoint, set the tone and make the judgments. All of Panorama's reporters were men of strong personality and independent opinion and their films reflected their own personalities; none of them succumbed to the rule of the backroom.

Extraordinarily, despite the presence of Day, Kee, and Mossman, Panorama in the public mind *was* Dimbleby. When Mossman reported on the City, and the next day that harbinger of rich men's gloom, the stock market, suddenly tumbled, it was described in the *Guardian* as 'Dimbleby's Dip'. And although he frequently did 'light' items (he engaged in an ice-cream-eating contest with Francis Williams, swallowed a midget transmitter to record the goings-on inside his stomach, and demonstrated the American craze for balloon jumping—leaping fifteen feet off the ground in the process) it was as guarantor to the public that the contents of Panorama mattered that he was most valued by his colleagues. They had no illusions about the public's response to them: it was Dimbleby who gave them their audience—which in the early sixties still hovered only a little below ten million people each week.

He was at his most distinctive on those occasions which demanded a subtle blend of portentousness and reassurance; when the prestige of Panorama (and of the BBC) depended on his approach and his manner. His gift was to preside over imminent catastrophe and yet convince that while he was there the worst would never happen. It was his natural inclination always to reduce emotions—to comfort where others would shock.

On October 22nd 1962 he opened Panorama with the brief item of news that 'In just three hours time, President Kennedy will speak on American television on a subject—I quote—"of the highest national urgency". Later he interrupted the programme to report that Robin Day had telephoned from Washington with news that the President was almost certainly to announce the 'full-scale naval blockade of Cuba,' and that it seemed that Kennedy was prepared to go, 'to the brink to prevent Communism getting a permanent foothold in the Western hemisphere.' Next evening, in a Panorama Special, he acted (in the words of the Head of Talks, Leonard Miall) 'as a national ombudsman or restorer of national confidence'. If he was ever (as Grace Wyndham-Goldie thought) 'a kind of living embodiment of stability, a reassuring symbol that somewhere at the heart of disturbance lies a basic kindliness and an enduring commonsense' it showed in that programme. While the world waited to see whether the Soviet fleet would turn away or risk nuclear war, he sat in the studio as calmly as ever: 'I am aware that a great many people today are extremely worried and frightened by what has happened, and have some awful feeling that something dreadful may happen quite quickly, suddenly' he informed Alun Gwyn-Jones, the Defence Correspondent of *The Times* and later Lord Chalfont. He then asked, 'Do you think that there is reason at all for short-term, immediate nerves on this?' So weightily rhetorical was the question that Gwyn-Jones was almost bound to answer 'No'. A week later, in some relief, he introduced the programme by asking: 'Was it then the most dangerous week in the whole history of mankind—I suppose it was—but we're through it— and where are we now? That's something to which we shall seek the answer tonight . . .' And Panorama, like the rest of the world, took a deep breath and carried on.

With reporters like Kee and Mossman and later John Morgan, who in the eyes of the Establishment was a man of dangerously left-wing commitment, Richard Dimbleby not only gave prestige to Panorama but he became its sheltering umbrella. Left-wing critics of the programme frequently fell into the trap: identifying Dimbleby's air of comforting reassurance with reactionary reporting, they berated the programme for its middle-class conservatism. Critics on the right, seeing in Morgan and Kee dangerous subversives, found themselves impotent in protest: no-one would take seriously their charges against 'leftie' reporters in a programme which enjoyed the presiding approval of Dimbleby.

Dimbleby's public persona not only gave reporters freedom to pursue liberal crusades, it put Panorama almost beyond attack. On the rare occasions when misguided individuals pressed their point against the programme, the BBC was able to react with almost arrogant assurance. In April 1960, in preparing notes for the defence of the programme against an imminent attack in the House of Lords, Leonard Miall wrote that Panorama

is responsible not to advertisers or Government censors. Programmes are balanced over the long run—not necessarily within each edition . . . the fact that seven million viewers or more and all the newspapers watch it regularly demands a sense of responsibility to the public, a responsibility to reveal truth.

The tone of Miall's note reflected a confidence which had infected the whole BBC, and which had grown steadily since the early days of Panorama. At the start of the Sixties, when for a brief moment, the BBC was filled with the spirit of freedom, Panorama had pushed back the frontiers, and in the Sixties it held them secure. Hugh Carlton-Greene, the Director-General who let that spirit loose, only felt free to transmit programmes like 'That Was the Week That Was' (which scandalised the Establishment) because of the balancing prestige of Richard Dimbleby's Window on the World.

An indication of his public status at this time—he was now almost beyond criticism in the public print—was that Grace Wyndham-Goldie refused to produce a new programme called 'Choice' unless he was willing to present it. Choice was to be the most delicate programme the BBC had ever produced; potentially much more dangerous to the Corporation than the late night satire shows. The pressures on Choice were to come not from politicians but Britain's businessmen. The programme, based on the magazine *Which?* was to provide consumer research, advising millions of viewers on 'best buys'. The Federation of British Industries warned the BBC that it ran the risk of major law suits; the Retail Distributors Association protested furiously; trade journals wrote in threatening terms of the anxieties of businessmen and the legal minefields into which the BBC was treading. The unstated warning was that if Choice made the slightest error, the might of British Industry would be roused against it: a mistake would be expensive. Grace Wyndham-Goldie took all the precautions she could; each programme script and videotape was to be vetted individually by no less than eight BBC lawyers. Even so, she said that the programme would be impossible without Richard Dimbleby to blunt the assaults of any industrial bullies. According to Wyndham-Goldie, once he had been assured that Choice was 'in the national interest', Dimbleby accepted the job, though not before a huge file had been filled with insurance forms against the possibility of his involvment in Court action. In the event, the risks were so great that Choice was forced to be more anodyne than Wyndham-Goldie had hoped: it was an adventure in television journalism but a cautious one.

One of the disconcerting consequences of Dimbleby's public position was that his smallest asides took on the aura of major editorial statements. When he indicated in an outside broadcast in July 1961 that he thought the British Government had behaved churlishly towards the Soviet cosmonaut, Yuri Gagarin, by sending only a civil servant to greet him at London Airport, his words were at once quoted in full in the national press. The BBC said that his words were not the Corporation's but his own; the press interpreted the BBC's remarks as a rebuke to Dimbleby; and the Director-General (who had never before spoken to him) felt bound to telephone personally to mollify him, assuring him that he was free to speak as he would, and that in no sense had the BBC apologised for him. In any case Dimbleby was unruffled— but gratified two days later when the spaceman was invited to a hastily arranged Government reception for him at the Hyde Park Hotel attended by the Prime Minister, the Foreign Secretary, and Lord Hailsham, then Minister of Science, whose civil servant had caused the fuss in the first place.

An unpalatable consequence of his pre-eminence was that he seemed in some ways 'too big' for Panorama. If he left the studio to make a film or record an interview, the 'story' was at once given disproportionate importance. To his growing frustration, he found himself restricted more and more to his chair. 'You know,' he once complained to Robin Day, 'they're trying to turn me into a bloody announcer.' 'That's me in my role as human parrot' he explained drily to a visiting journalist after he had finished a brief dubbing session introducing someone else's film. He was still a reporter, hating to be cocooned in an image which served the BBC well but reality (and himself) poorly. He argued and complained and the producers raised their hands in sympathetic impotence. On those infrequent occasions when he did report on film or 'live' on an outside broadcast, those who had come to believe their own myths about him were astonished. On his first visit to America at the end of 1959 he reported from Chicago and then New York, where he drove through the city in a police car at speed, his hair flying as he went, talked to street gangs, spoke gently to a mumbling junkie in skid row, slowly extracting the painful story of his short life. After the two programmes the *Listener* judged: 'Richard Dimbleby who scored an inner with his recent Chicago round-up hit the bull's-eye with a masterly report from New York.' Geoffrey Cox, the editor of ITN, and one of the shrewdest journalists of the day, wrote congratulating him on the brilliance of his pioneering report. But such forays were rare. Dimbleby was imprisoned in the studio.

In the studio too the frustrations grew. The crises of Suez and Hungary had demonstrated to the members of a sceptical and ignorant House of Commons that whether they liked it or not (and most did not) the television public was a force which could not for long be treated with the smiling disdain of an occasional Prime Ministerial or Party Political Broadcast. A large section of the public had come to rely on television, and Panorama in particular to put a confusing world into perspective. Suez had been the last feeble blow struck for a dying Empire; its consequences— the ridicule, the shame and the petrol-rationing—had diminished the standing of Parliament. It did not happen at once; but as Britain re-adjusted to the disconcerting reality of demise, people began to doubt and question. The process began in the Fifties and accelerated in the Sixties. Politicians, used to the easy distant supremacy of the House of Commons, could no longer ignore the new reality. One by one, and with much distrust they tiptoed forth from Westminster to Broadcasting House or Lime Grove to face the people. They expected, and for a time they received, deference. In the late Fifties it was still possible for a BBC reporter to greet the Prime Minister and the Foreign Secretary at London Airport and ask him: 'Have you anything to tell us, sir?' and for Harold Macmillan to turn to his colleague and ask him, 'Have we got anything to tell them,' and then turning back laconically to the reporter, 'No, I don't think we *have* got anything to tell you.' But with the gradual descent of the politicians into the studio, and the gradual assumption of their mortality, television established its own authority as a forum for political debate.

Richard Dimbleby, who had been the first interviewer in both radio and television, had learned his techniques in the Thirties and Forties when the microphone was feared and the camera was an intruder. In the early Fifties, in programmes like 'At Home', he had been the Corporation's foremost interviewer. When it still seemed miraculous that the Great would condescend to talk on television, he was the only man who was thought grand enough in his own right to ease their words on to the air. Many of those interviews now look not merely deferential but even obsequious; at the time they were greeted with rapturous approval by the critics, even by those who had attacked his Royal 'reverence'. When he visited the Duke of Norfolk and the two swopped harmless banalities about the history of the Howard family, it was thought to be a television breakthrough; and when he went to tea with Viscount Montgomery, the *Daily Herald* (not noted for its deference before the Establishment) thought the resulting programme a 'fascinating encounter'; the *Daily Mail* judged that 'it would have been remarkable had we seen only Monty and not his house: or only his house and not him. To have both was richness indeed'. When Dimbleby was 'At Home' with the Marquis of Bath the *Manchester Guardian* found the encounter 'highly entertaining'; only the *Listener* was upset, and that was because Dimbleby had failed to live up to the standards expected from television of that day: he had been discourteous enough to greet 'the lady of the house with a perfunctory "hello". That seemed to be pointing the fact of social change a little too crudely even for this jaunty occasion'.

When in 1955 he interviewed the Archbishop of Canterbury after Princess Margaret had let it be known that she would not marry Group Captain Peter Townsend, Dimbleby had television's first 'scoop' interview. Before a ritual tour of the Archbishop's

Palace he asked discreetly about the Church's attitude towards divorce (Townsend was a divorcee); and the Archbishop confirmed that it remained unchanged. 'I imagine that most people believe you, as Archbishop of Canterbury, were very closely connected with Princess Margaret's decision,' observed Dimbleby. 'Can you say something about it?' The Archbishop, Geoffrey Fisher (who was never averse to publicity) had much to say, the gist of it being that the Princess had made her decision alone: 'purely on the grounds of conscience'; that she had been constantly seeking to discover God's will; and that when the Father's will was made clear to her 'she did it, and that's not a bad thing for people to take note of'. A decade later, it would have been incumbent upon an interviewer to press a little harder, even to suggest (though not in so many words) that the Archbishop was talking sanctimonious nonsense. But in 1955 that was enough. The next day the front pages of every Fleet Street paper was filled with a verbatim record of the interview, and the *Evening News* judged that the programme had 'provided a supreme example of the impact of television when it goes out into the real world, and with mounting excitement, brings directly to us something that is both unexpected and significant . . . The sense of mounting tension riveted one's interest and made one wonder what on earth was coming next.'

By 1960, so fast had television grown up that the At Home technique had become embarrassingly irrelevant. Politicians filled the studio; and when they found it no more daunting than the soap-box, they came more freely. They adapted their techniques, learned not to make speeches but to be pithy and score points. Their purpose, though, was unchanged. Most of them still sought to propagate the half-truisms and old slogans upon which they assumed they had come to power. Although the BBC had rid itself of the fourteen-day rule, it was still required by Parliament to impose balance between the two parties. Its purpose was to ensure 'fairness'; its effect was to produce an interminable series of shouting matches between the conflicting parties for which each would subsequently (and with monstrous humbug) blame the BBC. In such an arena, the skills of the interviewer had to be quite other than those displayed by Richard Dimbleby 'At Home'.

As Panorama became recognised as the main forum for public political debate, television was sometimes thought to be unfair to politicians, to hector or bully them. Sometimes it was true.

More often, though, it was the reverse. Politicians could pick their moment when to appear; they frequently tried to pick their company; and even their questions. Ministers would cajole and then threaten if they could not have their way; the parties would lose their tempers or pretend to; all of them would promise to 'take the matter up at the highest level in the BBC'—and sometimes they did. It was unseemly but inevitable: at its best, the BBC stood firm; at its worst, it was craven.

Unappreciative of the intricacies of Parliamentary cut-and-thrust, by nature not combative, Richard Dimbleby had the plain man's contempt for the way television politicians behaved. Holding the Constitution in awe, he feared that they would bring Parliament into disrepute, and so threaten to tumble the pillars upon which democracy was founded. He could never understand that at the root of most political controversy (deeply buried under the compromises demanded by Parliamentary democracy) was a fundamental division of principle; like others after him, he believed that politicians should spend less time shouting at each other, and more time 'telling the country the truth'. It was a naive view of political life and one that did not fit him for the role of 'political' interviewer. It suited the BBC well. For in his aloof neutrality, he personified a Corporation which would allow controversy within its walls, but would stand impartial above the fray.

Dimbleby did not like 'tough' interviews. He detested what he regarded as the 'merciless' probing of programmes like 'Face to Face' where the interviewer, 'tries to strip people and tear them apart in public. It is unnecessary unless you are interviewing a monster, like Hitler and in that case I would have torn him apart long before we went on the air.' Although he did not say so, he found the manner of his new Panorama colleague, Robin Day, disconcerting: the style of the two men in the studio differed as much as their style behind the microphone at the State Opening of Parliament.

More than anyone else, Robin Day defined the art of the television interviewer. In the late Fifties, first on ITN and then in a short series called 'Tell the People', he began to master the craft at which he was to have no rival. 'He hunches forward, often in full close up, narrowing his eyes meaningfully behind glinting spectacles' wrote one critic to Day's evident delight, '. . . In the studio he puts his blunt loaded questions with the air of a proscecuting counsel at a murder trial. As he swings back to face the cameras, metaphorically blowing on his knuckles, one detects the muffled disturbance as his shaken victim is led away.' The writer over-estimated the effect of a Day interview on politicians (who generally relished his pugnacity) but he was the first interviewer to cross-examine politicians in their own terms, who understood the workings of Parliament, and (to Dimbleby's wonderment) found them obsessively fascinating.

In 1956, Richard Dimbleby had conducted an interview in the accepted manner of the day with the Prime Minister of Northern Ireland, introducing him with the words: 'Lord Brookeborough has come today from Belfast by air in reply to an invitation from us to speak in Panorama tonight. I don't need to tell you Prime Minister, we are very glad to have you.' When Lord Brookeborough showed an unexpected grasp of news value by telling Dimbleby that he had just heard that the IRA was attacking a police car 'quite near my home', Cecil Wilson in the *Daily Mail* described the moment as 'one of the most dramatic things I have ever heard in my own home'. And when Dimbleby asked 'What must be the actual feelings of your people in Northern Ireland about all this?' and 'Now what *is* this IRA?' and finally 'Why do you people of Northern Ireland wish so much to keep with us?', it occurred to no-one that the interview had been less than incisive.

Eight years later in 1964, Panorama observed the same courtesies. When Sir Alec Douglas-Home, the Prime Minister, appeared on the programme, he was witnessed first, on a videotape recording, being greeted by Dimbleby at the entrance of Lime Grove. As he entered the studio he exchanged pleasantries (Dimbleby: 'Good evening, sir, welcome to Panorama'; Douglas-Home: 'Nice to see you, how are you?) and only after the courtesies had been fully exchanged, did Robin Day take over to do the interview.

By then, however, the style of interview had changed utterly. In 1960 only four years after Dimbleby's Brookeborough interview, Robin Day had interviewed Ernest Marples, who was then Minister of Transport, and who had a rare gift for presenting gimmicks as ideas.

'Well Mr. Marples,' began Day, 'you have put yourself across to the public as a go-getter, as a Minister with energy and ideas, and you realise that unless road casualties are reduced, this reputation may boomerang.' It was hardly the gentlest beginning, but Day continued, 'Now what do you say to the criticism which has been made of you, that since you took office as Minister of Transport, you have talked too much and done too little?' As Marples gulped, Day prepared his next thrust: '. . . What new measures have you introduced to deal with this appalling rise in road casualties?' Marples rallied: 'Well, first of all, your question is based on an assumption that there's been appalling rise . . . But that's wrong . . . so I hope you'll withdraw the question.' Day: 'I certainly won't withdraw it Mr. Marples, because . . . there has been a very great increase in the road casualties . . .' Marples: 'No there hasn't. I'm sorry, you've got the facts wrong . . .' Day: 'Well now, whether its appalling or not Mr. Marples, what new safety measures have you introduced yourself?'

And later in the interview after Marples had suggested that his Department had been responsible for a number of road-safety suggestions, Day attacked again: 'Some of your earlier speeches when you became Minister didn't give this impression of powerlessness that you're now giving.' Marples: 'Quote one, quote one, and I bet you can't.' Day: 'Well I mean—I meant the general impression. I don't come armed with trick quotations.' Marples: 'Well, I don't know, but you asked.' Day: 'Don't you think that's a fair point?' Marples: 'No, I don't, because you can't quote one.' Day: 'Well, all right, I can't quote one at the moment, but don't you think that you gave the impression that you were going to do a terrific job in reforming the transport system?' Marples: 'I am.' Day: '. . . and now you find you can't do it because there's—' Marples: 'No, no, I—' Day: 'too much complication with the—' Marples: 'No, no, no, I—' Day: '—rival authorities.' Day's approach was important because it trumpeted—perhaps a little loudly—the beginning of the end of deference.

Dimbleby recognised Day's supremacy at his special craft and did not seek to emulate him. His dilemma was that while he granted that Day should be the programme's political interviewer, he wished to do all the 'major' interviews himself. Yet by the Sixties, major interviews were almost always political. Though it was gratifying to interview the Duke of Edinburgh, the King and Queen of Greece and King Hussein of Jordan, such interviews were not enough to keep him busy. He pressed to do more; and on the rare occasions when he was permitted to step down into the political arena he showed that his confidence in himself was not misplaced. Perhaps the most extraordinary encounter of that era on television was the confrontation between Sidney Greene and Ernest Marples on Panorama in October 1962. With Dimbleby in the chair, the interview started ordinarily enough. Sir Sidney Greene (leader of the National Union of Railwaymen) was in Brighton at the NUR's annual conference. Ernest Marples, still Minister of Transport, was in the studio. A one-day rail strike was promised for the middle of the week as a result of a complicated dispute over the issue of consultation about redundancies.

At the start of the interview both men confirmed that they could see no way to prevent the strike. Each explained his position; then they began to argue. Marples: 'They bunged in a strike notice.' Green: 'We didn't bung in anything.' For a moment it appeared that the interview would take a predictable course. But suddenly Marples said: 'All right, I'll make you an offer ... may I make this offer to you *now*—before a lot of people?' Will you and your executive go and see him [Dr. Beeching, the Chairman of British Railways] tomorrow ... do that and call off the strike and don't inconvenience the public.' It was a cheap gimmick, calculated to throw Greene, who rallied: 'Well, we don't want to inconvenience the public, and it's a bit of a novel method of trying to start negotiations in connection with the strike by a Minister doing it over television.' At once Dimbleby interrupted: 'Mr. Greene, could I intervene a moment—not to be a mediator, because that certainly is not my role but just to try and clarify this unexpected point that we've come to ... As I understand it, Minister, do you mean that you would be prepared to tell Dr. Beeching, as I presume you can do, or advise Dr. Beeching that he should meet Mr. Greene, if necessary tomorrow ... ?' Marples tried to retreat: 'Well, all I can do is to say what Dr. Beeching has said himself, not what I ask him to say.' Dimbleby: 'No, but you made an offer.'

With the interview over-running Dimbleby cut short a threatened altercation: 'There are a great many people listening at this moment who are going to be very seriously inconvenienced on Wednesday and I don't doubt have very strong feelings on the subject—one way or the other (he always preserved a scrupulous impartiality). Could we, for their benefit, just try to clarify what's happened in the last two or three minutes ... The Minister said that he would be prepared for a meeting tomorrow, at which, I've no doubt, Dr. Beeching would know that something had to be clarified on the question of consultation and precisely what it meant, I pressume, for the future. Now if that is the right reading, Mr. Greene, I'm not saying it is—I hope it is—would you be prepared to go to such a meeting?' Greene: 'I would be prepared, if we get this in black and white as to what it actually means, to place it before my Executive Committee and give consideration to going to the meeting with Dr. Beeching...' Dimbleby: 'Tomorrow?' Greene: 'Yes, if that's possible—it would have to be tomorrow, if the strike is going to commence by Wednesday.' Dimbleby: 'That's what was in my mind.' And, the point of contact thus made, he ended the interview, which had now overrun by nearly ten minutes, sounding much more like the Minister than Marples: 'Well the Minister has at any rate made a suggestion... you both through your respective channels will know how to follow it up if you wish to. May we, in the studio, thank you both.'

Afterwards, even those who had not forgotten that his journalistic instincts were powerful, were surprised by his handling of the unexpected drama. The next day *The Times*, almost suggesting that he should be made a Government Minister, noted that 'he seized on a debate which was steadily degenerating into a comic turn, and with a deftly placed question, turned it into a national issue'. And the Director of Television, Kenneth Adam, expressed his delight 'that *The Times* of all people, paid respectful tribute on Saturday to Richard Dimbleby's handling of the famous Marples–Greene item... it was gratifying that somebody besides ourselves (and millions of viewers) recognised his expertness and aplomb.' The leaders of the NUR and British Railways did meet the next day. But when the Marples gesture proved indeed to be a gimmick, (the Board's attitude had not altered), the strike went ahead. With few such opportunities to reveal his sharpness and little chance to report on film, Dimbleby's role in Panorama was severely restricted.

Yet in the early Sixties he dominated the programme—a fact which caused great pleasure to the BBC's senior executives but, which much irritated some younger members of the staff, who had been grumbling about him for some time. It was whispered in the corridors of Lime Grove by those who were restless for change that Dimbleby had served his purpose, that his time had passed. The public, they argued, no longer required his reassuring presence, his gently guiding hand, his omnipresent infallibility.

Some of them regarded his much-praised impartiality as a front for the Establishment. Others believed that the advance of television journalism was frustrated by his overpowering presence in the 'anchorman's chair'; that the programme was inflexible, artificially moulded to fit his presence.

In 1959 Michael Peacock had returned to Panorama after an unhappy period in outside broadcasts. Determined to stamp his imprint on the programme but uncertain how to do it, believing that the programme was too predictable and too ponderous, that previous producers had substituted fresh studio sets for fresh editorial thoughts, he wondered whether Dimbleby was really irreplaceable. The two men did not dislike each other, but their relationship had never been warm; Dimbleby's departure would cause Peacock no inward agony. He noised the prospect abroad. And then one evening in the summer of 1960, he invited the Panorama reporters round to his flat. Kee, Day and Mossman were there; they had dinner and talked about Panorama until after 3 a.m. According to Day it was a discussion 'of a pretty high general level' but Dimbleby's position was never mentioned. Peacock, however, gained the impression that the meeting felt that Panorama 'was moving towards a situation where the anchorman was no longer relevant; where if a film needed an introduction, it could be made by the reporter himself'. Afterwards, the meeting was to be remembered by those who were not there as an attempted Palace putsch—requiring the unity of producer and reporters if Dimbleby were to be toppled.

Whatever the aspirations or ambitions of Dimbleby's colleagues, whatever part they may have played, Peacock went alone to Grace Wyndham-Goldie to propose the removal of Richard Dimbleby. When roused, Wyndham-Goldie was a formidable opponent, and there were few who did not quail before the lash of her tongue—the more so because they knew she lacked all malice. She had chosen Dimbleby for Panorama; he had far exceeded even her expectations. She made it quite clear to Peacock, not only that Dimbleby would stay, but that he had been a foolish young man to suppose otherwise. There the matter should have been forgotten. Unfortunately the gossip flew, twisting the truth at every stage in its flight through Lime Grove. A few days later, Dimbleby heard a version of what Peacock had planned. He was furious and much wounded: the rumour confirmed his suspicions that the young men wanted to get rid of him, that he had become the figurehead he could not bear to be. He said nothing about it to Peacock, preferring to seem unmoved, and knowing that his producer had been firmly put down. Only once did he mention it publicly. Some months later after the BBC's party to celebrate his twenty-five years in Broadcasting, he met a colleague in the corridor who asked him if he had enjoyed the celebration. Dimbleby replied that it had all been most pleasant. 'Peacock,' he added, 'made a very delightful speech about me—somehow, though, he forgot to mention how he tried to kick me out.'

The knowledge that he was not yet replaceable did little to ease his frustration. He could not escape the feeling that, for all his pre-eminence, he was undervalued. And his misgivings were further aroused in 1962 when restless minds within the BBC canvassed the possibility of merging Tonight and Panorama: the prospect dismayed and alarmed him. He wrote a long memo on the subject to Grace Wyndham-Goldie in which he showed that he had lost none of the journalistic sharpness the BBC seemed unwilling to exploit.

I assume [he wrote drily] that there is no question of making a change simply for the sake of change. If, therefore, the news programme is to be better than the existing pair, it must combine their best points. Tonight has wit, verve and has a slightly brash, slightly 'undergraduate' attitude to life which a great many people find refreshing. Panorama has an authority that has not been equalled by any current affairs programme since broadcasting began, and this authority extends far beyond the shores of Britain . . . in amalgamating the two programmes, we may lose the essence of both. Although the comparison is not really fair, I cannot remember the amalgamation of any two newspapers where one did not become eventually a small name in the title-page of the other. A possible exception was the merge of the *Daily News* and the *Daily Chronicle*, which produced a weakling that died.

He indicated that if the new programme went ahead, he would want to work only with Paul Fox (who had just become Panorama's producer):

Although Paul Fox and I certainly have our disagreements, we get on excellently together and I have great respect for his

ability and his mastery of a rapidly changing situation. I find
that in emergencies, we have an almost telepathic knack of
deciding on the same course of action. I would very much like
to continue working with Fox, rather than with a stranger,
however efficient the latter may be.

To Dimbleby's great relief the idea was soon dropped, and he
was left alone with Panorama and Paul Fox.

Dimbleby's relationship with Fox (who was to become the
most important figure in the BBC by the end of the Sixties)
intrigued their colleagues and revealed much about both of them.
Fox was the BBC's greatest impresario, a man who could act as
toughly as he sometimes chose to speak. Dimbleby regarded him
as his one real friend in television. On the face of it, theirs was an
unlikely friendship: they seemed to represent quite different
strands in the BBC. Dimbleby had been bred in the old
Corporation traditions, had an unshakable faith in 'public service
broadcasting', and despised ITV; Fox was one of the BBC's new
men, with scant respect for Reithian myths and eager to challenge
ITV 'at the ratings game'. But they had much deeper character-
istics in common. Neither man had been to university; both
felt a little intellectually insecure among the glitter of bright
young graduates at Lime Grove; both had their deeper emotions
near the surface; and both shared an instinctive feel, which many
cleverer men lacked, for the needs of the audience. They were
both populists, inexhaustibly excited by the dramatic potential of
television. Fox determined to let Dimbleby play a bigger part in
Panorama. Their shared obsession with the Outside Broadcast
gave him the opportunity: Dimbleby was the only broadcaster
who could speak 'live' without notes in front of an outside
broadcast camera with the same unhurried authority that he had
in the studio. Fox believed that the O.B. would add a sense of
urgency to the programme; Dimbleby was still convinced that
it was the ideal means of bringing the momentous into the
sitting room, bringing people into closer contact with each other
across the geographical and political barriers of the world.

By the accident of events, it seemed for a brief moment in
the first few years of the Sixties that Dimbleby's belief was no
illusion. Not only did the technology stride forward (which in
itself created major occasions) but some historical moments
happened to occur on Monday nights. Even when they did not,

so powerful was Fox's Panorama that he could frequently commandeer the network for a Panorama 'special'. On other occasions he contrived (with the judicious use of film and studio interview) to construct a 'live' Panorama, introduced from the spot by Dimbleby. Though it proved to be a final fling for the Outside Broadcast, the Panoramas which Dimbleby introduced 'live' from France, Denmark, Italy, Germany and even the Solent and the Clyde had a verve (and the ever-present risk of technical catastrophe) which journalistically purer, editorially tighter programmes—all on film or neatly presented from the studio—lacked. From Germany, in particular, it was a memorable moment when Dimbleby stood at the edge of West Berlin, near the Brandenburg Gate, and pointed down at the nails driven into the street which marked the border between East and West —the frontier which he had sensed first in 1945 and upon which a fortnight later the Berlin Wall was to be constructed.

Especially memorable, however, were the first 'live' broadcasts from Moscow in 1961, and then to and from the United States a year later. The moves towards co-operation with Soviet television had been slow and painstaking, the pace coinciding with the rate of thaw in East–West relations. It was agreed for the first time in 1956 that a few selected Soviet commentators should be allowed to speak (in sound only) on the BBC. When the Russians launched Sputnik I, Boris Belitzky took part in a telephone conversation with Dimbleby in Panorama on the 'future of space'. In 1958, for Panorama again, Richard Dimbleby went to the Brussels exhibition, where he stood inside the Soviet Pavilion and opened the programme with the words (which gave him immense delight): 'I am speaking to you direct from a studio of Radio Moscow.' In 1960, when Moscow ceased jamming the BBC European Service, a group of Corporation officials went to Moscow to discuss the future coverage of scientific and sporting events. It was then agreed that on May 1st the BBC could transmit 'live', the May Day parade, to be followed that night by a 'Moscow' Panorama—both programmes to be done by Dimbleby across the Eurovision network.

By chance, while Paul Fox and others were in Moscow at the end of April preparing the final details of the May Day coverage, it was announced that Yuri Gagarin, the first man in space, had landed safely. The BBC men worked furiously in Moscow, and as a result British viewers watched Krushchev welcome Gagarin at Moscow Airport, with Richard Dimbleby in London to explain what was happening. A few days later he was in Moscow. He at once imagined himself back in the spy-land of his Turkish fantasies, accepting the drabness of the city and its slow service, in the fierce conviction that his every private word was being secretly recorded. If he had discovered otherwise, he would have been extremely disappointed.

In London, it had been agreed, much to his irritation, that he should share the May Day commentary with Boris Belitzky— though how it would be shared was to be decided on the spot. The two sides met at the Soviet Television Centre, and in the words of the British producer, Noble Wilson:

> the focus was on just two men: Dimbleby and Belitzky. The latter, feeling slightly uncomfortable, a radio man directed to work in the relatively unfamiliar medium of television on a programme of considerable political importance; the former, shadow-boxing gently, sniffing the political air, sizing up the problem. And the rest of us like so many seconds out of the ring.

Eventually Dimbleby suggested that the two men should work out their plans alone, and they left for another office, where according to Wilson 'Dimbleby managed to secure the commentary on most of the politically touchy parts of the parade'. However, Belitzsky was to cover that part of the procession in which a vast crowd of Soviet workers would pass through Red Square bearing placards with the slogans: 'Hands off Cuba' and 'Down with American Imperialism'.

The next morning (after an interminable wait for a lift at the hotel—which, explained Dimbleby in a loud voice, was why so many Russians read Dostoyevsky) the two commentators took up position on the top floor of the department store which runs along one side of Red Square. When the parade started, Dimbleby was on his best form. The phrases rolled forth. And he found himself intoxicated by the sight: row after row of weapons, of men and women, soldiers and workers—an army marching through the Square. 'Wave after wave follow from factories and farms, with floats illustrating the seven year plan,' he commented. 'It's like a moving balance sheet. In a sense it is the people reporting to the nation... If you've ever wondered about the people of the Soviet Union, well, you're looking at them now, jubilant... This is the truth, passing before your eyes, as it is happening.' Those who had expected or hoped for a hostile or propaganda-ridden commentary were aghast. The *Daily Worker*—which had once judged him 'God's gift to the Establishment' wondering if he would have been capable of turning out his fine phrases on behalf of a people's Government —was grudgingly delighted.

Noble Wilson, listening to Dimbleby's commentary, still worried about the slogans: what would Belitzky say? But at the moment the banners entered the Square, when he should have handed over the Belitzky, 'Richard "missed the place" and went straight on, translating the political slogans without emphasis and attracting attention to more interesting things. Then he switched off the mike, turned to Boris and said "Oh! I'm terribly sorry, Boris, you were supposed to do that bit!"' As the Parade ended Dimbleby informed Britain that he was 'flabbergasted, bewildered, stunned and dumbfounded' by what he had seen. In the evening, he introduced Panorama from the centre of the deserted Square. For the *Daily Mirror* the parade was 'the most massive television spectacle ever seen'; for the *Daily Herald* it was 'TV's finest hour'; for Richard Dimbleby the day had symbolised the meaning and purpose of broadcasting. That night he flew back to London, changed planes, and arrived in Rome the next morning three hours before the start of the State Visit by the Queen to Italy. 'No-one in television,' observed Peter Black in the *Daily Mail*, 'is nearer to being indispensable.' Before the end of the month, he had done three more Panoramas, a Royal Wedding (Princess Alexandra to Angus Ogilvy) and the first television interview with Prince Philip.

A little over a year later (in 1962), he stood in Brussels on behalf of sixteen European broadcasting services to welcome 'America to Europe'—in the first live transatlantic programme beamed by the satellite Telstar. A few days later, he was in New York about to become the first European to broadcast 'live' across the Atlantic by satellite. 'Good evening, Panorama—good evening, London,' he began with delighted portentousness, and continued an effortless commentary as the cameras swept around the New York skyline: 'There the Empire State Building, here and there perhaps I can identify a skyscraper for you as we look across the skyline. This type of view you have to get used to because it's quite breathtaking to a foreigner. There is the new white building, the Pan Am building, not yet finished . . . There's the Statue of Liberty . . .' What no-one in England knew was that Dimbleby's view was distinctly more breath-taking than they had imagined. A minute before transmission his monitor had gone 'dead'.

> There he was in mid-town Manhattan [wrote Paul Fox] the first Briton to televise live across the Atlantic, and he could not himself see any of the pictures that were being transmitted. He could not see whether the pictures the American director was selecting were of the New York skyline or the cops or the drugstore or the sidewalk. He had to guess and hope the transmission would follow the rehearsal. It did, fortunately.

The first Telstar transmissions across the Atlantic were watched on both sides with excitement and expectation. 'The Western World shrank to the size of a television screen' reported the *Daily Express*. In America Dimbleby became an overnight 'star'. Americans had seen his name and heard his voice from the Coronation, the State Opening of Parliament and Princess Margaret's Wedding. Now they had seen him in the electronic flesh. Thereafter when he went to the States he was stopped in the streets to sign autographs. He appeared on American television—on NBC and with Walter Cronkite on CBS. Newspapers devoted many columns to him; and—though Ed Murrow was still alive—the *New York Times* commented: 'He dominates Britain's television in a way that has no equivalent in the United States.' More than twenty-five years after Dimbleby had made his first broadcast, he was still at the peak of the profession he had dominated for much of that time. The boundaries, at the start of the Sixties, seemed limitless.

15

Illness Not Age

Do not go gentle into that good night.

DYLAN THOMAS

You do not die from being born, nor from having lived, nor from old age. You die from *something* ... There is no such thing as a natural death: nothing that happens to a man is ever natural, since his presence calls the world into question. All men must die: but for every man his death is an accident, and, even if he knows it and consents to it, an unjustifiable violation.

SIMONE DE BEAUVOIR

RICHARD DIMBLEBY FIRST NOTICED A SWELLING IN HIS groin in February 1960. In the hope it was not serious and the fear that it was, he ignored it. As the swelling grew, he became more anxious but did nothing about until six months later at the end of July when it could no longer be ignored. For the first time he told Dilys. She called the doctor who made a brief examination, said nothing but walked to the bedroom window and stared out. To save his discomfort my father told him that he knew it was cancer.

A few days later he entered St. Thomas's Hospital where he had an operation to remove his right testicle. The pathologist's report the next day confirmed what Dimbleby had instinctively known, that it was a seminoma—a form of cancer which is fast growing but highly susceptible to treatment by radiotherapy. The principle anxiety concerned the long delay between the time when he first noticed the symptom and the time that he summoned the doctor. If the growth had not spread to the abdomen he had roughly an eighty per cent chance of a complete cure; if it had spread, the likelihood of his survival beyond five years would be reduced to thirty per cent. As he had delayed six months, it was almost certain that the growth had reached the abdomen.

In the middle of August, Richard Dimbleby saw Dr. Ian Churchill-Davidson who ran the hospital's radiotherapy department. Churchill-Davidson, who was one of the country's most distinguished radiotherapists, was at once struck by the bearing of his patient at a moment of acute personal crisis. In a long career, he had already treated many patients. All of them had been frightened, and most of them had made it clear that they did not wish to know how ill they were or even whether the radiotherapy treatment he gave them was for cancer. He found that professional colleagues, whose reason must have known the truth, were able to protect themselves from their own knowledge by a blind faith in his treatment.

Richard Dimbleby was frightened and was not ashamed to admit it, but—unique in Churchill-Davidson's experience—so far from recoiling from the facts, his patient at once wanted to understand every detail of his illness and the treatment that Churchill-Davidson proposed to give him. The question of whether my father should be told the truth did not even arise in Churchill-Davidson's mind: 'Richard had to know. It would have been impossible to hide it from him.' Churchill-Davidson had treated famous and distinguished men before and was in no way over-awed by Dimbleby's name. He was, however, astonished at his patient's self-control, and the calm, detached curiosity with which he asked about his own case—almost as if he were discovering about someone else. He realised then that his patient was a man of unusual strength; and the quiet, shy, undramatic doctor was much affected: 'It was simple. You have to be a great human being to react as Richard did.' The two men took to each other at once.

My father decided at once that the BBC should know the truth. In September he was supposed to cover the closing ceremony of the Rome Olympics but throughout the month he was to undergo daily radiotherapy treatment; so the trip to Italy would have to be cancelled. The press had been told that his operation had been for a hernia; but he did not think he could persuade the BBC that he was attending hospital every day for four weeks merely for a hernia. In any case he felt a strong obligation to tell the truth to those colleagues who relied on him. He was greatly anxious, however, that the Corporation should be made aware that it was only the inconvenience of the treatment —and not its severity—which kept him from his work. The prospect that any of his colleagues should think that he was a finished man alarmed him. From the hospital he asked, through my mother, that only his close colleagues in the BBC should know the truth. In a warren of gossip, the request was honoured with integrity.

My parents had already taken the decision to tell the family. We were soon able to use the term 'cancer' without difficulty (at a time when it was as socially taboo as any blasphemy) and even to ask him about the treatment without embarrassment. As a result the fact of his illness became an unobtrusive part of our family life, causing no sudden drama or alarm; the pattern of our family existence was unchanged.

My father had just bought a small cottage in the village of Dittisham on the river Dart in Devon. For some time my parents had wanted to buy somewhere in the West Country to spend the holidays that he had promised my mother he would soon begin to take. Their plain little cottage was on the edge of the river so that at high tide the water slapped against the garden wall. The sitting room looked out over a wide bay dotted with boats towards thick-wooded hills and red-earth fields. Behind the house was a steep orchard of apples and plums. Snowdrops and daffodils covered the grass in spring. The village was out of the way of the tourist routes, quiet and beautiful in the thatched and white-washed Devon way. The trees, the gulls, the water and the rattling of rigging in the wind were the only sounds to disturb the peace. For my father it combined the cosiness of 'Sleepy Dell' and the high adventure of the sea: Dittisham was perfection. There, my parents romanced, when the television no longer required him, they would spend their last days.

While he recovered from the operation in hospital, we prepared the cottage for him: painting doors and floors and making a window seat so that he could sit there and look at the river. When he arrived, straight from hospital, he looked drawn and tired. He stayed much of the time in bed, and for the first time gave way (but only with my mother) to the terrible depression with which the knowledge of his cancer had filled him. He spoke to her of his dread of the future, about his fear for her and for his children, of the pain, of death—and she comforted him. Thus unburdened, his strength returned, and his spirits rose.

By the beginning of September he was ready to approach his first radiotherapy sessions determined that he would be cured.

In thirty-three days, he had twenty-five heavy doses of radio-therapy, irradiating his abdomen in the hope of destroying any growth that might have spread. The treatment was not painful but it tired him. He developed a severe cold (and subsequently had low resistance to infection) and on occasions he was violently sick. Yet by the time he was half way through the course, he was so relaxed that (to the amazement of the department) to pass the time he used to take a book inside the isolated chamber in which he was treated. Whenever possible he was treated at the end of the afternoon after the department had officially closed. He was always guiltily apologetic to the staff who thus had to stay late. According to Churchill-Davidson, he was so affection-ately regarded by the nurses, technicians and porters that: 'if I'd told them he had to be treated at two o'clock in the morning they would have come in quite happily.'

To avoid arousing public suspicion about his visits, he did not arrive through the main entrance of the hospital but more modestly through the V.D. clinic—where he delighted in startling a benchful of silent patients by saying in a loud voice to Dilys as they passed through, 'Right, you go that way; I go this way' pointing up at the signs which gave privacy to the unhappily afflicted of each sex. After his treatment it was his habit to go to the local pub or medical school club with Ian, where he would listen enthralled to other case histories or the anatomical reminiscences of calloused medical students. In the process he and his doctor became close friends. For the first time in his career Ian Churchill-Davidson found that he had allowed himself to become emotionally involved in the future of one of his patients. Until then, knowing well that by nature of the disease many of those he treated would subsequently die, he had always (against his natural inclination) preserved a necessary and proper profes-sional detachment. Now after many long evenings in the bar, sitting, talking and laughing with this patient, he realised that he could not bear to confront the prospect of Richard Dimbleby's death; he loved this man and he had to keep him alive.

On the last day of his month's treatment, when Dimbleby should have been resting, he wrote in jubilant capital letters in his diary, 'LAST TIME' and introduced that night's edition of Panorama. During the treatment he had taken part in five

Panoramas, two editions of Twenty Questions, and a 'special' with General Sir Brian Horrocks.

He continued to attend hospital regularly; at first every month, then every two months, and then (by a year after his first treatment) every three months. It was not until May 1962, eighteen months later, that he noticed a dull but persistent ache in his back. It was the evidence that the doctors had feared: the cancer had spread. He had two heavy doses of radiotherapy after which he felt acutely ill for some hours but which relieved the symptoms. By the beginning of 1963 he reported to St. Thomas's that he had not felt better for two years. But six weeks later, X-rays showed that the cancer had spread again both in his abdomen and his back. At this point Ian Churchill-Davidson knew that the chances of saving his friend's life were much reduced. Though nothing was said about it between them, my father knew enough about the disease to share that knowledge. At this stage most specialists would have prescribed palliative treatments which would relieve pain but which does not prevent the growth of the malignancy.

Ian Churchill-Davidson had no desire to keep his patient alive merely for the sake of it; he believed strongly that 'the quality of survival' mattered much more than the mere fact of existence. Those treatments which prolonged life at the cost of hideous side-effects filled him with disgust. Yet he was now so closely involved with Richard Dimbleby that he determined to eliminate the cancer. This meant much more rigorous and radical treatment under general anaesthetic, giving massive doses of radiotherapy in a high-pressure oxygen tank, in which conditions the cancer should have been much more susceptible to irradiation. On three occasions in March 1963, Richard Dimbleby was subjected to this process; after each one he presided over Panorama two days later.

He continued to go to the hospital. By the end of 1963 he had made fifty visits to St. Thomas's and had not yet missed a BBC engagement. In those three years he covered three Royal Weddings, three Trooping the Colours, three Remembrance Day services, a Royal Funeral, a Presidential Funeral, a Presidential Inauguration, a Papal Funeral, a Papal Visit to the Holy Land, Royal Visits to Sweden and Italy, budgets and by-elections, inaugural programmes from Moscow and New York, numerous other lesser outside broadcasts, several 'crisis' specials, more than one hundred and thirty Panoramas, and over a hundred editions of Twenty Questions. In the public mind he had become more than ever entrenched as a national figure in British life. More papers than before had urged 'Make him Sir Richard!', more spoke of him as 'a symbol of stability in our alarming world' and more began to treat him with uncritical acclaim. In addition they began to bestow upon him the supreme form of British affection—gentle irony. It affected several commentators. After Princess Alexandra's Wedding in April 1963 (just after his most severe bout of treatment) one wrote:

> Perhaps when the commentator is recognised to be the supreme factor that he is, they will give up using the inconvenient Abbey, and marry Prince Charles if not in Dimbleby's house, then at any rate in a vast television studio where there is no need to keep the microphones in the candlesticks.

A few weeks later in *Punch* Bernard Hollowood observed of Major Cooper's Space Orbit, 'The knowledge that Dimbleby was at the controls in Britain must surely have made Cooper supremely confident: nothing in space would have the frontery to disrupt one of the maestro's TV outings'.

In the summer of 1963 Dimbleby drove through Greece in the back of a jeep driven by King Paul with Queen Frederika at his side, while the local peasantry dutifully applauded. 'How nice,' wrote one critic, 'even if we at home take him too much for granted, these simple Greek islanders clearly know true worth when they see it.' And he went on to admit feeling: 'a twinge or two of reflected glory at the First Gentleman of Eurovision' proceeding on his way 'between thickening crowds and mounting applause'.

In the eyes of the BBC he could do little wrong. At the beginning of Panorama's summer break Paul Fox wrote to express:

> my profound appreciation of everything you have done for us and everything you mean to us. From the Marples/Green clash through the Bidault interview to the Greek Royals it has been a tough season for everyone and for you—as our shield and anchor—probably tougher than most. I am sure you know how deeply grateful we are to you not only for what you do, but the

enjoyable way you do it with us. Thank you for seeing us through Panorama; thank you for masterminding the Big Specials—from Cuba to the Test Ban Treaty. As ever, it was a pleasure—and an education—to have you with us.

By 1964, my father suffered much discomfort: little acute suffering, but enough aches and pains to wear a man down. And though he controlled the worry, it never left him. For fifteen years he had lived in the country, driving on average five hundred miles each week merely to get to his work and back. Even with the Rolls-Royce, even with Arthur his chauffeur, driving more frequently, the journey was becoming more than his tired body could stand. More than that, Danley Farm was now painfully quiet: the children had started to leave home; the stables had no horses; the tack room and the barn were empty; the pigs, the cows and chickens had long since gone. The Farm echoed with too many memories. After sad debate my parents decided to move nearer London. Realising that this was the beginning of the end of a too brief family life, but not being overburdened with sentimentality, they resolutely drove Danley Farm out of their minds. Suspecting that they would not greatly care for their new home, they bought a house on the end of Boulter's Island in the middle of the Thames just outside Maidenhead. It was a bizarre choice. Originally the house had been the principal Japanese exhibit at the British Exhibition sixty years before. Its design was inconvenient (which was why no-one else had bought it); its position was less than obviously desirable. It stood under fifty yards from a weir on one side, which drowned all other sound, and the lock-cut on the other where, less than about ten feet from the kitchen window, pleasure boats accelerating out of the lock sending wash over the lawn and fumes into the house. It was possible to reach the house only by water, which was always inconvenient, and when river mists fell—as they frequently did—extremely dangerous, since it was easy to lose the way and end up anxiously trying to escape the beckoning current of the weir.

It was this oddity that at first appealed to my father: even if he was no longer in the country, no-one could accuse him of joining the suburban rat-race. By means of a floating pontoon they moved all their furniture by the summer of 1964 (including a grand piano) across the lock-cut. However, the builders who had been instructed to gut the inside of the house had not yet completed its metamorphosis into an elegant island home. It was impossible to live inside the house. Undismayed, my father summoned his twenty-three foot motor-boat from Devon (whence it was brought by road), had it launched into the river, moored beside the island, and turned into a miniature houseboat. And while the carpenters, plumbers and decorators worked in the house, my father sat inside a small tent which was erected on the lawn to serve as his office. From all this, when he was well, he derived much satisfaction. He spent many hours before the 1964 General Election sitting outside his tent, a telephone by his side, a cigar in his mouth, a typewriter on a rickety card-table, notes on the grass around him, 'doing his homework' while the builders banged and the trip boats roared by.

Later he bought an elderly river cruiser which had been fashionable in Edwardian England and on Sunday afternoons joined the flotillas of pleasure craft which chugged up the river, energetically going nowhere. But the romance and excitement of the island which had taken his fancy when he felt strong, soon palled on a sick man. For a start, the river had changed from his boyhood; even from the summers in the early Fifties when he had idled slowly up the river on *Vabel*, crowding every other craft out of his way, playing captain of his yacht, shouting instructions and pretending to terrorise his friends who threw ropes poorly and then brought him cups of tea in mock-humility as atonement for their clumsiness; Then he had carefully edged *Vabel* into each lock, with a few inches on either side, pleased at his own precision, and pleased that the crowds which always gathered had seen him do it well: he waved back as they shouted hellos, and gave his orders.

By 1964, he had the same friends and he still had a boat, but the pleasure had gone. The weir soon seemed noisy, there were too many boats and they went too fast. The shouts of 'Hello Richard!', assuming a familiarity which he no longer wished, had lost their charm. He was tired of the constant recognition which in the country he had escaped. Sometimes he lost his temper with it. Then infuriated by passing heads peering into the dining room from the river a few feet away, he would leap up from lunch, rush out of the house and charge along the bank, shouting that they were washing the island away and demanding that they slow down. Since he did not wave his fist, his fans would exuberantly wave back at him, happy to have seen him, and speed on their way.

Such outbursts of spleen against 'his public', fired by disillusion, were sparked off by tiredness and pain. He was now expert at his own diagnosis, distinguishing between those aches which mattered and those which were just a passing irritation. He refused to slow down his life and his body now seemed always tired. By August, although he had had no apparent recurrence of growth in his abdomen or spine, he began to suffer intensely from a pain in his left shoulder which he had first felt early in the year, but had tried to ignore. He dosed himself on codeine, six or eight a day, for days at a time. He soon found it impossible to raise his shoulder. To his chagrin he was unable to dress himself and (though he would never speak to his children about it) my mother had to put his clothes on for him. The journeys across the lock-cut were slow, difficult and uncomfortable. At Lime Grove one day he could hardly hold back a scream when a well-meaning friend, who did not know of his illness, clapped him on the shoulder and asked him if he was feeling all right. He grimaced, smiled at the consideration and said he had a stiff neck. An enquiring journalist was told that he still had a back-injury which meant he had to attend hospital regularly. At home, to his subsequent mortification, he occasionally shouted at those around him. It was as much anxiety as pain. He was certain the cancer had spread, and he was aware of the implications of that: the radical treatment of fifteen months before had not eradicated the disease. As it happened, to his great (but momentary) relief, the doctors diagnosed a frozen shoulder. He was given cortisone, and five treatments with radiotherapy which relieved the pain. For the rest of the year he suffered intermittent discomfort but there was still no definite evidence that the three massive doses of radiation of the spring of 1963 had not been successful.

The evidence for the conclusion that Churchill-Davidson had always feared came in January 1965, when one of his pains in the back became more frequent and more severe. He was kept awake at night, and once more took eight codeine tablets a day to ease the pain. Between the fifteenth of January and the ninth of February he was given three doses of radiation to abdomen and spine. At the same time, to his alarm, he began to feel a tell-tale irritation on his scalp. Once again, he was certain that it was the start of a tumour. At St. Thomas's, unable to feel anything, the doctors concluded without great confidence that the pain may have been psychologically induced by the stress caused by the recurrence of the cancer elsewhere.

In the same period, Richard Dimbleby conducted four Panoramas and six other major programmes, the last of which, the funeral of Sir Winston Churchill was the most important public occasion since the Coronation. The funeral—'Operation Hopenot' as it had been known inside the BBC for years—was to be the most complex programme in the history of the BBC, involving forty cameras and four hours of continuous transmission. Dimbleby was to be the BBC's sole commentator for an event which was to attract a world audience of three hundred and fifty million people, the vast majority of which would experience the occasion through him.

The death of Churchill, long expected, was no less a shock for that. To the generation which had lived through the war, to those who had believed that he had saved Britain, it was a moment of great grief—grief for the man himself but also for the end of that Britain he seemed to stand for. Sharing the grief, sensing the mood, Richard Dimbleby first broadcast from Churchill's Lying-in-State in Westminster Hall, as the first of more than three hundred thousand people filed by to pay their last respects to the dead leader.

Evoking images and sentiments like those he had expressed fifteen years before at the Lying-in-State of King George VI, Dimbleby's voice was low and reverential. Again it was the presence of the public, more than the tableau itself, which most affected him, which gave him once more the assurance that his beliefs and attitudes and feelings were shared by the mass of the people. At such times, when the people rose to the occasion and paid their homage, he loved them and was much moved.

> I have stood for half-an-hour at a time today [he said as the camera fixed the passing faces] in the corner of this beautiful old building watching this silent flow of people, imagining who they were and where they came from, and realising that this is simply the nation, with its bare heads, and its scarves, and its plastic hoods, and its shopping bags, and its little puzzled children, and its older men and women who close their eyes for a moment as they pass, and those who are crying as they leave ...

It is not easy to pay your debt of gratitude. You must stand in the bitter night on the edge of the Thames, prepared to shuffle slowly along the South Bank and cross the full length of Lambeth Bridge, and move up, step by step, past the House of Lords until you reach St. Stephen's Tower. And then as you turn into the top of the ancient worn steps, these steps that lead you down into the Hall, and wait to take your place in the rustling procession, you have your first glimpse of the catafalque where the remains of Churchill lie. It is small and simple and still... And almost before you have time to take in even this detail, the beckoning white glove of the silent policeman tells you that you're delaying those behind you and you move on down the long unfolding carpet that deadens all sound and leads too soon to the bitter night outside. And for this you may wait hours, hours that are being given gladly by thousands upon thousands of people who are waiting outside now. And what have they done when they've passed by? Have they just seen something stirring and serene, something stored in the memory and told to little children in the years ahead? Or have they paused to pray for the soul of a great man, released from the imprisonment of enfeebled old age? Or are we all, as we gaze upon this very moving scene, trying to say 'thank you' in our hearts to the man whose inspiration saved us all?

They are changing the vigil... We shall never see Winston Churchill again, but we may do well to print this scene deep in our memories for many will talk of him that are yet unborn.

Three days later, after forty-eight hours of homework and rehearsal (starting at 4.30 a.m. on the second day) Richard Dimbleby continued to speak for millions of British people and millions more in the rest of the world. For his last great television commentary on Saturday 30th January, four out of five of the British who watched chose to hear the words of Richard Dimbleby as he sat in the commentary position in St. Paul's Cathedral.

The funeral of Sir Winston Churchill was a pageant from another age. From the beginning, instinctively, tenderly, Dimbleby reflected the sense of an ending, each phrase a resonance of time past. As Anthony Craxton's cameras swung over London, panning slowly, caressingly, from old monuments to new tower blocks, Richard Dimbleby guided the public into the past. From the Tower of London to the 'straight tall white steaming chimney of Bankside Power Station, pouring out its electricity where once Shakespeare's actors used to perform his plays', Dimbleby's unscripted words evoked careful images of permanence in change, inviting the world to share with him his security in the 'familiar and comforting' scenes of Westminster, Big Ben, the House of Commons, and 'ancient Westminster Hall where for these three days and nights hundreds of thousands of people have been passing the coffin on the catafalque'. While they waited for the state procession to begin, he guided the cameras along the funeral route, setting the scene, preparing the mood. And as the moment for the coffin to emerge from Westminster Hall drew near, he paused for a moment before giving his judgment that:

There have been funeral processions before, there have been state funerals of commoners before, and of those who are not commoners, there has not been I think in the whole history of our land a state funeral or an occasion which has touched the hearts of people quite as much as this one is doing today.

Then, on the chime of Big Ben at fifteen minutes before ten o'clock, the procession began; the ghosts of the past started to float across the screen. Elderly monarchs from ancient European regimes, old presidents and ex-presidents, the sad Churchill family, old Dukes and Duchesses, ageing prime ministers from across the world, the gnarled, wizened little outline of Earl Attlee, the tottering elegance of Lord Avon and Sir Harold Macmillan, an unbowed General de Gaulle, Generals Eisenhower and Slim, Army detachments who fought glorious campaigns long ago, and the Royal Marines playing Beethoven's Funeral March. The sheriffs, the City Marshal, the Lord Mayor of London, the Pursuivants, the Kings of Arms—all the ornaments of ceremony —were there as well; and, orchestrating the end of an era with the perfect dignity of the nation's undertaker, the Earl Marshal, the Duke of Norfolk, old before his time, but fittingly so.

As the procession wound slowly into the Cathedral, Richard Dimbleby, spoke of 'its richness, its colour, and its pride, and its intense solemnity and feeling and love'. Afterwards, when they had sung the Battle Hymn of the Republic', and when from the Whispering Gallery, Corporal Wilson of the Household Cavalry had sounded the Last Post, the Procession moved outside again to the steps of St. Paul's, where the old men stood together in the cold as if awaiting the last photocall of the British Empire.

After a little while, the funeral cortege set off slowly through the city for Tower Pier, with London: 'echoing the sound of these solemn funeral marches one after the other, set to the beat of this ceaseless slow tread of boots between the high buildings,' while, as the cameras looked down from on high, Dimbleby recalled the memories 'of those bitter days in the Second World War when Churchill was our champion, and these people below were fighting so bravely . . .'

At Tower Pier, as the coffin was placed on board the Trinity House Boat *Havengore*, Dimbleby still touched on the details: on the pipers playing their laments, the crowds lining Tower Bridge, the cranes on Hay's Wharf dipping in salute, the river on the last of the flood tide. As the boats left for Waterloo, he spoke almost in a whisper, with yearning, half-pausing at every word:

> How slowly they seem to creep away upstream towards the bridges of London— *Havengore* flying the flag of the Lord Warden of the Cinque Ports, the Trinity House boat remembering that Winston Churchill was an elder brother, and there behind, London—on this day of mourning; and the only movement on this bustling, thriving waterway of ours, this small flotilla. It seems almost to be drifting up the last of the tide at high water on its way to Waterloo . . .

At the station the bearer party took the coffin to Platform Eleven, still led by the Duke of Norfolk—'there's something so irrevocable and unalterable about the Earl Marshal's pace . . . one slow, steady, unchanging tread all the way on this last journey'— who watched it placed carefully on the train, while Dimbleby, his voice breaking with the emotion of the moment, said simply, 'We shall not—we shall not see it—again—after it's gone in'.

As the train moved off, the programme switched for its closing moments to Bladon where Churchill was to be buried in private. While remote control cameras watched over the graveyard of the parish church Richard Dimbleby spoke the last words of his commentary, reading the names on the headstones of the graves of 'John Harry Adams, and Percy Terry, and William Partlitt, and John Abbott, and Arthur Sawyer and two little unnamed children' which were beside the grave 'where his mother, whom he said was to him like the evening star, is buried'; beside the grave where Churchill would lie. Finally behind the church, looming in the distance he picked out Blenheim Palace: 'There as a boy he played. As a young man he took the train to Handborough, and a lift on the Estate cart up to the Palace. Here he returned in the days of his fame, here they bring him today to lie forever.' Richard Dimbleby had commentated for nearly five hours. Now he returned to Television Centre to record a two-and-a-half hour commentary for an edited version of the funeral that night.

Richard Dimbleby's public was Churchill's public, and he had spoken their emotions. Afterwards he received fifteen hundred letters, some unsigned ('to save you replying'), some barely literate, some from men who did not usually write such letters (like Sir Harold Nicholson and Noel Coward), and one which summed up the sentiments of all the others, saying 'You spoke for England'. Three of America's most distinguished broadcasters, Walter Cronkite, Ed Sevareid and Fred Friendly sent him a cable saying simply, 'We salute you'. His commentary had left many colleagues moved. One of them, the Director-General, Sir Hugh Greene wrote: 'It is really impossible to find words in which to give expression to one's admiration for your achievement on Saturday. On so many great occasions one feels that it was your "finest hour" and always, as on Saturday, there is still a finer hour to come.'

Had it been in his nature, Richard Dimbleby could perhaps have allowed himself the indulgence of basking in the praise so unstintingly heaped on him. He had proved again that he was at the peak of his profession. He was the master 'anchorman' and the master 'commentator'. He was engaged on average in two programmes each week. From television alone he was earning in excess of £15,000 a year. He was a famous and much-loved public man. Yet so far from relaxing, he drove himself even harder, compulsively, increasingly anxious about the future. His diary for seven weeks in the spring of 1965 gives some idea of the punishing schedule he set himself—at a time when he was in pain and the growth of the cancer could not much longer be restrained.

April	26th	Panorama
	27th	Fly to New York
	28th	New York filming
	29th	New York filming
	30th	Fly London
May	1st	Rehearsal at Television Centre for 'Early Bird' satellite inaugural programme
	2nd	Early Bird Inaugural Programme
	3rd	Panorama 'Live' from New York
	4th	Fly London
	5th	Prepare 'Victory in Europe' satellite programme
	6th	Dubbing session Lime Grove, 'Victory in Europe'.
	7th	Rehearsal 'Victory in Europe', War Cabinet Room, Whitehall.
	8th	Transmission 'Victory in Europe' (General Eisenhower, Walter Cronkite, New York; Field Marshal Montgomery, Richard Dimbleby, London).
	9th	At Home
	10th	Panorama
	11th	Prepare State Visit to Germany. To office at Richmond. Guide guests from Her Majesty's Household round TV Centre, then formal dinner.
	12th	At Home
	13th	St. Thomas's Hospital. Radiotherapy. Then office. Then BBC Kensington House (programme meeting).
	14th	Richmond office.
	15th	Fly Cologne, Germany.
	16th	Cologne—preparing 'Panorama from Germany'
	17th	'Panorama from Germany', 'Live'
	18th	Royal Visit to Germany starts. Commentary arrived at Cologne Airport. Then Special Report in evening.
	19th	To Wiesbaden. Special Report.
	20th	Coblentz. Outside Broadcast AM. Then evening Special Report.
	21st	Fly Frankfurt to Munich. Special Report.

May 22nd Fly London
     23rd At Home
     24th Panorama 'Live' from Sotheby's—'transatlantic sale'.
     25th Fly Cologne. Special Report.
     26th Fly Berlin. Special Report.
     27th Berlin. Outside Broadcast, Queen's arrival. Special Report.
     28th Fly Hamburg. Special Report.
     29th Hamburg. Queen ends visit. Fly London.
     30th At Home
     31st Panorama
June 1st St. Thomas's Hospital treatment.
      2nd Rest at home after treatment.
      3rd Fly Calais, then Dunkirk for 25th Anniversary programme.
      4th Dunkirk
      5th Dunkirk
      6th Dunkirk. '25th Anniversary' transmission. Fly London.
      7th Panorama
      8th St. Thomas's Hospital. Operation scalp tumour. Treatment to abdomen.
      9th Lunch with Lord Denning to discuss Magna Carta Anniversary Service at St. Paul's; then rehearsal in Cathedral; then meeting with Brigade Major organising 1965, Trooping the Colour.
     10th St. Paul's. Magna Carta Service, outside broadcast.
     11th See 1964, Trooping the Colour Film at BBC Kensington House. St. Thomas's Hospital treatment.
     12th Trooping the Colour, Outside Broadcast.
     13th At Home
     14th Panorama. Then St. Thomas's Hospital radiotherapy.

In that period, he had done more than twenty major programmes; he had made ten European and four transatlantic flights; he had endured five serious radiotherapy sessions, and an operation for the removal of a malignant tumour from his scalp.
The next month was spent attempting to halt a cancer which

had spread throughout his body and now extended from his groin to his scalp. Between the middle of June and the month of July he went to hospital nineteen times for radiotherapy and was given forty-three treatments to his abdomen, neck, scalp, ribs, spine, shoulders and lymphatic glands. Throughout the month, he continued to introduce Panorama.

As if the anxiety about the cancer was not enough to bear, my father had become increasingly worried about his professional future. On June 2nd, on his return from Germany, an article appeared in the *Financial Times* written by the distinguished critic, T. C. Worsley.

> That we can have too much of a good thing [wrote Mr. Worsley, in ignorance of Dimbleby's condition] is one of life's dreary but valid truisms; and it applies to even the most skilful of personality performers on the box, even to semi-sacred ones: even to Richard Dimbleby . . . He has suffered from over-use. He is in danger of becoming, even if he has not indeed become, something of a bore . . .

It was the first time that a critic had been so cruel for years. Had he felt sanguine, though he would have been hurt, my father might have dismissed the criticism as a cyclical occurrence; the sick man was shaken by them, and even more by what followed. Mr. Worsley was not merely making cheap jibes; nor was he to know that he was hitting a man who was falling; he had a serious point to make and he spared the niceties.

> . . . it is a fact that at last his gift of the gab—and it is quite a gift—has got the better of him . . . it is time to say frankly that Panorama, for instance, has no hope of recovering its lead position as a current affairs programme while Mr. Dimbleby remains in charge of it. He gets in its way. He imposes a formula, and this formula is worn out.

It was not just Panorama. On state occasions too, despite Dimbleby's unquestioned brilliance, the commentator's 'personal manner, his very personal manner, has become obtrusive; it has begun to get on our nerves; we have had enough of a good thing'. If Mr. Worsley's words lacked sensitivity, they were not without bite. According to him, the State Visit to Germany

N

revealed that 'the formula of this one-man panjandrum show is worn out. The medium has at last exhausted him in his present manifestation'. Although Mr. Worsley went on to suggest that Richard Dimbleby was too valuable to the Corporation to be discarded, it was by far the most damaging attack that had been made on him.

They were bitter words to read and they could not have been written at a more poignant moment. Now that he was so ill, the judgment of the *Financial Times* confirmed his own worst doubts; always acutely sensitive to the signs, he was, even before the article was written, half-ready to believe that he was a finished man. His obsession with work, his refusal to rest, sprang in part from his belief that what he did mattered greatly and in part from the fear that others thought it mattered very little. Mr. Worsley had not raised his voice in isolation, though he was the first to do so publicly. Others, no less forcible, but in private, judged that the day of the Outside Broadcast was done, that the Churchill Funeral was a final fling. They said too that the 'anchorman' was now irrelevant. According to this view (such is the vicious circularity of trends) Richard Dimbleby was an actor without a part, whose brilliance as a performer alone still gave him a stage. Some (including senior figures in the BBC) believed that almost single-handed Richard Dimbleby held up the advance of television; that it was merely because of Dimbleby that the art of the commentator and the craft of the anchorman—two anachronisms of the medium—had endured beyond their time. If it were true, it was a remarkable accolade— that one man should play Canute and win.

Richard Dimbleby, sensing this mood, was alarmed and depressed; and there was evidence to suggest that his fears were not ungrounded. In June, at the end of the last State Visit he covered—the first by a British Head of State since the War— he had broadcast in terms which revealed how important such occasions were to him, and in his opinion to the medium.

As the Queen left Hamburg watched by a huge crowd of German citizens to wave her away he quoted from the German song:

> '*Muss Ich Denn*
> *Muss Ich Denn,*
> *Muss Ich Denn*
> *Züm statërle Hinaus.*'

and translated, 'Do I have to, do I have to, do I *have* to leave the town,' and then spoke of the feelings of the German people:

> They longed to see a Queen and hoped to find her a friend. They longed to feel that this State Visit marked the end of years of bitterness and that it implied an understanding of Germany's position today—and, what is more, a promise of continued British support. In all these things they must surely be satisfied. As the Royal Yacht steams away down the Elbe with her Anglo-German escort, there are happy hearts in the Federal Republic of Germany tonight.

However, a few evenings earlier the true significance of the Queen's visit in the mind of the BBC had been cruelly demonstrated to him. The high point of the visit was to be the Monarch's visit to the Berlin Wall—a gesture of Anglo-German solidarity at the public point of confrontation between East and West. For those who had not been able to watch during the day, a special recording of her visit—the 'edited highlights'—was to be transmitted to Britain in the evening with a 'live' commentary by Dimbleby. It was due to start at 8.50 p.m. and end twenty-five minutes later at 9.15 p.m. with the Queen's inspection of the wall. There had been exasperating technical problems all week (Dimbleby had frequently to commentate 'blind' when his monitor failed at crucial moments); both he and the producer Richard Francis were anxious that on this important occasion all would go well. It was not to be. A few moments before they went on air, Dick Francis lost contact with London.

> Six minutes later [recorded Francis] one vision line and one sound line were re-opened and off we went. Richard was in good form and the delay soon seemed unimportant. But after two minutes, on another line, back came the message: London not receiving us. We checked back, they were getting neither sound nor vision. Reluctantly we stopped the videotape. 'Richard,' I said aloud, 'Hold everything. We're not on the air. London isn't getting us.'

'Jesus Wept!' exclaimed Dimbleby in exasperated exhaustion. Viewers in Britain sat up, amazed. Hundreds of them at once rang the BBC in protest. So far from a breakdown, the BBC in London had been receiving the broadcast perfectly. Richard Dimbleby's expletive had burst rudely in upon an otherwise flawless commentary. The dramatic effect was intense. To his chagrin, the next day he was in the Fleet Street headlines: 'So he *is* human after all' said the *Mirror*, summing up one view of the tea-pot storm: 'Dimbleby's two words upset the viewers' reported the *Daily Mail*, reflecting the opposite opinion. A poker-faced BBC released a Broadcasting House apology: 'We are sorry that personal remarks made by Richard Dimbleby when the programme broke down were overheard by the public. It was just one of those things and it is understandable in the circumstances.'

His return to London was delayed by an emergency landing at Amsterdam. It was not the first of his career; and in such situations he took it upon himself to cheer frightened passengers. On this occasion he walked back down the plane to a group of anxious London policemen (who had been on ceremonial duty in Germany) and said, 'Well, men, are you prepared to die bravely'—at which he avowed they at once cleared their throats and put on their helmets. At Heathrow, asked about his lapse, he felt bound to apologise: 'Jesus Wept is not a remark I usually make,' (for him 'damn and blast it' was a forceful expletive), 'I am not in the habit of swearing and I deplore blasphemy; I'm very sorry it was so public'. He was not universally forgiven. The *Bradford Telegraph* observed solemnly that his error was 'a warning to everybody not to say things in private that they would not say in public'. Thus delivered of that flatulence, the paper continued, 'Mr. Dimbleby with his high reputation for calm commentary cannot afford to show his irritation.' And the *Daily Mail*, while expressing sympathy for him, philosophised, 'In some mysterious way words we toss off without a moment's thought suddenly seem important, terrible weapons to hurt or infuriate other people'.

In the public mind the 'Jesus Wept' incident quite overshadowed the rest of his broadcast; it was what they remembered. Richard Dimbleby did not forget what was to him a much more outrageous incident. As a result of the delayed start, the programme would either have to overrun by ten minutes or be cut short. As Dimbleby measured his words towards the climax of the Queen's arrival at the Wall, the instruction came through that the programme would be faded out early—before the Queen reached the Wall, and he, his peroration. It was a decision that would have been unthinkable five years before.

'Richard for once was silent at the end of a programme' noted Francis. 'More precisely he was speechless—with anger. Anger not for himself, but because he hated any BBC programme to fail, particularly one like this.' But it had not just been the chaos which angered him. He was angry not only *for* the BBC, but *with* the BBC. To leave the Monarch stranded on her way to the Wall, was an insult to her, and an affront to his concept of broadcasting. No longer was the State Visit, the great Outside Broadcast, inviolable. The dream of 1950, that television would let nation speak peace unto nation, had been shattered by a faceless bureaucrat with a stopwatch somewhere in the bowels of the BBC. The words of the critic in the *Financial Times* were but a cruel refrain to his own lament.

As with the commentator, so with the anchorman. In Lime Grove, the voices that had murmured against him five years earlier now grumbled aloud. Dimbleby was in the way, why should he stay? Those who felt this rejoiced when it was announced that Panorama was to have a new producer, Jeremy Isaacs, who until then had worked for ITV. It was an unprecedented step for the public service to enter into the commercial market; that the BBC should hire the producer of This Week, the programme with which ITV dared challenge Panorama, and which until then the Corporation had affected not to notice, was to pay homage indeed.

The reputation of Jeremy Isaacs was considerable. By a judicious mixture of sentiment and sharpness (where Panorama—to its critics—seemed leaden and portentous) he had hauled an in- consequential programme high into the ratings. Moreover, he had done so by ousting the anchorman from This Week. Those who wished Dimbleby away wondered if Isaacs would seek to oust him too.

Anxious about 'the brash young man they've got from the "other side",' Dimbleby was even more worried when he read an unhappily exuberant interview with Isaacs in the *Daily Sketch*: 'I talk too much, I shout too much, I argue too much, I'm too dogmatic.' They were all traits that Dimbleby detested and feared. Moreover, it soon became known inside the BBC that Isaacs wished to do precisely as the BBC's 'young Turks' hoped. His desire to seek Dimbleby's removal from Panorama lacked malice, but he shared Worsley's view—Dimbleby imposed a formula, the formulas were exhausted, Dimbleby should go. But Richard Dimbleby was not easily removable. Paul Fox, who was now

Head of Current Affairs, spoke as firmly to Isaacs as Wyndham-Goldie had done to Peacock: Dimbleby *was* Panorama; Dimbleby would stay.

In June, Dimbleby met his new young producer. Though Isaacs would never be told this, he had just completed five continuous days of radiotherapy, and had come to have lunch with him at Lime Grove straight from St. Thomas's. He was feeling ill. Like all broadcasters who had never met him, Isaacs (who was not unduly humble) felt some nervousness at meeting the 'great man'. As Isaacs walked into the hospitality room with Paul Fox, Dimbleby got up from a chair in the corner and walked over to them. 'Ah!' he said with a smile that lacked any coldness, 'so you're the man who wants to get rid of me.' Isaacs, who warmed readily to others, was disarmed, and filled with gratitude. What could have been a frosty difficult occasion became a pleasant lunch.

Yet, as Dimbleby left the table to hurry to his office, before celebrating the 20th Anniversary of the United Nations that evening via Early Bird satellite to New York, he felt no relief. He hated 'unpleasantness', and in any case it was plain that Isaacs was no mere 'young upstart'—but he felt that Fox's stand was a postponement, not a reprieve. It was not mere paranoia. At the time, the Director of Television, Kenneth Adam, believed, and subsequently wrote for publication (though it did not in fact appear in print) that although Dimbleby was the supreme broadcaster in the history of radio and television, the era which he had dominated 'was already coming to an end'. According to Adam, Dimbleby's function would become irrelevant as a result of the growth in technology—which allowed the role of the commentator to be 'reduced', and the anchorman to be 'eliminated'. History has so far proved Adam wrong. Yet in a more profound sense an era *was* ending. Television would continue to devour commentators and anchormen; and the BBC would spend a decade in the search for 'another' Dimbleby—but he was not to be found, because Richard Dimbleby was much more than either commentator or anchorman. He had spoken on behalf of a generation, witnessing for them the great occasions and the terrible events of nearly thirty years; he had helped revolutionise radio, helped make television matter; he was better known in Britain than any other individual apart from the Monarch or Sir Winston Churchill; he was a greatly reverenced and much loved public figure.

In 1965, Dimbleby's future was not a question of technology or of journalism; it was not whether he would still be wanted by the BBC—though he feared it was. The real issue was whether he would any longer want to be wanted in the way in which they needed him. How long could he continue to be a patriarch? For how long would the public wish to be led gently, reassuringly by him through the muddle of the world? For how long would it share his patriotism, his love of ceremony, his devotion to monarchy, his belief in established order, his faith in the slow advance of the *status quo*—the values which even when he was silent were stated by his very presence? Or would he soon be eyeless in Gaza?

In 1965, all that Dimbleby cared for was under attack. Although the difference between the old Conservative Government and the new Labour Government already seemed to be more one of rhetoric than action, the arrival of the new order coincided with the acceleration of profound change. If the Fifties had witnessed the end of the myth that Britain was a great world power, then the Sixties saw the death of the illusion that she was a great moral force. The humiliation of Suez yielded to the shame of Rhodesia—and no-one cared. Disregarding delusions of international grandeur, the nation became preoccupied with local realities—where it was thought that means mattered more than ends, where the talk of all statesmen was in the language of economics, and of the movements of exports and imports or prices and wages.

It was a bleak world which all wished to escape; some into the fantasies of hippy-land, others by revolution, and even more by fighting for the rights which now transparently seemed to have been denied them. For years the country's leaders had spoken as if they were the architects of a Grand Design, and most had listened in wondering respect. Now the leaders had become the keepers of the nation's purse and most knew that the shares were unfair. The consensus, the illusion of national unity, began to crumble. Public protest, open dispute and even violent conflict proliferated: a middle-class morality, which had preached much of tolerance and justice, but had not been unduly dismayed by inequality, became discredited.

In this upheaval no institution was to be spared; preserving the past, they lost their prestige. Mockery and indifference replaced awe and loyalty. Touched by the mood, reflecting the conflict, the BBC could no longer speak with one voice, proclaiming common beliefs and shared values. It was the recognition of social *dis*harmony and national *dis*unity which produced the Indian Summer of freedom in which the broadcasters of the Sixties basked.

Richard Dimbleby had been the voice of the BBC, of a generation, even of Britain. But in the Sixties for whom was he to speak? For which BBC? What generation? Whose Britain? Although he did not put the questions so baldly, and though he interpreted the signs a little differently, Dimbleby was dismayed. 'Do you think television is going to stay important?' he asked sadly and rhetorically in the last interview he gave (with Peter Black), 'I can see it becoming just part of the wallpaper in five years time.' If there were no role for him in television he 'would just bow out' gracefully; he would never permit himself 'to be reduced to the level of an announcer'. Yet he added, seeking re-assurance, 'I think, don't you, that if the public know you and trust you, you can go on for ever, or until your voice goes!'

In July, as if to comfort his insecurity, he went to Sheffield University where the Chancellor, Lord Butler, bestowed on him Honorary Doctorate of Laws. For my father it was a supreme honour, prized more highly than any other public tribute that had been paid him; to him it was an accolade from the intellectual elite of the land for a man who had never been to university, and who had worked all his career in a medium which he was never quite sure was absolutely serious.

Little knowing how sick the new 'graduate' was, Professor Laughton, the University's Public Orator, introduced Richard Dimbleby with the words:

> If a national opinion poll were to be held to discover the personality whose disappearance from the television screen would leave the largest gap, the nation's choice might well fall on Richard Dimbleby. In the event of such a calamity, severe as would be the loss (especially on Monday evenings) of that expansive and reassuring presence, it would be still more grievous to lose the voice which for a quarter of a century, at great moments in our history, has expressed the thoughts and feelings of Everyman . . . If our ceremony today be regarded as an acknowledgement of the contribution which television can make to education in the widest sense, let it not escape notice that we have chosen to honour a man to whose good taste and

integrity, no less than his exceptional talents, television in this country owes much of its high repute.

After the ceremony there were not to be any speeches, but when the Vice-Chancellor proposed the toast of the new honorary graduates, it became clear that a speech would be required. 'All eyes turned to Dimbleby,' recorded one of those present, 'and a rattling of cutlery became louder and more insistent. Eventually he was drawn to his feet by the spontaneous demonstration of friendliness and regard, and spoke briefly and elegantly and with great sincerity. It was a beautiful piece of impromptu utterance, perfectly adapted to the occasion'.

In the car afterwards, he collapsed, half-fainting and exhausted. After a month of intensive radiotherapy he would better have been in bed, storing his strength. Yet he continued the losing struggle. At the end of July, he wrote to the Heads of Current Affairs and Outside Broadcasts about the radiotelephone which had been installed in his car—making him, to his delight, the first person in the country to have one. It was his last letter to the Corporation, and touchingly it contained much of the spirit of the first which he had written nearly thirty years before. Yet, though it was simple, it seemed to say more, to remind the BBC that he was not yet finished, that he should not be forgotten.

As a precaution against being 'un-get-at-able' in time of emergency [he wrote with an attempt at matter-of-factness which would have deceived no-one] I have had a radio-telephone fitted to my car. If you should need me urgently at any time and cannot find me at my office or home number, you should dial 141 and ask the radio phone service for 282002. If they cannot raise me at once, they will keep the call in hand until they find me.

Whatever the speculation about his future, he had made it clear that he was not yet ready to rest.

A few days later the family went to the cottage in Dittisham for the summer holiday. The treatment of June and July had given my father temporary relief. Although he was tired, and his back was tender from the treatment, and he could not easily walk far, he had little pain. For long hours he sat on a divan in front of the cottage, shading himself from the sun, dozing or reading the papers. Sometimes he leant over the wall with his binoculars, watching the boats, gleefully recounting the mishaps of seamanship which in August (when the river was filled with awkward holiday boats) were frequent; and frequently threatening to take action against the trip boats which went too fast through the mooring, while their skippers shouted through megaphones to their customers, their voices echoing across the water, 'And there on the left, you see the little bungalow at the end of the village, that is where the famous broadcaster Richard Dimbleby . . .' Usually they got it wrong: not believing that he could live in so inauspicious a dwelling, they moved him into a large and much more elegant house further along the shore.

We were joined in the middle of the holiday by Ian Churchill-Davidson, in whom my father had come to trust completely. His presence banished those moments of gloom which even my father's great strength could not withstand. With Ian there, he felt safe. I remember them, walking across the shingle, the tall shambling doctor glancing anxiously at his friend as my father walked with difficulty across the slippery stones, carrying a picnic basket, wearing an old battered straw-hat, his trousers rolled up nearly to his knees like a Bournemouth pensioner, wincing as he slipped but brushing off solicitous hands.

He still climbed into the dinghy with delicacy, careful to move his weight slowly, so as not to tip the boat. He sat amidships, surrounded by dogs and children, rowing out to the mooring with quick short dabs at the water, which is how one is supposed to row in a choppy sea. When we pointed out to him, as we always did, that the river was mirror-calm, he smiled at the family joke, and did not change his ways.

He had just acquired the latest in a line of motor-boats, an old converted naval launch with two one hundred horse-power diesel engines. He loved the water, but he had never particularly relished the sea, though he liked to think he did. Whenever the sea was a little rough, our trips were soon curtailed—lest others, he would explain, should feel frightened or seasick. However, for most of the time, that summer, the weather was fine. We went round to bays to picnic among the rocks; we went to Torbay to watch the power boats and to Salcombe, where twenty years before, at the end of the war, my father had seen the yachts begin to sail again.

One afternoon, however, we went too close to the tidal 'race' which runs off Start Point. Suddenly we found ourselves jolting against steep six-foot waves which could easily swamp a small boat; hundreds of gallons of green water poured onto the deck; the boat shuddered and we could only creep forward against the slamming of the sea. Knowing the weakness of my father's back, Ian looked at him in alarm as he stood at the wheel, his body jolting to the motion of the boat. Then David took the wheel, and my father stood to one side. After more than an hour of buffeting we emerged from the 'race', much relieved. Ian was astonished that his patient had suffered no harm.

Though we did not talk of it to each other, except in passing, and though we shared the common human capacity to protect ourselves from the remorseless logic of the truth—so that we never thought his failing would be final—we instinctively nurtured the moments of that holiday. He fought in fun with David, slapping at him, shouting: 'wicked boy, wicked boy', while his eldest son retreated in mock fear; he tried to restore order to an argumentative dinner table with a frown of loving sternness; and he presided over 'picnic point', as we called our secret corner of the river where the bank was shrouded by trees which let the sunlight dapple through. There we cooked sausages on a wood fire, and drank beer, and joked and teased and laughed; and some of the sausages burned, and the smoke eddied into everyone's eyes; and we took photographs. Yet when privately one of us, putting terrible pressure on him, took Ian on one side to say that Papa seemed so well, and would it be all right now, he hedged in discomfort and gave no answer; and then when we saw how his arms had withered, and the skin was loose on his hands, and his face under the tan was drawn, we touched him in passing and were reassured that his hand was firm and warm and alive. The holiday lasted a month—the longest he had taken in his life.

In September, as if symbolising the end of the old world and the start of the new, he introduced a programme to commemorate the 25th Anniversary of the Battle of Britain, and another, in the wake of President Johnson's grim declaration that 'This was Real War' on the American struggle in Vietnam. At the end of the month he opened the first Panorama of the autumn season, ten years after the first programme. In the *Sun*, Nancy Banks-Smith noticed: 'Isn't Richard Dimbleby less solid than he was? He seems to be all eyes.' And the *Daily Mirror* recorded that his smile and his 'casual but informed' appeal had gone. Instead, 'we have a taut face and a voice of cold urgency' and the critic did not like that. Others, observing that this was the first Panorama produced by Jeremy Isaacs, and that Dimbleby had little to do but say 'good evening' and 'good night', wondered if this was the beginning of his end.

In October, he flew to New York to report for Panorama on the arrival of Pope Paul at the United Nations, which was thought to symbolise a new era in the history of the Catholic Church. The Pope was given a warm welcome, and Dimbleby translated and paraphrased as he addressed the General Assembly:

We here celebrate the epilogue of a wearying pilgrimage in search of a conversation with the entire world, ever since the command was given to us—'Go, and bring the good news to all peoples.' Now, you here, represent all peoples. Allow us to tell you that we have a message to deliver to each one of you, and to all . . .

As always, before the programme, there had been briefings, and as always, Richard Dimbleby had been the principal presence—'how'd you reckon that's gonna make out Dick?' the American producers would ask him. By this time he had developed fever and was suffering from dysentery. He could eat nothing. Yet he went to two parties, and driving through New York along the Pope's route to the U.N. to make his usual meticulous preparations, he kept up a running commentary—'on our left we see . . . and over there, just behind the buildings where . . . and now we look . . . here's Tiffany's where His Holiness is not expected for breakfast'—mocking his own craft.

After the Panorama transmission from the U.N., feeling worse than ever but refusing to go to bed, he announced that he wished to see *Hello Dolly*, which was making a hit on Broadway. 'Any chance of two seats tonight?' enquired the BBC's New York office. 'You're kidding . . . Anyway who are they for?' 'Richard Dimbleby.' 'Mr. Dimbleby? Well now, Mr. Dimbleby we *can* accommodate.'

The next day he returned to London, but delayed by fog, the plane had to land at Shannon airport. He was now wretchedly ill. Together with a British M.P., he was offered a bed in the V.I.P. suite. The M.P. accepted with alacrity, but Dimbleby, noticing a mother with two children stranded from the same flight, suggested that they should take his place. No-one noticed the gesture, nor were they meant to: he sat on an airport bench until dawn, uncomplaining but silent.

Two days later at St. Thomas's it was recorded that he had complained of cramp in his left leg, that his hamstring muscles were wasting, that he had a continual sensation of spasm when he put his foot to the ground. X-rays suggested that the quiescent cancer was active again. He was tired and weak; he now found it difficult to walk up or down stairs. The doctors debated whether to give him more radiotherapy, but hoping that it was 'too early to expect the worst', concluded that the treatment might create more trouble than it resolved.

Richard Dimbleby introduced two more Panoramas, but on the 20th October he felt so ill that he could not leave his bed. For five days he stayed there, with his temperature hovering around 103 degrees, refusing to see the doctor. Finally on October 25th he cancelled an appointment for the first time in five years (to have dinner with the Archbishop of Canterbury), and for the first time since the programme had started, he was unable to introduce Panorama On that day, against his fierce will, my mother called the doctor, who insisted that my father should go to hospital at once. Refusing to have an ambulance, he crossed the lock-cut in a rowing boat, and was helped into the car which had been brought specially along the tow-path for him. Then as the car moved off, he ceremoniously waved his hand in the monarch's style at the silent, deserted cabin cruisers moored against the wet autumn river bank, explaining in self-mockery, 'I'm just saying farewell to my public.'

Three days later an exploratory operation confirmed the worst. The cancer had spread further, perforating his bowels. For his body still to function, it was necessary to perform a colostomy—which caused my father more anguish than any of the treatment of the last five years. He felt embarrassed, humiliated and disgusted by it; it violated his self-respect; and it was irrevocable.

Still fighting against his knowledge that his friend would never now leave hospital, Ian Churchill-Davidson continued the radiotherapy. Each day of the week for a fortnight, my father was wheeled through subterranean passages of the hospital to the radiotherapy department for treatment, smiling and joking with his old friends there, but becoming weaker and weaker. Soon the increasingly desperate attempts to keep him alive became counter-productive. He was sick, he had daily rigours, he caught pneumonia, his wound from the operation became infected. His pain could be relieved only with heavy drugs.

In the middle of this medical nightmare he was still able to discuss an issue which had become pressing. Should he let an anxious British public (he had received 3,000 letters of sympathy already) know the truth? Torn between a distaste for sensationalism and an urge to tell the truth, he finally asked David to announce why he was in hospital:

My father first contracted cancer over five years ago and has been undergoing treatment at various times since then. He has asked me to explain this because he is very strongly opposed to the idea of cancer being an unmentionable disease. The reason he has not mentioned it is that he has not lost a single day's work because of it. But as he expects to be away for a few weeks he thought that people ought to know why.

At once letters and phonecalls, in unprecedented spate, poured into the BBC. The Archbishop of Canterbury and Cardinal Heenan asked to see him but he was too tired; a woman came from the country with a basket of eggs; the Queen had a footman bring six bottles of champagne to his bedside; and as each sign of affection arrived, he murmured, half in tears: 'how kind, how very kind'. The press, reflecting the public shock and respect poured praise upon him. 'Richard Dimbleby is a man of courage,' wrote the *Daily Mirror*. 'He has broken one of the greatest taboos of this century. Cancer is an unmentionable subject. Until a few years ago, no popular paper would even print the word . . . We should be able to talk about cancer as we talk about measles. Perhaps we will now be able to.' And later, the editor of *Family Doctor*, after listing his own paper's attempts over twenty years to make cancer mentionable concluded that Richard Dimbleby had: 'done more than any of us in one characteristic gesture. Often it takes a public figure and one who is greatly admired by millions of people to set a trend in these matters.'

My father was at once gratified and frightened by the response. Reading all the papers, sensing that his action had been right, he nonetheless felt that they were all talking as if he were a dead man. Yet, as the first of 7,000 letters reached him, he realised for the first time that he was much loved.

My wife and children [wrote one] asked me to write to you and say how sorry we are that you are ill, and how much we miss you on Panorama. Who am I? Just an ordinary roadman from Berkshire. See you down my road one of these days. Yours faithfully, The Roadman.

My mother now rarely left his side. She cooked for him, bathed and cleaned him, helped him take the ever more painful effort to leave his bed and take exercise—without her, he was desolate. With her, he talked always of the future: of the children, of their plans for the new home in the country (which had already been bought to replace the mistake of the island), of the BBC, and of old friends. When we saw him, dreadfully weakened, he hid his fears, and talked and listened and asked questions with the same loving details and sometimes ran the back of his hand along his forehead to hide his tears. Sometimes he just held our hands.

With strangers, with doctors, nurses, maids and porters he preserved an absolute charm and dignity, forcing himself to wake up when the woman who cleaned the room entered, to ask her where she lived, what her husband did, how many children they had, what she wanted for them, whether she liked the job and how long were the hours. Doctors and nurses, who had seen much misery, who had seen nothing like this, were humbled by his fortitude. His own nurse, who for several years had cared only for terminal cancer cases, and who (like Ian) had until then resisted emotional involvement, found herself deeply committed—staying at his bedside when she should have gone home, refusing to go abroad when she should have taken up a new appointment, and distraught when she realised at last that there was no hope for him. To her, he was simply the bravest man she had ever met.

One of my father's letters came from Joan Marsden, Panorama's Floor Manager, who cheered him by informing him that she had of her own accord removed 'his' Chair from the studio, so that whatever the rivalry to succeed him, no-one should sit in it while he was away. My mother's reply gives some indication of how both he and she withstood their crisis.

Dear 'Mum',

Richard was so pleased to hear from you. He is constantly talking about you, always makes the effort to watch Monday's telly, and loved the 'Chair' story.

It was a ghastly week last week. He had pneumonia, then a

fistula developed, then new pains in the back. On Friday he went back to a blood transfusion, but on Saturday, blood having done its job, he was so very much better. It's no good saying how he is because he changes day to day but he *never*, bless him, loses his sense of humour. When told that an old dear of 100 had called in person to ask after him, he said: 'Blimey! shows where *my* sex appeal lies'.

Please tell all his Panorama friends how very touched Richard is by their enquiries and kindness. He can't quite believe, you know, that everyone cares so much.

St. Thomas's is marvellous and I am allowed to help in a small way with the nursing and can cook the little he eats in the way he likes. They're terribly understanding. It's marvellous to be able to be with him.

Keep that Chair for him—I *know* he'll be back. With love, Dilys.

At the beginning of December, when his return seemed improbable, the BBC made the generous and sensitive gesture of paying him in advance for the Panoramas of the first quarter of 1966. My parents were much touched. In the middle of the month, my mother wrote to the Corporation: 'It is difficult to express our great appreciation for the generosity shown by the BBC. Would you please thank everybody responsible . . . I wish I could give you some encouraging news of Richard but I am afraid it is not very good at the moment.'

He was now deteriorating rapidly, though still he fought. On the 14th, Ian persuaded his colleagues to try one more operation, which showed conclusively that there was no more to be done. On the 18th December, distraught, Ian Churchill-Davidson accepted defeat and personally took the decision to put him onto a combination of drugs which would relieve anxiety and pain, but end his resistance. Gradually he relaxed, and became drowsy. Still, though, he read the papers and talked with the family.

On the 19th, the only person from outside the family he wished to see, Paul Fox, came to visit him. They talked of television, of Panorama, of the previous week's programme, and he made such an effort that Paul Fox even felt able to suggest that he might like to say Panorama's 'Happy Christmas' the next night; but, my father, who now looked close to death, did not wish to have others see him like that, and refused.

The next day he performed a ritual that he carried out for many years, signing the cards on the boxes of chocolates which he had always had specially prepared for the girls who worked on Panorama. A frail hand, which collapsed across the card, wrote to Joan Marsden, 'For you. Sorry cannot do better!' That night at the end of Panorama, James Mossman spoke of his courage and sent him the good wishes of friends and colleagues. My father watched, much moved, in silent tears.

Two days later on Wednesday 22nd December, he emerged briefly from a heavy sleep. His doctors came in to see him, in the hope that their reassuring presence should make him feel all was well. Once more, summoning his last reserves, when he should have been in a deep sleep, he tried to make conversation. Then he decided to tell a joke. It was long and complicated and half way through he lost his way. In anguish, my mother prompted him to the end. When he had finished, he fell back to sleep.

He died a little after nine o'clock that night, aged fifty-two, leaving a terrible emptiness in the lives of those who loved him.

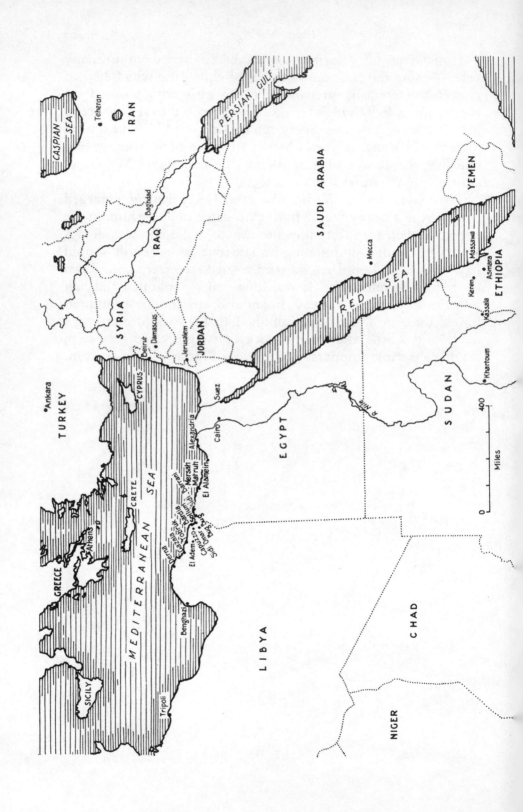

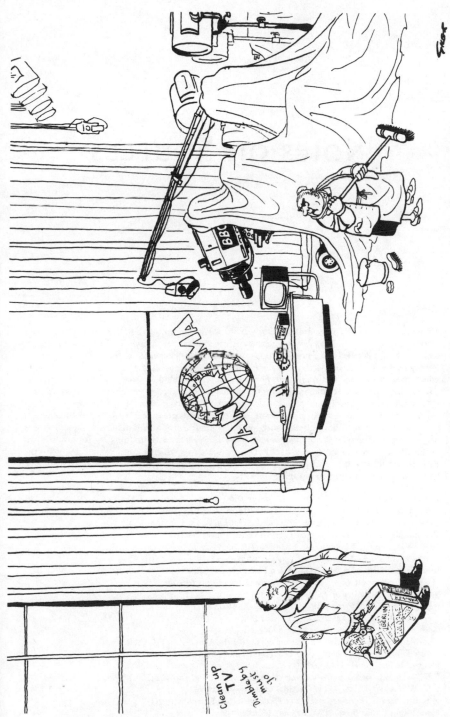

'Of course they're all on strike! Language like you bin using what else do you expect?'

Notes on Sources

Throughout the book I have drawn heavily from Richard Dimbleby's broadcasts, articles, war diaries, letters, and books. Except where it has seemed necessary I have tried not to burden the reader with the detailed reference for each of these sources. He wrote at different times for the *Sunday Despatch*, the *Daily Mail*, the *Daily Herald*, and various weekly magazines. The two books which have been most useful are *The Frontiers Are Green* (Hodder and Stoughton 1943), and *The Waiting Year* (Hodder and Stoughton 1944). I have been saved many hours of research by the BBC publication *Richard Dimbleby, Broadcaster*, which is a collection of articles written by his colleagues within a few weeks of his death, and edited with great skill by Leonard Miall into a continuous narrative. I have quoted anecdotes and judgments from it. The first three volumes of Asa Brigg's *History of Broadcasting in the United Kingdom* are required reading for any student of the BBC. They contain a wealth of detailed research to which I am indebted. Likewise the BBC Handbooks for the entire period are invaluable. I list below some of the books which I have found particularly useful or enjoyable.

Corelli Barnett, *The Desert Generals* (Kimber 1960).
Peter Black, *The Mirror in the Corner* (Hutchinson 1972).
George Dangerfield, *The Strange Death of Liberal England* (MacGibbon and Kee 1966).
Robin Day, *Television—A Personal Report* (Hutchinson 1961).
BBC War Report, *6 June 1944 to 5 May 1945* (OUP 1946).
Lionel Fielden, *The Natural Bent* (Deutch 1960).
John Hilton, *Rich Man Poor Man* (Allen and Unwin 1944).
Harman Grisewood, *One Thing At A Time* (Hutchinson 1968).
Stuart Hood, *A Survey of TV* (Heinemann).
Alan Moorehead, *African Trilogy* (Hamish Hamilton 1944).
Cornelius Ryan, *The Last Battle* (Collins 1966).
C. A. Lewis, *Broadcasting From Within* (Newnes 1924).
Thomas Jones, *A Diary With Letters 1931–50* (Keith Middlemass Ed. OUP 1954).
Hugh Thomas, *The Spanish Civil War* (Eyre and Spottiswoode 1961).
Henry Maule, *Spearhead General* (Odhams 1961).
J. C. W. Reith, *Broadcast Over Britain* (Hodder and Stoughton 1924).
J. C. W. Reith, *Into the Wind* (Hodder and Stoughton 1949).
Anthony Smith, *The Shadow In The Cave* (Allen and Unwin 1973)
Hans Rumpf, *The Bombing of Germany* (Muller 1963).

Index